SCREENING, BRIEF INTERVENTION,

AND

REFERRAL TO TREATMENT

FOR **SUBSTANCE USE**

SCREENING, BRIEF INTERVENTION, AND REFERRAL TO TREATMENT FOR SUBSTANCE USE

A Practitioner's Guide

Edited by
M. Dolores Cimini and Jessica L. Martin

AMERICAN PSYCHOLOGICAL ASSOCIATION
PUBLISHING

Published by
American Psychological Association
750 First Street, NE
Washington, DC 20002
https://www.apa.org

Order Department
https://www.apa.org/pubs/books
order@apa.org

In the U.K., Europe, Africa, and the Middle East, copies may be ordered from Eurospan
https://www.eurospanbookstore.com/apa
info@eurospangroup.com

Typeset in Meridien and Ortodoxa by Circle Graphics, Inc., Reisterstown, MD

Printer: Sheridan Books, Chelsea, MI
Cover Designer: Mercury Publishing Services, Inc., Rockville, MD

Library of Congress Cataloging-in-Publication Data

Names: Cimini, M. Dolores, editor. | Martin, Jessica Leigh, 1991- editor. |
  American Psychological Association, issuing body.
Title: Screening, brief intervention, and referral to treatment for
  substance use : a practitioner's guide / edited by M. Dolores Cimini and
  Jessica L. Martin.
Description: Washington, DC : American Psychological Association, [2020] |
  Includes bibliographical references and index.
Identifiers: LCCN 2020001925 (print) | LCCN 2020001926 (ebook) |
  ISBN 9781433832017 (paperback) | ISBN 9781433832031 (ebook)
Subjects: LCSH: Substance abuse—Diagnosis. | Substance abuse—Treatment. |
  Evidence-based psychiatry.
Classification: LCC RC564 .S38 2020 (print) | LCC RC564 (ebook) |
  DDC 362.29—dc23
LC record available at https://lccn.loc.gov/2020001925
LC ebook record available at https://lccn.loc.gov/2020001926

http://dx.doi.org/10.1037/0000199-000

Printed in the United States of America

10 9 8 7 6 5 4 3 2 1

This book is dedicated to my parents and mentors,
who have instilled in me the desire to learn,
the curiosity to expand my horizons, and the courage to persist
despite sometimes insurmountable challenges and barriers.
—M. DOLORES CIMINI

To my parents and my husband, who, in their own ways,
helped foster the ambition, confidence, and perseverance
necessary to complete a project such as this.
And to Charlotte, my dream come true.
—JESSICA L. MARTIN

CONTENTS

CONTRIBUTORS

Jason J. Burrow-Sánchez, PhD, Department of Educational Psychology, University of Utah, Salt Lake City

M. Dolores Cimini, PhD, Center for Behavioral Health Promotion and Applied Research, University at Albany, State University of New York, Albany

Jessica M. Cronce, PhD, Department of Counseling Psychology and Human Services, College of Education, University of Oregon, Eugene

Carlo C. DiClemente, PhD, ABPP, Psychology Department, University of Maryland Baltimore County, Baltimore

Peter P. Ehlinger, BA, Department of Counseling Psychology and Human Services, College of Education, University of Oregon, Eugene

Heather J. Gotham, PhD, Department of Psychiatry & Behavioral Sciences and Center for Behavioral Health Services and Implementation Research, Division of Public Mental Health & Population Sciences, Stanford University School of Medicine, Stanford, CA

Gregory R. Hancock, PhD, Department of Human Development and Quantitative Methodology and Center for Integrated Latent Variable Research, University of Maryland, College Park

Brett Harris, DrPH, Department of Health Policy, Management and Behavior, School of Public Health, University at Albany, State University of New York, Rensselaer

Alec Howard, MPH, University of Pittsburgh School of Pharmacy, Pittsburgh, PA

Joseph Hyde, MA, LMHC, CAS, JBS International, Inc., Rockville, MD

Jody Kamon, PhD, Center for Behavioral Health Integration (C4BHI), Middlebury, VT

Sandeep Kapoor, MD, MS-HPPL, Division of General Internal Medicine, Department of Emergency Medicine, Department of Psychiatry/Behavioral Health, Northwell Health, New Hyde Park, NY, and Donald and Barbara Zucker School of Medicine at Hofstra/Northwell Health, Hempstead, NY

Sharon Levy, MD, MPH, Harvard Medical School; Adolescent Substance Use and Addiction Program, Division of Developmental Medicine, Boston Children's Hospital, Boston, MA

Mary A. Marchetti, BS, Department of Counseling Psychology and Human Services, College of Education, University of Oregon, Eugene

Jessica L. Martin, PhD, Department of Educational and Counseling Psychology, University at Albany, State University of New York, Albany

Brianna Mintz, MS, Department of Counseling Psychology and Human Services, College of Education, University of Oregon, Eugene

Marjean Nielsen, MPP, School of Dentistry, University of Utah, Salt Lake City

Alexandra Nowalk, MPH, CPH, CHES, University of Pittsburgh School of Pharmacy, Pittsburgh, PA

Megan A. O'Grady, PhD, Division of Health Services Research, Center on Addiction, New York, NY and Department of Psychiatry, Icahn School of Medicine at Mount Sinai, New York, NY

Michael V. Pantalon, PhD, Department of Emergency Medicine, Yale School of Medicine, New Haven, CT

Mary Piepmeier, MA, Columbia University School of Social Work, New York, NY

Janice Pringle, PhD, University of Pittsburgh School of Pharmacy, Pittsburgh, PA

James F. Schaus, MD, University of Central Florida College of Medicine, Orlando

Miriam A. Schizer, MD, MPH, Harvard Medical School; Adolescent Substance Use and Addiction Program, Division of Developmental Medicine, Boston Children's Hospital, Boston, MA

Mary Schmidt-Owens, PhD, Student Health Services, University of Central Florida, Orlando

Lawrence Schonfeld, PhD, Department of Mental Health Law and Policy, Louis de la Parte Florida Mental Health Institute, University of South Florida, Tampa

Matthew Taylor, PhD, University of Pittsburgh School of Pharmacy, Pittsburgh, PA

Win Turner, PhD, LADC, School of Social Welfare, Stony Brook University, Stony Brook, NY; Center for Behavioral Health Integration (C4BHI), Middlebury, VT

Elissa R. Weitzman, ScD, MSc, Harvard Medical School; Division of Adolescent/Young Adult Medicine, Boston Children's Hospital, Boston, MA

Allen Zweben, PhD, Columbia University School of Social Work, New York, NY

ACKNOWLEDGMENTS

The idea for a book addressing the application of screening, brief intervention, and referral to treatment (SBIRT) across diverse health care settings and with a wide range of populations would not have become a reality without the support of grant funding and dedicated government project officers from agencies that permitted us to explore new avenues for discovery, plant seeds for innovation, and pursue a journey aimed to achieve excellence, both within our institution and beyond. We thank our government project officers and grants management staff members from the National Institute on Alcohol Abuse and Alcoholism, the National Institute on Drug Abuse, the Substance Abuse and Mental Health Services Administration (Center for Mental Health Services, Center for Substance Abuse Prevention, and Center for Substance Abuse Treatment), the U.S. Department of Education, and the New York State Office of Addiction Services and Supports for the opportunities afforded to us.

We thank our colleagues from the University at Albany Center for Behavioral Health Promotion and Applied Research and Counseling and Psychological Services, who so capably made contributions to the development and evaluation of innovative evidence-based SBIRT strategies and engaged in countless hours testing interventions with fidelity while faced with the multiple and competing demands that exist within university-based student service settings. Special thanks to Estela M. Rivero, PhD, Assistant Vice President for Student Affairs and Director, University at Albany Counseling and Psychological Services, for her vision and support of the implementation of innovative practices within these settings.

Finally, we express our deepest gratitude to Morgan Boyle, Dana Bozek, Yaya Tineo Cabrera, Margeaux Cannon, Melissa Ertl, Alicia McDonough, Rena Pazienza, Emily Planz, the student members of Dr. Martin's lab, and the Health and Addictive Behaviors Investigative Team for their hard work providing editorial assistance on the chapters within this volume.

SCREENING, BRIEF INTERVENTION, AND REFERRAL TO TREATMENT FOR SUBSTANCE USE

Introduction

M. Dolores Cimini and Jessica L. Martin

As part of our training as psychologists, a great deal of time and attention was focused on clinical assessment and intervention with individuals within a diagnostic and psychotherapeutic environment, with almost exclusive attention to diagnostic categories such as depression, anxiety, and other conditions in the more "traditional" mental health arena. Less attention was paid to how we, as professionals, might use our knowledge and skills to intervene within the domain of substance use assessment and treatment to enhance the health and resilience and mitigate the risks faced by individuals with whom we worked. To many psychologists and allied mental health professionals in training, it appeared as if the area of substance use diagnoses and treatment was relegated to a special practice silo, and we were, as a result, discouraged from entering this diagnostic and treatment territory when working with our patients and clients.

Though our training may have taken place within silos, the experiences of our patients and clients have not paralleled this reality. We cannot deny that patients and clients are coming to us with increasingly complex mental health and substance use concerns that, by definition, interface with each other. Likewise, we also cannot deny the priority that we must place in understanding and addressing the needs of the whole person in front of us, inclusive of any issues associated with substance use. No matter what our training may be or where our professional interests lie, it is incumbent on each of us to move beyond our comfort zone and gain a more expansive understanding of

http://dx.doi.org/10.1037/0000199-001
Screening, Brief Intervention, and Referral to Treatment for Substance Use: A Practitioner's Guide,
M. D. Cimini and J. L. Martin (Editors)

the complexity, challenges, and unexplored opportunities that a comprehensive approach—one that includes a broader understanding of substance use assessment and treatment—may offer us.

Screening, brief intervention, and referral to treatment (SBIRT) is a comprehensive, integrated, public health approach to the delivery of early intervention and treatment services for persons engaging in risky substance use and those with alcohol and other substance use disorders and co-occurring mental health disorders. Primary care centers, hospitals, emergency departments, college campuses, schools, and other community settings provide ideal opportunities for early intervention with at-risk patients and clients before more severe consequences occur. SBIRT comprises three components:

- *Screening* quickly assesses the severity of alcohol and other substance use and identifies the appropriate level of treatment.

- *Brief intervention* focuses on increasing insight and awareness regarding alcohol and other substance use and comorbid psychiatric conditions and enhancing motivation toward behavioral change as indicated.

- *Referral to treatment* provides those identified as needing more extensive treatment with access to specialty care.

To date, health care providers such as physicians, surgeons, nurses, and social workers, who often work on interdisciplinary health care teams with psychologists, have been trained in and use SBIRT to a far greater extent than psychologists. Few psychologists are aware of SBIRT as an evidence-based skill set that can effectively engage patients and clients in conversations about substance use, reduce substance use, and prevent serious negative consequences. Given that the majority of patients and clients report substance use (e.g., alcohol consumption, tobacco and marijuana use), it is imperative that psychologists increase their knowledge of SBIRT and build skills to deliver it in diverse health care settings to more effectively prevent and intervene with substance use.

OVERVIEW OF THE BOOK

In light of the timeliness and critical importance of disseminating information regarding SBIRT to psychologists and allied health care professionals, this volume

- describes the research supporting the efficacy of SBIRT within behavioral health care settings and other service delivery environments;

- provides an overview of motivational interviewing (MI), the theoretical framework for SBIRT, and outlines how practitioners may use MI techniques to deliver target population–relevant and responsive brief interventions addressing alcohol and other substance use;

- discusses the selection and use of the most appropriate screening tools and methods for assessing alcohol and other substance use among diverse target populations across the life span;

- explains how SBIRT may be implemented in a number of service delivery settings, such as primary care settings, colleges and universities, comprehensive health care settings, and other practice environments;

- highlights how SBIRT can be used for different target populations, such as adolescents, older adults, and marginalized populations; and

- describes technological advances in training and delivering SBIRT, as well as strategies to address the challenges associated with SBIRT training and implementation.

The researchers who wrote chapters for this volume describe their investigations of SBIRT and provide practical tips for the application of their findings to a variety of clinical practice settings. Likewise, the practitioners who contributed to this volume discuss how their work and success in promoting the behavioral health of their patients and clients was informed by substance use research in general and SBIRT best practices in particular. This book also addresses special topics regarding the translation of SBIRT research to practice, such as the delivery of interventions with fidelity and cultural and population-specific considerations in the development and implementation of evidence-based SBIRT practices within a wide range of intervention settings.

Part I of this volume focuses on strategies and tools for SBIRT implementation. In Chapter 1, Carlo C. Di Clemente provides an overview of SBIRT, the research supporting the effectiveness of SBIRT, and an exploration of the settings in which it is delivered. Chapters 2 and 3, by James F. Schaus and Mary Schmidt-Owens, respectively, will give the reader an overview of tools and strategies for conducting SBIRT for alcohol use and tobacco use. Chapter 4, by Allen Zweben and Mary Piepmeier, and Chapter 5, by Janice Pringle, Alexandra Nowalk, Alec Howard, and Matthew Taylor, focus on MI and the use of this framework to deliver brief interventions after screening for alcohol and drug use.

Subsequent chapters discuss the implementation of SBIRT within different settings and with diverse populations. In Chapter 6, Megan A. O'Grady and Sandeep Kapoor highlight the implementation of SBIRT in medical and integrated care settings. Chapters 7 and 8 address the unique challenges associated with SBIRT implementation in college student and adolescent populations based on the work of research teams led by Jessica M. Cronce at the University of Oregon and Sharon Levy at Boston Children's Hospital. In Chapter 9, Jason J. Burrow-Sánchez and Marjean Nielsen explore factors to be considered when SBIRT is conducted with populations representing racial and ethnic diversity. In Chapter 10, Lawrence Schonfeld describes the delivery of SBIRT with older adults, highlighting important clinical considerations when working with this population.

The remainder of the book addresses special issues and new frontiers in the practice of SBIRT, such as the use of technology to deliver and provide training in SBIRT (Chapter 11: Michael V. Pantalon & Heather J. Gotham), SBIRT for cannabis use in a changing legal landscape (Chapter 12: Win Turner, Joseph Hyde, Jody Kamon, & Gregory R. Hancock), the integration of SBIRT training in graduate programs in psychology based on our work conducted under a 3-year grant funded by the Substance Abuse and Mental Health Services Administration (Chapter 13: Jessica L. Martin and M. Dolores Cimini), and the role of public policy in advancing SBIRT implementation and dissemination (Chapter 14: Brett Harris).

The development of this book represents a career-long culmination of the journey we have shared in expanding our understanding of the increasingly complex behavioral health needs of our patients and clients, developing strategies and interventions to address these challenges, and helping to promote clients' resilience. Each of the colleagues involved in this project helped shape our work along the way and taught us the meaning of dedication, persistence, and excellence. In this spirit, we express our deepest thanks to the chapter authors of this volume, who generously shared their scholarship and practical suggestions with readers. Each of them has made a significant footprint within our nation's understanding of SBIRT best practices, and we are honored to have them as our colleagues and book contributors.

SCREENING, BRIEF INTERVENTION, AND REFERRAL TO TREATMENT TOOLS AND TECHNIQUES

1

Screening, Brief Intervention, and Referral to Treatment

An Efficacious Public Health Approach to Substance Use Prevention and Treatment

Carlo C. DiClemente

This chapter lays the foundation for understanding the three key elements of SBIRT: screening, brief intervention, and referral to treatment. After a brief review of the historical roots of this practice, I explore how SBIRT made its way into public health and health care. The barriers and the benefits of both identifying and implementing this practice are discussed. Before offering a brief overview of the effectiveness of SBIRT interventions by substance and setting, I attempt to define the effective ingredients of SBIRT and then offer a view of implementation challenges and a perspective on what is needed to fulfill the promise of SBIRT for substance misuse prevention and intervention.

SUBSTANCE USE IN HEALTH CARE AND PUBLIC HEALTH SETTINGS

Substance use is a prevalent activity in our current society and has been for many centuries. Substances derived from plants, herbs, and flowers or manufactured in legal or illegal factories have been sought after and used by most civilized populations (Carlson, 2006). Some substances, such as alcohol, nicotine, caffeine, and marijuana, are extremely popular and helpful for relaxation, socializing, and perceived stress management. Others have been created as medicinal aids and, when used properly, treat chronic pain, anxiety, depression, serious mental illness, and attention-deficit/hyperactivity

http://dx.doi.org/10.1037/0000199-002
Screening, Brief Intervention, and Referral to Treatment for Substance Use: A Practitioner's Guide,
M. D. Cimini and J. L. Martin (Editors)

disorders. Society has had a love–hate relationship with substances for many years. However, the scope and impact of substance use on individuals, families, and society have reached a point of crisis in the United States with the opioid epidemic; cheap, powerful synthetics; novel delivery systems; and legalization of previously illegal substances.

This chapter focuses on substance misuse, noting how substances with salutary purposes can become harmful, destructive, and deadly. Misuse of substances can result in significant harm to individuals, families, and society. Substances have the power to change behavior and the brain in ways that cause dysfunction, disability, disease, and death; the prevalence and significance of such consequences warrant greater attention.

UNDERSTANDING SUBSTANCES OF ABUSE

Substances that can lead to problematic use and substance use disorders seem to share the following characteristics. First, they affect brain functioning and neurotransmitter activity. The brain accommodates to the presence of these substances. This neuroadaptation often creates a need to continue to use or use more of the substance to feel "normal" and function. Continued use results in significant withdrawal symptoms when access is denied. Second, these substances can disrupt self-regulation, affecting the executive cognitive function and affect regulation of the individual. Finally, these substances, when taken in ever-larger amounts and used more frequently, disrupt pleasure and pain systems and become essential and ubiquitous in the individual's life (DiClemente, 2018).

The path to excessive use and the end state that we call *addiction* cannot be predicted by personal characteristics, setting, access, or family and peer influences. However, there is a journey into misuse and addiction that follows a pathway that can be described using the heuristic framework of stages of change (DiClemente, 2018). Individuals who are exposed to substances do not become excessive users or develop severe substance use disorders (SUDs) overnight. SUDs develop over time and follow a behavior change process. Individuals begin considering use and experimenting, find reasons to continue use, become significantly exposed to the substance and both utilitarian and dysfunctional elements, continue exposure, and increase quantity and frequency of use. They then find themselves with a serious SUD that is difficult to modify or stop. At this point, individuals may enter the stages of recovery, most often beginning in precontemplation (i.e., where they do not see the need for change and are not concerned about the substance-using behavior). Movement forward to contemplation, preparation, and action begin a road to recovery that is often circuitous and takes significant effort and persistence.

The consequences and complications created by SUDs cost society billions of dollars annually (National Institute on Drug Abuse [NIDA], 2018;

U.S. Department of Health and Human Services [USDHHS], 2016). Costs are not only those associated with premature death and disability but also include crime, accidents and injuries, emergency care, and a variety of other societal problems, such as domestic violence, suicide, HIV/AIDS, and medical problems (e.g., cancer, hepatitis, cardiovascular issues, lung disease). In a recent report, the World Health Organization (2017) indicated that 70% of worldwide mortality was caused not by infections, but by chronic diseases attributable to lifestyle behaviors, with substance use as one of the most important contributors. The opioid overdose crisis in the United States and other countries highlights the extensive costs in human suffering, medical resources, and criminal activity caused by substances.

PREVENTION AND TREATMENT

Two often-separate approaches address substance use problems. One is prevention focused on limiting experimentation and initiation among youth, and the other is treatment focused on stopping or modifying substance use among people with a use disorder. In reality, prevention and treatment are two sides of the same coin (DiClemente, 2018). Terms such as *early intervention*, *harm reduction*, and *teachable moments* have brought addressing substance use into mainstream health care. SBIRT is part of this movement to address substance use and misuse whenever and wherever a health care or social service provider interacts with an individual (Agerwala & McCance-Katz, 2012). The aim is to change the goal of "zero tolerance" from one that is oriented toward criminal justice (punishing every occasion of drug use) to a proactive, provider-oriented goal; there should be no tolerance for any provider interaction with a substance user that does not include addressing the substance use. It is a matter of life and death.

This is not a completely new concept. For many years, medical history checklists often included questions about drinking and smoking, most often with little probing of responses. More recently, smoking was included as a vital sign in health records (USDHHS, 1996). However, discussion of substance use often was cursory and considered outside the purview of the general medical community. Dealing with substance misuse was seen as the responsibility of substance use prevention and treatment specialists. Motivation to change was the responsibility of the person using substances who had to ask for help.

Thankfully, medical and social service systems have been changing. Professional groups have begun to set standards of practice that include screening and addressing substance use. The federal health care and research agencies (NIDA, National Institute on Alcoholism and Alcohol Abuse [NIAAA], Substance Abuse and Mental Health Services Administration [SAMHSA]) have encouraged and endorsed screening and provide screening instruments on their websites. Medical professionals (from physicians to dentists, nurses to social workers) are being instructed in their training programs on how to screen for, advise, and refer for a variety of substances from tobacco to illegal drugs. Nonprescription use of prescription medications has become a focus of monitoring and intervention in both the medical and pharmacy communities as well as in the criminal justice system (NIDA, 2018). For psychologists and psychotherapists, SBIRT should be encouraged as a standard practice in assessment and treatment settings (schools, private practice employment assistance programs) and research screening.

There are many barriers still to overcome (Holland, Pringle, & Barbetti, 2009). Because most individuals use substances and many do so to excess at times, it can be difficult for providers to probe the substance use patterns of patients.[1] Those behaviors often are viewed as personal choices and outside the purview of the provider, unless substance use is clearly a focus of the encounter. There is also stigma related to substance misuse that interferes with the veracity of the patient and the comfort of the provider. Often, providers fear the reaction of the person seeking services; that is, providers fear the client may get angry, avoid the provider, or drop out of care. These fears persist despite evidence demonstrating that patients would not consider it offensive to be asked about medications and substance use, including alcohol, especially if there were a rationale for those questions (Holland et al., 2009). Finally, many providers do not feel adequately trained to intervene in this area. Although SAMHSA has funded over 20 projects to teach and incorporate SBIRT into medical residency training, the sustainability of these programs leaves much to be desired (SAMHSA, 2015). Overcoming these barriers is a critical component to adopting the SBIRT protocol among providers.

SBIRT is an innovative protocol to help providers from many different disciplines and specialties to address substance use among the populations they serve in a respectful, caring, and effective manner. It is not a miracle intervention (Babor et al., 2007). SBIRT simply offers awareness, motivational considerations, and opportunity for a referral to individuals at all stages of initiation of problematic use, as well as those experiencing moderate to severe use disorders. What follows is a detailed description of key elements of SBIRT and ways to incorporate this simple, well-established procedure into various practice settings.

A SHORT HISTORY OF SCREENING AND BRIEF INTERVENTIONS

SBIRT is composed of three central components. The first is to provide sensitive and comprehensive screening for substance use and misuse. The second is to provide a brief intervention after the screening. This brief intervention

---

[1]In this chapter, *provider* refers to medical and other health professionals, as well as social service providers. The terms *patient* and *client* are used interchangeably to indicate anyone who is seeking services from one of these types of providers. This is done to avoid using multiple terms throughout the chapter.

should support appropriate use or motivate consideration of change for risky or disordered use. If there is a need for further assessment or referral to specialized addiction treatment, the third component of the SBIRT model includes providing such referrals to appropriate resources in the most effective manner possible.

Although screening is a common practice in health care settings, screening typically involves questions or lab work related to the presenting problem and only peripherally touches on substance use. Although screening for tobacco is often required, typically screening for alcohol, illegal substances, and non-prescription use of medications is ignored. To correct for this error, SBIRT requires a simple yet detailed questioning about the use of specific substances during one's lifetime and in the recent past (3 or 6 months, past year). This information can be gathered via a self-report form or in-person with a provider or staff member.

Screening should be informative and can trigger self-monitoring of the behavior. Just becoming mindful of quantity and frequency of use can lead to reductions (Kazdin, 1974). In tobacco research studies, participants reduced the number of cigarettes smoked when asked to monitor their smoking (Foxx & Brown, 1979). In a screening where individuals must identify how often and how much they used specific substances, their awareness is increased, and that can promote serious consideration regarding their pattern of use.

Early versions of screening protocols were designed to include giving advice. Training medical professionals for tobacco screening often used the five A's (ask, advise, assess, assist, and arrange for a follow-up; USDHHS, 1996). Although an efficacious protocol, it was difficult to get providers to implement all five A's. Many would ask and advise, but few would complete the entire protocol (Dixon et al., 2009). The prevalence of smokers reporting that providers had asked and advised them to quit smoking increased, however, and some attributed their quitting to this intervention (Stead, Bergson, & Lancaster, 2008).

In the 1980s, Miller, Sovereign, and Krege (1988) introduced the "Drinker's Checkup" that included an assessment of alcohol use and an objective assessment of risk that left it up to the drinker to decide what to do about the drinking. The results indicated that after this assessment and feedback, individuals reduced their drinking significantly. Miller's work, along with the success of a briefer advice intervention for drinking in a trial by Orford and Edwards (1977), led to the focus on briefer interventions focused on alcohol use that can shift motivation.

Support for this emphasis on brief interventions came from the development of the construct of the stages of change from the transtheoretical model (TTM). The TTM redefined denial and resistance as early stages of an intentional change process (Prochaska & DiClemente, 1984). The authors identified pre-action stages that different types of interventions could influence (Prochaska & DiClemente, 1984). These stages indicated key tasks that, if activated, would help move individuals forward toward behavior change (Center for Substance Abuse Treatment, 1999).

Individuals in precontemplation (i.e., not currently seriously consider-ing change) had to become interested and concerned about the behavior or the need to change to move forward to the next stage, contemplation. Once considering, an evaluation of the risks and benefits helped individuals move toward a decision to change. Once they decided to change, the individual created the commitment and plan to implement the change during the prepa-ration stage. Finally, individuals would move into the action stage where they initiated changes, revised plans, and established patterns of new behavior. Sustaining changes over time would lead to the maintenance stage. Viewing change from this perspective allowed providers to consider what types of interventions could promote movement through the stages and prevent relapse. Brief interventions became a way of promoting movement through the change process.

In 1991, Miller and Rollnick described motivational interviewing (MI) as an intervention that prepared people for change. This approach dovetailed nicely with the tasks of the early stages of change. The description of the spirit and strategies of this approach lent itself well to brief interventions that could help individuals complete early-stage tasks and move toward behavior change (DiClemente & Velasquez, 2002). Miller and Rollnick designed the MI approach to help individuals talk themselves into changing behaviors. This combination of objective feedback and motivational communication became the core of a new approach to intervening with substance use that was briefer and could be used in a variety of settings with both risky use and use disorders.

Once the field realized that one did not have to wait until someone "hit rock bottom" to make an impact on motivation and behavior, the impor-tance of early intervention increased. There was increased awareness that natural events could promote change and that natural or self-directed change was an important phenomenon (DiClemente, 2006). The search was on for settings and opportunities to provide brief interventions that could become "teachable moments" (i.e., when screening, feedback, and a motivational conversation could promote behavior change or accepting help).

SBIRT was an innovative way to build a protocol with the potential for use in a variety of opportunistic settings. The primary focus initially was on medical settings, especially ones wherein individuals may present with substance-related illnesses or injuries, such as emergency departments and trauma units. SBIRT was a logical extension of tobacco screening, which became a vital sign evaluated in every medical visit (Dwinnells, 2015). Supported by funding from SAMHSA, the National Institutes of Health, and other entities, research, evaluation, and training of SBIRT blossomed in medical centers and among nurses and other multidisciplinary health care providers. Funding supported incorporating screening for substance use problems into residency training for primary as well as specialty care (SAMHSA, 2017). The SBIRT protocol was used with adolescents and in schools (Mitchell, Gryczynski, O'Grady, & Schwartz, 2013), as well as other settings (e.g., obstetrics, HIV screening, mental health clinics).

As with every implementation of an innovative approach, there were both successes and "learning opportunities" (Babor et al., 2007). Key barriers for implementation included (a) time (not enough time to complete the intervention), (b) training (not appropriately trained to do this type of brief intervention), (c) reaction (patients and families would become angry and uncooperative), and (d) overidentification (these patients did not look like they had a substance abuse problem, or the interviewers drank, so they were not comfortable talking about this topic). Another barrier was the belief that SBIRT was a waste of time and would do no good because addictions are difficult to conquer. A final barrier to the adoption of the SBIRT protocol was that outcomes varied and often resulted in reduction rather than total abstinence. That is, patients would change one, but not all, substance risk behaviors. Abstinence-only beliefs and stigmatized views of illegal drug users complicate the adoption of SBIRT as well. Thus, even after training, implementation has been difficult, with medical systems often trying to find providers other than medical professionals to implement SBIRT or attempting to create self-report and automated, technology-driven feedback systems.

DEFINING SBIRT

This section highlights the key elements for providing SBIRT effectively and efficiently. Each of the SBIRT components offers challenges for proper understanding and implementation. The nuances of the elements of the protocol make implementation more challenging. A solid understanding of the practices related to each element of the SBIRT intervention is critical.

Screening

There is a significant difference between screening and assessment. Screening should be substantive and gather enough information to be able to offer some guidance. However, it is not a comprehensive diagnostic assessment. If we turn a screening into an assessment, we make it harder for the provider to deliver, interpret, and react to information when SBIRT is offered in these opportunistic settings. Simplicity is an important element of screening for both the provider and the patient. Patients do not mind being asked some screening questions in the service of comprehensive care but can react to extensive questions about a topic that is not a focus of the visit. Providers should resist becoming substance abuse assessors.

What makes for adequate screening? The objective of the screen is to get actionable information, to get enough information to compare current behavior with some norms or important health values. That would mean avoiding simple yes or no answers to vague questions such as, "Are you a drug abuser?" and not asking "loaded" screening questions such as, "You drink socially, right?" Screens should allow providers to get a sense of the quantity and frequency of use.

Lifetime use questions allow the screener to know about any use and can be particularly helpful when individuals have stopped recently or may be at risk of relapse. Specific questions about recent use over the past 3, 6, or 12 months allow the screener to contextualize the current pattern of quantity and/or frequency of use. Because some individuals use multiple substances (e.g., smoke and drink, use OxyContin and marijuana), it is important to get a sense of quantity and frequency of use for each substance. With some substances, it is easier to define quantity (e.g., standard drinks of alcohol). Specificity about quantity is important. One 64-ounce drink of 80 proof liquor is not equal to 64 ounces of beer. When it is difficult to get a sense of how much is being used, as with marijuana or cocaine, because of a lack of uniform dose and potency, frequency and sometimes amount of time using can be helpful. This information allows the provider to compare the current use with guidelines (e.g., levels of tobacco consumption that indicate dependence [10 cigarettes per day, initiating the first cigarette of the day immediately after waking]) or to use norms (e.g., exceeding medication dosages).

There are many different screening instruments available for use. Some focus more on consequences of use and offer a somewhat indirect approach to problematic use of substances, such as the CAGE (Mayfield, McLeod, & Hall, 1974), the Michigan Alcoholism Screening Test (Selzer, 1971), the NIDA modified ASSIST (NIDA, n.d.), the Drug Abuse Screening Test (Skinner, 1982), and more recent computerized self-administered screens for multiple substances (Adam et al., 2019). However, direct questioning about quantity and frequency during specific time frames enhances efficiency and interpretability for providers who are not substance use specialists.

Brief Intervention

Once the screening is completed, the brief motivational communication intervention should occur, as appropriate. In my experience, it is best to complete the entire screening before doing the brief intervention. If providers discuss each substance when screened, they run the risk of using all their allotted time on just one or two substances and not having enough time to discuss the substance that may present the greatest risk. Completing the screen for all substance use allows the provider to get an overview of use and then follow up in the brief intervention by targeting one or more of the riskier substances used.

A brief intervention can be many different things (Babor et al., 2007; Bernstein et al., 2009). It can be a simple statement of advice or feedback such as, "I understand you have been smoking regularly for the past 10 years. As your doctor, I have to recommend that you quit smoking in the interest of your health. I have a number of resources to help when you want to quit." Alternatively, interventions can focus on how the substance use interacts with a current condition of concern: "Your high blood pressure is a serious condition, and drinking at the levels you are drinking is exacerbating the condition. My best advice is to cut down significantly on your drinking, and then we can check it again." In another setting, the statement could be different: "Your depressive symptoms seem to be getting worse and may be exacerbated by your level of drinking. Have you thought about reducing your drinking to see whether your depressive symptoms improve?" Even better is a communication that first indicates affirmation of the patient and then offers feedback—for example, "I want to thank you for being so open with me about your drinking. It is the only way I can really help. Thank you again for your honesty." Following that affirmation, the provider could discuss the role of alcohol use in liver function abnormalities. These advice-giving feedback scenarios represent one type of brief intervention.

A more sophisticated motivational approach to brief intervention would be to begin a dialogue about the specific substance use and explore any concerns or motivation to change the behavior. This is more consistent with the MI approach (Miller & Rollnick, 1991). Practitioners have to learn to avoid stigma and create a respectful client-centered conversation using MI strategies of open-ended questions, affirmation, reflections, and summaries to increase motivation for change and promote movement through the stages of change.

Many risk assessment protocols proceed from identification of risk (low, moderate, or severe) to referral. This leads to many failed referrals and is not an efficient use of provider time. A more efficient approach is to move from risk assessment to readiness before moving forward to a referral. Readiness is a moderating factor in accessing a referral even when the referral is to a provider in the same building or agency (DiClemente, 2018). Acknowledgment of risk is not equivalent to motivation for treatment or further assessment.

Assessing readiness should be an important element of the brief intervention. A readiness ruler is a simple tool to assist the provider in evaluating motivation and guiding the intervention. The client response to the question, "On a scale from 1 (*not ready*) to 10 (*very ready*), how ready are you to talk to one of our behavior health providers about your cocaine use?" The response to this question should guide the provider either to provide a brief intervention and follow-up or to provide a referral. The brief intervention for a low readiness score would focus on increasing interest and concern and evoking reasons for change and change talk. A higher score should start a conversation affirming the motivation, discussing the importance of planning, and making an offer of resources to help. At the heart of the brief intervention is the belief that you can make a difference no matter what the motivation. However, the outcome for every risk assessment does not have to be a formal referral.

Referral to Assessment or Treatment

Referrals are an integral part of medical treatment and other types of behavioral health treatments, often done in a routine manner. The patient gets a slip of paper with one or more providers recommended for getting specialty care (e.g., dermatologist, orthopedist, cardiologist). It is up to the patient to follow through on the call and appointment. For acute care, this often works well enough because patients are motivated to resolve the immediate health concern; however, there is still often a lack of follow-through. Effective referral involves more than simply giving a list of providers and phone numbers or addresses.

Referrals for chronic conditions and SUDs are challenging. Motivation and stage of change status are not static—they are fluid. Someone who screens positive for risky drinking may express concern, offer reasons for modifying drinking in the provider's office, and accept a referral. However, once they leave the office, motivation may diminish and undermine the referral. Thus, how referrals are made can be critical.

Referrals have been categorized as cold, warm, and hot. A *hot* referral or handoff involves making a definitive and personal connection between the patient and the referral source. For example, the provider may introduce the person to the appropriate provider within their agency. A *warm* handoff involves some type of engagement between the patient and the new provider. Giving a detailed description of what to expect and endorsing the provider, as well as making some contact with the provider ahead of time, would constitute a warm handoff. Last, offering a name and phone number or a list of providers constitutes a *cold* handoff or referral. Personal knowledge of the services and personnel and established links with referral sources would greatly enhance the ability to provide the hot handoff.

The NIAAA (2014) published a treatment guide for families and persons facing alcohol use issues. Their guide details the questions to ask and the dimensions to look for to find the right type of treatment provider for individuals or loved ones. Although there is no recommendation for a single provider, this strategy helps empower families and patients to make informed choices. The SBIRT provider should be knowledgeable about some reputable and available resources. A referral plan, like a treatment plan, must be effective, acceptable, and accessible (DiClemente, 2018). This type of preparation will make warm or hot referrals more likely.

EVALUATION OF SBIRT: AN OVERVIEW

This section provides a brief overview of the effectiveness and implementation of SBIRT for different types of substance use problems across different settings. Although there are many studies of SBIRT, findings concerning feasibility and efficacy are limited for some substances and settings. Implementation of SBIRT in each study differs in terms of which substances are screened, what constituted the brief intervention, and how the referral was made (DiClemente, Corno, Graydon, Wiprovnick, & Knoblach, 2017). Implementation often differs by type of professional implementing the protocol (e.g., physician, nurse, social worker, technical assistant, addiction specialist).

Finally, studies are of varying rigor and evaluate myriad outcomes, including feasibility and acceptability of reduction and abstinence. The following review highlights findings across substances and settings and offers an informed and personal view of the status of the empirical support for SBIRT with individual substances and in various settings. Areas where there is a need for additional evidence and research are highlighted.

The following overview relies heavily on a recent review of screening and brief interventions and treatments (Babor, Del Boca, & Bray, 2017) and a review of reviews of motivational interventions with various substances of abuse (DiClemente et al., 2017). Both reviews posit that screening and brief motivational interventions are moderately to strongly supported as efficacious and cost-effective for the most common substances of abuse (alcohol, tobacco, and marijuana). Research related to drugs such as cocaine, heroin, prescription opiates, and other types of substances is less extensive, and the outcomes are positive but not always as significant (Glass et al., 2015; Madras et al., 2009; Saitz et al., 2014). There is substantial evidence that these types of interventions promote a process of change and can initiate or accelerate the modification of addictive behaviors, and there is little evidence that screening or brief advice or motivational intervention have any untoward effects. A brief review of substances and settings where SBIRT has been used follows.

Alcohol

The vast majority of studies on brief motivational interventions and screening focus on alcohol use. From the brief intervention studies of Miller and colleagues (1988) to the large World Health Organization multicountry study, screening and brief interventions have demonstrated efficacy or effectiveness in promoting changes in drinking and drinking-related risk behaviors for adults and adolescents (Babor & Higgins-Biddle, 2000). Screening in high-risk settings such as emergency departments has a long history of successful trials (Bernstein et al., 2009); SBIRT now is a required activity for certification of Level 1 trauma units (American College of Surgeons, Committee on Trauma, 2006). The U.S. Preventive Services Task Force (USPSTF) included the following statement in its recommendations: "Behavioral counseling interventions for risky/harmful alcohol use among adult primary care patients can provide an effective public health approach to reducing risky/harmful drinking" (Whitlock, Polen, Green, Orleans, & Klein, 2004, p. 557). A Cochrane review found that brief interventions targeting drinking have significant support in primary care settings but seem weaker in hospital settings (Kaner et al., 2009; McQueen, Howe, Allan, Mains, & Hardy, 2011).

Tobacco

Tobacco screening has a long history as well. Since the 1980s, there have been efforts to screen every patient for tobacco use in medical settings. Current rates of screening for tobacco use in physicians' offices exceed 65% (Jamal, Dube, Malarcher, Shaw, & Engstrom, 2012). Efficacy of SBIRT for tobacco use has been supported by Cochrane Reviews and numerous research studies (e.g., Lindson-Hawley, Thompson, & Begh, 2015; Lundahl et al., 2013).

A recent review of motivational interventions with tobacco indicated that there was substantial support for the effectiveness of brief interventions for tobacco for adolescents and adults (Hettema & Hendricks, 2010). However, evidence for the efficacy of SBIRT with pregnant women smokers had mixed results (DiClemente et al., 2017). In addition, DiClemente and colleagues' (2017) review of reviews found that there was significant and strong support for larger effect sizes when primary care physicians and general practitioners delivered SBIRT and better outcomes when there was a higher quality of intervention. The USPSTF has given its highest-level recommendation (Grade A) to clinicians treating adults and pregnant women who smoke for screening, advising, and offering assistance via behavioral and Food and Drug Administration approved medications (Siu, 2015).

Marijuana

The marijuana literature also provides evidence for the effectiveness of SBIRT. DiClemente and colleagues (2017) concluded that across multiple reviews, there was strong support for brief interventions for reducing marijuana use. However, more intensive interventions seemed to outperform these briefer interventions. A large trial in an emergency department also demonstrated effectiveness for marijuana screening and brief intervention for adolescents (Bernstein et al., 2009).

Other Illegal Drugs

Studies on the effectiveness of SBIRT with other illegal drugs (cocaine, methamphetamine, and heroin) are too few to make a substantive conclusion. A Cochrane review did not support the effectiveness of brief interventions for cocaine use (Minozzi, Saulle, De Crescenzo, & Amato, 2016). The U.S. Preventive Services Task Force (USPSTF, 2019) stated that there is currently insufficient evidence to recommend illicit drug use screening for adults, adolescents, and pregnant women. Other studies have found some support for adding brief motivational interventions to treatment programs, and some studies offer minimal support for the effectiveness of SBIRT with other types of substances (DiClemente et al., 2017). However, screening for substance use for prevention with individuals initiating problematic use has shown positive effects on prevention outcomes (Mitchell et al., 2012). Effectiveness of SBIRT for these types of illegal substances may have more to do with making an effective referral as opposed to using screening and brief intervention without a referral. Indeed, at least one study suggested that the quality of the referral practices impacts treatment outcomes (Agerwala & McCance-Katz, 2012). However, overall support for SBIRT for illicit drug use is mixed and insufficient due to a number of factors that include the quality of implementation, type of substance, and lack of studies compared with alcohol, tobacco, and marijuana. Clearly, there is a need for additional well-implemented and controlled studies.

Nonprescription Use of Prescription Medications

The onset of the opiate crisis has raised awareness that many individuals develop SUDs by using prescription medications in a manner not prescribed (Griggs, Weiner, & Feldman, 2015). Misuse of prescription opioids, central nervous system depressants, and stimulants represents a significant problem. In 2017, an estimated 18 million individuals in the United States (6% of individuals age 12 or older) reported misuse of prescription medication at least once in the past year (NIDA, 2018; SAMHSA, 2018). Besides opioids, other prescription medications that are often misused include prescription stimulants, tranquilizers, and sedatives.

Screening for nonprescription use of prescription medications is a vital prevention and early intervention tool and should be included in SBIRT training, delivery, and research. School-based health clinics (both high school and college), as well as other health providers, will often see individuals who are misusing prescription medications come in for other health problems, which provides an ideal opportunity to address the nonprescription use of prescription medications (Mitchell et al., 2012).

Individual states have begun deploying prescription drug monitoring programs that can access records of prescriptions obtained by patients to curb "doctor shopping" and reduce prescription misuse. Physicians are using these programs to screen for patients misusing medications. There are mixed findings in the use of this approach for reducing the prevalence of misuse (Griggs, Weiner, & Feldman, 2015). However, according to many professionals, these systems have reduced access to prescription medications. One unintended, negative effect has been that monitoring and restriction of access to prescription medications have contributed to the increased cost of illegal prescription medications and increased the use of lower-cost heroin and fentanyl in the United States.

SBIRT IN VARIOUS SETTINGS

Originally, SBIRT and its precursors were viewed as intervention tools to be used in primary care settings, particularly targeting tobacco and alcohol use (Fleming et al., 2002). SBIRT for alcohol in emergency departments and trauma units generated significant amounts of effectiveness research and thereby moved into standard practice (Bernstein et al., 2009; Gentilello et al., 1999; Soderstrom et al., 2007). Hospital settings became the next target for SBIRT for tobacco and substance use, with funding for trials across the

United States (Rigotti, Munafo, & Stead, 2008). As this happened, the type of provider using SBIRT shifted from physicians to nurses, medical assistants, pulmonary staff, medical technicians, and social workers. Hospital-based programs were successful in connecting smokers with quit lines and getting substance-using individuals to a substance abuse provider for additional assessment and/or treatment. SAMHSA then became a major funder of initiatives to incorporate SBIRT training into medical residency, nursing, and social work training programs. These training programs have been initiated across the United States and have supported the creation of training materials that are available online to facilitate the implementation of SBIRT by many different types of providers (Oregon Health and Science University, n.d.; University of Maryland School of Medicine, n.d.).

Massive efforts to establish SBIRT as a first line of intervention for alcohol, tobacco, and other drugs across multiple medical settings (e.g., primary care, family medicine, emergency departments, specialty care) have yielded mixed results (Babor et al., 2017). Often, funded projects have allowed SBIRT to be initiated in various settings. However, once projects were completed and funding ended, SBIRT has not always been continued. Unfortunately, practitioners and programs often relapsed back to standard practice and implemented only the minimum amount of screening or referral required by accrediting bodies or medical provider policies.

Effective referral and patient engagement in brief interventions and treatment programs have been challenging. One complicating factor is that many different types of screening and interventions are recommended in these settings. Screenings for domestic violence, depression, other mental health conditions, and HIV and infectious disease risk compete for the precious time of medical providers.

Suffice it to say, the implementation of SBIRT practices has been launched successfully across many different settings, and a multidisciplinary array of providers have been trained. However, full and sustained implementation has been successful only for certain substances (primarily alcohol and tobacco) and in settings with implementation champions on staff, individuals convinced of the value and committed to the practice of SBIRT. The uptake, spread, and engagement of providers and programs have been less than hoped for, limiting the promise of prevention and early intervention for substance abuse using the SBIRT protocol.

IMPLEMENTATION, IMPORTANCE, AND IMPACT OF SBIRT

Viewing substance use initiation and recovery from the stages of change framework (DiClemente, 2018), it appears that screening and a brief intervention can interrupt the initiation process. As youth and adults move into preparation, action, and maintenance stages of problematic patterns of substance use, a trusted professional at an opportune moment asking about this pattern, listening carefully to the answers, exploring motivational considerations, and offering clear and respectful advice and support for needed assistance can interrupt initiation. Prevention and early intervention as patterns of problematic use develop are critical functions of SBIRT.

Similarly, for individuals whose problematic patterns of use continue and become moderate to severe SUDs, the same approach can offer these addicted individuals a lifeline and help them move through the stages of recovery. Tasks of the early stages of precontemplation and contemplation for recovery include generating interest and concern about a need for change and fostering decisional consideration that can tip the decision balance toward change. SBIRT interventions performed competently have the potential to instigate movement through these early stages. For individuals with ambivalence or an emerging decision to make a change, SBIRT interventions have supported the decision and offered some ideas for a plan to disrupt and modify the problematic pattern of substance use significantly (e.g., cutting down, talking to a counselor, calling a quit line, asking spouse or family to help).

SBIRT for substance use can be a "tipping point" (Gladwell, 2000) to foster movement through the process of change. Brief interventions alone have resulted in significant modification of substance use (Soderstrom et al., 2007). It is important to point out that the brief intervention does not produce the change but rather stimulates the patient to consider and act to create change. There are many events in the lives of substance users that can influence them to make a change. Personal experiences, feedback from family and friends, death of a friend, and medical events are all events that can promote changing one's behavior (DiClemente, 2006) and often happen by chance. Establishing an SBIRT protocol represents an attempt to create such a tipping point to interfere with the initiation of substance use and to instigate recovery from disordered use.

The promise of substance use prevention and early intervention that can interrupt initiation and promote recovery has not been fully realized with SBIRT. Significant barriers continue to limit progress. Provider time and reluctance have interfered with implementation. As the economics of providing care make the time allocated to each patient shorter, the demands of addressing multiple risk factors increase, and the ever-increasing focus on specialty care grows, SBIRT for substance use is viewed as a luxury and not a necessity. Many do not see screening for substance use as something they are prepared to do by training or temperament. Others still believe it will not be effective and that it could alienate patients. Stigma continues to impact implementation.

Systems of care face barriers and have difficulty seeing where the screening fits in, who should do it, and how to create a viable referral system for the different types of substances screened. Screening and intervening with tobacco and alcohol lead the way in creating system approaches, and other substances are often way behind. We must develop viable and sustainable ways to implement SBIRT if we are to see the promise of SBIRT for the reduction of hazardous and harmful substance use fulfilled (SAMHSA, 2013).

Developing, implementing, and sustaining an effective SBIRT protocol in any setting requires a systemic perspective (Babor et al., 2007). In many settings, one or more providers, convinced of the value of SBIRT, are committed to screening and intervention with every one of their patients. These champions, however effective in their practices, represent outliers and not the systemic commitment needed to create a viable and sustainable universal screening program. Administration and staff must find space, train and motivate providers, set the policy, and make it clear to patients that, in this setting, SBIRT is standard practice ("We ask everybody"). Current staff and new hires should be oriented to and initiated into this practice. Sustaining change requires that the new behavior become a normative part of the agency culture.

CONCLUSION

The field of substance misuse prevention and treatment has progressed in many ways over the past 40 years. Addiction is best understood as a chronic disease or disorder rather than a moral failing. We have a better understanding of relapse and recycling through the change process as learning processes. Motivation now is understood to involve movement through a series of tasks or stages needed to create and maintain change. Substance users are no longer condemned to wait until the inexorable accumulation of consequences provides enough motivation to move them into recovery. Harm reduction is recognized as a valuable tool. We have more medications that can assist individuals struggling with certain SUDs to navigate the difficult action stage of change.

Added to this list must be the awareness that highlighting substance use behavior and offering a brief intervention that is motivational, supportive, and presented in a respectful manner can significantly alter the course of substance use initiation and recovery. Hopefully, the next 10 years will see that the implementation of SBIRT for substance use is well-established, effective, and standard practice in many of the most opportunistic settings described in this chapter. Only then will we be able to see a substantial downturn in the prevalence, consequences, economic costs, and human suffering caused by substance misuse and disorders.

RESOURCES

- General information on SBIRT: https://www.samhsa.gov/sbirt

- SBIRT training resources: http://www.integration.samhsa.gov/clinical-practice/sbirt/training-other-resources

- SBIRT toolkit and resources for clients, professionals, and organizers: https://ireta.org/resources/sbirt-toolkit/

- Some webinars on the effectiveness of SBIRT: https://ireta.org/resources/what-is-the-evidence-for-drug-sbirt-in-general-health-settings-and-what-does-it-mean/

- University of Maryland, SBIRT/MD3 website: http://www.sbirt.umaryland.edu/

- MDQuit website information on SBIRT: http://mdquit.org/cessation-programs/screening-brief-intervention-and-referral-treatment-sbirt

- Information on Medicare and Medicaid coverage of SBIRT services: https://www.cms.gov/Outreach-and-Education/Medicare-Learning-Network-MLN/MLNProducts/downloads/SBIRT_Factsheet_ICN904084.pdf

- White paper on evidence for SBIRT effectiveness (2011): https://www.samhsa.gov/sites/default/files/sbirtwhitepaper_0.pdf

- Some information on the effectiveness of SBIRT screening and assessment tools: http://iusbirt.org/articles/effectiveness-of-screening-assessment-tools/

REFERENCES

Adam, A., Schwartz, R. P., Wu, L. T., Subramaniam, G., Laska, E., Sharma, G., . . . McNeely, J. (2019). Electronic self-administered screening for substance use in adult primary care patients: Feasibility and acceptability of the tobacco, alcohol, prescription medication, and other substance use (myTAPS) screening tool. *Addiction Science & Clinical Practice, 14,* 39. http://dx.doi.org/10.1186/s13722-019-0167-z

Agerwala, S. M., & McCance-Katz, E. F. (2012). Integrating screening, brief intervention, and referral to treatment (SBIRT) into clinical practice settings: A brief review. *Journal of Psychoactive Drugs, 44,* 307–317. http://dx.doi.org/10.1080/02791072.2012.720169

American College of Surgeons, Committee on Trauma. (2006). *Resources for optimal care of the injured patient: 2006.* Chicago, IL: Author.

Babor, T. F., Del Boca, F., & Bray, J. W. (2017). Screening, brief intervention and referral to treatment: Implications of SAMHSA's SBIRT initiative for substance abuse policy and practice. *Addiction, 112*(Suppl. 2), 110–117. http://dx.doi.org/10.1111/add.13675

Babor, T. F., & Higgins-Biddle, J. C. (2000). Alcohol screening and brief intervention: Dissemination strategies for medical practice and public health. *Addiction, 95,* 677–686. http://dx.doi.org/10.1046/j.1360-0443.2000.9556773.x

Babor, T. F., McRee, B. G., Kassebaum, P. A., Grimaldi, P. L., Ahmed, K., & Bray, J. (2007). Screening, brief intervention, and referral to treatment (SBIRT): Toward a public health approach to the management of substance abuse. *Substance Abuse, 28,* 7–30. http://dx.doi.org/10.1300/J465v28n03_03

Bernstein, E., Topp, D., Shaw, E., Girard, C., Pressman, K., Woolcock, E., & Bernstein, J. (2009). A preliminary report of knowledge translation: Lessons from taking screening and brief intervention techniques from the research setting into regional systems of care. *Academic Emergency Medicine, 16,* 1225–1233. http://dx.doi.org/10.1111/j.1553-2712.2009.00516.x

Carlson, R. G. (2006). Ethnography and applied substance misuse research. In W. R. Miller & K. M. Carroll (Eds.), *Rethinking substance abuse: What the science shows and what we should do about it* (pp. 201–219). New York, NY: Guilford Press.

Center for Substance Abuse Treatment. (1999). *Enhancing motivation for change in substance abuse treatment* (DHHS Publication No. (SMA) 99-3354). Retrieved from https://www.ncbi.nlm.nih.gov/books/NBK64967/

DiClemente, C. C. (2006). Natural change and the troublesome use of substances. In W. R. Miller & K. M. Carroll (Eds.), *Rethinking substance abuse: What the science shows and what we should do about it* (pp. 81–96). New York, NY: Guilford Press.

DiClemente, C. C. (2018). *Addiction and change: How addictions develop and addicted people recover* (2nd ed.). New York, NY: Guilford Press.

DiClemente, C. C., Corno, C. M., Graydon, M. M., Wiprovnick, A. E., & Knoblach, D. J. (2017). Motivational interviewing, enhancement, and brief interventions over the last decade: A review of reviews of efficacy and effectiveness. *Psychology of Addictive Behaviors, 31*, 862–887. http://dx.doi.org/10.1037/adb0000318

DiClemente, C. C., & Velasquez, M. (2002). Motivational interviewing and the stages of change. In W. R. Miller & S. Rollnick (Eds.), *Motivational interviewing: Preparing people for change* (2nd ed., pp. 201–216). New York, NY: Guilford Press.

Dixon, L. B., Medoff, D., Goldberg, R., Lucksted, A., Kreyenbuhl, J., DiClemente, C., . . . Afful, J. (2009). Is implementation of the 5 A's of smoking cessation at community mental health centers effective for reduction of smoking by patients with serious mental illness? *The American Journal on Addictions, 18*, 386–392.

Dwinnells, R. (2015). SBIRT as a vital sign for behavioral health identification, diagnosis, and referral in community health care. *Annals of Family Medicine, 13*, 261–263. http://dx.doi.org/10.1370/afm.1776

Fleming, M. F., Mundt, M. P., French, M. T., Manwell, L. B., Stauffacher, E. A., & Barry, K. L. (2002). Brief physician advice for problem drinkers: Long-term efficacy and benefit–cost analysis. *Alcoholism: Clinical and Experimental Research, 26*, 36–43. http://dx.doi.org/10.1111/j.1530-0277.2002.tb02429.x

Foxx, R. M., & Brown, R. A. (1979). Nicotine fading and self-monitoring for cigarette abstinence or controlled smoking. *Journal of Applied Behavior Analysis, 12*, 111–125. http://dx.doi.org/10.1901/jaba.1979.12-111

Gentilello, L. M., Rivara, F. P., Donovan, D. M., Jurkovich, G. J., Daranciang, E., Dunn, C. W., . . . Ries, R. R. (1999). Alcohol interventions in a trauma center as a means of reducing the risk of injury recurrence. *Annals of Surgery, 230*, 473–480. http://dx.doi.org/10.1097/00000658-199910000-00003

Gladwell, M. (2000). *The tipping point: How little things can make a big difference*. Boston, MA: Little, Brown.

Glass, J. E., Hamilton, A. M., Powell, B. J., Perron, B. E., Brown, R. T., & Ilgen, M. A. (2015). Specialty substance use disorder services following brief alcohol intervention: A meta-analysis of randomized controlled trials. *Addiction, 110*, 1404–1415. http://dx.doi.org/10.1111/add.12950

Griggs, C. A., Weiner, S. G., & Feldman, J. A. (2015). Prescription drug monitoring programs: Examining limitations and future approaches. *The Western Journal of Emergency Medicine, 16*, 67–70. http://dx.doi.org/10.5811/westjem.2014.10.24197

Hettema, J. E., & Hendricks, P. S. (2010). Motivational interviewing for smoking cessation: A meta-analytic review. *Journal of Consulting and Clinical Psychology, 78*, 868–884. http://dx.doi.org/10.1037/a0021498

Holland, C. L., Pringle, J. L., & Barbetti, V. (2009). Identification of physician barriers to the application of screening and brief intervention for problem alcohol and drug use. *Alcoholism Treatment Quarterly, 27*, 174–183. http://dx.doi.org/10.1080/07347320902784890

Jamal, A., Dube, S. R., Malarcher, A. M., Shaw, L., & Engstrom, M. C. (2012). Tobacco use screening and counseling during physician office visits among adults—National Ambulatory Medical Care Survey and National Health Interview Survey, United States, 2005–2009. *Morbidity and Mortality Weekly Report Supplements, 61*, 38–45.

Kaner, E. F., Dickinson, H. O., Beyer, F., Pienaar, E., Schlesinger, C., Campbell, F., . . . Heather, N. (2009). The effectiveness of brief alcohol interventions in primary care settings: A systematic review. *Drug and Alcohol Review, 28,* 301–323. http://dx.doi.org/10.1111/j.1465-3362.2009.00071.x

Kazdin, A. E. (1974). Reactive self-monitoring: The effects of response desirability, goal setting, and feedback. *Journal of Consulting and Clinical Psychology, 42,* 704–716. http://dx.doi.org/10.1037/h0037050

Lindson-Hawley, N., Thompson, T. P., & Begh, R. (2015). Motivational interviewing for smoking cessation. *Cochrane Database of Systematic Reviews.* http://dx.doi.org/10.1002/14651858.CD006936.pub3

Lundahl, B., Moleni, T., Burke, B. L., Butters, R., Tollefson, D., Butler, C., & Rollnick, S. (2013). Motivational interviewing in medical care settings: A systematic review and meta-analysis of randomized controlled trials. *Patient Education and Counseling, 93,* 157–168. http://dx.doi.org/10.1016/j.pec.2013.07.012

Madras, B. K., Compton, W. M., Avula, D., Stegbauer, T., Stein, J. B., & Clark, H. W. (2009). Screening, brief interventions, referral to treatment (SBIRT) for illicit drug and alcohol use at multiple healthcare sites: Comparison at intake and 6 months later. *Drug and Alcohol Dependence, 99,* 280–295. http://dx.doi.org/10.1016/j.drugalcdep.2008.08.003

Mayfield, D., McLeod, G., & Hall, P. (1974). The CAGE Questionnaire: Validation of a new alcoholism screening instrument. *The American Journal of Psychiatry, 131,* 1121–1123.

McQueen, J., Howe, T. E., Allan, L., Mains, D., & Hardy, V. (2011). Brief interventions for heavy alcohol users admitted to general hospital wards. *Cochrane Database of Systematic Reviews.* http://dx.doi.org/10.1002/14651858.CD005191.pub3

Miller, W. R., & Rollnick, S. (1991). *Motivational interviewing: Preparing people to change addictive behavior.* New York, NY: Guilford Press.

Miller, W. R., Sovereign, R. G., & Krege, B. (1988). Motivational interviewing with problem drinkers: II. The Drinker's Check-up as a preventive intervention. *Behavioural Psychotherapy, 16,* 251–268. http://dx.doi.org/10.1017/S0141347300014129

Minozzi, S., Saulle, R., De Crescenzo, F., & Amato, L. (2016). Psychosocial interventions for psychostimulant misuse. *Cochrane Database of Systematic Reviews.* http://dx.doi.org/10.1002/14651858.CD011866

Mitchell, S. G., Gryczynski, J., Gonzales, A., Moseley, A., Peterson, T., O'Grady, K. E., & Schwartz, R. P. (2012). Screening, brief intervention, and referral to treatment (SBIRT) for substance use in a school-based program: Services and outcomes. *The American Journal on Addictions, 21*(Suppl. 1), S5–S13. http://dx.doi.org/10.1111/j.1521-0391.2012.00299.x

Mitchell, S. G., Gryczynski, J., O'Grady, K. E., & Schwartz, R. P. (2013). SBIRT for adolescent drug and alcohol use: Current status and future directions. *Journal of Substance Abuse Treatment, 44,* 463–472. http://dx.doi.org/10.1016/j.jsat.2012.11.005

National Institute on Alcohol Abuse and Alcoholism. (2014). *Treatment for alcohol problems: Finding and getting help* (NIH Publication No. 14-7974). Retrieved from https://pubs.niaaa.nih.gov/publications/Treatment/treatment.htm

National Institute on Drug Abuse. (n.d.). *NIDA drug screening tool.* Retrieved from https://www.drugabuse.gov/nmassist/

National Institute on Drug Abuse. (2018). *Misuse of prescription drugs.* Retrieved from https://www.drugabuse.gov/publications/research-reports/misuse-prescription-drugs

Oregon Health and Science University. (n.d.). *SBIRT Oregon.* Retrieved from https://www.sbirtoregon.org/

Orford, J., & Edwards, G. (1977). *Alcoholism: A comparison of treatment and advice, with a study of influence of marriage* (Maudsley Monograph No. 26). New York, NY: Oxford University Press.

Prochaska, J. O., & DiClemente, C. C. (1984). *The transtheoretical approach: Crossing the traditional boundaries of therapy*. Malabar, FL: Krieger.

Rigotti, N. A., Munafo, M. R., & Stead, L. F. (2008). Smoking cessation interventions for hospitalized smokers: A systematic review. *Archives of Internal Medicine, 168*, 1950–1960. http://dx.doi.org/10.1001/archinte.168.18.1950

Saitz, R., Palfai, T. P., Cheng, D. M., Alford, D. P., Bernstein, J. A., Lloyd-Travaglini, C. A., . . . Samet, J. H. (2014, August 6). Screening and brief intervention for drug use in primary care: The ASPIRE randomized clinical trial. *JAMA, 312*, 502–513. http://dx.doi.org/10.1001/jama.2014.7862

Selzer, M. L. (1971). The Michigan Alcoholism Screening Test: The quest for a new diagnostic instrument. *The American Journal of Psychiatry, 127*, 1653–1658. http://dx.doi.org/10.1176/ajp.127.12.1653

Siu, A. L. (2015). Behavioral and pharmacotherapy interventions for tobacco smoking cessation in adults, including pregnant women: U.S. Preventive Services Task Force recommendation statement. *Annals of Internal Medicine, 163*, 622–634. http://dx.doi.org/10.7326/M15-2023

Skinner, H. A. (1982). The Drug Abuse Screening Test. *Addictive Behaviors, 7*, 363–371. http://dx.doi.org/10.1016/0306-4603(82)90005-3

Soderstrom, C. A., DiClemente, C. C., Dischinger, P. C., Hebel, J. R., McDuff, D. R., Auman, K. M., & Kufera, J. A. (2007). A controlled trial of brief intervention versus brief advice for at-risk drinking trauma center patients. *The Journal of Trauma: Injury, Infection, and Critical Care, 62*, 1102–1112. http://dx.doi.org/10.1097/TA.0b013e31804bdb26

Stead, L. F., Bergson, G., & Lancaster, T. (2008). Physician advice for smoking cessation. *Cochrane Database of Systematic Reviews*. http://dx.doi.org/10.1002/14651858.CD000165.pub3

Substance Abuse and Mental Health Services Administration. (2013). *Systems-level implementation of screening, brief intervention, and referral to treatment* (HHS Publication No. SMA 13-4741). Retrieved from https://www.integration.samhsa.gov/sbirt/tap33.pdf

Substance Abuse and Mental Health Services Administration. (2015). *Behavioral health trends in the United States: Results from the 2014 National Survey on Drug Use and Health* (HHS Publication No. SMA 15-4927, NSDUH Series H-50). Retrieved from https://www.samhsa.gov/data/sites/default/files/NSDUH-FRR1-2014/NSDUH-FRR1-2014.pdf

Substance Abuse and Mental Health Services Administration. (2017). *Screening, brief intervention, and referral to treatment*. Retrieved from http://www.samhsa.gov/sbirt

Substance Abuse and Mental Health Services Administration. (2018). *Results from the 2017 National Survey on Drug Use and Health: Detailed tables*. Retrieved from https://www.samhsa.gov/data/report/2017-nsduh-detailed-tables

University of Maryland School of Medicine. (n.d.). MarylanD M.D.s Making a Difference (MD3). *University of Maryland School of Medicine*. Retrieved from http://www.sbirt.umaryland.edu/

U.S. Department of Health and Human Services. (1996). *Smoking cessation: Clinical practice guidelines*. Rockville, MD: Public Health Service, Agency for Health Care Policy and Research.

U.S. Department of Health and Human Services. (2016). *Facing addiction in America: The Surgeon General's report on alcohol, drugs, and health*. Washington, DC: Author.

U.S. Preventive Services Task Force. (2019). *Drug use, illicit: Screening*. Retrieved from https://www.uspreventiveservicestaskforce.org/Page/Document/UpdateSummary-Final/drug-use-illicit-screening

Whitlock, E. P., Polen, M. R., Green, C. A., Orleans, T., & Klein, J. (2004). Behavioral counseling interventions in primary care to reduce risky/harmful alcohol use by adults: A summary of the evidence for the U.S. Preventive Services Task Force. *Annals of Internal Medicine, 140,* 557–568. http://dx.doi.org/10.7326/0003-4819-140-7-200404060-00017

World Health Organization. (2017). *World health statistics 2017: Monitoring health for the SDGs, sustainable development goals.* Retrieved from https://apps.who.int/iris/handle/10665/255336

2

Approaches to Screening for Alcohol Misuse in Primary Health Care

James F. Schaus

The U.S. Preventive Services Task Force (USPSTF) recommends screening for unhealthy alcohol use in primary care settings in adults 18 years or older, including pregnant women, and providing persons engaged in risky or hazardous drinking with brief behavioral counseling interventions to reduce unhealthy alcohol use (Curry et al., 2018). It is important to assess for possible alcohol use disorder (AUD) because treatment and referral often require urgent action. An AUD is defined by the *Diagnostic and Statistical Manual of Mental Disorders* (5th ed.; *DSM–5*; American Psychiatric Association, 2013) as a maladaptive pattern of alcohol use leading to clinically significant impairment or distress, as manifested by two or more of 11 alcohol-related experiences within 1 year. Severity is based on the number of symptoms, from mild (two to three symptoms) to moderate (four to five symptoms) to severe (six or more symptoms).

This chapter covers the principles of comprehensive preventive screening, highlighting unhealthy alcohol use patterns and related consequences experienced by various patient populations and age groups, and the importance of choosing appropriate alcohol screening methods in these disparate populations. The screening, brief intervention, and referral to treatment (SBIRT) screening model proposed by the Substance Abuse Mental Health Services Administration (SAMHSA; 2013) and the National Institute of Alcohol Abuse and Alcoholism (NIAAA) recommended screening methods are discussed in the chapter.

---

http://dx.doi.org/10.1037/0000199-003
Screening, Brief Intervention, and Referral to Treatment for Substance Use: A Practitioner's Guide,
M. D. Cimini and J. L. Martin (Editors)

Health care settings, including primary medical, psychiatric, psycho-therapeutic, and mental health counseling, provide ideal opportunities to conduct routine universal alcohol screening. Routine screening substantially improves the detection of unhealthy alcohol use, including "at-risk" drinking, heavy episodic drinking, and AUD. In this chapter, alcohol screening is discussed in the context of routine clinical practice because patients frequently present with the consequences of unhealthy alcohol use. This chapter also provides recommended evidence-based screening tools leading to brief intervention methods in various clinical settings, focusing on high-risk populations. I also discuss ways to transition from a positive alcohol screen to an effective and efficient brief intervention, using the principles of motivational interviewing.

PRINCIPLES OF PREVENTIVE SCREENING

Routine screening for unhealthy alcohol use is a major component of disease prevention in the primary health care setting. The stages of disease prevention are divided into primary, secondary, and tertiary screening efforts. Across a patient's life span, the prevention of disease begins in the primary prevention stage with the attempt to remove risk factors before the adverse behavior begins. However, most screening efforts in clinical practice target the secondary prevention stage, at a time in the life span when early use of alcohol has already begun, but harmful or frequent use patterns are not yet firmly established. Adolescence and early adulthood are critical times for secondary prevention and alcohol screening, which identifies early harmful use and consequences and helps set the stage for behavior change. Screening efforts are specifically applied to detect current use, and it is critical to use a screening tool that accurately and efficiently identifies early unhealthy drinking patterns. Tertiary prevention is used in the later stages of the life span when disease progression has already occurred and prevention efforts are targeted at reducing complications of the disease or behavior.

The decision to implement routine preventive screening is complex and difficult, often decided by a practice leadership group considering commitment to various preventive services. Routine screening is a commitment of time, expense, clinician training, and intention to sustain a comprehensive preventive health program. Putting prevention into practice goes beyond the primary function of a medical or mental health care practice when the function is defined as responding to the patient's presenting complaints. Although routine screening is ultimately in the patient's best interest, it is primarily driven by the health care provider and health care system and not the individual. The patient-centered practice places the patient's perceived reason for seeking care as paramount and incorporates routine screening as a secondary but highly important component of practice. The patient should perceive the screening questions as related to their overall general health and wellness, and screenings are most impactful when related to their present-ing complaint.

The screen may also be conducted on a case-by-case basis by individual clinicians, incorporated into routine patient history taking, or done episodically as it applies to the presenting complaint. For example, inquiry regarding alco-hol use is a frequent component of patient history and essential information for any patient presenting with respiratory, cardiovascular, gastrointestinal, or mental health complaints. Often, the same screening instrument used for routine universal screening is used in the context of routine patient history taking, giving consistent and reproducible information at various points.

Alcohol screening questions are ideally posed in a general preventive health screening questionnaire given at the initial visit and updated period-ically. This places sensitive alcohol screening questions in the context of other health questions, somewhat decreasing the stigma that might be present had the same question been asked as an isolated screening question. More honest responses to alcohol screening may be elicited with the use of self-report questionnaires, rather than in response to direct questions asked verbally by a clinician or other health care personnel. The frequency and periodicity of repeating the screening questions are often difficult to deter-mine and are not well established. The USPSTF does not state the optimal screening interval to repeat screening for unhealthy alcohol use in adults. If the alcohol screen is used too often as a routine at every health care visit, there is the risk that the patient will experience "questionnaire fatigue" and perceive this as repetitive and intrusive, compromising patient engage-ment and honesty of response. At our student health service, we routinely screen all patients for alcohol use at initial presentation and update their responses annually.

When choosing a particular subject for routine screening conducted across your patient population, consider whether it meets the criteria of being prevalent, harmful, and potentially amenable to various levels of treatment, including brief or extended counseling. Screening for unhealthy alcohol use meets all these criteria, and there are various brief evidence-based screening instruments available for this purpose. The ideal screening tool is inexpen-sive, brief, easy to administer, appropriate for the specific target population, and evidence based. For example, there are distinct evidence-based alcohol screening tools that should be used for various target populations, such as the CRAFFT screening test for adolescents (Knight, Sherritt, Harris, Gates, & Chang, 2003), high-risk drinking screening for adolescents or college students, and the CAGE questionnaire for screening older adults for AUD (Ewing, 1984). The choice of an evidence-based screening tool is made considering recent scientific evidence and an assessment of sufficient reliability by panels of experts, such as the USPSTF.

Brief and efficient screening tools that retain quality psychometric proper-ties are preferred over more lengthy instruments, and brevity is appreciated by providers, patients, and clients. For example, the information garnered from the brief Alcohol Use Disorders Identification Test—Consumption (AUDIT–C; Bush, Kivlahan, McDonell, Fihn, & Bradley, 1998) screening tool is often preferable to the lengthier full 10-question Alcohol Use Disorders Identification Test (AUDIT; Babor & Grant, 1989), considering time to complete and interpret. Because there are many competing agendas within the limited time frame of a health care visit, the time it takes to complete the survey instrument, ease of administration, and interpretation of results are important considerations in choosing the most appropriate screening instrument.

The decision to screen is usually based on the recommendation from a panel of experts such as the USPSTF, government agencies such as SAMHSA and NIAAA, or the Centers for Disease Control and Prevention. Grade A or B recommendations from these agencies, although not a mandate, serve as highly influential advice from panels of experts that have carefully considered the potential benefits, harms, and expense involved in routine health screening. USPSTF, for example, assigns one of five letter grades (A, B, C, D, or I) for strength of recommendation, and the various grades communicate the relative importance to clinicians of adopting a screening recommendation. A Grade A recommendation represents high certainty that the net benefit of screening is substantial, and a Grade B recommendation represents high certainty that the net benefit is moderate or there is moderate certainty that the net benefit is moderate to substantial.

SENSITIVITY AND SPECIFICITY OF SCREENING INSTRUMENTS

The screening instrument should have good psychometric properties, with high reliability and established validity. The term *sensitivity* refers to the ability of a test to correctly identify those people in a population who actually have the disorder. A highly sensitive test is desirable when the cost of missing people who do have the condition (a "false negative" result) is high. For example, the failure of a screening test to correctly identify a commercial airline pilot who exhibits frequent high-risk drinking could have potentially catastrophic results. *Specificity* is a test's ability to identify people in a population who do not have the disorder under investigation. A highly specific screening test is desirable when the cost of misclassification (a "false positive" result) is high. For example, a person could be unjustly denied insurance or other benefits due to a false-positive screening result for current alcohol misuse. A screening test with high sensitivity and a negative result essentially rules out the problem with a high degree of confidence (a mnemonic device to remember this is SNOUT—for sensitivity out). A screening test with high specificity and a positive result essentially rules in the problem with a high degree of confidence (the mnemonic is SPIN—for specificity in).

Ideally, a screening test should be both highly sensitive and specific. However, there is often a difficult choice to be made between these two test properties. Particular cutoff scores for specific tests determine the level of sensitivity and specificity. When choosing a specific cutoff score of a screening test, one must decide the desired level of confidence in ruling out or ruling in a particular condition.

A screening tool is often the first step of a multistage alcohol assessment process, and the initial screening tool and corresponding threshold should have a high sensitivity, perhaps erring on the side of identifying many patients who prove on secondary assessment to not be experiencing significant problems or who are not at significant risk. The use of a brief initial screening instrument with high sensitivity ensures that you reach the greatest number of patients possibly experiencing unhealthy alcohol use; following up with secondary assessment assures specificity.

ALCOHOL SCREENING TOOLS AND METHODS

Brief questions about typical recent alcohol consumption are being increasingly used as a first stage or prescreening attempt and are attractive due to their brevity and relative high sensitivity. A positive screening resulting from initial screening questions then leads to more detailed secondary assessments of alcohol-related consequences. Results of a more complete screening may also indicate that a diagnosis of a substance use disorder should be considered, but alcohol screenings do not indicate the definite presence or absence of AUD. For all the tools described in the next sections, a "standard drink" contains 14 grams of pure alcohol: 12 ounces of beer, 5 ounces of wine, or 1.5 ounces of 80-proof distilled spirits.

"5/4" Definition of High-Risk Drinking

My colleagues and I (Schaus, Sole, McCoy, Mullett, Bolden, et al., 2009) sought to identify the best rapid routine screening tool to be used in a college student health center to detect high-risk drinking and ultimately reduce alcohol-related harms. We characterized the drinking patterns of students presenting to a student health center and screening positive for the "5/4" definition of high-risk drinking, assessed their alcohol-related harms, and stratified the risk of experiencing harms. The 5/4 definition is more than five drinks in 2 hours for men or more than four drinks in 2 hours for women on one occasion. The study population was stratified into one of three groups based on self-reported alcohol use: nonheavy, heavy, and heavy and frequent drinkers. The students in the heavy and frequent group made up 20% of the sample but experienced 31% of the harms. From a public health perspective, a resource-limited intervention program has to target interventions to those with the greatest burden of disease, potentially requiring a more intense intervention or referral. The study concluded that the 5/4 screening question accurately identified college students already experiencing significant alcohol-related harms and that the addition of a frequency question (drinking 3 or more days per week) to the 5/4 question identified those students at highest risk and in greatest need of intervention. We have used this brief two-question alcohol screen for many years at our college health center as part of our comprehensive preventive college health questionnaire.

The USPSTF recommended screening for unhealthy alcohol use in primary care settings and determined that one- to three-item screening instruments have the best accuracy and utility for assessing unhealthy alcohol use in adults 18 years or older, including the AUDIT–C, the NIAAA Single Alcohol Screening Question, and the NIAAA three-question screen.

NIAAA-Recommended Single-Item Alcohol Screening Questionnaire

The NIAAA-recommended Single-Item Alcohol Screening Questionnaire (SASQ) has sensitivity ranging from 73% to 88% and specificity ranging from 74% to 100% for detecting the full spectrum of unhealthy alcohol use (Curry et al., 2018). The single question is "How many times in the past year have you had 5 or 4 (males or females, respectively) or more drinks in a day?"

NIAAA-Recommended Three-Question Screen

The three-question screen is used when evaluating the patient's typical drinking patterns and enables the provider to relate the NIAAA recommended advice not to exceed maximum drinking limits.

1. How many days per week do you drink alcohol?
2. On a typical day when you drink, how many drinks do you have?
3. What is the maximum number of drinks you had on any given day in the past month?

   This initial screen defines recommended maximum drinking limits:

- For men up to age 65, no more than four drinks in a day, and no more than 14 drinks in a week.
- For women and men over age 65, no more than three drinks in a day, and no more than seven drinks in a week.

Alcohol Use Disorders Identification Test—Consumption

The AUDIT–C (Bush et al., 1998) is composed of the first three consumption questions from the full 10-question AUDIT questionnaire (Babor & Grant, 1989). The third question of the AUDIT–C is somewhat variable, with some versions using five or more drinks and others using six or more drinks on one occasion:

1. How often did you have a drink containing alcohol in the past year?

   never (0), monthly or less (1), 2 to 4 times a month (2), 2 to 3 times a week (3), 4 or more times per week (4)

2. How many drinks did you have on a typical day when you were drinking in the past year?

   1 to 2 drinks (0), 3 to 4 drinks (1), 5 to 6 drinks (2), 7 to 9 drinks (3), 10 or more drinks (4)

3. How often did you have 6 or more drinks on one occasion in the past year?

   never (0), less than monthly (1), monthly (2), weekly (3), or daily or almost daily (4)

Scores range from 0 to 12. The score is negative if all points come from Question 1.

Research comparing the AUDIT and the AUDIT–C for alcohol screening in college students determined that both performed well for at-risk drinking detection (DeMartini & Carey, 2012). The briefer AUDIT–C performed significantly better than the full AUDIT when screening for at-risk drinking females. The AUDIT–C is preferred when both genders have to be assessed, and a suggested AUDIT–C cut off score of 5 should be used for females and 7 for males in college settings. Another recent study examined the AUDIT–C for detecting at-risk drinking among students who used on-campus primary care services (Campbell & Maisto, 2018). They found that the AUDIT–C significantly correlated with measures of alcohol consumption and negative drinking consequences and also supported a cutoff score of 5 for females and 7 for males. These cutoff scores are higher than those recommended based on research for other populations such as veterans and community primary care settings, with recommended cutoff scores of 3 for females and 4 for males (Bradley et al., 2007).

Alcohol Use Disorders Identification Test

The AUDIT (Babor & Grant, 1989) is a 10-question alcohol use questionnaire developed by the World Health Organization in 1970 that has components of consumption, alcohol-related harms, and assessment of alcohol misuse and dependence. The AUDIT does a good job assessing individuals with chronic alcohol problems, but it is not specifically designed to detect heavy episodic drinking patterns seen in college students. This 10-item scale has four possible answers for each question, from 0 to 4, giving a maximum possible score of 40. The cutoff score appropriate for college students is a matter of disagreement and ranges from a cutoff score of 6 to 11, with sensitivity of 80% at a score of 6. Another study demonstrated a sensitivity of 84% at a cutoff score of 11 (Aertgeerts et al., 2000). Kokotailo et al. (2004) suggested that a cutoff score of 8 resulted in a sensitivity of 82% and specificity of 78% with criteria for high risk heavy episodic drinking as opposed to a diagnosis of alcohol use disorders. It is perhaps too lengthy (i.e., it takes approximately 5 minutes to complete) to be used as an initial first stage alcohol screen, but the use of the AUDIT as a secondary assessment after a positive brief initial screen improves specificity.

1. How often do you have a drink containing alcohol?

   Never • Monthly or less • 2 to 4 times a month • 2 to 3 times a week • 4 or more times a week

2. How many standard drinks containing alcohol do you have on a typical day when drinking?

   1 or 2 • 3 or 4 • 5 or 6 • 7 to 9 • 10 or more

3. How often do you have six or more drinks on one occasion?

   Never • Less than monthly • Monthly • Weekly • Daily or almost daily

4. During the past year, how often have you found that you were not able to stop drinking once you had started?

   Never • Less than monthly • Monthly • Weekly • Daily or almost daily

5. During the past year, how often have you failed to do what was normally expected of you because of drinking?

   Never • Less than monthly • Monthly • Weekly • Daily or almost daily

6. During the past year, how often have you needed a drink in the morning to get yourself going after a heavy drinking session?

   Never • Less than monthly • Monthly • Weekly • Daily or almost daily

7. During the past year, how often have you had a feeling of guilt or remorse after drinking?

   Never • Less than monthly • Monthly • Weekly • Daily or almost daily

8. During the past year, have you been unable to remember what happened the night before because you had been drinking?

   Never • Less than monthly • Monthly • Weekly • Daily or almost daily

9. Have you or someone else been injured as a result of your drinking?

   No • Yes, but not in the past year • Yes, during the past year

10. Has a relative or friend, doctor or other health worker been concerned about your drinking or suggested you cut down?

    No • Yes, but not in the past year • Yes, during the past year

For Questions 9 and 10, which only have three responses, the scoring is 0, 2, and 4. For the general adult population, a score of 8 or more is associated with harmful or hazardous drinking. A score of 13 or more in women and 15 or more in men is likely to indicate alcohol dependence.

CRAFFT

The CRAFFT (Knight et al., 2003) was developed for use with adolescents and contains questions relating to both alcohol and drug use. If a conjoint screen for adolescents is desired, this tool efficiently combines alcohol and drug-related questions in a single brief, validated, six-question screen. The CRAFFT has adequate psychometric properties for detecting AUD and substance use disorders and is recommended by the American Academy of Pediatrics for use with adolescents:

C: Have you ever ridden in a *car* driven by someone (including yourself) who was "high" or had been using alcohol or drugs?
R: Do you ever use alcohol or drugs to *relax*, feel better about yourself, or fit in?
A: Do you ever use alcohol/drugs while you are by yourself, *alone*?
F: Do you ever *forget* things you did while using alcohol or drugs?
F: Do your family or *friends* ever tell you that you should cut down on your drinking or drug use?
T: Have you gotten into *trouble* while you were using alcohol or drugs?

Answering yes to two or more questions is highly predictive of an alcohol or drug-related disorder.

CAGE

The CAGE (Ewing, 1984) is a four-question questionnaire for adults to screen for chronic problem drinking and AUD. The CAGE lacks sensitivity to detect high-risk drinking and other alcohol misuse experienced by adolescents and college students:

C: Have you ever felt you should *cut down* on your drinking?
A: Have people *annoyed* you by criticizing your drinking?
G: Have you ever felt bad or *guilty* about your drinking?
E: *Eye opener*—have you ever had a drink first thing in the morning to steady your nerves or to get rid of a hangover?

Two or more positive responses are considered a positive test and indicate further assessment is warranted.

CUGE

The CUGE (Van Den Bruel, Aertgeerts, Hoppenbrouwers, Roelants, & Buntinx, 2004) is a brief screening instrument with simple yes or no answers and is most useful for screening for problem drinking in college students. At a cutoff of one positive answer, it has a sensitivity of 91% and specificity of 76.3%, acceptable for an initial screening instrument.

1. Have you ever felt you should cut down on your drinking?

2. Have you ever been under the influence of alcohol in a situation where it increased your chances of getting hurt (for example, when riding a bicycle, driving a car or operating a machine)?

3. Have you ever felt bad or guilty about your drinking?

4. Have you ever had a drink in the morning to get rid of a hangover?

CAPS–r

The CAPS–r (College Alcohol Problems Scale—revised; Maddock, Laforge, Rossi, & O'Hare, 2001), a revision of the original 20-item CAPS (O'Hare, 1997), is a short, reliable eight-item screening instrument measuring alcohol-related negative consequences in two main categories of social and personal problems and takes approximately three minutes to complete. It has demonstrated good reliability and concurrent validity in college student populations and is highly correlated with the original CAPS with little loss of information in the shorter revision. Although it was primarily designed to assess negative consequences of drinking as an outcome measure of research and program effectiveness, it can also be used as a clinical screening tool where a brief consequences inventory can be used to facilitate the transition to a brief intervention. The CAPS–r consists of eight items; participants are asked to indicate how often each item occurred as a result of drinking in the last year, and it is measured using a six-point Likert scale format. The scale can also be combined with alcohol quantity and frequency measures for a comprehensive assessment of alcohol use and consequences:

> In the past year, as a result of drinking alcoholic beverages I . . .

> (Social problems)

> 1. engaged in unplanned sexual activity.
> 2. drove under the influence.
> 3. did not use protection when engaging in sex.
> 4. engaged in illegal activities associated with drug use.

> (Personal problems)

> 1. felt sad, blue, or depressed.
> 2. was nervous or irritable.
> 3. felt bad about myself.
> 4. had problems with appetite or sleeping.

EVIDENCE-BASED SCREENING IN VARIOUS TARGET POPULATIONS

SBIRT is an evidence-based practice used to identify, reduce, and prevent problematic substance use and alcohol and drug use disorders. It consists of three major components: screening to assess a patient for risky substance use behavior using standardized screening tools, engaging the individual in a brief intervention providing feedback and using motivational interviewing techniques to induce behavior change, and referral to treatment for those who need additional services. The SBIRT model recommends using a brief one- to three-question initial screen such as the NIAAA three-question screen and, if positive, proceeding to further assessment using the 10-question AUDIT. The NIAAA clinicians guide "Helping Patients Who Drink Too Much" (U.S. Department of Health and Human Services, 2005) provides an efficient step-by-step approach, enabling the clinician to obtain an increasingly detailed drinking history. It typically takes less than 5 minutes to complete and documents the number of drinking occasions over the past year, the typical amount consumed per occasion, and the number of binge drinking episodes. The NIAAA defines gender-specific criteria for at-risk alcohol consumption by both typical weekly consumption and single-day consumption. In a typical week, males who drink at least 14 drinks and females who drink at least seven drinks are considered at-risk drinkers. In a single day, males who consume at least five drinks and females who consume at least four drinks are considered at risk.

It is important to assess for possible AUD because treatment and referral often require urgent action. An AUD is defined by the *DSM–5* as a maladaptive pattern of alcohol use leading to clinically significant impairment or distress, as manifested by two or more of 11 alcohol-related experiences within 1 year. Severity is based on the number of symptoms, from mild (two to three symptoms) to moderate (four to five symptoms) to severe (six or more symptoms).

With adolescent and college student populations, and in other special circumstances, however, research indicates that clinicians have to be aware of several factors affecting screen decisions.

College Students' High-Risk Episodic Drinking

Heavy episodic drinking by college students is the most serious public health problem on college campuses (Wechsler, Dowdall, Maenner, Gledhill-Hoyt, & Lee, 1998). Alcohol misuse and related harms among college students primarily involve high-risk drinking, often referred to as *binge drinking*. NIAAA defines binge drinking as a pattern of drinking that brings blood alcohol concentration levels to 0.08 g/dL. This typically occurs after four drinks for women and five drinks for men in about 2 hours. The four College Alcohol Studies conducted at Harvard School of Public Health showed the rate of binge drinking among college students to be approximately 43%; this number held relatively steady between 1993 and 2001 (Wechsler et al., 2002). In 2005, SAMHSA found a similar prevalence rate of 44.7% in college students reporting five or more drinks per occasion. The 2016 Monitoring the Future Study at the University of Michigan showed a significant decrease in binge drinking rates among college students, with a reported prevalence of 32% having consumed five or more drinks in a row at least once in the previous 2 weeks. There has been a 24% proportional decrease in reported binge drinking rates among college students from 1991 to 2016, from 43% to 32% (Schulenberg et al., 2016).

According to Hingson, Zha, and Weitzman (2009), an estimated 1,825 college students age 18 to 24 die each year of alcohol-related injuries. An estimated 600,000 are injured each year due to drinking, and the secondary effects include 696,000 who were hit or assaulted by a drinking student. According to SAMHSA, an estimated 29% of the college student population has driven under the influence of alcohol in the past year. It is estimated that there are 97,000 victims of alcohol-related sexual assault or date rape at colleges each year. The link between alcohol, sexual assaults, and driving under the influence is evidence that binge drinking among college students is not only harmful to the people drinking but also to many others in their communities.

According to a study conducted by Foote, Wilkens, and Vavagiakis (2004), surveying 249 college health centers, only 32% conducted routine alcohol screening. Only 12% used standardized screening instruments, predominantly the CAGE, which is an inappropriate screening tool for the college population because it is not designed to primarily screen for episodic high-risk drinking. A more recent study showed some improvement, with 44% of colleges reporting using at least one formal alcohol screening tool (Winters et al., 2011). However, less than half of this group (44%) also reported using one of the most favorable tools validated for use with college students (AUDIT, CUGE, CAPS).

Despite high rates of high-risk drinking among the college student population, students often do not seek treatment for alcohol problems. The National Epidemiologic Survey on Alcohol and Related Conditions showed that despite higher rates of AUDs among college students compared with their noncollege peers, college students were significantly less likely to seek or receive treatment (Blanco et al., 2008). Routine alcohol screening is therefore essential to detect students who fail to self-identify drinking problems and seek treatment on their own initiative, providing opportunities to intervene and prevent harmful consequences and the establishment of lifelong harmful drinking patterns.

As individual- and population-level initiatives take hold on college campuses, prevalence rates for high-risk drinking have begun to decline. Among those individual level initiatives is SBIRT, conducted on college campuses at various venues, including college student health and counseling centers, credited with influencing a recent decline and movement toward safer levels of alcohol consumption. Expanding use and expertise in SBIRT by the professional staff at student health and counseling centers is expected to result in further declines in high-risk drinking rates and alcohol-related harms and should now be the routine standard of care. Approximately 20% of college students need intervention or treatment for alcohol misuse, but most problem drinkers do not think they have a problem and never seek counseling (Weitzman, Nelson, Seibring, & Wechsler, 2005). The continuing challenge is to get the largest number of students screened and then get these students into counseling. We have the proper evidence-based alcohol screening tools and must continue to find better ways and venues to apply these tools (Larimer & Cronce, 2007). The NIAAA states that single question quantity and frequency screening instruments are appropriate initial screens for episodic high-risk drinking among college students and have been validated in various health care settings.

Adolescents

The current USPSTF recommendation (Curry et al., 2018) states that the evidence is insufficient to recommend screening and brief counseling interventions for alcohol use in adolescents aged 12 to 17. However, the lack of research evidence does not rule out the potential effectiveness of screening and brief interventions for this population. For example, it is recognized that this population experiences frequent high-risk behaviors, including heavy episodic drinking and alcohol-related injuries, which are a leading cause of death among adolescents. Research has indicated that heavy alcohol use during adolescence could interfere with normal brain development and increase the risk of developing an AUD in later life. Screening adolescents for alcohol use is an opportunity for primary and early secondary prevention, potentially preventing a lifetime of high-risk exposure and consequences. For these reasons, the American Academy of Pediatrics supports alcohol screening and brief counseling for adolescents and specifically recommends the use of the CRAFFT screening tool.

People With Co-Occurring Mental Health and Psychiatric Conditions

AUD is common in this population and is a frequent cause and effect for various mental health diagnoses and a frequent contributing factor in exacerbations of existing mental health conditions. According to *DSM–5*, it is essential to screen for alcohol use and AUD whenever a patient presents with mental health conditions in the primary health care setting (Kranzler & Soyka, 2018). It is the standard of care to assess alcohol use in outpatient psychiatry, psychology, and counseling settings, adopting the biopsychosocial model of care. Alcohol is a psychoactive substance with dose-related alterations in cognition, memory, judgment, impulsivity, and other aspects of abnormal and high-risk behavior. All psychotropic medications have potential alcohol interactions and alcohol-related side effects, and a detailed inquiry about recent alcohol use must be conducted whenever psychotropic medications are prescribed. Alcohol has well-known effects on sleeping, with alterations in initiation and maintenance of sleep, and lack of sleep further exacerbates existing mental health problems

People With Alcohol-Related Medical Complications

Alcohol misuse is a contributing cause of myriad medical conditions affecting all organ systems of the body and is associated with significant psychological consequences and lack of social well-being. Consequences of unhealthy drinking seen in general medical settings frequently include traumatic injury, hypertension, gastrointestinal symptoms, liver disease, cardiac symptoms, and neurological symptoms. Behavioral health consequences include anxiety, depression, suicidality, comorbid substance use disorders, sleep disturbances, and social and legal problems.

Alcohol-related chronic liver disease (cirrhosis) is relatively common in the adult primary care setting. Failure to assess and address alcohol use in a patient experiencing liver disease has significant consequences with progression to irreversible end-stage cirrhosis. Early detection of AUD could alter the trajectory of liver disease and prevent a progressive decline in hepatic function. It is imperative to screen for severe AUD in any patient presenting with circumstances of abrupt cessation or withdrawal from alcohol because this may result in hallucinations, seizures, and death (Tetrault & O'Connor, 2018).

People With a Family History of Alcohol Use Disorder

An essential component of the secondary assessment of alcohol misuse is obtaining a family history of possible AUD because this places patients at higher risk of developing alcohol-related problems and severe AUD due to established genetic component and hereditary effects. A family history of AUD can also serve as a deterrent; patients frequently express fear and avoidance of alcohol because they have observed other family members struggle with alcohol misuse and alcohol-related disease. One must assess current alcohol use patterns whenever a patient describes a family history of AUD.

TRANSITIONING FROM A POSITIVE ALCOHOL SCREEN TO AN EFFECTIVE AND EFFICIENT BRIEF INTERVENTION

The transtheoretical (stages of change) model (Prochaska, DiClemente, & Norcross, 1992) assesses the individual's motivation for change so that the health care provider can select the optimal counseling approach. It is important to assess the patient's perceived readiness to change and proceed to an intervention depending on the patient's current perceived stage of change, from early precontemplation through contemplation, preparation, action, and maintenance stages.

The transition from screening to brief intervention uses the techniques of motivational interviewing, remaining patient-centered and nonjudgmental (Rollnick, Miller, & Butler, 2008). Individuals presenting with a positive alcohol screen are often in the precontemplative stage, where they have no intention to take action within the foreseeable future and may be unaware of the need to change. They may be underestimating the benefits or overestimating the cost of change, and there may be inertia accompanied by a general reluctance to consider change. It is tempting to emphasize the consequences of continuing the high-risk or harmful behavior, but it is imperative to avoid confrontation and the resistance that might be brought on by an aggressive educational approach. This often has the unintended effect of reducing the patient's openness to discussion.

The transition from the positive screen should begin with asking permission to discuss the results of the alcohol screen. The clinician should then state that the alcohol screen is routinely conducted and important in the context of preventive health and the assessment of the individual's overall health. After a brief further assessment of type, quantity, and frequency of alcohol consumption, the provider attempts to increase the precontemplative patient's awareness by eliciting the pros and cons of the behavior—for example, "What do you like about drinking? What do you not like about drinking?" The clinician is trying to affect decisional balance and move the patient toward contemplation and action stages. The discussion often involves addressing obstacles for positive change and a progression in patients' change talk by increasingly stating the pros versus the cons of changing their behavior. The principles of motivational interviewing include the use of open-ended questions, affirmations with validation of patients' interest in changing, reflective statements reassuring patients that they are being heard, and summarizations that set the stage for patients' "change talk" (Rollnick et al., 2008).

The USPSTF and a recent Cochrane review (Kaner et al., 2018) suggested that several 10- to 15-minute counseling appointments are most effective for reducing alcohol consumption. My colleagues and I (Schaus, Sole, McCoy, Mullett, & O'Brien, 2009) conducted an NIAAA-funded randomized controlled trial to test the efficacy of brief interventions delivered by providers to college students within a student health center. There were 363 participants that had screened positive for the 5/4 definition of high-risk drinking at initial enrollment to the student health service, and they were randomized to a control or intervention group. The intervention was two 20-minute brief interventions delivered by four specially trained providers. The brief intervention used the motivational interviewing framework and proceeded from a positive alcohol screen to further discussion only after addressing patients' presenting complaints and then obtaining permission to discuss alcohol use as it related to their complaint.

The brief intervention was founded in the BASICS curriculum (Dimeff, Baer, Kivlahan, & Marlatt, 1999) and provided personalized feedback with norms clarification, comparing the students' use with that of their peers. The focus of the intervention was on harm reduction and promoting protective factors. The goals for behavior change were set by the student, with the provider inducing change talk and encouraging self-efficacy. The results of the randomized controlled trial showed statistically significant reductions in alcohol use and alcohol-related harms in the treatment group compared with the control group. A similar larger study was conducted at multiple student health centers and also demonstrated positive intervention effects (Fleming et al., 2010).

TRANSITIONING FROM THE PRESENTING COMPLAINT TO BRIEF INTERVENTION

The provider should assess alcohol use whenever a patient's complaint has a potential alcohol-related cause or effect. Examples include complaints of obesity, insomnia, traumatic injury, sexually transmitted diseases, and mental health problems. Unhealthy alcohol use is often associated with uncontrolled hypertension, insomnia, mood disorders, sexual dysfunction, unintentional injuries, and interpersonal problems. A patient may present with these gateway issues and provide an important opportunity for further inquiry and discussion about alcohol use as a contributing factor. The principle of patient-centered care is applied when the patient is allowed to fully express their primary reason for seeking health care advice and transitioning to a discussion about alcohol use as it relates to their presenting complaint or problem. This transition often overcomes the stigma and barrier to open honest discussion that may be in place had the provider not related the alcohol inquiry to the patient's presenting complaint. For example, if patients present with complaints of obesity and a desire for weight loss, they may be more open to a discussion regarding alcohol use if approached from the standpoint of the caloric content of their recent drinking pattern. The patient presenting with a traumatic injury or sexually transmitted disease that occurred as a result of an alcohol-related alteration in judgment presents an opportunity to discuss and consider the role that alcohol may be playing in placing them at higher risk of future injury or disease, capitalizing on the "teachable moment."

CONCLUSION

In summary, the USPSTF recommends using a brief and validated alcohol screening test, specifically the AUDIT–C, for detecting the full spectrum of unhealthy alcohol use across multiple populations, or the SASQ for episodic heavy drinking, followed by an assessment of typical drinking patterns. When patients screen positive, clinicians should conduct a more in-depth assessment to confirm unhealthy alcohol use and determine the next steps of care.

Screening and brief intervention are widely recommended for primary care settings and considered a top prevention priority but are challenging and have not been widely implemented in clinical settings (Babor et al., 2005; Funk et al., 2005). There are many barriers to increasing provider use of routine screening in health care settings, including overcoming alcohol-related stigma and perceptions by clinicians that screening and brief interventions are beyond their scope of care and level of training and will not significantly impact unhealthy alcohol use and consequences. Optimal methods of implementing programs that comprehensively address these and other barriers remain elusive (Williams et al., 2016).

Future research is needed to study novel methods of conducting screening via the web or mobile devices and incorporating screening into electronic health records. Patients who screen positive should be offered effective intervention options delivered in a patient-centered manner at the time of the initial screening or as sequential doses of intervention via continuity of care with a trusted clinician.

REFERENCES

Aertgeerts, B., Buntinx, F., Bande-Knops, J., Vandermeulen, C., Roelants, M., Ansoms, S., & Fevery, J. (2000). The value of CAGE, CUGE, and AUDIT in screening for alcohol abuse and dependence among college freshmen. *Alcoholism: Clinical and Experimental Research, 24,* 53–57. http://dx.doi.org/10.1111/j.1530-0277.2000.tb04553.x

American Psychiatric Association. (2013). *Diagnostic and statistical manual of mental disorders* (5th ed.). Arlington, VA: Author.

Babor, T. F., & Grant, M. (1989). From clinical research to secondary prevention: International collaboration in the development of the Alcohol Disorders Identification Test (AUDIT). *Alcohol Health and Research World, 13,* 371–374.

Babor, T. F., Higgins-Biddle, J. C., Dauser, D., Higgins, P., & Burleson, J. A. (2005). Alcohol screening and brief intervention in primary care settings: Implementation models and predictors. *Journal of Studies on Alcohol, 66,* 361–368. http://dx.doi.org/10.15288/jsa.2005.66.361

Blanco, C., Okuda, M., Wright, C., Hasin, D. S., Grant, B. F., Liu, S. M., & Olfson, M. (2008). Mental health of college students and their non-college-attending peers: Results from the National Epidemiologic Study on Alcohol and Related Conditions. *Archives of General Psychiatry, 65,* 1429–1437. http://dx.doi.org/10.1001/archpsyc.65.12.1429

Bradley, K. A., DeBenedetti, A. F., Volk, R. J., Williams, E. C., Frank, D., & Kivlahan, D. R. (2007). AUDIT–C as a brief screen for alcohol misuse in primary care. *Alcoholism: Clinical and Experimental Research, 31,* 1208–1217. http://dx.doi.org/10.1111/j.1530-0277.2007.00403.x

Bush, K., Kivlahan, D. R., McDonell, M. B., Fihn, S. D., & Bradley, K. A. (1998). The AUDIT alcohol consumption questions (AUDIT–C): An effective brief screening test for problem drinking. *Archives of Internal Medicine, 158,* 1789–1795. http://dx.doi.org/10.1001/archinte.158.16.1789

Campbell, C. E., & Maisto, S. A. (2018). Validity of the AUDIT–C screen for at-risk drinking among students utilizing university primary care. *Journal of American College Health, 66,* 774–782. http://dx.doi.org/10.1080/07448481.2018.1453514

Curry, S. J., Krist, A. H., Owens, D. K., Barry, M. J., Caughey, A. B., Davidson, K. W., . . . Wong, J. B. (2018, November 13). Screening and behavioral counseling interventions to reduce unhealthy alcohol use in adolescents and adults: U.S. Preventive Services Task Force Recommendation Statement. *JAMA, 320,* 1899–1909. http://dx.doi.org/10.1001/jama.2018.16789

DeMartini, K. S., & Carey, K. B. (2012). Optimizing the use of the AUDIT for alcohol screening in college students. *Psychological Assessment, 24,* 954–963. http://dx.doi.org/10.1037/a0028519

Dimeff, L. A., Baer, J. S., Kivlahan, D. R., & Marlatt, G. A. (1999). *Brief Alcohol Screening and Intervention for College Students (BASICS): A harm reduction approach.* New York, NY: Guilford Press.

Ewing, J. A. (1984, October 12). Detecting alcoholism: The CAGE Questionnaire. *JAMA, 252*(14), 1905–1907. http://dx.doi.org/10.1001/jama.1984.03350140051025

Fleming, M. F., Balousek, S. L., Grossberg, P. M., Mundt, M. P., Brown, D., Wiegel, J. R., . . . Saewyc, E. M. (2010). Brief physician advice for heavy drinking college students: A randomized controlled trial in college health clinics. *Journal of Studies on Alcohol and Drugs, 71,* 23–31. http://dx.doi.org/10.15288/jsad.2010.71.23

Foote, J., Wilkens, C., & Vavagiakis, P. (2004). A national survey of alcohol screening and referral in college health centers. *Journal of American College Health, 52,* 149–157.

Funk, M., Wutzke, S., Kaner, E., Anderson, P., Pas, L., McCormick, R., . . . Saunders, J. (2005). A multicountry controlled trial of strategies to promote dissemination and implementation of brief alcohol intervention in primary health care: Findings of a World Health Organization collaborative study. *Journal of Studies on Alcohol, 66,* 379–388. http://dx.doi.org/10.15288/jsa.2005.66.379

Hingson, R. W., Zha, W., & Weitzman, E. R. (2009). Magnitude of and trends in alcohol-related mortality and morbidity among U.S. college students ages 18–24, 1998–2005. *Journal of Studies on Alcohol and Drugs, Supplement, S16,* 12–20. http://dx.doi.org/10.15288/jsads.2009.s16.12

Kaner, E. F., Beyer, F. R., Muirhead, C., Campbell, F., Pienaar, E. D., Bertholet, N., . . . Burnand, B. (2018). Effectiveness of brief alcohol interventions in primary care populations. *Cochrane Database of Systematic Reviews.* http://dx.doi.org/10.1002/14651858.CD004148.pub4

Knight, J. R., Sherritt, L., Harris, S. K., Gates, E. C., & Chang, G. (2003). Validity of brief alcohol screening tests among adolescents: A comparison of the AUDIT, POSIT, CAGE, and CRAFFT. *Alcoholism: Clinical and Experimental Research, 27,* 67–73. http://dx.doi.org/10.1111/j.1530-0277.2003.tb02723.x

Kokotailo, P. K., Egan, J., Gangnon, R., Brown, D., Mundt, M., & Fleming, M. (2004). Validity of the Alcohol Use Disorders Identification Test in college students. *Alcoholism: Clinical and Experimental Research, 28,* 914–920. http://dx.doi.org/10.1097/01.ALC.0000128239.87611.F5

Kranzler, H. R., & Soyka, M. (2018, August 28). Diagnosis and pharmacotherapy of alcohol use disorder: A review. *JAMA, 320,* 815–824. http://dx.doi.org/10.1001/jama.2018.11406

Larimer, M. E., & Cronce, J. M. (2007). Identification, prevention, and treatment revisited: Individual-focused college drinking prevention strategies 1999–2006. *Addictive Behaviors, 32,* 2439–2468. http://dx.doi.org/10.1016/j.addbeh.2007.05.006

Maddock, J. E., Laforge, R. G., Rossi, J. S., & O'Hare, T. (2001). The college alcohol problems scale. *Addictive Behaviors, 26,* 385–398. http://dx.doi.org/10.1016/S0306-4603(00)00116-7

O'Hare, T. (1997). Measuring problem drinking in first time offenders. Development and validation of the College Alcohol Problem Scale (CAPS). *Journal of Substance Abuse Treatment, 14,* 383–387. http://dx.doi.org/10.1016/S0740-5472(97)00033-0

Prochaska, J. O., DiClemente, C. C., & Norcross, J. C. (1992). In search of how people change. Applications to addictive behaviors. *American Psychologist, 47,* 1102–1114. http://dx.doi.org/10.1037/0003-066X.47.9.1102

Rollnick, S., Miller, W. R., & Butler, C. C. (2008). *Motivational interviewing in health care: Helping patients change behavior.* New York, NY: Guilford Press.

Schaus, J. F., Sole, M. L., McCoy, T. P., Mullett, N., Bolden, J., Sivasithamparam, J., & O'Brien, M. C. (2009). Screening for high-risk drinking in a college student health center: Characterizing students based on quantity, frequency, and harms. *Journal of Studies on Alcohol and Drugs, Supplement, S16,* 34–44. http://dx.doi.org/10.15288/jsads.2009.s16.34

Schaus, J. F., Sole, M. L., McCoy, T. P., Mullett, N., & O'Brien, M. C. (2009). Alcohol screening and brief intervention in a college student health center: A randomized controlled trial. *Journal of Studies on Alcohol and Drugs, S16,* 131–142. http://dx.doi.org/10.15288/jsads.2009.s16.131

Schulenberg, J. E., Johnston, L. D., O'Malley, P. M., Backman, J. G., Miech, R. A., & Patrick, M. E. (2016). *Monitoring the future national survey results on drug use, 1975–2016: Vol. II. Secondary school students.* Ann Arbor: Institute for Social Research, The University of Michigan.

Substance Abuse and Mental Health Services Administration. (2013). *Systems-level implementation of screening, brief intervention, and referral to treatment* (HHS Publication No. (SMA) 13-4741). Retrieved from https://store.samhsa.gov/product/TAP-33-Systems-Level-Implementation-of-Screening-Brief-Intervention-and-Referral-to-Treatment-SBIRT/SMA13-4741

Tetrault, J. M., & O'Connor, P. G. (2018). *Risky drinking and alcohol use disorder: Epidemiology, pathogenesis, clinical manifestations, course, assessment, and diagnosis.* Retrieved from https://www.uptodate.com/contents/risky-drinking-and-alcohol-use-disorder-epidemiology-pathogenesis-clinical-manifestations-course-assessment-and-diagnosis

U.S. Department of Health and Human Services. (2005). *Helping patients who drink too much: A clinician's guide.* Retrieved from https://www.integration.samhsa.gov/clinical-practice/Helping_Patients_Who_Drink_Too_Much.pdf

Van Den Bruel, A., Aertgeerts, B., Hoppenbrouwers, K., Roelants, M., & Buntinx, F. (2004). CUGE: A screening instrument for alcohol abuse and dependence in students. *Alcohol and Alcoholism, 39,* 439–444. http://dx.doi.org/10.1093/alcalc/agh077

Wechsler, H., Dowdall, G. W., Maenner, G., Gledhill-Hoyt, J., & Lee, H. (1998). Changes in binge drinking and related problems among American college students between 1993 and 1997: Results of the Harvard School of Public Health College Alcohol Study. *Journal of American College Health, 47,* 57–68. http://dx.doi.org/10.1080/07448489809595621

Wechsler, H., Lee, J. E., Kuo, M., Seibring, M., Nelson, T. F., & Lee, H. (2002). Trends in college binge drinking during a period of increased prevention efforts. Findings from 4 Harvard School of Public Health College Alcohol Study surveys: 1993–2001. *Journal of American College Health, 50,* 203–217. http://dx.doi.org/10.1080/07448480209595713

Weitzman, E. R., Nelson, T. F., Seibring, M., & Wechsler, H. (2005). *Needing, seeking and receiving treatment for alcohol problems in college.* Cambridge, MA: Center for Substance Abuse Treatment, Substance Abuse and Mental Health Services Administration, Harvard School of Public Health.

Williams, E. C., Achtmeyer, C. E., Young, J. P., Rittmueller, S. E., Ludman, E. J., Lapham, G. T., . . . Bradley, K. A. (2016). Local implementation of alcohol screening and brief intervention at five Veterans Health Administration primary care clinics: Perspectives of clinical and administrative staff. *Journal of Substance Abuse Treatment, 60,* 27–35. http://dx.doi.org/10.1016/j.jsat.2015.07.011

Winters, K. C., Toomey, T., Nelson, T. F., Erickson, D., Lenk, K., & Miazga, M. (2011). Screening for alcohol problems among 4-year colleges and universities. *Journal of American College Health, 59,* 350–357. http://dx.doi.org/10.1080/07448481.2010.509380

3

Screening and Intervention for Tobacco Use

Mary Schmidt-Owens

Tobacco control efforts dating back to the early 1960s made a huge impact on the health, social, and financial burdens of society, resulting in a significant reduction in tobacco users. In 1965, current smokers outnumbered former smokers three to one, whereas there are now more former smokers than current smokers (U.S. Department of Health and Human Services, 2008). Despite this, tobacco use continues to be the chief preventable cause of disease, disability, and death in the United States (Mokdad, Marks, Stroup, & Gerberding, 2004).

Historically, smoking was viewed as a habit rather than a chronic disease contributor, and there were no scientifically validated treatments for tobacco use or dependence. Currently, there are many effective treatment programs, from pharmacological medications to free online programs, whereby one can create a personalized web-based quit plan, track progress, and access blogs for sharing success stories. Health care providers are encouraged to screen for tobacco use, offer smoking cessation counseling, and provide pharmacotherapy when appropriate (U.S. Department of Health and Human Services, 2008). In this chapter, I discuss the prevalence of tobacco product use and current trends, as well as effective methods to assess current tobacco use and identify a person's readiness to change. and identify best practices for tobacco prevention and treatment.

http://dx.doi.org/10.1037/0000199-004
Screening, Brief Intervention, and Referral to Treatment for Substance Use: A Practitioner's Guide,
M. D. Cimini and J. L. Martin (Editors)

A BRIEF HISTORY OF TOBACCO USE

The ingestion and inhalation of tobacco for medical purposes, tribal rituals, and pleasure date back centuries. Evidence of the negative effects of smoking began to surface in the 1930s, 1940s, and 1950s. At that time, research started to confirm relationships between cigarette smoking and lung cancer, bronchitis, emphysema, and coronary heart disease (U.S. Department of Health Education and Welfare, 1964). In 1957, Surgeon General Leroy E. Burney declared that the official position of the U.S. Public Health Service was that the evidence pointed to a causal relationship between smoking and lung cancer (U.S. Department of Health Education and Welfare, 1964). In the mid-1960s, published medical findings confirmed the statistical relationship of smoking to lung cancer and other serious diseases such as bronchitis, emphysema, and coronary heart disease. These findings made it impossible for the public to ignore the dangers of tobacco. From that point forward, research on the negative health consequences associated with tobacco use helped support policy changes, initiate warning labels on cigarette packaging, and introduce restrictions on tobacco advertising and even influenced tobacco product production. A behavior that was historically looked on as being "glamorous" became viewed as a health threat. Cigarette companies tried to challenge the scientific research linking tobacco use to multiple health consequences and diseases but were not successful (Bero, 2005; Drope & Chapman, 2001; Grüning, Gilmore, & McKee, 2006).

PREVALENCE RATES AND CONSEQUENCES OF TOBACCO USE

Self-reported adult smoking peaked in 1954 at 45% and remained at 40% or more through the early 1970s (Dugan, 2018). Since that time, the rates for cigarette smoking have declined. According to Wang et al. (2018), the proportion of U.S. adults who reported smoking cigarettes was 20.9% in 2005 and declined to 14% in 2017.

In 2017, 19.3% of adults aged 18 years and older (approximately one in five) reported current use of some type of tobacco product, and 19% of these adults reported using multiple tobacco products. The use of any combustible tobacco products was 16.7%. Because of heightened curiosity, flavoring, cost, convenience, simulation of cigarettes, and as a method to quit smoking, e-cigarettes, combined with traditional cigarettes, were reported as the most commonly used multiple tobacco product (King, Gammon, Marynak, & Rogers, 2018). Multiple tobacco product users are at increased risk of nicotine addiction and dependence (U.S. Department of Health and Human Services, 2014a). Studies have reported that men are more likely to use tobacco products than women (nearly 24.8% vs. 14.2%, respectively). The current tobacco product use rates by age are as follows: 18.3% of adults age 18 to 24 years old, 22.5% of adults age 25 to 44, 21.3% of adults age 45 to 64, and 11% of adults 65 and older (Wang et al., 2018).

Tobacco Use Among Adolescents and Young Adults

Adolescence and young adulthood is a particularly vulnerable period when both healthy and unhealthy behaviors start to develop. During adolescence, experimentation, social pressure, and overall self-image and self-likeness are just a few of the key elements that contribute to one's decision-making process. These early behavioral decisions begin to shape the foundation of a lifetime of behavior patterns.

Despite all the research, warning labels, and education about the harmful effects of use, each day, approximately 3,450 young people between the ages of 12 and 17 smoke their first cigarette (U.S. Department of Health and Human Services, 2004). Supporting data indicates that approximately 90% of adult smokers began smoking as adolescents (U.S. Department of Health and Human Services, 2014a). E-cigarettes are one of the more popular forms of tobacco products, and research has suggested that their use may serve as a gateway product for preteens and teens who then go on to use other tobacco products, including cigarettes (National Institute on Drug Abuse [NIDA], 2018b, 2018c). One study showed that students who had used e-cigarettes by the time they started ninth grade were more likely than others to start smoking cigarettes and other smoking tobacco products within the next year (Leventhal et al., 2015). In 2012, approximately 6.7% of middle school students and 23.3% of high school students reported using a tobacco product within the past 30 days (Centers for Disease Control [CDC], 2013). More recent data have indicated that e-cigarette use among middle and high school went from 2.12 million in 2017 to 3.62 million in 2018 (Cullen et al., 2018). Social environmental, psychological, and genetic factors all play a role in tobacco use. Motivation to begin and continue to use tobacco is influenced by factors including the use of tobacco and approval of tobacco use by peers and siblings, parents or guardians who smoke, accessibility of tobacco products, and exposure to tobacco use promotional campaigns (Healthy People, 2014).

Health Consequences of Tobacco Use

Cigarette smoking remains the leading cause of preventable disease, disability, and death in the United States, accounting for more than 480,000 deaths (from either cigarette smoking and/or secondhand smoke exposure) every year, or about one in five total deaths (U.S. Department of Health and Human Services, 2014a). Smokers die, on average, approximately 13 to 14 years earlier than people who have never smoked (CDC, 2008). More deaths are caused each year by tobacco use than by all deaths from HIV, illegal drugs, alcohol use, motor vehicle injuries, suicides, and murders combined (CDC, 2008; Mokdad et al., 2004). Furthermore, for every person who dies from tobacco-related causes, another 20 experience at least one serious tobacco-related illness (CDC, 2003). Illnesses associated with tobacco use (of any form) include several forms of cancer, lung disease, gum disease, stroke, coronary heart disease, and pregnancy complications (including preterm delivery and low birth rates; CDC, 2003). Smoking tobacco causes an estimated 90% of all lung cancer deaths in men and 80% of all lung cancer deaths in women (U.S. Department of Health and Human Services, 2004). Inhalation of secondhand smoke also poses health threats. The secondhand smoke from cigarettes and cigars has been shown to cause heart disease, lung cancer, asthma, respiratory infections, ear infections, and sudden infant death syndrome (U.S. Department of Health and Human Services, 2006).

Vulnerable populations, such as alcohol and illicit drug users and adults with a psychiatric diagnosis or illness, a group estimated to account for nearly 50% of cigarettes sold in the United States, have a higher prevalence of tobacco dependence (Prochaska, 2010). Some contributing factors for this increase in use among these populations include the reinforcing mood-altering effects of nicotine, a shared environment or genetic factors, and reduced coping for cessation efforts. Tobacco use is the leading cause of death in patients with psychiatric illnesses or addictive disorders; therefore, it has to be a treatment priority in mental health and addiction treatment settings (Prochaska, 2010). Emerging evidence indicates that the treatment of tobacco dependence among these vulnerable populations can improve addiction treatment and mental health outcomes (Prochaska, 2010).

CURRENT TRENDS IN TOBACCO USE

Despite the intense marketing efforts, particularly aimed at youth, the overall percentage of tobacco users continues on a downward trend. Unfortunately, with the decline in cigarette use, other tobacco products are flooding the market. According to Tobacco Free Kids (2019), current tobacco products include the following:

- typical cigarettes (including loose tobacco leaf, either hand rolled, cigarette, or pipe),

- combustible tobacco products (tobacco products that are designed to be smoked including cigars, cigarillos, little cigars, blunts, and bidis or beedis),

- electronic cigarettes (e-cigarette) and other electronic nicotine delivery systems (ENDS) products (electronic and/or battery-operated devices designed to deliver an inhaled dose of nicotine or other substances), and

- hookah, shisha, and water pipes (a single or multistemmed instrument for vaporizing and smoking flavored tobacco or other products in which the vapor or smoke is passed through a water basin, often made from glass, before inhalation).

ENDS have become highly sought-after products due to the belief that they are much safer than traditional cigarettes (Kaisar, Prasad, Liles, & Cucullo, 2016). E-cigarettes, although marketed as an alternative to smoking tobacco that produces harmless water vapor with no adverse impact on indoor air quality, have been found, in actuality, to emit chemicals that pose health threats directly to the user (American Academy of Family Physicians, 2019). Nicotine, flavorings, and tiny tin and lead particles have been found in the vapor and liquid that is delivered to the lungs. Some of the labels on e-cigarettes contradict these research findings, which is misleading to the user and, as a result, puts the user at risk of contracting cancer and other lung diseases such as asthma or chronic obstructive pulmonary disease (Mark, 2019). A newer e-cigarette that hit the U.S. market in 2015 is the "JUUL." JUULs are shaped like a USB flash drive and contain pods of liquid. According to the manufacturer, a single JUUL pod contains as much nicotine as a pack of 20 regular cigarettes (Bach, 2018; U.S. Department of Health and Human Services, 2016).

Inadequate research and lack of regulatory guidelines for both the manufacturing process and the content of the vaping solutions of e-cigarettes and other ENDS have become major concerns, especially because these products still lack U.S. Food and Drug Administration (FDA) approval (Walley & Jenssen, 2015). The CDC, FDA, state and local health departments, and other clinical and public health agencies are investigating negative health effects of e-cigarette, or vaping, products. Recent lung injuries, which in some cases resulted in death, have been linked with the use of e-cigarette, or vaping, products containing vitamin E acetate as the chemical of concern (CDC, 2019). However, the evidence is not yet sufficient to rule out other chemicals of concern. The CDC (2019) recommended not to use THC-containing e-cigarette, or vaping, products; that people not buy any type of e-cigarette, or vaping, products, particularly those containing THC from informal sources (i.e., friends, family, online dealers); and not to modify or add any substances (such as vitamin E acetate) to e-cigarette, or vaping, products that are not intended by the manufacturer. Because the specific cause or causes of lung injury are not yet known, the recommendation by the CDC is to refrain from the use of all e-cigarette, or vaping, products (Blount et al., 2019).

THE ADDICTIVE NATURE OF TOBACCO

Nicotine, one of the more than 4,000 chemicals found in the smoke from tobacco products, is recognized as one of the most frequently used addictive drugs. It is a naturally occurring colorless liquid that turns brown when burned and acquires the odor of tobacco when exposed to air (NIDA, 2018b). By inhaling tobacco smoke, the average smoker takes in 1 to 2 milligrams of nicotine per cigarette. A typical smoker will take 10 puffs on a cigarette over the roughly five minutes that the cigarette is lit (Hoffmann & Hoffmann, 1997). For persons who smoke a pack (20 cigarettes) a day, this equates to 200 "hits" of nicotine to the brain each day. Research published by NIDA (2018a, b) revealed the following physiological changes that take place once nicotine enters the body. When cigarette smoke enters the lungs, nicotine is absorbed rapidly, within 10 seconds of inhalation, into the bloodstream and enters the brain, stimulating the adrenal glands to release the hormone epinephrine (adrenaline). Epinephrine stimulates the central nervous system and increases blood pressure, breathing, and heart rate. Nicotine also affects brain function by activating the brain reward circuits and increasing levels of the feel-good chemical dopamine. When dopamine is released, it gives a brief "hit" or "buzz" to the user. Once the nicotine buzz passes, the receptors are eager for more, resulting in the user taking another puff or hit. The nicotine increases levels of dopamine in these reward circuits, which reinforces the behavior of taking the drug. Repeated exposure alters the brain circuits' sensitivity to dopamine and leads to changes in other brain circuits involved in learning, stress, and self-control (NIDA, 2018a, b). In addition, habitual use results in the user building up a tolerance to the nicotine; a given dose of the nicotine produces less effect, and increasing doses are required to achieve a similar "euphoric" or "pleasurable" response. For those who do not inhale the smoke—such as cigar and pipe smokers and smokeless tobacco users—nicotine is absorbed through mucous membranes in the mouth and reaches peak blood and brain levels more slowly (NIDA, 2018b).

For many tobacco users, the long-term brain changes induced by continued nicotine exposure results in addiction, which involves withdrawal symptoms when not using tobacco, and difficulty adhering to any type of resolution to quit (NIDA, 2018a, b). Nicotine addiction is a treatable disease; however, one must know the nature of addiction to treat the disease successfully. Although the onset of addiction begins with the voluntary act of using some type of drug (e.g., cigarettes), the continued repetition can lead to involuntary use to the point that the behavior is driven by a compulsive craving for the drug. The drug begins to control the user rather than the user controlling the use of the drug. At this point, the user's body becomes dependent on having nicotine in the system, and being without nicotine for too long can cause a regular user to experience irritability, craving, depression, anxiety, cognitive and attention deficits, sleep disturbances, and increased appetite (NIDA, 2018a, b). These "withdrawal" symptoms may begin within a few hours after the last cigarette, quickly driving the user back to using tobacco. A chronic disease model recognizes the long-term nature of the addiction with an expectation that patients cycle through abstinence and relapse, requiring ongoing care by a clinician as opposed to acute care (U.S. Department of Health and Human Services, 2008). For many users, repeated treatment is required before long-term abstinence can be achieved.

The frequency and quantity of the use of nicotine products are two factors that impact how difficult the quitting process may be. Not only does it involve the addiction to nicotine but also the behavioral factors associated with nicotine dependence. The behavioral factors, including the smell, feel, and sight of the product (e.g., a cigarette) and the obtaining, handling, lighting, and "smoking," are all associated with the pleasurable effects and can make withdrawal or cravings worse (Brauer et al., 2001). These factors become "cues to smoke" along with other activities, such as driving a car, finishing a meal, drinking a cup of coffee, or talking on the phone. The activity triggers cravings that often persist until the smoker is satisfied by smoking the cigarette. Cessation programs that address both the addictive properties and behavioral components of tobacco addiction have been shown to be effective (Larzelere & Williams, 2012). Nicotine replacement therapies such as gum, patches, inhalers, and other medications approved for the treatment of nicotine addiction may help alleviate the physiological aspects of withdrawal and block the reinforcing effects of the nicotine (Stead et al., 2012). Behavioral therapies can help identify the triggers of cravings and provide strategies to avoid and manage the feelings and activities associated with the cravings.

E-cigarette companies advertise that the "e-cig" is safer than traditional cigarettes because they do not burn tobacco. Some research has found that e-cigarettes deliver less nicotine on average than traditional cigarettes, but the users may change puffing patterns to compensate (Schroeder & Hoffman, 2014). Users believe that e-cigarette products are less harmful than traditional cigarettes, and many report using them to help quit smoking traditional cigarettes (England, Bunnell, Pechacek, Tong, & McAfee, 2015). The U.S. Preventive Services Task Force (USPSTF; 2019) recently concluded that the current evidence is insufficient to recommend ENDS for tobacco cessation in adults and recommended that clinicians direct patients who smoke to cessation programs with established effectiveness and safety, rather than recommending or condoning the use of ENDS in place of traditional cigarettes.

USPSTF "GRADE A" RECOMMENDATION FOR TOBACCO SCREENING

Preventing tobacco use and helping those who use tobacco to quit can improve the overall health and well-being of people of all ages (Healthy People, 2014). The USPSTF recognizes that there is no safe level of tobacco use and, therefore, strongly recommends with a Grade "A" recommendation that clinicians screen all adults for tobacco use and provide tobacco cessation interventions for those who use any tobacco products. The USPSTF assigns one of five letter grades (A, B, C, D, or I) to each of its recommendations to describe the recommendation's strength. Describing the strength of a recommendation is an important part of communicating its importance to clinicians and other users. An "A" grade means that the USPSTF (2019) strongly endorses the recommendation with a high level of certainty. The USPSTF defines *certainty* as the likelihood that the USPSTF assessment of the net benefit of a preventive service is correct. The *net benefit* is defined as benefit minus harm of the preventive services as implemented in a general, primary care population. The USPSTF assigns a certainty level based on the nature of the overall evidence available to assess the net benefit of a preventive service. The USPSTF (2019) found evidence, based on results from well-designed, well-conducted studies in representative primary care populations, that the routine screen by clinicians improves important health outcomes and concludes that benefits substantially outweigh harms. The goal is for every health care provider to use routine screening to identify tobacco use and to advise every patient using any form of tobacco products to quit (USPSTF, 2019).

SBIRT FOR TOBACCO USERS

The Substance Abuse and Mental Health Services Administration (SAMHSA) recommends universal substance use screening, brief intervention, and referral to treatment (SBIRT) as part of routine health care (Levy & Williams, 2016). Opportunities to screen whenever and wherever individuals receive medical care can increase the identification of users of tobacco and other nicotine delivery systems. During the patient interaction, SBIRT must be conducted with sensitivity to the various patient population abilities, vulnerabilities, and needs. It is important to "meet the patient where they are" in their readiness to change behavior regarding tobacco (and/or other ENDS) use.

Screening

Universal tobacco screening, assessment, and intervention are widely accepted due to recommendations made by the USPSTF (2019) and because tobacco use may be associated with, cause, or exacerbate a patient's presenting concerns or symptoms. The *Clinical Practice Guideline for Treating Tobacco Use and Dependence* (U.S. Department of Health and Human Services, 2008) recommended that every clinician ask patients two key questions: (a) "Do you smoke?" and, in the case of a yes response, (b) "Do you want to quit?" An alternative to the closed question "Do you want to quit?" would be to acknowledge the behavior and then advise to quit. An example is "I see that you currently smoke cigarettes. I would advise you to take one of the smoking cessation classes offered in our office (in the community) and determine whether you are ready to quit." "Asking" and "advising" are two of the five major components of the five A's (discussed further in the next section) of a brief intervention. Open-ended dialogue is recommended, as opposed to close-ended questions, to assess the patient's stage of change (Searight, 2018).

Clinicians can use a validated brief screening tool, such as the Screening to Brief Intervention (Levy et al., 2014) or Brief Screener for Tobacco, Alcohol, and Other Drugs (Kelly, Gryczynski, Mitchell, Kirk, O'Grady, & Schwartz, 2014) to gain further knowledge about the level of addiction. These two screening tools include questions about tobacco use, frequency, quantity, and patterns of use. The clinician is then able to respond to the screening results and facilitate care through brief intervention and referral to treatment practices.

Brief Intervention—The Five A's Approach

Brief intervention is a conversation that focuses on encouraging healthy choices so that the risk behavior (i.e., tobacco or ENDS use) is prevented, reduced, or stopped (Levy & Williams, 2016). The health care system provides multiple opportunities for facilitating brief interventions, which can motivate the tobacco user to quit. Studies have shown that obtaining tobacco use status while measuring the vital signs, including blood pressure, body temperature, respiration rate, and pulse rate, increased smoking cessation recommendations by the provider and decreased rates of tobacco use among patients (Anczak & Nogler, 2003). A common approach to screening and brief intervention has been summarized as the five A's (ask, advise, assess, assist, arrange; Searight, 2018; U.S. Department of Health and Human Services, 2008, 2014b).

The five A's include the following:

- *Asking* every patient at every visit about tobacco use, including the current amount.

- *Advising* them to quit through clear, unambiguous, personalized messages that associate the patient's tobacco use to their other health conditions (e.g., asthma). The benefits of quitting should be emphasized. Follow-up discussions at each subsequent visit may increase the patient's compliance with advice.

- *Assessing* their willingness to make a quit attempt and current stage of behavior change (Prochaska & DiClemente, 1992). Patients bring different levels of ambivalence, readiness, and motivation to quit. The clinician can influence the change continuum at each visit by using motivational interviewing techniques that avoid confrontation and using empathy and respect for patients' autonomy, helping to build their self-efficacy to quit. Assessment might also include perceived barriers to quitting, smoking history, current level of nicotine dependence, and previous attempts to decrease or quit tobacco use.

- *Assisting* them in their effort to quit by advising about possible pharmacotherapy interventions and helping them anticipate obstacles to cessation, including nicotine withdrawal symptoms, depression, and weight gain. It is important to determine a timeline for quitting, including setting a specific quit date.

- *Arranging* follow-up and support, including multiple patient contacts offering further advice and reassurance.

The five A's framework is a useful strategy for screening and engaging patients that allows clinicians to transition from a positive screen to assisting and arranging an effective plan for long-term smoking cessation (U.S. Department of Health and Human Services, 2008).

Assessing Stage of Change

One of the key components of the five A's approach is to assess individuals' willingness to change their behavior. Using the transtheoretical model of behavior change, developed by Prochaska and DiClemente (1992), the clinician can assess the patient's motivation and determine his or her specific stage of change (defined later). Once identified, the clinician can move the patient toward initiating action or support ongoing health behavior change, whichever is more appropriate (Searight, 2018).

The five stages of change are as follows:

- *Precontemplation.* The smoker is not seriously considering quitting in the next 6 months. Smokers in this stage overestimate the benefits of smoking, underestimate the risks, and avoid information to help them change (Anczak & Nogler, 2003). In this stage, the clinician's role is primarily to advise and inform the patient.

- *Contemplation.* Smokers are beginning to evaluate their behavior and are seriously planning to quit smoking in the next 6 months, though not immediately, and no quit date is set. Smokers in this stage are weighing the cost and benefits and are open to education and feedback about tobacco use. Clinicians should emphasize the negative effects of smoking (Anczak & Nogler, 2003).

- *Preparation.* The smoker is planning to quit, and a stop date has been set in the next month. Assistance in initiating steps toward cessation is pursued (e.g., delaying the first cigarette of the morning, cutting down, informing family and friends). Interventions to assist patients in this stage to quit smoking include focusing on nicotine replacement therapies (NRT) and developing behavior modification skills (Anczak & Nogler, 2003).

- *Action.* Individuals have taken steps to stop smoking. Smokers may quit by using medication and NRT, behavior modification, willpower, an informal quitting strategy, or a combination of some or all these methods (Anczak & Nogler, 2003). This is the most frequent stage for relapse, which varies with therapy, coffee and alcohol consumption, history of depression, and gender (Anczak & Nogler, 2003). High initial relapse occurs within the first 2 to 3 weeks and then tapers off during the next 2 to 3 months (Anczak & Nogler, 2003). Thus, initial and continued support is important.

- *Maintenance.* At this stage, the individuals have not smoked for 6 months. Successful individuals are avoiding relapse. Relapse is common; the most successful quitters relapse and cycle through the stages an average of three to four times before becoming free from cigarettes (Anczak & Nogler, 2003).

Referral to Treatment—Treating Tobacco Use and Dependence

Referral to treatment describes the facilitative process through which patients identified as needing more extensive evaluation and treatment can access the appropriate services (Levy & Williams, 2016). In the context of tobacco or ENDS users, the clinician may determine a treatment plan based on the screening and brief intervention outcomes. Treatment could include any of the following: cessation medication (unless contraindicated), counseling, support, verbal reinforcement, and motivation enhancement techniques, as well as arranging follow-up contact either with on-site programs or via a referral to online or community resources.

Treating Tobacco Use and Dependence: Update 2008 (U.S. Department of Health and Human Services, 2008) provides recommendations from a panel of experts from federal government and nonprofit organizations. The document contains strategies and recommendations designed to assist clinicians, tobacco dependence treatment specialists, and health care administrators, insurers, and purchasers in delivering and supporting effective treatments for tobacco use and dependence. The overarching goal of the recommendations is for clinicians to strongly recommend the use of tobacco dependence counseling and medication treatments to patients who use tobacco and that health systems, insurers, and purchasers assist clinicians in making such effective treatments available (U.S. Department of Health and Human Services, 2008). The key recommendations include the following:

- Tobacco dependence is a chronic disease that often requires repeated intervention and multiple attempts to quit. Effective treatments exist, however, that can significantly increase rates of long-term abstinence.

- It is essential that clinicians and health care delivery systems consistently identify and document tobacco use status and treat every tobacco user seen in a health care setting.

- Tobacco dependence treatments are effective across a broad range of populations. Clinicians should encourage every patient willing to make a quit attempt to use recommended counseling and medications.

- Brief tobacco dependence treatment is effective. Clinicians should offer every patient who uses tobacco at least the brief treatments, including NRT (e.g., patch, gum, or lozenges) and supplementary materials, including information on quit lines (800-QUIT-NOW), and provide a supportive environment which reinforces the user's willingness to quit.

- Individual, group, and telephone counseling are effective, and their effectiveness increases with treatment intensity. Two components of counseling are especially effective, and clinicians should use these when counseling patients making a quit attempt:
  - practical counseling (problem solving, skills training) and
  - social support delivered as part of treatment.

- Numerous effective medications are available for tobacco dependence, and clinicians should encourage their use by all patients attempting to quit smoking—except when medically contraindicated or with specific populations for which there is insufficient evidence of effectiveness (i.e., pregnant women, smokeless tobacco users, light smokers, adolescents). Clinicians also should consider the use of certain combinations of medications depending on the patient and level of need. Seven first-line medications (five nicotine and two nonnicotine) reliably increase long-term smoking abstinence rates:

– bupropion SR,

– nicotine gum,

– nicotine inhalers,

– nicotine lozenges,

– nicotine nasal spray,

– nicotine patches, and

– varenicline.

- Counseling and medication are effective when used by themselves for treating tobacco dependence. The combination of counseling and medication, however, is more effective than either alone. Thus, clinicians should encourage all individuals making a quit attempt to use both counseling and medication.

- Telephone quit line counseling is effective with diverse populations and has a broad reach. Therefore, both clinicians and health care delivery systems should ensure patient access to quit lines and promote quit line use.

- If a tobacco user is unwilling to make a quit attempt, the clinician can use the transtheoretical model to move the user from one stage to the next (i.e., precontemplation to contemplation).

- Tobacco dependence treatments are both clinically effective and highly cost-effective relative to interventions for other clinical disorders. Providing medical insurance coverage for these treatments increases quit rates. Insurers and purchasers should ensure that all insurance plans include the counseling and medication identified as effective be covered as a benefit.

CONCLUSION

The harmful effects of tobacco and other ENDS have been proven through numerous well-conducted studies. Unfortunately, the knowledge of this research and the facts mentioned throughout this chapter have not reached 100% of those currently using tobacco or ENDS products. In addition, according to the CDC (2013), thousands of young people start using tobacco and/or ENDS products every day.

The overall mission of screening for tobacco product use, determining readiness to change, and providing evidence-based brief interventions and treatment are key elements of a comprehensive tobacco control program.

Clinicians play a key role in identifying tobacco users and connecting them with the resources that will best help that individual to quit. When there is successful synergy between these elements, tobacco users can get the help they need to achieve long-term success and ultimately increase their health and quality of life.

REFERENCES

American Academy of Family Physicians. (2019). *Bolster policy on tobacco, ENDS, secondhand smoke, says AAFP: Letter supports robust taxation and flavor regulation, among other tactics*. Retrieved from https://www.aafp.org/news/government-medicine/20190212tobaccoletter.html

Anczak, J. D., & Nogler, R. A., II. (2003). Tobacco cessation in primary care: Maximizing intervention strategies. *Clinical Medicine & Research, 1*, 201–216. http://dx.doi.org/10.3121/cmr.1.3.201

Bach, L. (2018). *JUUL and youth: Rising e-cigarette popularity*. Retrieved from https://www.tobaccofreekids.org/assets/factsheets/0394.pdf

Bero, L. (2005). Public health chronicles: Tobacco industry manipulation of research. *Public Health Reports, 120*, 200–208. http://dx.doi.org/10.1177/003335490512000215

Blount, B. C., Karwowski, M. P., Morel-Espinosa, M., Rees, J., Sosnoff, C., Cowan, E., . . . Pirkle, J. L. (2019). Evaluation of bronchoalveolar lavage fluid from patients in an outbreak of e-cigarette, or vaping, product use-associated lung injury—10 states, August–October 2019. *Morbidity and Mortality Weekly Report, 68*(45), 1040–1041. http://dx.doi.org/10.15585/mmwr.mm6845e2

Brauer, L. H., Behm, F. M., Lane, J. D., Westman, E. C., Perkins, C., & Rose, J. E. (2001). Individual differences in smoking reward from de-nicotinized cigarettes. *Nicotine & Tobacco Research, 3*, 101–109. http://dx.doi.org/10.1080/14622200123249

Centers for Disease Control and Prevention. (2003). Cigarette smoking-attributable morbidity—United States, 2000. *Morbidity and Mortality Weekly Report, 52*, 842–844. https://www.cdc.gov/mmwr/preview/mmwrhtml/mm5235a4.htm

Centers for Disease Control and Prevention. (2008). Smoking-attributable mortality, years of potential life lost, and productivity losses—United States, 2000–2004. (2008). *Morbidity and Mortality Weekly Report, 57*, 1226–1228.

Centers for Disease Control and Prevention. (2013). Tobacco product use among middle and high school students—United States, 2011 and 2012. *Morbidity and Mortality Weekly Report, 62*, 893–897.

Centers for Disease Control and Prevention. (2019). *Outbreak of lung injury associated with the use of e-cigarette, or vaping, products*. Retrieved from https://www.cdc.gov/tobacco/basic_information/e-cigarettes/severe-lung-disease.html

Cullen, K. A., Ambrose, B. K., Gentzke, A. S., Apelberg, B. J., Jamal, A., & King, B. A. (2018). Notes from the field: Use of electronic cigarettes and any tobacco product among middle and high school students—United States, 2011–2018. *Morbidity and Mortality Weekly Report, 67*, 1276–1277. http://dx.doi.org/10.15585/mmwr.mm6745a5

Drope, J., & Chapman, S. (2001). Tobacco industry efforts at discrediting scientific knowledge of environmental tobacco smoke: A review of internal industry documents. *Journal of Epidemiology and Community Health, 55*, 588–594. http://dx.doi.org/10.1136/jech.55.8.588

Dugan, A. (2018). *In U.S., smoking rate hits new low at 16%*. Retrieved from https://news.gallup.com/poll/237908/smoking-rate-hits-new-low.aspx

England, L. J., Bunnell, R. E., Pechacek, T. F., Tong, V. T., & McAfee, T. A. (2015). Nicotine and the developing human: A neglected element in the electronic cigarette debate. *American Journal of Preventive Medicine, 49*, 286–293. http://dx.doi.org/10.1016/j.amepre.2015.01.015

Grüning, T., Gilmore, A. B., & McKee, M. (2006). Tobacco industry influence on science and scientists in Germany. *American Journal of Public Health, 96*, 20–32. http://dx.doi.org/10.2105/AJPH.2004.061507

Healthy People. (2014). *Tobacco use across the life stages*. Retrieved from https://www.healthypeople.gov/2020/leading-health-indicators/2020-lhi-topics/Tobacco/determinants

Hoffmann, D., & Hoffmann, I. (1997). The changing cigarette, 1950–1995. *Journal of Toxicology and Environmental Health, 50*, 307–364. http://dx.doi.org/10.1080/009841097160393

Kaisar, M. A., Prasad, S., Liles, T., & Cucullo, L. (2016). A decade of e-cigarettes: Limited research and unresolved safety concerns. *Toxicology, 365*, 67–75. http://dx.doi.org/10.1016/j.tox.2016.07.020

Kelly, S. M., Gryczynski, J., Mitchell, S. G., Kirk, A., O'Grady, K. E., & Schwartz, R. P. (2014). Validity of brief screening instrument for adolescent tobacco, alcohol, and drug use. *Pediatrics, 133*, 819–826. http://dx.doi.org/10.1542/peds.2013-2346

King, B. A., Gammon, D. G., Marynak, K. L., & Rogers, T. (2018, October 2). Electronic cigarette sales in the United States, 2013–2017. *JAMA, 320*, 1379–1380. http://dx.doi.org/10.1001/jama.2018.10488

Larzelere, M. M., & Williams, D. E. (2012). Promoting smoking cessation. *American Family Physician, 85*, 591–598.

Leventhal, A. M., Strong, D. R., Kirkpatrick, M. G., Unger, J. B., Sussman, S., Riggs, N. R., . . . Audrain-McGovern, J. (2015, August 18). Association of electronic cigarette use with initiation of combustible tobacco product smoking in early adolescence. *JAMA, 314*, 700–707. http://dx.doi.org/10.1001/jama.2015.8950

Levy, S., Weiss, R., Sherritt, L., Ziemnik, R., Spalding, A., Van Hook, S., & Shrier, L. A. (2014). An electronic screen for triaging adolescent substance use by risk levels. *JAMA Pediatrics, 168*, 822–828. http://dx.doi.org/10.1001/jamapediatrics.2014.774

Levy, S. J., & Williams, J. F. (2016). Substance use screening, brief intervention, and referral to treatment. *Pediatrics, 138*, e1–e15. http://dx.doi.org/10.1542/peds.2016-1211

Mark, A. M. (2019). A look at e-cigarettes. *The Journal of the American Dental Association, 150*, 236. http://dx.doi.org/10.1016/j.adaj.2019.01.020

Mokdad, A. H., Marks, J. S., Stroup, D. F., & Gerberding, J. L. (2004, March 10). Actual causes of death in the United States, 2000. *JAMA, 291*, 1238–1245. http://dx.doi.org/10.1001/jama.291.10.1238

National Institute on Drug Abuse. (2018a). *Cigarettes and other tobacco products*. Retrieved from https://www.drugabuse.gov/publications/drugfacts/cigarettes-other-tobacco-products

National Institute on Drug Abuse. (2018b). *Tobacco, nicotine, and e-cigarettes*. Retrieved from https://www.drugabuse.gov/node/pdf/1344/tobacco-nicotine-and-e-cigarettes

National Institute on Drug Abuse. (2018c). *Vaping devices (electronic cigarettes)*. Retrieved from https://www.drugabuse.gov/publications/drugfacts/electronic-cigarettes-e-cigarettes

Prochaska, J. J. (2010). Failure to treat tobacco use in mental health and addiction treatment settings: A form of harm reduction? *Drug and Alcohol Dependence, 110*, 177–182. http://dx.doi.org/10.1016/j.drugalcdep.2010.03.002

Prochaska, J., & DiClemente, C. (1992). *Stages of change in the modification of problem behaviors*. Newbury Park, CA: SAGE.

Schroeder, M. J., & Hoffman, A. C. (2014). Electronic cigarettes and nicotine clinical pharmacology. *Tobacco Control, 23*, ii30–ii35. http://dx.doi.org/10.1136/tobaccocontrol-2013-051469

Searight, H. R. (2018). Counseling patients in primary care: Evidence-based strategies. *American Family Physician, 98*, 719–728.

Stead, L. F., Perera, R., Bullen, C., Mant, D., Hartmann-Boyce, J., Cahill, K., & Lancaster, T. (2012). Nicotine replacement therapy for smoking cessation. *Cochrane Database of Systematic Reviews, 11.* https://www.ncbi.nlm.nih.gov/pubmed/23152200

Tobacco Free Kids. (2019). *Tobacco control laws: Type of tobacco product.* Retrieved from https://www.tobaccocontrollaws.org/litigation/browse/tobacco-type/

U.S. Department of Health and Human Services. (2004). *The health consequences of smoking: A report of the surgeon general.* Atlanta, GA: Centers for Disease Control and Prevention.

U.S. Department of Health and Human Services. (2006). *The health consequences of involuntary exposure to tobacco smoke: A report of the Surgeon General.* Atlanta, GA: Author.

U.S. Department of Health and Human Services. (2008). *Treating tobacco use and dependence: 2008 update.* Retrieved from http://www.tobaccoprogram.org/clientuploads/documents/Consumer%20Materials/Clinicians%20Systems%20Mat/2008-Guidelines.pdf

U.S. Department of Health and Human Services. (2014a). *Best practices for comprehensive tobacco control programs.* Retrieved from https://www.cdc.gov/tobacco/stateandcommunity/best_practices/pdfs/2014/comprehensive.pdf

U.S. Department of Health and Human Services. (2014b). *The health consequences of smoking—50 years of progress: A report of the Surgeon General.* Atlanta, GA: Centers for Disease Control and Prevention.

U.S. Department of Health and Human Services. (2016). *E-cigarette use among youth and young adults: A report of the Surgeon General.* Atlanta, GA: Author.

U.S. Department of Health Education and Welfare. (1964). *Smoking and health: Report of the Advisory Committee to the Surgeon General.* Washington, DC: U.S. Government Printing Office.

U.S. Preventive Services Task Force. (2019). *Tobacco smoking cessation in adults, including pregnant women: Behavioral and pharmacotherapy interventions.* Retrieved from https://www.uspreventiveservicestaskforce.org/Page/Document/RecommendationStatementFinal/tobacco-use-in-adults-and-pregnant-women-counseling-and-interventions1

Walley, S. C., & Jenssen, B. P. (2015). Electronic nicotine delivery systems. *Pediatrics, 136,* 1018–1026. http://dx.doi.org/10.1542/peds.2015-3222

Wang, T. W., Asman, K., Gentzke, A. S., Cullen, K. A., Holder-Hayes, E., Reyes-Guzman, C., . . . King, B. A. (2018). Tobacco product use among adults—United States, 2017. *Morbidity and Mortality Weekly Report, 67,* 1225–1232. http://dx.doi.org/10.15585/mmwr.mm6744a2

4

Motivational Interviewing and Screening, Brief Intervention, and Referral to Treatment

Allen Zweben and Mary Piepmeier

Most people with addiction problems interact with health care and other service systems in settings not specifically related to treating these problems (Substance Abuse and Mental Health Services Administration [SAMHSA], 2018). Such settings may include emergency or trauma units (e.g., acute injuries; White, Slater, Ng, Hingson, & Breslow, 2018), outpatient treatment (mental health; Brady & Sinha, 2005; Dickey, Normand, Weiss, Drake, & Azeni, 2002; Grant et al., 2004; National Institute on Drug Abuse [NIDA], 2018), the criminal justice system (legal troubles; Chang, Lichtenstein, Larsson, & Fazel, 2015; Fazel, Bains, & Doll, 2006), school-based counseling services (poor academic performance and early school dropouts; Cox, Zhang, Johnson, & Bender, 2007; Diego, Field, & Sanders, 2003; Townsend, Flisher, & King, 2007), and child protection services (child maltreatment and neglect; Famularo, Kinscherff, & Fenton, 1992). Although alcohol and drug use may not be the primary reason for these visits, substance use often contributes to these pressing concerns (Moyer, Finney, Swearingen, & Vergun, 2002; Rollnick, Miller, & Butler, 2008). Active involvement in these nonspecialty programs can be a valuable opportunity for early intervention or secondary prevention of substance use problems (Babor et al., 2007; Bray, Del Boca, McRee, Hayashi, & Babor, 2017).

It is now widely recognized that brief intervention can be an effective approach in addressing substance use problems in nonspecialty settings where universal screenings are conducted for risky or hazardous drinking,

http://dx.doi.org/10.1037/0000199-005
Screening, Brief Intervention, and Referral to Treatment for Substance Use: A Practitioner's Guide,
M. D. Cimini and J. L. Martin (Editors)

tobacco use, and/or misuse of prescription or illicit drugs. A positive screen triggers a brief intervention followed by a referral to specialized addiction treatment services, if required (Babor & Higgins-Biddle, 2000; Bischof et al., 2008; Institute of Medicine, 1990; National Institute on Alcohol Abuse and Alcoholism, 2005; NIDA, 2010; Smith et al., 2001). This chapter covers early support for, and evolution of, screening and brief intervention approaches in health care and other nonspecialty settings. We discuss how motivational interviewing can be readily adapted and integrated into brief intervention approaches to address earlier deficiencies in this treatment model more effectively and, at the same time, help to sustain the benefits derived from the approach　.

EVOLUTION OF BRIEF INTERVENTION APPROACHES

Acknowledging the potential impact of expanding brief intervention, the World Health Organization initiated a screening and brief intervention project in 1980 aimed at identifying and intervening with individuals with hazardous and harmful alcohol use (Bray et al., 2017). The development of brief intervention led to the initiation of a nationwide demonstration project for screening, brief intervention, and referral to treatment (SBIRT) in 2003. The project was funded by SAMHSA and included illicit and prescription drugs, tobacco, alcohol, and mental health conditions (Bray et al., 2017). Referral to treatment was incorporated as a mechanism to streamline access to the full spectrum of services for individuals with substance use disorders (Bray et al., 2017; Jonas et al., 2012). Underlying these changes is the perspective that substance abuse is a public health concern and should, therefore, be addressed in settings beyond the boundaries of specialized addiction treatment services.

The format of brief intervention (BI) may range from a few minutes of counseling and advice to one or more 15- to 60-minute sessions (Bien, Miller, & Tonigan, 1993; Miller & Sanchez, 1994; Viner, Christie, Taylor, & Hey, 2003). BI sessions comprise the following: (a) giving individualized feedback on the severity and magnitude of substance use problems, (b) identifying a menu of options to address the misuse, and (c) giving clear advice on behavior change. This information is presented using an empathic, person-centered counseling style that emphasizes the person's autonomy and potential for making behavioral changes. The primary goals of the BI are to evoke and facilitate commitment to, and support, action steps for behavior change. Individuals in need of continued support (as indicated by endorsing more severe alcohol or drug use problems) or those who are unable to make use of or who lack access to the current services are often referred to intensive outpatient or residential addiction treatment clinics for specialized addiction services.

LIMITATIONS OF THE BRIEF INTERVENTION MODEL

The main limitation of the BI model is that it fails to address lack of client readiness for change. To illustrate, in an ideal situation, a visit to a non-specialty setting, such as an emergency department (ED) for an acute injury or a primary care clinic for a medical condition, may be the catalyst for uncovering an underlying ambivalence about addressing substance use behaviors. Individuals may discover that ongoing alcohol and/or drug use may be affecting their employability (e.g., inability to maintain a steady job), mental health condition (e.g., increasing symptoms of anxiety or depression), and/or family hardships (e.g., marital conflict). Individuals may recognize that they cannot continue their current drinking or drug use practices (i.e., present state) and, at the same time, become what they consider to be effective parents (e.g., desirable state; Miller, Forcehimes, & Zweben, 2019). Such a situation signals the message that change is necessary to reconcile the disparity between the individual's present and desirable states as a beginning step in addressing the co-occurring conditions. For many clients, providing feedback in conjunction with constructive advice and support can be effective in facilitating clinically meaningful change.

However, in nonspecialty settings, for some clients with substance use issues, giving information and offering opportunities for taking steps toward change may not be sufficient to produce positive behavioral change (Aldridge, Dowd, & Bray, 2017; Sterling, Ross, & Weisner, 2016). For example, individuals entering the ED due to an injury from a motor vehicle accident are likely to be focused on the primary reason for their visit, the acute injury. They may be unable to make or have not yet made the connection between the car accident and heavy alcohol use, even though substance use played a salient role in creating or exacerbating the presenting concerns. Individuals having difficulties in reconciling discrepancies between their present state and their desirable state of functioning will likely see little or no reason for needing or making behavioral change (e.g., "I'm not like those alcoholics you see that need a drink in the morning. I only drink at night, so I don't see how I have a real problem").

In the past, a client who did not acknowledge an identifiable problem was seen by providers as being "in denial." Clients were stigmatized and labeled as "hard to reach" or "difficult to treat," with the expectation that they had to "hit rock bottom" before recognizing, desiring, or becoming committed to change. Over the years, as research and clinical standards improved, the addiction field has moved away from these pejorative perspectives toward seeing clients in need of help. The current perspective views motivation for behavioral change as a state rather than a trait (Miller, 1983). That is, in the right context and environment, a person's thoughts and feelings about behavioral change are modifiable.

A critical component in assuming the state-based perspective is the emphasis placed on the relationship between the client and the provider. A provider must gain the trust of the client to be able to form a collaborative, helping relationship for enhancing and supporting a client's commitment to change. Not surprisingly, many treatment providers find it challenging to accept and resolve clients' reluctance or ambivalence regarding their problem drinking and/or drug use. At the same time, attempts to persuade individuals to seek treatment for substance use behaviors—especially when the individuals themselves have not verbalized readiness or commitment to change—can be seen as dealing with the provider's needs and not what clients need or want for themselves. Situations like these are likely to provoke defensive reactions, create discord in the professional relationship, and result in poor treatment outcomes (Miller & Rollnick, 2013).

For example, Glass et al. (2016) conducted a rigorously designed meta-analysis of 13 randomized controlled trials to assess clients' specialized alcohol treatment use following single or multiple BI sessions. The sample consisted of clients who were identified opportunistically among varied health care settings, including EDs and medical inpatient units, and endorsed risky drinking and/or alcohol-related medical problems. Trial participants were randomized to one of two conditions: (a) brief alcohol intervention session(s) or (b) a control group, which ranged from no intervention to receiving hand-outs and general health advice. Surprisingly, higher rates of posttreatment alcohol-related care use were not significantly associated with receiving BI compared with the control group.

These findings call into question the efficacy of BI as a referral adherence strategy to increase the use of specialized treatment for non-help-seeking clients with alcohol problems seen in nonspecialty settings. The data suggest that motivational interviewing skills such as rapport building, emphasizing autonomy, evoking acceptance, and facilitating change talk are needed to identify and clarify the aforementioned disparities between clients' and providers' ideas about help-seeking behavior (Aldridge et al., 2017; Glass et al., 2016; Simioni, Cottencin, & Rolland, 2015; Turner et al., 2017), rectify clients' uncertainties about treatment, and facilitate commitment to enter and remain in requisite treatment.

MOTIVATIONAL INTERVIEWING: SETTING THE STAGE FOR HEALTH BEHAVIOR CHANGE

Motivational interviewing (MI), a person-centered counseling style that empha-sizes an equal and collaborative partnership between the client and provider, can set the stage for improving help-seeking behavior. MI can help raise clients' awareness of their alcohol and/or drug use problems and facilitate movement toward a stronger commitment to behavior change (Miller, Forcehimes, & Zweben, 2011). MI is useful in guiding clients to acknowledge ambivalence about substance use and related problems. It can help resolve discrepancies between their substance use and personal priorities, values, and goals in pursuit of what is intrinsic to their best self-interest. The client's autonomy over deciding on realistic goals and carrying out those goals is honored throughout the MI sessions. Furthermore, as a form of communication style, MI can be readily incorporated into a BI session.

To illustrate, Barnett et al. (2010) randomly assigned clients with alcohol-related injuries presenting in an ED to have a single session of counselor-involved brief motivational intervention (BMI) or to receive written personal feedback involving minimal counselor contact. Eligible clients had either a score of 8 or higher on the Alcohol Use Disorders Test or reported alcohol use 6 hours before the ER visit. Aside from a written personal feedback report, BMI counselors focused on building rapport and clients' self-efficacy during the sessions. MI micro-skills, including affirmations and reflections, were used to identify and resolve the client's ambivalence about changing drinking behaviors and strengthen the commitment to change. All clients received two telephone booster sessions that took place 1 and 3 months after the initial session.

This trial was unique to BI efficacy trials in that investigators conducted a moderator analysis to study factors impacting treatment outcomes. The investigators analyzed such moderators as alcohol intake before the event of the injury, attribution of the alcohol use to the injury event, and client readiness to change at the time of ED treatment. Treatment outcomes included alcohol consumption patterns and the number of alcohol-related injuries at the 12-month follow-up. The findings indicated that clients who (a) drank before the injury event, (b) attributed the injury event to alcohol use, and (c) had high levels of readiness to change performed as well in BMI as in the minimal care condition. In contrast, clients who (a) did not drink before the injury event, (b) did not attribute the injury event to alcohol use, and (c) had moderate to low levels of readiness to change performed better in BMI than in the minimal feedback session. Failure to attribute the alcohol event to the medical emergency was also associated with lower levels of readiness to change. These data underscore the importance of having a more intimate, person-centered intervention for individuals who do not readily attribute alcohol consumption to the problems that originally brought them to the ED. Furthermore, the investigators suggested that concerned reactions by family and friends and the minimal hospital intervention may have served as an effective "teachable moment" for the clients (Barnett et al., 2010). Hence, individuals who possess an awareness of the risks associated with alcohol use (i.e., the injury event) may not require help beyond what is conventionally offered in an ED setting.

Adapting Brief Motivational Interviewing to Clients' Capacities and Needs

In a recent meta-analysis, DiClemente, Corno, Graydon, Wiprovnick, and Knoblach (2017) pointed out that current evidence shows that BMI may be an important ingredient in shifting attitudes, intention, and preparation for change but may not be adequate to engender actual behavior change. BMI may be useful in resolving ambivalence about the potential of behavior change, but something more or different is needed to facilitate the actualization of behavior change (DiClemente et al., 2017; Richter & Ellerbeck, 2015). Thus, we must consider which elements or processes associated with BMI need improvement to facilitate behavioral health change (Aldridge et al., 2017; Del Boca, McRee, Vendetti, & Damon, 2017; Dunn, Deroo, & Rivara, 2001; Jonas et al., 2012).

In response to this challenge, Lee et al. (2010) posited that outcomes derived from BMI would be considerably improved if more focus was placed on the planning process. The planning process, the final step of the four processes of MI, involves eliciting original ideas from the client (reflecting individual needs) and evaluating all available options for next steps (affirming capacity) to collectively devise a clear plan of action toward behavior change. The overall aim of the study was to determine whether the level of quality of the change plan would have a positive effect on posttreatment outcomes. Another aim was to determine whether differences in levels of readiness to change would affect treatment outcomes.

Participants were recruited from an ED while seeking medical treatment for alcohol-related injuries and were randomly assigned to one of three conditions: a single BMI session, a BMI session plus a booster session, or standard ED care (assessment only). Clients in the two BMI conditions were exposed to fundamentals of an MI intervention by receiving individualized feedback, conducting a decisional balance (weighing pros and cons), and creating a well-thought-out change plan for attainable change goals. The creation of a high-quality change plan meant special attention was devoted to identifying detailed action steps and strategies to maintain treatment goals in the posttreatment period. The providers encouraged the clients to take responsibility for different aspects of the change plan to strengthen the client's commitment to change.

To test the hypothesis that levels of readiness and quality of change plan affect treatment outcomes, investigators examined outcomes related to the two BMI conditions (individuals in the ED condition did not complete a change plan and thus were not included in the analysis). Clients in the BMI condition were divided into four groups depending on their level of readiness to change and the quality of the change plan: (a) high readiness to change alcohol use and high quality of change plan, (b) high readiness to change alcohol use and low-quality change plan, (c) low readiness to change alcohol use and high-quality change plan, or (d) low readiness to change alcohol use and low-quality change plan.

Findings at 12 months posttreatment showed differential benefits (i.e., fewer alcohol-related consequences) for individuals with high readiness to change and who completed high-quality change plans. Pretreatment readiness also improved outcomes, but the relationship decayed when the effects of the change plan were introduced into the analysis. In other words, the quality of the change plan produced benefits beyond what was offered by the level of readiness or change plan alone. The authors concluded that improved levels of readiness followed by detailed and comprehensive planning might be "interrelated and synergistic events" as part of the MI process (Lee et al., 2010, p. 731).

The implication is that BMI could potentially produce improved treatment outcomes when greater emphasis is placed on developing a comprehensive "high-quality" change plan. More specifically, considerable effort should be given to establishing a specified change goal (i.e., drinking reduction), identifying practical strategies to achieve and maintain that goal, and finding solutions to potential barriers that might interfere with momentum toward attaining the goal. These issues should be addressed within an MI framework that has been effectively used in resolving underlying ambivalence and facilitating a commitment to change (see the section Incorporating Motivational Interviewing Into Brief Intervention).

Using Brief Motivational Intervention With Reactive Clients

Although we continue to explore improvements to the efficacy of BMI, it is important to consider that not all clients will be receptive to BMI. Some individuals will remain strongly reactive or unwilling to change the status quo related to stopping or reducing substance use. Under such circumstances, it may be useful to incorporate the client's perspective of the situation and shift the discussion to exploring other options related to the client's interest in and capacity for change. For example, a client may observe recurring familial conflict when they drink at home and could actively reduce the chances of continued conflict by avoiding alcohol use at home. Other clients may exercise the option of finding a designated driver to avoid drunk driving. Allowing clients to survey different areas in their life that are negatively impacted by their substance use may open windows of opportunity for initiating small steps (i.e., proximal goals) leading to greater awareness and acceptance of having substance use problems, increasing self-efficacy about change, and improving willingness to change—factors linked to abstaining or cutting down on drinking and drug use (Miller et al., 2011).

INCORPORATING MOTIVATIONAL INTERVIEWING INTO BRIEF INTERVENTION

The process of integrating MI into BI begins with assessing client readiness for change. From there, it can be divided into four functions: (a) building rapport and engaging the client in a collaborative relationship, (b) forging a consensus about treatment goals, (c) encouraging and supporting commitment for change, and (d) sustaining behavioral change. Although each constitutes a distinguishable feature of MI, taken as a whole, they are not discrete in practice; each is viewed as an ongoing process that is constantly unfolding and evolving with engagement skills used throughout the intervention process (Miller et al., 2019).

Assessing Client Readiness for Change

Client readiness is a highly variable phenomenon that fluctuates across time, settings, and circumstances. When assessing a client's readiness, the central issue to consider is "where the client is" at a given moment in time. The following questions are not asked directly but are considered in forging a therapeutic alliance with clients. The issues covered are based on what clients are willing, ready, and able to discuss in the initial interview. Some clients may be ready, willing, and able to discuss plans for changing their drinking or drug use. Others may still be unaware of risks and harms associated with the substance use behaviors, and consequently, we may have to spend more time obtaining a consensus about treatment goals and strategies. We typically do not use standardized measures because they tend to interfere with the rapport-building process. The following questions and issues are considered in determining client readiness to change.

- Do they recognize the benefits and risks associated with changing or not changing substance use behaviors?

- Do they attribute the reason(s) that brought them to the setting (e.g., alcohol-related injury) to substance use behaviors (risks)?

- Do they believe that changing the substance use behavior will have a positive impact on their current situation (e.g., improve economic status; benefits)?

- How willing are they to carrying out an agreed-on treatment plan (commitment)?

- Do they have the confidence (or have the capacity to build confidence) to take the necessary steps to change substance use behaviors (confidence)?

Once you have gauged the client's level of readiness, then you can determine what kinds of strategies will be most effective at facilitating attitudinal and behavioral change, as you proceed through the next four steps.

Rapport Building: Engaging the Client in a Collaborative Relationship

The main objective in rapport building is to engage with the client in a meaningful, goal-orientated conversation. Fostering a solid, collaborative relationship and an equal partnership is fundamental to improving treatment outcomes (Anderson, Ogles, Patterson, Lambert, & Vermeersch, 2009; Kim, Wampold,

& Bolt, 2006; Moyers & Miller, 2013; Norcross & Lambert, 2011). You can initiate the conversation by orienting the client to the reasons for the appointment while clarifying your role and the client's part in actively contributing to the treatment process. It is important to listen attentively to accurately reflect the client's comments, questions, and/or concerns about the process. Avoid questioning the client's uncertainties about treatment ("Why do you feel that you don't need to be here?"). These questions often engender distrust, defensiveness, or stonewalling. Clients who arrive with preexisting feelings of ambivalence about having and/or changing their substance use may be particularly vulnerable to these circumstances (Miller, Benefield, & Tonigan, 1993).

The relational component of MI is captured in the term *MI spirit*, which is defined by four active ingredients that characterize the guidance of a person toward change: collaboration, evocation, acceptance, and compassion (Miller & Rollnick, 2013). *Collaboration* is a partnership in which both the therapist and the provider are working as a team toward an agreed-on goal. It is centered on forming a working alliance to share feedback on such issues as the severity levels of substance use and related consequences (e.g., family conflicts). The provider does not present the information as "the expert," but rather as a person who is present in the moment and is genuinely working toward gaining a comprehensive and compassionate understanding of the client's perspective. MI spirit provides the context and social environment to help move the person along the continuum of change.

The second component, *evocation*, is a method of yielding collaborative responses. Evocation is used to increase a client's speech in favor of change (i.e., *change talk*); doing so helps to soften or reduce speech in favor of not changing (i.e., *sustain talk*). Verbalizing change is linked with language favoring movement in a positive direction (e.g., preparatory change talk: "I would," "I want," "I will"; and mobilizing change talk: "I am committed to," "I made plans to," "I am doing").

Contrary to change talk is sustain talk, which is language favoring the status quo (e.g., "I don't need to do anything different right now," "My friends drink way more than I do," "I need to drink to help me relax"). Using strategies that increase change talk while avoiding those that increase sustain talk increase the likelihood that health behavior change will occur (Campbell, Adamson, & Carter, 2010; Gaume, Bertholet, Faouzi, Gmel, & Daeppen, 2013; Morgenstern et al., 2012; Moyers, Martin, Houck, Christopher, & Tonigan, 2009; Walker, Stephens, Rowland, & Roffman, 2011). In other words, you should purposefully and strategically tip the balance of the scale in favor of change talk over sustain talk.

The third and fourth components of MI spirit are acceptance and compassion. The practice of *acceptance* means that the client's autonomy and potential for change are readily acknowledged and supported. The client must explicitly understand that he or she is the one in the driver's seat with regard to decision making, goal setting, and carrying out any actual change in behavior. *Compassion* involves the provider communicating genuine care and concern for the person and a desire to help improve his or her well-being. Taken together, these components of MI spirit encompass a humanistic approach to help reduce the stigma associated with substance use problems and ensure that the client feels accepted, valued, and worthy of positive change (Miller et al., 2019).

Forging a Consensus About Treatment Goals

MI strategies are used to form a consensus about treatment goals that are pertinent to the specific circumstances and conditions of the client (Zweben & Zuckoff, 2002). A shared agreement on the established goal allows clients to know they are in control over their choices and actions. It further empowers clients to undertake the necessary action steps for behavior change. As mentioned earlier, identifying and accomplishing even a minor goal can become a beginning step in the right direction. In some cases, just providing a comfortable and welcoming environment for clients to fully express uncertainties and anxieties about change can help improve levels of readiness and facilitate behavior change. A welcoming environment allows clients an opportunity to clarify priorities, make necessary modifications in treatment goals, and cope with other challenges that often arise during treatment.

Four specified MI strategies are valuable tools in facilitating a productive exchange between client and provider and help move clients further along the continuum of change (i.e., preparation, commitment, and action). These strategies include open-ended questioning, affirming, reflecting, and summarizing. MI strategies are known by the acronym OARS (Miller & Rollnick, 2013).

Open-Ended Questioning
Open-ended questions are useful to understand and clarify the client's perspective of their current situation, condition, or circumstances surrounding substance use behavior (e.g., "Can you tell me more?"). In determining what kind of help would be most beneficial, you might consider asking the following open-ended questions: "What kinds of help have been useful to you in the past or would be useful to you in the near future?" "What would it take to gain access to these services?" "What would help you maintain involvement in these needed services?"

A useful way to determine the appropriateness of a question is to ask yourself whether the client's response is going to deepen your understanding of the person's perspectives without causing negative reactions and/or discord in the therapeutic relationship. For example, exploring only the negative consequences of risky or hazardous drinking or drug use can undermine the self-efficacy and confidence of the client. Therefore, it might be helpful to mitigate these negative responses by posing a series of questions about the benefits of not drinking or not using drugs as well.

Affirming

It is common to focus on the negative aspects of the client's current behavior in need of change. However, *affirming* personal abilities or strengths gives the provider a better opportunity to pivot the conversation in a more positive direction. Affirmations are most effective in positively reinforcing and empowering the client to envision his or her potential change. Affirmations can be separated from praise insofar as you do not interject the statement with your own opinion or judgment (e.g., "I think," "I am impressed"). Listen for the client's utterances that uncover specific strengths, abilities, and positive behavioral changes and reflect back what you hear (e.g., "You put in a lot of hard work into planning, which shows an honest commitment to your treatment goal," "It takes a lot of strength and courage to reach out to your family for help"). In short, affirmations accurately and genuinely represent information the client has shared with you.

Reflecting

The most integral skill in fostering a nonjudgmental and supportive environment when conducting MI is the practice of *reflecting*. Reflections paraphrase the client's words and move further ahead by considering what the person means but has not yet shared. For example, instead of merely repeating what the client has said (*simple reflection*), effective reflections capture what the client might be thinking but not verbalizing (*complex reflection*). In essence, you are hypothesizing the meaning behind the client's words and experiences in the form of a reflection.

In general, reflecting is a useful strategy for communicating that you do not have an agenda separate from the client's needs (i.e., a person-centered approach). It also serves as a mechanism to promote further introspection of self on the part of the client. Your entire focus is on following (or *tracking*) and seeking a better understanding of the individual's perspectives and experiences with respect to substance use and related behaviors (Miller & Rollnick, 2013). Reflections also provide a foundation to cultivate collaboration in preparation, commitment, and taking action in the direction of change. Complex reflections have been shown to be a statistically significant predictor in postintervention for drinking (Tollison et al., 2008), cannabis use (McCambridge, Day, Thomas, & Strang, 2011), and HIV medication adherence (Thrasher et al., 2006).

Summarizing

Summarizing entails collecting comments and thoughts between yourself and the client in a series of reflections. They can be used to link different observations or comments made by the client and incorporate them into one coherent and cogent message. At the same time, summaries that use the client's words about current and past experiences can bring about an increased understanding and insight about the situation (e.g., "You reported that boredom often leads to drinking. You also mentioned that playing sports in the past alleviated feelings of boredom. It sounds like keeping yourself occupied with playing sports may help in addressing your current drinking"). Summarizing can also be a way to transition from one process to the next along the readiness continuum. For example, you may decide to move on to the planning process after the client demonstrated a strong commitment to change (e.g., "You've stated many times the reasons for your commitment to this goal. I am wondering now, taking all the reasons into consideration, what you envision as a next step").

Encouraging and Supporting a Commitment to Change

MI is distinct in evoking change talk, as well as reducing sustain talk. Reducing sustain talk and increasing change talk together have been shown to be important mechanisms of change in MI process research, including alcohol and drug use reduction (Apodaca & Longabaugh, 2009; Moyers, Houck, Glynn, Hallgren, & Manuel, 2017). Specific strategies can help enhance and encourage continued change talk and reduce the frequency of sustain talk.

With respect to change talk, affirming clients' behavioral changes and asking them to elaborate on the details of undertaking behavioral change can strategically perpetuate continued change talk. For example, the client may say, "I haven't had a drink in 2 weeks, and I feel great." The provider responds, "Your hard work toward achieving your goal is paying off. Can you tell me what benefits you've experienced so far from not drinking the past 2 weeks?" Here, the provider emphasizes the client's behavioral steps toward change while giving the client a chance to elaborate on the positive effects of said change.

It is also important to distinguish and listen for both *preparatory* (e.g., "I am thinking about applying for a job") and *mobilizing* change talk (e.g., "I have a job interview tomorrow"), and respond accordingly, liberally offering both affirmations and reflections. Reflecting and affirming specific behavioral changes moves the client's speech toward more explicit statements about and action steps toward change. Reframing the content of open-ended questions (e.g., "What do you think are some of the reasons your family wants you to quit?"), emphasizing optimism (e.g., "What would life be like when you stop drinking?"), and affirming client autonomy (e.g., "You have showed great resilience during this difficult time") can also be helpful.

Equally as important as evoking change talk is reducing sustain talk. One approach to reducing sustain talk is to normalize the client's situation. Clients often feel discouraged by setbacks or situations that are preventing them from progressing. Normalizing highlights the commonality of the client's struggles to improve optimism about change. You should be mindful of not using MI strategies that have the potential for soliciting or increasing sustain talk. For example, using decisional balancing (e.g., "Can you share with me the pros and cons of changing your drinking practices?") when the person is still ambivalent about changing substance use tends to increase sustain talk (Miller et al., 2019). Such an approach is best used when the client has already expressed a commitment to change. Instead, you should expend efforts on strategies tailored to evoke change talk (see the earlier discussion). In addition, you should not introduce other struggles the client may be having unless the client brings them up independently: "In the past, you have had trouble drinking on the job. Is that still a problem?" In other words, it is also important to stay focused on clients' strengths rather than deficiencies.

Helping Clients Sustain Behavioral Change

One of the most challenging aspects of addiction treatment is helping the client sustain benefits achieved in a treatment program. Consequently, there is a need to consider potential obstacles to change the individual may encounter. As mentioned earlier, it is important to develop and implement a coherent and thoughtful plan to forestall potential obstacles or barriers in the pathways to change. Again, the client and provider working alongside each other as equal partners (i.e., MI spirit) can be productive in planning for the client's future.

When addressing future planning, you might consider asking individuals what they envision happening after leaving the program and how they might respond to these issues. ("What do you envision happening after leaving the program?" "Together, let's review your options for managing these new challenges once you complete treatment"). Clients who have difficulty responding to these questions might benefit from information about potential challenges awaiting them after termination from the program (e.g., finding housing and employment, making child care arrangements, and handling financial stressors). However, it is critical that you ask permission before sharing information with the client. Asking permission allows the client to take ownership of the information being shared (i.e., supporting autonomy). It also moves you further away from the "expert" role and demonstrates that you are an equal partner in the process. It is useful to assess the individual's understanding of the shared information to strengthen sustainability. This helps to acknowledge and value the client's perspective of the issues while honoring their autonomy in the exchange.

CONCLUSION

The following are a number of take-home messages offered for your consideration. First, BMI should be adapted or tailored to clients' capacities, resources, and needs (Barnett et al., 2010; Bien et al., 1993; Dunn et al., 2001; Landy, Davey, Quintero, Pecora, & McShane, 2016; Moyer et al., 2002). Second, non-help-seeking clients seen in nonspecialty settings who evidence a low readiness for change and have high severity of alcohol and drug use problems may gain additional benefits from BMI, especially as a referral adherence strategy. As demonstrated in the meta-analysis by Glass et al. (2016), many will need additional help (e.g., medication-assisted treatment) following BI. Third, MI techniques, such as open-ended questioning, reflecting, affirming, summarizing, normalizing, and promoting optimism, can be effective in softening and reducing sustain talk and eliciting change talk, factors that, in turn, bolster a commitment to change. Fourth, in accordance with an MI framework, it would help clients if practitioners place a greater focus on the benefits of change (e.g., improved relationships and better quality of life) rather than on the risks of not changing (e.g., elevated liver enzymes and legal issues). In summary, you should be pragmatic, flexible, and mindful in using BMI with individuals with substance use problems.

REFERENCES

Aldridge, A., Dowd, W., & Bray, J. (2017). The relative impact of brief treatment versus brief intervention in primary health-care screening programs for substance use disorders. *Addiction, 112*, 54–64. http://dx.doi.org/10.1111/add.13653

Anderson, T., Ogles, B. M., Patterson, C. L., Lambert, M. J., & Vermeersch, D. A. (2009). Therapist effects: Facilitative interpersonal skills as a predictor of therapist success. *Journal of Clinical Psychology, 65*, 755–768. http://dx.doi.org/10.1002/jclp.20583

Apodaca, T. R., & Longabaugh, R. (2009). Mechanisms of change in motivational interviewing: A review and preliminary evaluation of the evidence. *Addiction, 104*, 705–715. http://dx.doi.org/10.1111/j.1360-0443.2009.02527.x

Babor, T. F., & Higgins-Biddle, J. C. (2000). Alcohol screening and brief intervention: Dissemination strategies for medical practice and public health. *Addiction, 95*, 677–686. http://dx.doi.org/10.1046/j.1360-0443.2000.9556773.x

Babor, T. F., McRee, B. G., Kassebaum, P. A., Grimaldi, P. L., Ahmed, K., & Bray, J. (2007). Screening, Brief Intervention, and Referral to Treatment (SBIRT): Toward a public health approach to the management of substance abuse. *Substance Abuse, 28*, 7–30. http://dx.doi.org/10.1300/J465v28n03_03

Barnett, N. P., Apodaca, T. R., Magill, M., Colby, S. M., Gwaltney, C., Rohsenow, D. J., & Monti, P. M. (2010). Moderators and mediators of two brief interventions for alcohol in the emergency department. *Addiction, 105*, 452–465. http://dx.doi.org/10.1111/j.1360-0443.2009.02814.x

Bien, T. H., Miller, W. R., & Tonigan, J. S. (1993). Brief interventions for alcohol problems: A review. *Addiction, 88*, 315–336. http://dx.doi.org/10.1111/j.1360-0443.1993.tb00820.x

Bischof, G., Grothues, J. M., Reinhardt, S., Meyer, C., John, U., & Rumpf, H.-J. (2008). Evaluation of a telephone-based stepped care intervention for alcohol-related disorders: A randomized controlled trial. *Drug and Alcohol Dependence, 93*, 244–251. http://dx.doi.org/10.1016/j.drugalcdep.2007.10.003

Brady, K. T., & Sinha, R. (2005). Co-occurring mental and substance use disorders: The neurobiological effects of chronic stress. *The American Journal of Psychiatry, 162*, 1483–1493. http://dx.doi.org/10.1176/appi.ajp.162.8.1483

Bray, J. W., Del Boca, F. K., McRee, B. G., Hayashi, S. W., & Babor, T. F. (2017). Screening, Brief Intervention and Referral to Treatment (SBIRT): Rationale, program overview and cross-site evaluation. *Addiction, 112*, 3–11. http://dx.doi.org/10.1111/add.13676

Campbell, S. D., Adamson, S. J., & Carter, J. D. (2010). Client language during motivational enhancement therapy and alcohol use outcome. *Behavioural and Cognitive Psychotherapy, 38*, 399–415. http://dx.doi.org/10.1017/S1352465810000263

Chang, Z., Lichtenstein, P., Larsson, H., & Fazel, S. (2015). Substance use disorders, psychiatric disorders, and mortality after release from prison: A nationwide longitudinal cohort study. *The Lancet Psychiatry, 2*, 422–430. http://dx.doi.org/10.1016/S2215-0366(15)00088-7

Cox, R. G., Zhang, L., Johnson, W. D., & Bender, D. R. (2007). Academic performance and substance use: Findings from a state survey of public high school students. *The Journal of School Health, 77*, 109–115. http://dx.doi.org/10.1111/j.1746-1561.2007.00179.x

Del Boca, F. K., McRee, B., Vendetti, J., & Damon, D. (2017). The SBIRT program matrix: A conceptual framework for program implementation and evaluation. *Addiction, 112*, 12–22. http://dx.doi.org/10.1111/add.13656

Dickey, B., Normand, S.-L. T., Weiss, R. D., Drake, R. E., & Azeni, H. (2002). Medical morbidity, mental illness, and substance use disorders. *Psychiatric Services, 53*, 861–867. http://dx.doi.org/10.1176/appi.ps.53.7.861

DiClemente, C. C., Corno, C. M., Graydon, M. M., Wiprovnick, A. E., & Knoblach, D. J. (2017). Motivational interviewing, enhancement, and brief interventions over the last decade: A review of reviews of efficacy and effectiveness. *Psychology of Addictive Behaviors, 31*, 862–887. http://dx.doi.org/10.1037/adb0000318

Diego, M. A., Field, T. M., & Sanders, C. E. (2003). Academic performance, popularity, and depression predict adolescent substance use. *Adolescence, 38*, 35–42.

Dunn, C., Deroo, L., & Rivara, F. P. (2001). The use of brief interventions adapted from motivational interviewing across behavioral domains: A systematic review. *Addiction, 96*, 1725–1742. http://dx.doi.org/10.1046/j.1360-0443.2001.961217253.x

Famularo, R., Kinscherff, R., & Fenton, T. (1992). Parental substance abuse and the nature of child maltreatment. *Child Abuse & Neglect, 16*, 475–483. http://dx.doi.org/10.1016/0145-2134(92)90064-X

Fazel, S., Bains, P., & Doll, H. (2006). Substance abuse and dependence in prisoners: A systematic review. *Addiction, 101*, 181–191. http://dx.doi.org/10.1111/j.1360-0443.2006.01316.x

Gaume, J., Bertholet, N., Faouzi, M., Gmel, G., & Daeppen, J.-B. (2013). Does change talk during brief motivational interventions with young men predict change in alcohol use? *Journal of Substance Abuse Treatment, 44*, 177–185. http://dx.doi.org/10.1016/j.jsat.2012.04.005

Glass, J. E., Hamilton, A. M., Powell, B. J., Perron, B. E., Brown, R. T., & Ilgen, M. A. (2016). Revisiting our review of Screening, Brief Intervention and Referral to Treatment (SBIRT): Meta-analytical results still point to no efficacy in increasing the use of substance use disorder services. *Addiction, 111*, 181–183. http://dx.doi.org/10.1111/add.13146

Grant, B. F., Stinson, F. S., Dawson, D. A., Chou, S. P., Dufour, M. C., Compton, W., . . . Kaplan, K. (2004). Prevalence and co-occurrence of substance use disorders and independent mood and anxiety disorders: Results from the National Epidemiologic Survey on Alcohol and Related Conditions. *Archives of General Psychiatry, 61*, 807–816. http://dx.doi.org/10.1001/archpsyc.61.8.807

Institute of Medicine. (1990). *Broadening the base of treatment for alcohol problems.* Washington, DC: National Academy of Sciences Press.

Jonas, D. E., Garbutt, J. C., Amick, H. R., Brown, J. M., Brownley, K. A., Council, C. L., . . . Harris, R. P. (2012). Behavioral counseling after screening for alcohol misuse in primary care: A systematic review and meta-analysis for the U.S. Preventive Services Task Force. *Annals of Internal Medicine, 157*, 645–654. http://dx.doi.org/10.7326/0003-4819-157-9-201211060-00544

Kim, D.-M., Wampold, B. E., & Bolt, D. M. (2006). Therapist effects in psychotherapy: A random-effects modeling of the National Institute of Mental Health Treatment of Depression Collaborative Research Program data. *Psychotherapy Research, 16*, 161–172. http://dx.doi.org/10.1080/10503300500264911

Landy, M. S., Davey, C. J., Quintero, D., Pecora, A., & McShane, K. E. (2016). A systematic review on the effectiveness of brief interventions for alcohol misuse among adults in emergency departments. *Journal of Substance Abuse Treatment, 61,* 1–12. http://dx.doi.org/10.1016/j.jsat.2015.08.004

Lee, C. S., Baird, J., Longabaugh, R., Nirenberg, T. D., Mello, M. J., & Woolard, R. (2010). Change plan as an active ingredient of brief motivational interventions for reducing negative consequences of drinking in hazardous drinking emergency-department patients. *Journal of Studies on Alcohol and Drugs, 71,* 726–733. http://dx.doi.org/10.15288/jsad.2010.71.726

McCambridge, J., Day, M., Thomas, B. A., & Strang, J. (2011). Fidelity to motivational interviewing and subsequent cannabis cessation among adolescents. *Addictive Behaviors, 36,* 749–754. http://dx.doi.org/10.1016/j.addbeh.2011.03.002

Miller, W. R. (1983). Motivational interviewing with problem drinkers. *Behavioural and Cognitive Psychotherapy, 11,* 147–172. http://dx.doi.org/10.1017/S0141347300006583

Miller, W. R., Benefield, R. G., & Tonigan, J. S. (1993). Enhancing motivation for change in problem drinking: A controlled comparison of two therapist styles. *Journal of Consulting and Clinical Psychology, 61,* 455–461. http://dx.doi.org/10.1037/0022-006X.61.3.455

Miller, W. R., Forcehimes, A. A., & Zweben, A. (2011). *Treating addiction: A guide for professionals.* New York, NY: Guilford Press.

Miller, W. R., Forcehimes, A. A., & Zweben, A. (2019). *Treating addiction: A guide for professionals* (2nd ed.). New York, NY: Guilford Press.

Miller, W. R., & Rollnick, S. (2013). *Motivational interviewing: Helping people change* (3rd ed.). New York, NY: Guilford Press.

Miller, W. R., & Sanchez, V. C. (1994). Motivating young adults for treatment and lifestyle change. In G. S. Howard & P. E. Nathan (Eds.), *Alcohol use and misuse by young adults* (pp. 55–81). Notre Dame, IN: University of Notre Dame Press.

Morgenstern, J., Kuerbis, A., Amrhein, P., Hail, L., Lynch, K., & McKay, J. R. (2012). Motivational interviewing: A pilot test of active ingredients and mechanisms of change. *Psychology of Addictive Behaviors, 26,* 859–869. http://dx.doi.org/10.1037/a0029674

Moyer, A., Finney, J. W., Swearingen, C. E., & Vergun, P. (2002). Brief interventions for alcohol problems: A meta-analytic review of controlled investigations in treatment-seeking and non-treatment-seeking populations. *Addiction, 97,* 279–292. http://dx.doi.org/10.1046/j.1360-0443.2002.00018.x

Moyers, T. B., Houck, J., Glynn, L. H., Hallgren, K. A., & Manuel, J. K. (2017). A randomized controlled trial to influence client language in substance use disorder treatment. *Drug and Alcohol Dependence, 172,* 43–50. http://dx.doi.org/10.1016/j.drugalcdep.2016.11.036

Moyers, T. B., Martin, T., Houck, J. M., Christopher, P. J., & Tonigan, J. S. (2009). From in-session behaviors to drinking outcomes: A causal chain for motivational interviewing. *Journal of Consulting and Clinical Psychology, 77,* 1113–1124. http://dx.doi.org/10.1037/a0017189

Moyers, T. B., & Miller, W. R. (2013). Is low therapist empathy toxic? *Psychology of Addictive Behaviors, 27,* 878–884. http://dx.doi.org/10.1037/a0030274

National Institute on Alcohol Abuse and Alcoholism. (2005). *Helping patients who drink too much: A clinician's guide.* Retrieved from https://www.integration.samhsa.gov/clinical-practice/Helping_Patients_Who_Drink_Too_Much.pdf

National Institute on Drug Abuse. (2010). *Resource guide: Screening for drug use in general medical settings.* Retrieved from https://www.drugabuse.gov/publications/resource-guide-screening-drug-use-in-general-medical-settings/nida-quick-screen

National Institute on Drug Abuse. (2018). *Comorbidity: Substance use disorders and other mental illnesses.* Retrieved from https://www.drugabuse.gov/publications/drugfacts/comorbidity-substance-use-disorders-other-mental-illnesses

Norcross, J. C., & Lambert, M. J. (2011). Psychotherapy relationships that work II. *Psychotherapy, 48,* 4–8. http://dx.doi.org/10.1037/a0022180

Richter, K. P., & Ellerbeck, E. F. (2015). It's time to change the default for tobacco treatment. *Addiction, 110,* 381–386. http://dx.doi.org/10.1111/add.12734

Rollnick, S., Miller, W. R., & Butler, C. C. (2008). *Motivational interviewing in health care: Helping patients change behavior.* New York, NY: Guilford Press.

Simioni, N., Cottencin, O., & Rolland, B. (2015). Interventions for increasing subsequent alcohol treatment utilisation among patients with alcohol use disorders from somatic inpatient settings: A systematic review. *Alcohol and Alcoholism, 50,* 420–429. http://dx.doi.org/10.1093/alcalc/agv017

Smith, S. S., Jorenby, D. E., Fiore, M. C., Anderson, J. E., Mielke, M. M., Beach, K. E., . . . Baker, T. B. (2001). Strike while the iron is hot: Can stepped-care treatments resurrect relapsing smokers? *Journal of Consulting and Clinical Psychology, 69,* 429–439. http://dx.doi.org/10.1037/0022-006X.69.3.429

Sterling, S. A., Ross, T. B., & Weisner, C. (2016). Large-scale implementation of alcohol SBIRT in adult primary care in an integrated health care delivery system: Lessons from the field. *Journal of Patient-Centered Research and Reviews, 3,* 186–187. http://dx.doi.org/10.17294/2330-0698.1317

Substance Abuse and Mental Health Services Administration. (2018). *2017 National Survey on Drug Use and Health (NSDUH) releases.* Retrieved from https://www.samhsa.gov/data/nsduh/reports-detailed-tables-2017-NSDUH

Thrasher, A. D., Golin, C. E., Earp, J. A. L., Tien, H., Porter, C., & Howie, L. (2006). Motivational interviewing to support antiretroviral therapy adherence: The role of quality counseling. *Patient Education and Counseling, 62,* 64–71. http://dx.doi.org/10.1016/j.pec.2005.06.003

Tollison, S. J., Lee, C. M., Neighbors, C., Neil, T. A., Olson, N. D., & Larimer, M. E. (2008). Questions and reflections: The use of motivational interviewing microskills in a peer-led brief alcohol intervention for college students. *Behavior Therapy, 39,* 183–194. http://dx.doi.org/10.1016/j.beth.2007.07.001

Townsend, L., Flisher, A. J., & King, G. (2007). A systematic review of the relationship between high school dropout and substance use. *Clinical Child and Family Psychology Review, 10,* 295–317. http://dx.doi.org/10.1007/s10567-007-0023-7

Turner, B. J., McCann, B. S., Dunn, C. W., Darnell, D. A., Beam, C. R., Kleiber, B., . . . Fukunaga, R. (2017). Examining the reach of a brief alcohol intervention service in routine practice at a level 1 trauma center. *Journal of Substance Abuse Treatment, 79,* 29–33. http://dx.doi.org/10.1016/j.jsat.2017.05.011

Viner, R. M., Christie, D., Taylor, V., & Hey, S. (2003). Motivational/solution-focused intervention improves HbA1c in adolescents with Type 1 diabetes: A pilot study. *Diabetic Medicine, 20,* 739–742. http://dx.doi.org/10.1046/j.1464-5491.2003.00995.x

Walker, D., Stephens, R., Rowland, J., & Roffman, R. (2011). The influence of client behavior during motivational interviewing on marijuana treatment outcome. *Addictive Behaviors, 36,* 669–673. http://dx.doi.org/10.1016/j.addbeh.2011.01.009

White, A. M., Slater, M. E., Ng, G., Hingson, R., & Breslow, R. (2018). Trends in alcohol-related emergency department visits in the United States: Results from the Nationwide Emergency Department Sample, 2006 to 2014. *Alcoholism, Clinical and Experimental Research, 42,* 352–359. http://dx.doi.org/10.1111/acer.13559

Zweben, A., & Zuckoff, A. (2002). Motivational interviewing and treatment adherence. In W. R. Miller & S. Rollnick (Eds.), *Motivational interviewing: Preparing people for change* (2nd ed., pp. 299–319). New York, NY: Guilford Press.

5

Approaches to Brief Interventions

Janice Pringle, Alexandra Nowalk, Alec Howard, and Matthew Taylor

Brief intervention (BI) is a core component of screening, brief intervention, and referral to treatment (SBIRT)—an evidence-based, public health practice that aims to reduce risks associated with harmful and hazardous substance use behaviors (Babor, Del Boca, & Bray, 2017). Specifically, BIs are time-limited, patient-centered conversations structured to facilitate effective behavior change. Rooted in basic motivational interviewing (MI) principles, effective BIs work by addressing an individual's internal ambivalence toward behavior change and connecting this change to individual values (Babor et al., 2007; Shetty, Murphy, Zigler, Yamashita, & Belin, 2011). BIs are a form of early intervention for those individuals who are at an elevated risk for physical, social, or mental consequences resulting from risky substance use, as well as those who do not meet formal diagnostic criteria for a substance use disorder (SUD; American Psychiatric Association, 2013). Through an early intervention process, BIs aim to prevent the escalation of individuals' substance use into the development of an SUD.

BIs are implemented in various clinical settings, including emergency departments (EDs; D'Onofrio et al., 2012), primary care (Hargraves et al., 2017), federally qualified health centers (Barbosa et al., 2018), outpatient settings (Barbosa, Cowell, Bray, & Aldridge, 2015), pharmacies (Pringle, Boyer, Conklin, McCullough, & Aldridge, 2014), university-based student health centers (Fleming et al., 2010), and behavioral health clinics (Rahm et al., 2015), among others. Several organizations, including the Substance Abuse and Mental Health Services Administration (SAMHSA; 2013), Centers for

http://dx.doi.org/10.1037/0000199-006
Screening, Brief Intervention, and Referral to Treatment for Substance Use: A Practitioner's Guide,
M. D. Cimini and J. L. Martin (Editors)

Disease Control and Prevention (CDC; 2014), and U.S. Preventive Services Task Force (USPSTF; Curry et al., 2018; USPSTF, 2019), recommend the systematic application of BIs within primary care as one of the top preventive care approaches (on par with mammograms and colonoscopies).

BIs are effective for reducing substance use, including alcohol (D'Onofrio et al., 2012; Kaner et al., 2018), tobacco (Klemperer, Hughes, Solomon, Callas, & Fingar, 2017), marijuana (Laporte et al., 2017; Walker et al., 2016), opioids (Bowman, Eiserman, Beletsky, Stancliff, & Bruce, 2013; Darker et al., 2016), and other drugs (Smout et al., 2010). The literature on the association between BIs and reduction in risky alcohol use is more extensive (Kaner et al., 2018), but evidence for the effectiveness of BIs to reduce drug use at various severity levels is growing (Humeniuk et al., 2012; Madras et al., 2009). Consequently, as of September 2019, the USPSTF was finalizing a recommendation statement on screening adults, age 18 years and older, for illicit drug use in primary care settings when implemented with an appropriate intervention (USPSTF, 2019). Moreover, the USPSTF has previously published a recommendation statement on screening for unhealthy alcohol use in primary care settings in adults 18 years or older, including pregnant women, and providing persons engaged in risky or hazardous drinking with brief behavioral counseling interventions (Curry et al., 2018).

Further, BIs are associated with reductions in negative medical consequences and downstream health care costs (Pringle et al., 2018). More recently, BIs have been applied to engage individuals with specialty addiction treatment (Cherpitel et al., 2010; D'Onofrio et al., 2017). BIs are effective for several populations, including adolescents (Tanner-Smith & Lipsey, 2015), pregnant women (M. J. O'Connor & Whaley, 2007), and patients with chronic medical conditions (Timko, Kong, Vittorio, & Cucciare, 2016). Despite these positive research findings, the routine use of screening and BI in many clinical settings remains underutilized (Holland, Pringle, & Barbetti, 2009; Rahm et al., 2015; Vendetti et al., 2017). In this chapter, we examine common BI models, clinical applications in various health care settings, billing and reimbursement considerations, and the connection between BIs and connecting patients to appropriate treatment services.

CORE COMPONENTS OF BRIEF INTERVENTIONS

Core components of effective BIs consist of personalized feedback, motivational techniques, and an action plan (E. A. O'Connor et al., 2018). More specifically, BIs place emphasis on a harm reduction approach that (a) provides individuals with feedback on the risks associated with substance use; (b) uses motivational techniques to explore positive and negative consequences related to individuals' substance use level; and (c) sets realistic goals with a specific, mutually agreed-on action plan (if appropriate to an individual's stage of change) that reduces individuals' risks for substance use–related harms (Babor et al., 2007).

Typically, a BI begins with the practitioner asking for permission to provide feedback on the individual's screening results. Asking permission is necessary because it establishes rapport with the individual, respects their individual autonomy, maintains focus on the individual, and allows an individual to discuss their substance use in personal terms. When permission is granted, the practitioner then provides a simple, factual statement about the individual's risk of harm and links the individual's screening results with a specific medical, mental health, or other concern. For example, if an individual is a heavy drinker with hypertension, the practitioner can provide feedback to the patient and inform them that their drinking habits place them at a higher risk of hypertension and cardiovascular disease. Providing feedback in this manner frames substance use as a medical issue that can be addressed during a routine office visit. Finally, the practitioner pauses for and perhaps invites a reaction from the individual before moving the BI forward. Allowing for reactions after providing feedback allows time and space for the individual to reflect and encourages the individual to take responsibility and control of the conversation.

In addition, effective BIs adopt the spirit, strategies, and skills of MI (Dunn, Deroo, & Rivara, 2001; E. A. O'Connor et al., 2018; see also Chapter 3, this volume). Throughout a BI, the practitioner uses MI techniques, including using open-ended questions, affirmations, reflections, and summaries to reduce *sustain talk* (i.e., reasons against change that support the maintenance of the status quo) and increase *change talk* (i.e., personal statements that support change; Miller & Rollnick, 2013). Open-ended questions allow practitioners to explore substance use by evoking personal feelings about substance use, soliciting additional information, and encouraging individuals to elaborate on their situation. Affirmations help practitioners increase an individual's confidence in their ability to change by emphasizing their strengths, promoting areas under their control, and respecting their autonomy. Reflections serve as an "auditory mirror" that help assure individuals the practitioner is engaged and actively listening to their concerns. Summaries move the BI forward, confirm the practitioner understands the individual's narrative, clarify potential conflict between the patient and provider, focus on modifiable risk factors (e.g., behaviors, attitudes, beliefs), and reinforce positive beliefs about the patient's ability to change.

Further motivational techniques essential to effective BIs include (a) practicing empathy and understanding an individual's rationale for their actions, (b) supporting an individual's self-efficacy through affirmation and positive reinforcement of past attempts at behavior change, (c) developing discrepancy by creating a disconnect between the individual's current behavior and their future goals, and (d) reducing discord (Miller & Rollnick, 2013). *Discord* refers to a potential breakdown in the working alliance between the practitioner and the individual and is best avoided by refraining from confrontation, labeling, stereotyping, or forcing individuals to accept a diagnosis or follow specific advice. Table 5.1 provides examples of how practitioners can effectively handle discord.

TABLE 5.1. Strategies for Reducing Discord

Strategy	Example language
Reflect	"I can see why you feel that way."
Apologize	"I'm sorry if I offended you. I'm not trying to push you to change anything you don't want to change."
Affirm	"I appreciate you coming in today. It must have been difficult for you."
Shift focus	"I'd really like to hear your thoughts about. . . ."

For behavior change to be achieved and sustained, change must be important to individuals, and they must feel confident they can realistically make the change. In some cases, individuals feel confident they can make a change but may not find this change valuable (i.e., "I can quit anytime I want to, but I don't feel my smoking is really a problem"). Using motivational techniques allows a practitioner to explore the individual's motivations for behavior change more in-depth and increases the likelihood behavior change will occur. Conversely, an individual may find behavior change important but possess little confidence to execute change (i.e., "I know I have to set a better example for my daughter, but all past attempts to quit have failed"). In this example, to increase self-efficacy to change, the practitioner would affirm the individual's reasons for change and use one or more strategies to build the patient's confidence. Building the individual's confidence often involves helping the patient agree to small changes coupled with affirming the patient's past and current ability to make changes.

One strategy to assess an individual's readiness to change is using a *readiness* or *confidence ruler* during the BI, which involves using open-ended questions to assess the extent to which change is important to the individual and the individual's confidence in changing their substance use (Hesse, 2006). The practitioner should first ask about importance because confidence in changing is irrelevant if behavior change is not important to the individual. Subsequently, the practitioner asks individuals how they would rate their readiness or confidence to change a specific behavior by saying, for example, "On a scale of 1 to 10, how confident are you that you can change your drinking habits?" After the individual selects a number for importance and a number for confidence, the practitioner affirms the individual's response and follows up with another open-ended question to further explore options for the behavior change that the individual is willing and able to accept. If a patient selects 6 on the ruler, the practitioner responds, "That's great. Why did you select 6 instead of 2?" Asking patients about their number choices provides them with an opportunity to share personal motivations for changing their behavior and is important for increasing change talk (i.e., reasons against maintaining the status quo). Figure 5.1 provides an example of using a readiness or confidence ruler.

The final core component of effective BIs is developing an action plan consisting of specific goals. As a harm-reduction approach, the primary outcome for effective BIs should be incremental reductions in substance-related harms

FIGURE 5.1. Readiness and Confidence Ruler

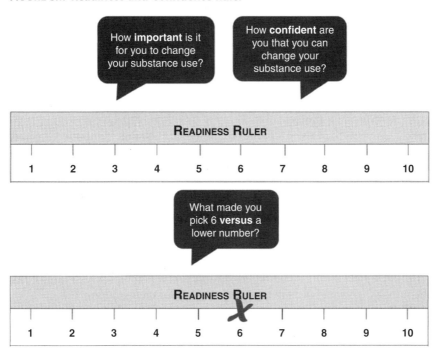

Note. Example showing use of a tool during a brief intervention to better elicit patient readiness or confidence to change substance use–related behaviors.

that are sustained over time (Gryczynski et al., 2011; Jonas et al., 2012). Practitioners can work collaboratively with individuals to set realistic and measurable goals for changing substance use behaviors that can reduce individuals' risk. Goals that are realistic match the individuals' current motivations, confidence level, and social circumstances, which influence how to implement their behavior change (Shetty et al., 2011). Setting measurable goals helps the patient quantify behavior change and serves to hold the individual accountable for progress toward change. For example, a practitioner can use open-ended questions to have individuals explicitly state by how much they will reduce their use (e.g., quantity, frequency) and by when (daily, weekly, monthly, etc.), rather than agreeing to merely "cut back" on their substance use. For individuals in the precontemplation or contemplation stages, an action plan may consist of simply monitoring use at first. For others, the action plan may include strategies to begin reducing use. Although characteristics of individual action plans vary, plans should be relevant, specific, and realistic and ultimately lead to achievable goals. When creating a plan for change, the practitioner can list options, offer guidance, and provide affirmation to the individual.

At the conclusion of the BI, the practitioner ensures the individual is capable and prepared to effectively carry out the agreed-on plan for behavior change (Rollnick, Mason, & Butler, 1999). First, the individual must possess the confidence and self-efficacy necessary to make a behavior change. Second, the individual must take responsibility for the plan and be autonomous in making a behavior change. Finally, the individual must have adequate resources and support to make the change. Follow-up is included in the plan as a means to measure progress, resolve barriers to change, and hold the individual accountable for taking steps toward behavior change.

Ultimately, effective BIs require practitioners to view the development of SUDs as similar to that of other chronic diseases. Chronic diseases evolve from a continuum of risk and time, where risk can change (both increase and decrease). Intervening in chronic disease development is best accomplished as early as possible in the risk progression and involves empowering the individual to learn how to best manage their risk. BIs will not always result in abstinence from substance use because that is not a realistic goal for all individuals. Practitioners must respect individuals' autonomy to make informed decisions about their health. Ideally, the practitioner can provide BIs to the patient over time that will support persistent and consistent risk reduction. Effective BIs are about meeting individuals where they are and empowering them to discover and pursue their motivations for change.

COMMON BRIEF INTERVENTION MODELS IN HEALTH CARE SETTINGS

Various BI models exist, all of which are associated with positive changes in substance use behaviors. Research regarding specific characteristics that lead to differential outcomes between models is limited, however (E. A. O'Connor et al., 2018). Rather, practitioners recognize shared components of effective BIs, as discussed in the previous section. The following section provides an overview of common BI models and the empirical support for each.

Feedback–Responsibility–Advice–Menu–Empathy–Self-Efficacy

Feedback–responsibility–advice–menu–empathy–self-efficacy (FRAMES), developed in the 1990s, synthesizes six common elements of successful BIs based on MI principles (Bien, Miller, & Tonigan, 1993; McQueen, Howe, Allan, Mains, & Hardy, 2011). First, the practitioner reviews screening results and provides the individual with *feedback* on their personal risk of substance-use related harms. Throughout the conversation, the practitioner emphasizes the individual's autonomy and *responsibility* for making their own choices, including whether to change behaviors related to their substance use. In addition, the practitioner offers the individual *advice* about how they can reduce their risk in the form of a *menu* of options for possible behavior changes. The practitioner exhibits *empathy* during the BI encounter and ensures the individual feels understood. Finally, the practitioner affirms individuals' *self-efficacy* and their ability to implement the agreed-on behavior change successfully. Some studies have demonstrated the FRAMES model to be effective at reducing substance use, particularly alcohol use, in both EDs and primary care settings (McQueen, Howe, Ballinger, & Godwin, 2015). Compared with other models, FRAMES leads to similar reductions in substance use (Aalto et al., 2000; Rubio, Jiménez-Arriero, Martínez, Ponce, & Palomo, 2010).

Feedback–Listening–Options

Feedback–listening–options (FLO) is a BI model endorsed by the CDC (2014) to address risky alcohol use. The practitioner begins the BI encounter by providing the individual with simple, factual *feedback* on their risk level. When providing feedback, practitioners are straightforward when introducing the topic and briefly disclose their concern for the individual's risk level using a collaborative approach. On sharing their feedback, the practitioner uses open-ended questions and actively *listens* to the individual verbalize personal motivations for behavior change. Listening allows the practitioner to understand the individual's perspective, motivations, and struggles with change better. More specifically, listening prompts the individual to verbalize their understanding of their risk level, their responsibility for personal choices, their ability to choose different behaviors, the relative importance of new behaviors, and their level of confidence in achieving specific behaviors. Finally, the practitioner explores *options* for behavior change that are realistic and important to the individual. Exploring options encourages patients to explore different choices that will reduce their risk of harm and to commit to the most important and realistic options for behavior change. In comparison to other models, FLO can be more effectively incorporated into medical curricula and clinical workflows.

Brief Negotiated Interview

The Brief Negotiated Interview (BNI) is based on MI principles and consists of a semistructured interview process that can be completed in 5 to 15 minutes (D'Onofrio et al., 2012). The practitioner opens the conversation by building rapport with the individual, raising the subject of substance use, and exploring what the individual identifies as the pros and cons of their substance use. Next, the practitioner provides the individual with feedback on their substance use and level of risk of harm. Once the individual reacts to the practitioner's feedback, the practitioner uses open-ended questions, affirmations, summarizations, and reflective listening to explore options and build the individual's readiness to change. Finally, the practitioner collaborates with the individual to negotiate a realistic plan for behavior change consistent with their stage of change to reduce the individual's risk of substance-related harm.

The BNI was first used with Project ASSERT (Alcohol and Substance abuse Services and Educating providers to Refer patients to Treatment), which implemented routine screening and BIs for adult ED patients ($n = 7,118$) at Boston

Medical Center from 1995 to 1996 (Bernstein, Bernstein, & Levenson, 1997). Significant reductions in alcohol and drug use were reported in follow-up patients (*n* = 245), and a majority of those patients were satisfied with the services they received. Practitioners can be successfully trained to proficiency using this model (D'Onofrio, Pantalon, Degutis, Fiellin, & O'Connor, 2005). More recently, the BNI has been used to initiate medication-assisted treatment and disseminate naloxone among patients with a potential opioid use disorder in the ED (D'Onofrio et al., 2015).

Permission-Open-Ended Questions-Listening Reflectively-Affirmations-Roll With Ambivalence-Summary

According to the permission-open-ended questions-listening reflectively-affirmations-roll with ambivalence-summary model (Pringle et al., 2014), before engaging in a BI, the practitioner asks the individual *permission* to discuss their substance use to establish rapport and demonstrate respect for the individual's autonomy. During the BI, the practitioner uses *open-ended questions* to elicit information from the individual and move the conversation forward. In addition, the practitioner *listens reflectively* through verbal confirmation and nonverbal body language. Methods for conveying reflective listening include maintaining eye contact, mirroring facial expressions, leaning forward and orienting toward the individual, maintaining an open and relaxed posture, taking occasional notes, and avoiding fidgeting or distracting movements. Furthermore, the practitioner *affirms* the individual's strengths, which helps build trust, increases the individual's confidence, and supports the individual's commitment to positive behavior change. The practitioner also helps the patient identify areas for possible behavior change that the patient can realistically control (i.e., modifiable risk factors). If discord emerges, the practitioner *rolls with resistance* using MI principles. Finally, the practitioner *summarizes* the individual's motivations for change and transitions to goal setting. When providing a summary, the practitioner explores possible options for behavior change and listens for action steps patients are willing to take to reduce their risk.

CLINICAL APPLICATION IN HEALTH CARE SETTINGS

Regardless of the model or setting, BIs typically last between 5 to 15 minutes (Jonas et al., 2012). BIs can be administered as discrete, one-time interventions or as a series of interventions over time. Implementing BIs over time is not feasible in clinical settings such as EDs and urgent care settings where patients do not have an established relationship with a provider and are not monitored over time. Although repeated BIs have an increased likelihood of leading to sustained behavior changes (Gryczynski et al., 2011; Jonas et al., 2012), one-time interventions can impact an individual's substance use (Humeniuk et al., 2012; O'Donnell et al., 2014).

Evidence supports the administration of BIs via trained providers or electronic methods (e.g., computers, text messages, tablets; Baumann et al., 2018; Kay-Lambkin, Baker, Lewin, & Carr, 2009). Practitioners who can be trained to conduct BIs include physicians, physicians' assistants, nurses, social workers, mental health counselors, psychologists, behavioral health specialists, dentists, physical and occupational therapists, and pharmacists (Duong, O'Sullivan, Satre, Soskin, & Satterfield, 2016; Kalu et al., 2016; Moore et al., 2017; Pringle, Kearney, Rickard-Aasen, Campopiano, & Gordon, 2017; Stanton, Atherton, Toriello, & Hodgson, 2012; Tanner, Wilhelm, Rossie, & Metcalf, 2012). Clinical staff who can be reimbursed for providing BIs vary by state and provider status for their profession (Institute for Research Education & Training in Addictions, 2018).

Practitioners are encouraged to undergo training before conducting BIs. Unfortunately, formal training for evidence-based substance use interventions is lacking in the graduate school curricula for most health care professionals (Pringle, Kearney, et al., 2017). To address this knowledge gap in the work-force, SAMHSA has funded SBIRT training for 31 medical residency and other professional programs (e.g., social work psychologists) across the United States since 2003 (SAMHSA, 2017b). Common components of training programs include knowledge building through online modules and opportunities for skill practice via precepted workshops with standardized patients or case studies (Duong et al., 2016; Giudice et al., 2015; Kalu et al., 2016; Moore et al., 2017; Pringle, Kearney, et al., 2017; Stanton et al., 2012; Stoner, Mikko, & Carpenter, 2014; Tanner et al., 2012). Trained moderators can assess MI skill proficiency using a standard proficiency checklist and provide trainees with real-time feedback (Pringle, Seale, et al., 2017). Thus, training provides practitioners with the opportunity to gain knowledge and practice skills necessary for implementing a BI model with fidelity.

Several barriers exist that may prevent large-scale uptake of BIs to address substance use in clinical practice, including issues with billing and reimbursement. Currently, BIs are reimbursed using a fee-for-service structure in many states. Approximately 16 states recognize Medicaid reimbursement, and 31 states have at least one commercial insurer that offers reimbursement using standard Current Procedural Terminology (CPT) codes (Institute for Research Education & Training in Addictions, 2018; SAMHSA, 2018). Despite the widespread availability of these billing codes, their routine use has been relatively low in most states (Anderson & Bhang, 2009; Winkle, 2016). The cost to deliver a BI varies greatly depending on length of time, practitioner, and setting, with costs ranging from $3.14 (Zarkin, Bray, Davis, Babor, & Higgins-Biddle, 2003) to $243.01 (Quanbeck, Lang, Enami, & Brown, 2010) per BI (an average of $48 per BI lasting 13.75 minutes; Bray, Zarkin, Hinde, & Mills, 2012). Further, billing codes only offer reimbursement for BIs that last for at least 15 minutes, which is above the average amount of time allotted for BIs in many practice settings. As such, current billing codes do not cover the "true" costs of delivering BIs. In addition, many practitioners do not have

TABLE 5.2. Healthcare Common Procedure Coding System for Brief Interventions

Payer	Code	Description	Fee schedule
Commercial insurance	CPT 99408	Alcohol and/or substance abuse structured screening and brief intervention services; 15 to 30 minutes	$33.41
	CPT 99409	Alcohol and/or substance abuse structured screening and brief intervention services; greater than 30 minutes	$65.51
Medicare	G0396	Alcohol and/or substance abuse structured screening and brief intervention services; 15 to 30 minutes	$29.42
	G0397	Alcohol and/or substance abuse structured screening and brief intervention services; greater than 30 minutes	$57.69
Medicaid	H0049	Alcohol and/or drug screening	$24.00
	H0050	Alcohol and/or drug screening, brief intervention, per 15 minutes	$48.00

adequate time to perform BIs due to competing clinical priorities (Hargraves et al., 2017; Rahm et al., 2015). Table 5.2 provides an overview of payers, codes, description of services, and fee schedule for screening and BIs.

Despite these barriers, managed care organizations (MCOs) are testing additional financial structures where SBIRT services are part of a bundled service and cost arrangement. These bundles include the provision of SBIRT services within per member, per month rates applied across a larger patient population in a full or partially capitated risk arrangement system (Gateway Health, 2018; SAMHSA, 2017a; Takach, Purington, & Osius, 2010; Washington State Health Care Authority, 2019). Further, quality indicators, such as the Health Effectiveness Data Information Set Unhealthy Alcohol Use Screening and Follow-Up (National Committee for Quality Assurance, 2018) released in 2018, will increase the likelihood MCOs will encourage their primary care networks to implement BIs in clinical practice. Regardless of how BIs are reimbursed, their applications within myriad health care settings are likely to increase and become part of standard care practice in the coming years.

BRIEF INTERVENTION AND BRIEF TREATMENT

Patients can also be engaged during a BI with a provider to access brief treatment (BT), a distinct level of care according to the American Society of Addiction Medicine (2015). When an individual is at high risk of developing an SUD, BT can be an effective type of early intervention. BT can be applied in various health care settings and is effective in helping to reduce alcohol use (Moyer, Finney, Swearingen, & Vergun, 2002) and illicit drug use (Aldridge, Dowd, & Bray, 2017), including marijuana use (Stephens, Roffman, & Curtin,

2000). BT typically includes cognitive behavior therapy and motivational enhancement therapy and places emphasis on identifying triggers for substance use and providing additional social support for the individual. Recently, BT has increased in popularity because it "offers a more flexible, accessible, less expensive and less stigmatized service than traditional therapy" (Aldridge et al., 2017, p. 55). Furthermore, research has shown that individuals who are administered BT are more likely and willing to access specialty addiction treatment (Krupski et al., 2010).

In contrast with BI, BT is typically administered by a formally trained and certified addiction or behavioral health specialist during one to 12 sessions that are each 30 to 60 minutes in duration (Aldridge et al., 2017). For billing purposes, BT is classified as a structured substance abuse screening and BI greater than 30 minutes (see Table 5.2). Unfortunately, this classification presents challenges with billing and reimbursement because the current fee-for-service reimbursement rates do not cover the full cost of providing BT. For example, CPT code 99409 reimburses providers $65.51 per session greater than 30 minutes, but estimates suggest that BT actually costs $75.54 per session to administer (Barbosa et al., 2017).

CONCLUSION

BIs can be used to engage an individual with an SUD and introduce the need for a referral to specialized treatment. Specifically, the practitioner would use a BI to (a) connect the patient's screening results and current office visit to the need for specialized treatment, (b) set the tone by displaying genuine interest with active listening, (c) display a nonjudgmental demeanor, and (d) explain their role and concern as the individual's health care provider. During the BI, the practitioner would explore possible treatment options ranging from those offered in a standard clinical setting (e.g., medication-assisted treatment) to intensive inpatient services. Depending on his or her background and training, the practitioner need not necessarily be the one to provide the individual with a diagnosis or determine the level of specialized treatment necessary. Practitioners not trained to diagnose should recognize the need for referral and immediately connect the individual with another professional who could appropriately assess the individual's needs. This process, commonly known as a *warm handoff*, helps individuals navigate the complex treatment system and could be used to help the individual acquire additional services (e.g., transportation, housing, mental health services). An individual who receives these services when needed through more effective care coordination is much more likely to engage in substance use treatment (Mussulman et al., 2018; Pace et al., 2018).

After an individual is enrolled in specialty treatment, a practitioner can also use BIs to facilitate follow-up with the individual (Pace et al., 2018). In this situation, a practitioner would use a BI to explore the individual's successes and barriers to remaining in recovery. Practitioners should recognize that recovery is a lifelong journey with the potential for relapse and remission, similar to other chronic diseases (U.S. Department of Health and Human Services, 2016). To help mitigate the likelihood of an individual's relapse, practitioners can use BI during treatment and provide strategies to better manage triggers and cravings (i.e., people, places, objects, situations, or feelings that remind individuals of their substance use).

REFERENCES

Aalto, M., Saksanen, R., Laine, P., Forsström, R., Raikaa, M., Kiviluoto, M., . . . Sillanaukee, P. (2000). Brief intervention for female heavy drinkers in routine general practice: A 3-year randomized, controlled study. *Alcoholism: Clinical and Experimental Research, 24,* 1680–1686. http://dx.doi.org/10.1111/j.1530-0277.2000.tb01969.x

Aldridge, A., Dowd, W., & Bray, J. (2017). The relative impact of brief treatment versus brief intervention in primary health-care screening programs for substance use disorders. *Addiction, 112,* 54–64. http://dx.doi.org/10.1111/add.13653

American Psychiatric Association. (2013). *Diagnostic and statistical manual of mental disorders* (5th ed.). Washington, DC: Author.

American Society of Addiction Medicine. (2015). *What is the ASAM criteria?* Retrieved from https://www.asam.org/quality-practice/guidelines-and-consensus-documents/the-asam-criteria/about

Anderson, T., & Bhang, E. (2009). *Medicaid reimbursement for screening and brief intervention: Massachusetts' preparations.* Retrieved from https://www.integration.samhsa.gov/clinical-practice/sbirt/Medicaid_Reimbursement_for_screening_and_brief_intervention.pdf

Babor, T. F., Del Boca, F., & Bray, J. W. (2017). Screening, Brief Intervention and Referral to Treatment: Implications of SAMHSA's SBIRT initiative for substance abuse policy and practice. *Addiction, 112,* 110–117. http://dx.doi.org/10.1111/add.13675

Babor, T. F., McRee, B. G., Kassebaum, P. A., Grimaldi, P. L., Ahmed, K., & Bray, J. (2007). Screening, Brief Intervention, and Referral to Treatment (SBIRT): Toward a public health approach to the management of substance abuse. *Substance Abuse, 28*(3), 7–30. http://dx.doi.org/10.1300/J465v28n03_03

Barbosa, C., Cowell, A., Bray, J., & Aldridge, A. (2015). The cost-effectiveness of alcohol Screening, Brief Intervention, and Referral to Treatment (SBIRT) in emergency and outpatient medical settings. *Journal of Substance Abuse Treatment, 53,* 1–8. http://dx.doi.org/10.1016/j.jsat.2015.01.003

Barbosa, C., Cowell, A., Dowd, W., Landwehr, J., Aldridge, A., & Bray, J. (2017). The cost-effectiveness of brief intervention versus brief treatment of Screening, Brief Intervention and Referral to Treatment (SBIRT) in the United States. *Addiction, 112,* 73–81. http://dx.doi.org/10.1111/add.13658

Barbosa, C., Wedehase, B., Dunlap, L., Mitchell, S. G., Dusek, K., Schwartz, R. P., . . . Brown, B. S. (2018). Start-up costs of SBIRT implementation for adolescents in urban U.S. federally qualified health centers. *Journal of Studies on Alcohol and Drugs, 79,* 447–454. http://dx.doi.org/10.15288/jsad.2018.79.447

Baumann, S., Gaertner, B., Haberecht, K., Bischof, G., John, U., & Freyer-Adam, J. (2018). How alcohol use problem severity affects the outcome of brief intervention delivered in-person versus through computer-generated feedback letters. *Drug and Alcohol Dependence, 183,* 82–88. http://dx.doi.org/10.1016/j.drugalcdep.2017.10.032

Bernstein, E., Bernstein, J., & Levenson, S. (1997). Project ASSERT: An ED-based intervention to increase access to primary care, preventive services, and the substance abuse treatment system. *Annals of Emergency Medicine, 30,* 181–189. http://dx.doi.org/10.1016/S0196-0644(97)70140-9

Bien, T. H., Miller, W. R., & Tonigan, J. S. (1993). Brief interventions for alcohol problems: A review. *Addiction, 88,* 315–336. http://dx.doi.org/10.1111/j.1360-0443.1993.tb00820.x

Bowman, S., Eiserman, J., Beletsky, L., Stancliff, S., & Bruce, R. D. (2013). Reducing the health consequences of opioid addiction in primary care. *The American Journal of Medicine, 126,* 565–571. http://dx.doi.org/10.1016/j.amjmed.2012.11.031

Bray, J. W., Zarkin, G. A., Hinde, J. M., & Mills, M. J. (2012). Costs of alcohol screening and brief intervention in medical settings: A review of the literature. *Journal of Studies on Alcohol and Drugs, 73,* 911–919. http://dx.doi.org/10.15288/jsad.2012.73.911

Centers for Disease Control and Prevention. (2014). *Planning and implementing screening and brief intervention for risky alcohol use: A step-by-step guide for primary care practices.* Retrieved from https://www.cdc.gov/ncbddd/fasd/documents/alcoholsbiimplementationguide.pdf

Cherpitel, C. J., Korcha, R. A., Moskalewicz, J., Swiatkiewicz, G., Ye, Y., & Bond, J. (2010). Screening, brief intervention, and referral to treatment (SBIRT): 12-month outcomes of a randomized controlled clinical trial in a Polish emergency department. *Alcoholism: Clinical and Experimental Research, 34,* 1922–1928. http://dx.doi.org/10.1111/j.1530-0277.2010.01281.x

Curry, S. J., Krist, A. H., Owens, D. K., Barry, M. J., Caughey, A. B., Davidson, K. W., . . . Wong, J. B. (2018). Screening and behavioral counseling interventions to reduce unhealthy alcohol use in adolescents and adults: US preventive services task force recommendation statement. *JAMA, 320,* 1899–1909. http://dx.doi.org/10.1001/jama.2018.16789

Darker, C., Sweeney, B., Keenan, E., Whiston, L., Anderson, R., & Barry, J. (2016). Tailoring a brief intervention for illicit drug use and alcohol use in Irish methadone maintained opiate dependent patients: A qualitative process. *BMC Psychiatry, 16,* 373. http://dx.doi.org/10.1186/s12888-016-1082-4

D'Onofrio, G., Chawarski, M. C., O'Connor, P. G., Pantalon, M. V., Busch, S. H., Owens, P. H., . . . Fiellin, D. A. (2017). Emergency department-initiated buprenorphine for opioid dependence with continuation in primary care: Outcomes during and after intervention. *Journal of General Internal Medicine, 32,* 660–666. http://dx.doi.org/10.1007/s11606-017-3993-2

D'Onofrio, G., Fiellin, D. A., Pantalon, M. V., Chawarski, M. C., Owens, P. H., Degutis, L. C., . . . O'Connor, P. G. (2012). A brief intervention reduces hazardous and harmful drinking in emergency department patients. *Annals of Emergency Medicine, 60,* 181–192. http://dx.doi.org/10.1016/j.annemergmed.2012.02.006

D'Onofrio, G., O'Connor, P. G., Pantalon, M. V., Chawarski, M. C., Busch, S. H., Owens, P. H., . . . Fiellin, D. A. (2015). Emergency department-initiated buprenorphine/naloxone treatment for opioid dependence: A randomized clinical trial. *JAMA, 313,* 1636–1644. http://dx.doi.org/10.1001/jama.2015.3474

D'Onofrio, G., Pantalon, M. V., Degutis, L. C., Fiellin, D. A., & O'Connor, P. G. (2005). Development and implementation of an emergency practitioner-performed brief intervention for hazardous and harmful drinkers in the emergency department. *Academic Emergency Medicine, 12,* 249–256.

Dunn, C., Deroo, L., & Rivara, F. P. (2001). The use of brief interventions adapted from motivational interviewing across behavioral domains: A systematic review. *Addiction, 96,* 1725–1742. http://dx.doi.org/10.1046/j.1360-0443.2001.961217253.x

Duong, D. K., O'Sullivan, P. S., Satre, D. D., Soskin, P., & Satterfield, J. (2016). Social workers as workplace-based instructors of alcohol and drug Screening, Brief Intervention, and Referral to Treatment (SBIRT) for emergency medicine residents. *Teaching and Learning in Medicine, 28,* 303–313. http://dx.doi.org/10.1080/10401334.2016.1164049

Fleming, M. F., Balousek, S. L., Grossberg, P. M., Mundt, M. P., Brown, D., Wiegel, J. R., . . . Saewyc, E. M. (2010). Brief physician advice for heavy drinking college students: A randomized controlled trial in college health clinics. *Journal of Studies on Alcohol and Drugs, 71*, 23–31. http://dx.doi.org/10.15288/jsad.2010.71.23

Gateway Health. (2018). *SBIRT for substance use disorders: Provider education, billing, and resource reference guide*. Retrieved from https://www.gatewayhealthplan.com/Portals/0/provider_forms/SBIRT_Provider_Resource_Guide.pdf

Giudice, E. L., Lewin, L. O., Welsh, C., Crouch, T. B., Wright, K. S., Delahanty, J., & DiClemente, C. C. (2015). Online versus in-person Screening, Brief Intervention, and Referral to Treatment training in pediatrics residents. *Journal of Graduate Medical Education, 7*, 53–58. http://dx.doi.org/10.4300/JGME-D-14-00367.1

Gryczynski, J., Mitchell, S. G., Peterson, T. R., Gonzales, A., Moseley, A., & Schwartz, R. P. (2011). The relationship between services delivered and substance use outcomes in New Mexico's Screening, Brief Intervention, Referral and Treatment (SBIRT) Initiative. *Drug and Alcohol Dependence, 118*, 152–157. http://dx.doi.org/10.1016/j.drugalcdep.2011.03.012

Hargraves, D., White, C., Frederick, R., Cinibulk, M., Peters, M., Young, A., & Elder, N. (2017). Implementing SBIRT (Screening, Brief Intervention and Referral to Treatment) in primary care: Lessons learned from a multi-practice evaluation portfolio. *Public Health Reviews, 38*, 31. http://dx.doi.org/10.1186/s40985-017-0077-0

Hesse, M. (2006). The Readiness Ruler as a measure of readiness to change poly-drug use in drug abusers. *Harm Reduction Journal, 3*, 3. http://dx.doi.org/10.1186/1477-7517-3-3

Holland, C. L., Pringle, J. L., & Barbetti, V. (2009). Identification of physician barriers to the application of screening and brief intervention for problem alcohol and drug use. *Alcoholism Treatment Quarterly, 27*, 174–183. http://dx.doi.org/10.1080/07347320902784890

Humeniuk, R., Ali, R., Babor, T., Souza-Formigoni, M. L., de Lacerda, R. B., Ling, W., . . . Vendetti, J. (2012). A randomized controlled trial of a brief intervention for illicit drugs linked to the Alcohol, Smoking and Substance Involvement Screening Test (ASSIST) in clients recruited from primary health-care settings in four countries. *Addiction, 107*, 957–966. http://dx.doi.org/10.1111/j.1360-0443.2011.03740.x

Institute for Research Education & Training in Addictions. (2018). *By itself, reimbursement doesn't expand SBIRT*. Retrieved from https://ireta.org/resources/by-itself-reimbursement-doesnt-expand-sbirt/

Jonas, D. E., Garbutt, J. C., Amick, H. R., Brown, J. M., Brownley, K. A., Council, C. L., . . . Harris, R. P. (2012). Behavioral counseling after screening for alcohol misuse in primary care: A systematic review and meta-analysis for the U.S. Preventive Services Task Force. *Annals of Internal Medicine, 157*, 645–654. http://dx.doi.org/10.7326/0003-4819-157-9-201211060-00544

Kalu, N., Cain, G., McLaurin-Jones, T., Scott, D., Kwagyan, J., Fassassi, C., . . . Taylor, R. E. (2016). Impact of a multicomponent screening, brief intervention, and referral to treatment (SBIRT) training curriculum on a medical residency program. *Substance Abuse, 37*, 242–247. http://dx.doi.org/10.1080/08897077.2015.1035841

Kaner, E. F., Beyer, F. R., Muirhead, C., Campbell, F., Pienaar, E. D., Bertholet, N., . . . Burnand, B. (2018). Effectiveness of brief alcohol interventions in primary care populations. *Cochrane Database of Systematic Reviews*. http://dx.doi.org/10.1002/14651858.CD004148.pub4

Kay-Lambkin, F. J., Baker, A. L., Lewin, T. J., & Carr, V. J. (2009). Computer-based psychological treatment for comorbid depression and problematic alcohol and/or cannabis use: A randomized controlled trial of clinical efficacy. *Addiction, 104*, 378–388. http://dx.doi.org/10.1111/j.1360-0443.2008.02444.x

Klemperer, E. M., Hughes, J. R., Solomon, L. J., Callas, P. W., & Fingar, J. R. (2017). Motivational, reduction and usual care interventions for smokers who are not ready to quit: A randomized controlled trial. *Addiction, 112,* 146–155. http://dx.doi.org/ 10.1111/add.13594

Krupski, A., Sears, J. M., Joesch, J. M., Estee, S., He, L., Dunn, C., . . . Ries, R. (2010). Impact of brief interventions and brief treatment on admissions to chemical dependency treatment. *Drug and Alcohol Dependence, 110,* 126–136. http://dx.doi.org/ 10.1016/j.drugalcdep.2010.02.018

Laporte, C., Vaillant-Roussel, H., Pereira, B., Blanc, O., Eschalier, B., Kinouani, S., . . . Vorilhon, P. (2017). Cannabis and young users—A brief intervention to reduce their consumption (CANABIC): A cluster randomized controlled trial in primary care. *Annals of Family Medicine, 15,* 131–139. http://dx.doi.org/10.1370/afm.2003

Madras, B. K., Compton, W. M., Avula, D., Stegbauer, T., Stein, J. B., & Clark, H. W. (2009). Screening, brief interventions, referral to treatment (SBIRT) for illicit drug and alcohol use at multiple healthcare sites: Comparison at intake and 6 months later. *Drug and Alcohol Dependence, 99,* 280–295. http://dx.doi.org/10.1016/j.drugalcdep. 2008.08.003

McQueen, J., Howe, T. E., Allan, L., Mains, D., & Hardy, V. (2011). Brief interventions for heavy alcohol users admitted to general hospital wards. *Cochrane Database of Systematic Reviews.* http://dx.doi.org/10.1002/14651858.CD005191.pub3

McQueen, J. M., Howe, T. E., Ballinger, C., & Godwin, J. (2015). Effectiveness of alcohol brief intervention in a general hospital: A randomized controlled trial. *Journal of Studies on Alcohol and Drugs, 76,* 838–844. http://dx.doi.org/10.15288/ jsad.2015.76.838

Miller, W. R., & Rollnick, S. (2013). *Motivational interviewing: Helping people change* (3rd ed.). New York, NY: Guilford Press.

Moore, J., Goodman, P., Selway, J., Hawkins-Walsh, E., Merritt, J., & Dombrowski, J. (2017). SBIRT education for nurse practitioner students: Integration into an MSN program. *The Journal of Nursing Education, 56,* 725–732. http://dx.doi.org/10.3928/ 01484834-20171120-04

Moyer, A., Finney, J. W., Swearingen, C. E., & Vergun, P. (2002). Brief interventions for alcohol problems: A meta-analytic review of controlled investigations in treatment-seeking and non-treatment-seeking populations. *Addiction, 97,* 279–292. http://dx.doi.org/10.1046/j.1360-0443.2002.00018.x

Mussulman, L. M., Faseru, B., Fitzgerald, S., Nazir, N., Patel, V., & Richter, K. P. (2018). A randomized, controlled pilot study of warm handoff versus fax referral for hospital-initiated smoking cessation among people living with HIV/AIDS. *Addictive Behaviors, 78,* 205–208. http://dx.doi.org/10.1016/j.addbeh.2017.11.035

National Committee for Quality Assurance. (2018). *Unhealthy alcohol use screening and follow-up.* Retrieved from https://www.ncqa.org/hedis/measures/unhealthy-alcohol-use-screening-and-follow-up/

O'Connor, E. A., Perdue, L. A., Senger, C. A., Rushkin, M., Patnode, C. D., Bean, S. I., & Jonas, D. E. (2018). *Screening and behavioral counseling interventions to reduce unhealthy alcohol use in adolescents and adults: An updated systematic review for the U.S. Preventive Services Task Force* (AHRQ Publication No. 18-05242-EF-1). Retrieved from https://www.ncbi.nlm.nih.gov/books/NBK534916/pdf/Bookshelf_NBK534916.pdf

O'Connor, M. J., & Whaley, S. E. (2007). Brief intervention for alcohol use by pregnant women. *American Journal of Public Health, 97,* 252–258. http://dx.doi.org/10.2105/ AJPH.2005.077222

O'Donnell, A., Anderson, P., Newbury-Birch, D., Schulte, B., Schmidt, C., Reimer, J., & Kaner, E. (2014). The impact of brief alcohol interventions in primary healthcare: A systematic review of reviews. *Alcohol and Alcoholism, 49,* 66–78. http://dx.doi.org/ 10.1093/alcalc/agt170

Pace, C. A., Gergen-Barnett, K., Veidis, A., D'Afflitti, J., Worcester, J., Fernandez, P., & Lasser, K. E. (2018). Warm handoffs and attendance at initial integrated behavioral health appointments. *Annals of Family Medicine, 16*, 346–348. http://dx.doi.org/10.1370/afm.2263

Pringle, J. L., Boyer, A., Conklin, M. H., McCullough, J. W., & Aldridge, A. (2014). The Pennsylvania Project: Pharmacist intervention improved medication adherence and reduced health care costs. *Health Affairs, 33*, 1444–1452. http://dx.doi.org/10.1377/hlthaff.2013.1398

Pringle, J. L., Kearney, S. M., Rickard-Aasen, S., Campopiano, M. M., & Gordon, A. J. (2017). A statewide screening, brief intervention, and referral to treatment (SBIRT) curriculum for medical residents: Differential implementation strategies in heterogeneous medical residency programs. *Substance Abuse, 38*, 161–167. http://dx.doi.org/10.1080/08897077.2017.1288195

Pringle, J. L., Kelley, D. K., Kearney, S. M., Aldridge, A., Dowd, W., Johnjulio, W., . . . Lovelace, J. (2018). Screening, brief intervention, and referral to treatment in the emergency department: An examination of health care utilization and costs. *Medical Care, 56*, 146–152. http://dx.doi.org/10.1097/MLR.0000000000000859

Pringle, J. L., Seale, J. P., Shellenberger, S., Grasso, K. M., Kowalchuk, A., Laufman, L., . . . Aldridge, A. (2017). Development and evaluation of two instruments for assessing screening, brief intervention, and referral to treatment (SBIRT) competency. *Substance Abuse, 38*, 43–47. http://dx.doi.org/10.1080/08897077.2016.1152343

Quanbeck, A., Lang, K., Enami, K., & Brown, R. L. (2010). A cost-benefit analysis of Wisconsin's screening, brief intervention, and referral to treatment program: Adding the employer's perspective. *Wisconsin Medical Journal, 109*, 9–14.

Rahm, A. K., Boggs, J. M., Martin, C., Price, D. W., Beck, A., Backer, T. E., & Dearing, J. W. (2015). Facilitators and barriers to implementing screening, brief intervention, and referral to treatment (SBIRT) in primary care in integrated health care settings. *Substance Abuse, 36*, 281–288. http://dx.doi.org/10.1080/08897077.2014.951140

Rollnick, S., Mason, P., & Butler, C. (1999). *Health behavior change: A guide for practitioners.* New York, NY: Churchill Livingstone.

Rubio, G., Jiménez-Arriero, M. A., Martínez, I., Ponce, G., & Palomo, T. (2010). Efficacy of physician-delivered brief counseling intervention for binge drinkers. *The American Journal of Medicine, 123*, 72–78. http://dx.doi.org/10.1016/j.amjmed.2009.08.012

Shetty, V., Murphy, D. A., Zigler, C., Yamashita, D.-D. R., & Belin, T. R. (2011). Randomized controlled trial of personalized motivational interventions in substance using patients with facial injuries. *Journal of Oral and Maxillofacial Surgery, 69*, 2396–2411. http://dx.doi.org/10.1016/j.joms.2010.12.040

Smout, M. F., Longo, M., Harrison, S., Minniti, R., Cahill, S., Wickes, W., & White, J. M. (2010). The Psychostimulant Check-Up: A pilot study of a brief intervention to reduce illicit stimulant use. *Drug and Alcohol Review, 29*, 169–176. http://dx.doi.org/10.1111/j.1465-3362.2009.00133.x

Stanton, M. R., Atherton, W. L., Toriello, P. J., & Hodgson, J. L. (2012). Implementation of a "learner-driven" curriculum: A screening, brief intervention, and referral to treatment (SBIRT) interdisciplinary primary care model. *Substance Abuse, 33*, 312–315. http://dx.doi.org/10.1080/08897077.2011.640140

Stephens, R. S., Roffman, R. A., & Curtin, L. (2000). Comparison of extended versus brief treatments for marijuana use. *Journal of Consulting and Clinical Psychology, 68*, 898–908. http://dx.doi.org/10.1037/0022-006X.68.5.898

Stoner, S. A., Mikko, A. T., & Carpenter, K. M. (2014). Web-based training for primary care providers on screening, brief intervention, and referral to treatment (SBIRT) for alcohol, tobacco, and other drugs. *Journal of Substance Abuse Treatment, 47*, 362–370. http://dx.doi.org/10.1016/j.jsat.2014.06.009

Substance Abuse and Mental Health Services Administration. (2013). *Systems-level implementation of screening, brief intervention, and referral to treatment* (HHS Publication No. (SMA) 13-4741). Retrieved from https://www.integration.samhsa.gov/sbirt/tap33.pdf

Substance Abuse and Mental Health Services Administration. (2017a). *Coding for screening and brief intervention reimbursement*. Retrieved from https://www.samhsa.gov/sbirt/coding-reimbursement

Substance Abuse and Mental Health Services Administration. (2017b). *Screening, brief intervention, and referral to treatment (SBIRT) grantees*. Retrieved from https://www.samhsa.gov/sbirt/grantees

Substance Abuse and Mental Health Services Administration. (2018). *Paying for primary care and behavioral health services provided in integrated care settings*. Retrieved from https://www.integration.samhsa.gov/financing/billing-tools#billing%20worksheets

Takach, M., Purington, K., & Osius, E. (2010). *A tale of two systems: A look at state efforts to integrate primary care and behavioral health in safety net settings*. Retrieved from http://www.tnpcaeducation.org/resourcelibrary/clinical/TwoSystems_0.pdf

Tanner, T. B., Wilhelm, S. E., Rossie, K. M., & Metcalf, M. P. (2012). Web-based SBIRT skills training for health professional students and primary care providers. *Substance Abuse, 33*, 316–320. http://dx.doi.org/10.1080/08897077.2011.640151

Tanner-Smith, E. E., & Lipsey, M. W. (2015). Brief alcohol interventions for adolescents and young adults: A systematic review and meta-analysis. *Journal of Substance Abuse Treatment, 51*, 1–18. http://dx.doi.org/10.1016/j.jsat.2014.09.001

Timko, C., Kong, C., Vittorio, L., & Cucciare, M. A. (2016). Screening and brief intervention for unhealthy substance use in patients with chronic medical conditions: A systematic review. *Journal of Clinical Nursing, 25*, 3131–3143. http://dx.doi.org/10.1111/jocn.13244

U.S. Department of Health and Human Services. (2016). *Facing addiction in America: The Surgeon General's report on alcohol, drugs, and health*. Retrieved from https://addiction.surgeongeneral.gov/sites/default/files/surgeon-generals-report.pdf

U.S. Preventive Services Task Force. (2019). *Illicit drug use, including nonmedical use of prescription drugs: Screening*. Retrieved from https://www.uspreventiveservicestaskforce.org/Page/Document/draft-recommendation-statement/drug-use-in-adolescents-and-adults-including-pregnant-women-screening

Vendetti, J., Gmyrek, A., Damon, D., Singh, M., McRee, B., & Del Boca, F. (2017). Screening, brief intervention and referral to treatment (SBIRT): Implementation barriers, facilitators and model migration. *Addiction, 112*, 23–33. http://dx.doi.org/10.1111/add.13652

Walker, D. D., Stephens, R. S., Blevins, C. E., Banes, K. E., Matthews, L., & Roffman, R. A. (2016). Augmenting brief interventions for adolescent marijuana users: The impact of motivational check-ins. *Journal of Consulting and Clinical Psychology, 84*, 983–992. http://dx.doi.org/10.1037/ccp0000094

Washington State Health Care Authority. (2019). *Early and Periodic Screening Diagnosis and Treatment (EPSDT) program billing guide*. Retrieved from https://www.hca.wa.gov/assets/billers-and-providers/EPSDT-bi-20190101.pdf

Winkle, J. (2016). *The story behind Oregon's SBIRT incentive measure and its impact on implementation*. Retrieved from https://my.ireta.org/sites/ireta.org/files/Winkle%20webinar%20handouts.pdf

Zarkin, G. A., Bray, J. W., Davis, K. L., Babor, T. F., & Higgins-Biddle, J. C. (2003). The costs of screening and brief intervention for risky alcohol use. *Journal of Studies on Alcohol, 64*, 849–857. http://dx.doi.org/10.15288/jsa.2003.64.849

II

SCREENING, BRIEF INTERVENTION, AND REFERRAL TO TREATMENT IN DIFFERENT HEALTH CARE SETTINGS AND WITH DIVERSE POPULATIONS

6

Screening, Brief Intervention, and Referral to Treatment in Medical and Integrated Care Settings

Megan A. O'Grady and Sandeep Kapoor

Health care reform efforts in the United States have led to unprecedented changes and opportunities for the way that substance use is addressed in health care settings. These efforts include the integration of care for substance use and behavioral health with traditional medical care. Screening, brief intervention, and referral to treatment (SBIRT) is a model that can be used in health care settings as part of integration efforts to identify and begin to address risky substance use (Sacks et al., 2016). SBIRT seizes the opportunity to address substance use among patients as part of routine, usual medical care. Uptake of substance use screening and brief intervention (BI) is recommended by a number of organizations in the United States (e.g., Substance Abuse and Mental Health Services Administration; SAMHSA). This chapter first provides an overview of SBIRT research in primary care, emergency department (ED), and other practice settings. Second, the chapter reviews clinical considerations, practical tips, and research on implementing SBIRT. Finally, we project the future of SBIRT in medical and integrated care settings, including innovations to the model, use of technology, and areas where more research is needed.

SUMMARY OF THE RESEARCH EVIDENCE

The strongest evidence for SBIRT efficacy comes from studies conducted in primary care that target reductions in alcohol use among people who are

http://dx.doi.org/10.1037/0000199-007
Screening, Brief Intervention, and Referral to Treatment for Substance Use: A Practitioner's Guide, M. D. Cimini and J. L. Martin (Editors)

not dependent on alcohol (Álvarez-Bueno, Rodríguez-Martín, García-Ortiz, Gómez-Marcos, & Martínez-Vizcaíno, 2015; Kaner et al., 2018). For example, BIs among hazardous drinkers have been shown to reduce weekly drinking amounts and increase the number of people who drink within recommended health limits. However, as is discussed in more detail later in the chapter, there is currently no clear evidence that SBIRT systematically reduces drug use in any medical setting (Hingson & Compton, 2014), though some studies have shown promising results (Bernstein & D'Onofrio, 2017; Gelberg et al., 2015).

The U.S. Preventive Service Task Force (USPSTF), on the basis of an extensive review of the scientific literature, recently renewed their recommendation that adults 18 years and older be screened for unhealthy alcohol use in primary care settings and that brief behavioral counseling be provided to those who drink in risky or hazardous ways (USPSTF, 2018). Reviews have suggested that BIs in primary care settings lasting no longer than 15 minutes with repeated brief follow-ups may be most effective compared with longer or single-session programs (Álvarez-Bueno et al., 2015). The USPSTF has also recently issued a draft statement recommending screening for illicit drug use in adults 18 years or older, suggesting that such screening be implemented in primary care when diagnostic, treatment, and other care services can also be offered or referred (USPSTF, 2019).

There are significant opportunities to intervene in the ED for substance use problems (Hawk & D'Onofrio, 2018). However, reviews find that ED-delivered BIs may not be effective in consistently reducing alcohol use, especially in the long term, but may reduce some alcohol-related negative consequences (Landy, Davey, Quintero, Pecora, & McShane, 2016; Wilson, Heather, & Kaner, 2011). In addition, there may be differences in outcomes for injured and noninjured patients, such that noninjured ED patients may have better BI outcomes (Elzerbi, Donoghue, Boniface, & Drummond, 2017). Although there may be some benefits, clarity is needed to identify the patients who benefit the most from ED-based BI.

Most SBIRT studies have been conducted in primary care and EDs. However, SBIRT could be useful in other settings. For example, mental health settings may be promising, given the comorbidity between substance use and mental health problems. As such, BI conducted in an outpatient psychiatry clinic among patients being treated for depression showed that patients reduced their drinking at 3-month follow-up (Satre, Delucchi, Lichtmacher, Sterling, & Weisner, 2013). Other settings also show potential, including dentistry, obstetrics, and long-term care (Neff et al., 2015; Wright et al., 2016). More research and practice examples are needed in settings other than primary care and EDs to determine best clinical practices and outcomes.

Cost-effectiveness research on SBIRT for alcohol has suggested that it can generate cost savings in ED and primary care settings (Barbosa, Cowell, Bray, & Aldridge, 2015). In primary care, cost estimates for SBIRT targeting drug use tend to be similar to those for alcohol (Zarkin, Bray, Hinde, & Saitz, 2015). Results from a large demonstration project suggested that SBIRT can be sustained by health insurance payments under a variety of staffing models; however, this varies by health care setting type (Cowell, Dowd, Mills, Hinde, & Bray, 2017).

CLINICAL CONSIDERATIONS

The very nature of SBIRT makes it a multicomponent intervention. Therefore, there are multiple clinical decision points when developing an SBIRT program in any medical or integrated care setting. Each component of SBIRT should be carefully planned, as described in the following sections.

Screening

The goal of screening is to identify patients with substance misuse or a substance use disorder (SUD). In selecting an evidence-based screening tool, the following considerations should be taken into account: (a) patient population, (b) clinical workflow, (c) integration into electronic health record (EHR), and (d) administration method (e.g., patient self-report, practitioner delivered, paper, or electronic based). Decisions should be driven by the needs and resources of the setting. For example, there are screening tools targeted to different populations (e.g., adolescents, pregnant women) and that differ in length. Screening tools should be appropriate for clinical workflows and be easily integrated in an EHR.

Multiple evidence-based screening tools are available and validated for use in medical settings. These screening tools are capable of assessing negative consequences, symptoms, and substance use patterns. Popular tools include the Alcohol Use Disorders Identification Test (AUDIT; Saunders, Aasland, Babor, de la Fuente, & Grant, 1993) and the Alcohol Smoking and Substance Involvement Screening Test (WHO ASSIST Working Group, 2002). Validated single-item and other brief screening tools are also available (McNeely et al., 2015; Smith, Schmidt, Allensworth-Davies, & Saitz, 2010). Single-item (e.g., the National Institute on Alcohol Abuse and Alcoholism screening test, Smith et al., 2010) and brief screening (e.g., AUDIT–C, Bradley et al., 2007) tools have been successfully built into EHRs to improve implementation (Mertens et al., 2015; Williams et al., 2016).

Brief Intervention

BIs focus on increasing a patient's insight and awareness about their substance use. A number of models have been used in medical settings, many of which include (a) providing feedback about use patterns, health risks, and recommended healthy limits; (b) increasing motivation by discussing readiness to change and pros and cons of use; and (c) setting goals and activities to make changes from multiple options (D'Onofrio, Pantalon, Degutis, Fiellin, &

O'Connor, 2005). Among these models, different degrees of motivational interviewing (MI) may be incorporated, and they may vary in content and length (Hettema et al., 2018). Clinical teams in medical settings are already familiar with counseling patients on a variety of health-related topics (e.g., medication management, diet). Highlighting the similarities can enhance the motivation and comfort of clinical providers in providing BIs for substance use.

Referrals

Patients whose screening scores indicate a possible SUD are then referred to treatment internally in the medical setting or externally. Medical providers often do not know where or how to refer patients and may lack an understanding of the landscape of addiction treatment. Best practices in developing referral protocols include proactive identification of internal or external local addiction treatment providers and the establishment of cross-collaborative communication between health care and addiction treatment settings. Other best practices include the use of MI techniques to help patients with ambivalence engage in treatment, assistance with intake appointment scheduling and transportation, follow-up after appointments, and ongoing contact with addiction treatment providers (SAMHSA, 2013).

IMPLEMENTATION OF SBIRT

Despite being a major public health issue, substance use remains under-addressed in health care settings (Office of the Surgeon General, 2016). A 2017 report indicated that only one in six binge drinkers in the United States are asked about alcohol use and advised to cut down by a health professional (McKnight-Eily et al., 2017). Implementation of SBIRT by primary care and ED providers is sporadic at best (Bandara, Samples, Crum, & Saloner, 2018; Broderick, Kaplan, Martini, & Caruso, 2015; Glass, Bohnert, & Brown, 2016; Harris & Yu, 2016; O'Donnell, Wallace, & Kaner, 2014), despite state and federal government promotion of the practice, availability of numerous implementation and clinical SBIRT guides, and widespread training efforts.

Barriers and Facilitators to SBIRT Implementation

There are well-documented barriers that have limited the widespread, sustained adoption of SBIRT, yet facilitators exist that have been found to improve implementation (McNeely et al., 2018; Rahm et al., 2015; Vendetti, Gmyrek, et al., 2017). Implementation science frameworks highlight the multilevel factors that may impede SBIRT implementation (Damschroder et al., 2009; Del Boca, McRee, Vendetti, & Damon, 2017). These can be divided into provider-, patient- and, system-level factors.

Providers often express support for and positive attitudes about conducting substance use screening (Derges et al., 2017; Harris & Yu, 2016; McNeely et al., 2018; Williams et al., 2016). However, a number of provider-level factors can decrease the likelihood that they conduct SBIRT. These include lack of training and comfort in addressing patient substance use problems, time constraints, low fidelity to SBIRT procedures, unsupportive peer clinical norms, and competing priorities (Clemence et al., 2016; Derges et al., 2017; Rahm et al., 2015; Williams et al., 2015). SBIRT can be conducted by a wide range of health professionals (e.g., psychologists, social workers, nurses, physicians). Provider barriers may differ by professional discipline, perceived role, SBIRT setting, and training emphasis (Wamsley, Satterfield, Curtis, Lundgren, & Satre, 2018).

Health care systems must make changes to support SBIRT implementation; offering training to providers in the absence of other supports is unlikely to lead to successful implementation. System-level factors that affect implementation include lack of organizational or leadership support and insufficient resources or physical space to implement SBIRT practices (Derges et al., 2017; McNeely et al., 2018; Rahm et al., 2015; Williams et al., 2016). Finally, there are patient-level factors relevant to implementation. Patients may be less likely to receive SBIRT depending on demographics (e.g., age, sex) or presence of other health problems (Bachhuber et al., 2017; Hodgson et al., 2016). Patients may feel stigma or discomfort in disclosing substance use or having it documented in the EHR (McNeely et al., 2018; Rahm et al., 2015; Spear, Shedlin, Gilberti, Fiellin, & McNeely, 2016).

A number of facilitators to implementation have been identified (Derges et al., 2017; Gorpland & McPherson, 2015; Hargraves et al., 2017; Nunes, Richmond, Marzano, Swenson, & Lockhart, 2017; Vendetti, Gmyrek, et al., 2017). These include having a practice champion to promote SBIRT and using an interprofessional team to conduct SBIRT. Additional facilitators include integrating screening tools into the EHR, having clear staff roles and protocols, carefully building SBIRT into the workflow, developing strong referral relationships, and building leadership and organizational support. Holding ongoing training is also important.

Practical Considerations

It is vital to understand that SBIRT protocols and workflows are fairly easy to develop; however, without stakeholder buy-in and motivated and educated staff, SBIRT will be difficult to implement and sustain. Identifying key stakeholders from the frontline to members of leadership is imperative to gain buy-in and increase motivation to conduct SBIRT. Moreover, proper EHR integration of SBIRT screening tools, documentation, and electronic guidance and prompts will ensure that services are efficiently and effectively integrated (Johnson, Woychek, Vaughan, & Seale, 2013). EHR integration enhances the ability to monitor implementation using extracted data. These data can be shared with clinical staff, compliance departments, and other stakeholders to maintain buy-in and make adjustments to protocols.

An SBIRT implementation time frame must allow for system and provider-level barriers to be addressed (e.g., 6 or more months). Time should be taken to address staff expectations and concerns about SBIRT implementation. Doing this provides an opportunity to reinforce the idea that a successful SBIRT program will rely heavily on whether staff approach patients with empathy and clinical skill when conducting SBIRT. Variations in fidelity to SBIRT procedures are to be expected as programs roll out. Research has suggested that sustained fidelity to motivational interventions is difficult (Hall, Staiger, Simpson, Best, & Lubman, 2016). Fidelity should be monitored and used to drive training offerings and iteration of protocols. Depending on how it is conducted, fidelity monitoring can be expensive and time-consuming. There are direct (e.g., observation, audio or videotape) or indirect (e.g., patient exit interviews) methods that range in resources needed, accuracy, and potential for bias (Allen, Shelton, Emmons, & Linnan, 2017). Proficiency checklists are available that can assist with SBIRT fidelity monitoring (Reho, Agley, DeSalle, & Gassman, 2016; Vendetti, McRee, & Del Boca, 2017).

THE FUTURE OF SBIRT IN MEDICAL SETTINGS: INNOVATIONS TO THE SBIRT MODEL

When thinking of SBIRT, one may typically think of a one-time intervention, conducted in person, with little attention focused on other behavioral health issues. However, as SBIRT continues to be studied and implemented, innovations to the original model are developing. These include models that monitor patients over longer periods, provide more care in primary care, integrate mental health screening, initiate medication, and use technology.

Providing Substance Use Care Within the Medical Setting

Researchers and practitioners acknowledge that enhancements to the traditional SBIRT model have to be made to better address alcohol and drug-related care in health care settings. Recent recommendations for primary care include screening all adults for alcohol and other drug use and offering brief counseling as appropriate at least annually, assessing for and managing SUD symptoms in primary care rather than making external referrals, using shared decision making to determine best treatment options (e.g., medications, counseling, referral), and conducting long-term monitoring for patients with SUD symptoms (National Council for Behavioral Health, 2018). These suggestions come from early research indicating that alcohol use disorders (AUDs) can be successfully managed in primary care (Oslin et al., 2014), though more recent studies have highlighted challenges to this practice (Bradley et al., 2018).

A slightly more structured practice, collaborative care, focuses on measurement-based practice. Trained primary care and behavioral health professionals provide evidence-based medication and/or psychosocial treatment, supported by psychiatric case consultation and treatment adjustment for nonimprovement. Collaborative care has only recently been applied to substance use, having originally been developed for depression care. Results from a randomized trial found that, relative to usual care, a collaborative care intervention increased both the proportion of patients receiving evidence-based treatment for opioid use disorder (OUD) and AUD and the number achieving abstinence from opioids or alcohol at 6 months (Watkins et al., 2017). A recent study also suggested that doing collaborative care from the ED for patients who misuse prescription drugs is feasible (Whiteside et al., 2017). These studies highlight the notion that traditional SBIRT can be extended to become a more comprehensive intervention.

Integration of SBIRT With Other Mental Health Interventions

SBIRT has historically been studied and implemented without consideration for how it could be implemented as part of a more comprehensive behavioral health intervention (McCambridge & Saitz, 2017). However, addressing substance use alone may not be practical or efficient. Substance use screening can be conducted with depression screening (Brown et al., 2014; Burdick & Kessler, 2017; Dwinnells & Misik, 2017) or screening for other concerns, such as anxiety, sleep problems, chronic pain, or intimate partner violence (Kene et al., 2018). Depending on the workflow and setting, practitioners may consider opportunities to screen for multiple issues. There are few examples in the literature of SBIRT being conducted in mental health settings; however, BIs have shown positive outcomes among people in psychiatric inpatient units (Graham et al., 2016). More research is needed to determine how SBIRT and other motivational BIs may be integrated with mental health screening and treatment and how these integrations occur in behavioral health versus primary care or other health care settings.

Initiation of Medications for Opioid Use Disorder and Alcohol Use Disorder

Several U.S. Food and Drug Administration–approved medications are now available to treat OUD and AUD. Although most patients will not meet the criteria for a disorder, a small percentage will and may benefit from medication. A newer approach, screening, treatment initiation, and referral (STIR), incorporates initiation of medication for OUD into the SBIRT model (Bernstein & D'Onofrio, 2017). Findings from studies on STIR, though limited, are encouraging. For example, initiation of buprenorphine for OUD in an ED resulted in greater engagement in treatment and greater self-reported abstinence (D'Onofrio et al., 2015). STIR may offer new, clinically effective approaches by building initiation of medication onto the traditional SBIRT model for patients with AUD or OUD.

Technology-Based SBIRT

Using technology to deliver potentially low-cost, time-saving, high-fidelity SBIRT programs may be a compelling way to increase uptake of SBIRT in health care settings (Blow et al., 2017; Harris & Knight, 2014; Nair, Newton, Shakeshaft, Wallace, & Teesson, 2015). Computerized SBIRT for alcohol use appears to be feasible for delivery in medical settings and acceptable among patients, and findings demonstrate promise for reducing alcohol use (Harris & Knight, 2014; Nair et al., 2015). Other unique models are being tested, including computerized referral from the ED (Haskins et al., 2017) and primary care–facilitated linkage to web-based SBIRT for patients to access after, rather than during, the medical visit (Anderson et al., 2016; Wallace et al., 2017). Moreover, computer-guided, clinician-facing products have recently been developed to help health care practitioners incorporate SBIRT skills more easily into clinical practice, including mobile device applications and clinician dashboards (Levesque, Umanzor, & de Aguiar, 2018; O'Grady, Kapoor, Gilmer, et al., 2019; Satre, Ly, Wamsley, Curtis, & Satterfield, 2017).

Telehealth models are also being studied. The Remote Brief Intervention and Referral to Treatment (R-BIRT) consultation service is designed to connect ED patients with health coaches by telephone or two-way video during their ED visit (Boudreaux, Haskins, Harralson, & Bernstein, 2015). Once connected, an R-BIRT health coach conducts BIRT, guided by software and an interactive referral generator. Initial acceptability and feasibility for this model have been established, and efficacy and cost-effectiveness now have to be established (Boudreaux et al., 2015). However, other research has found that telehealth models with injured ED patients did not reduce alcohol use (Mello et al., 2016). Therefore, the most effective telehealth models and the patients most likely to benefit from them should be carefully investigated in future research.

ADVANCING SBIRT IN MEDICAL AND INTEGRATED CARE SETTINGS

There are a number of research gaps that should be addressed to advance SBIRT clinical practice and implementation. A few of these gaps are highlighted next. These include referral to treatment, drug use, SBIRT delivery by mental health professionals, and implementation models.

Referral to Treatment

Referral typically occurs if screening results signal the need for further assessment and, if appropriate, intake into formal SUD treatment (SAMHSA, 2013). A linkage between the health care setting and an external SUD treatment program is often required. A referral can vary, from giving the patient a list of facilities that they can contact on their own, to "warmer" handoffs in which health care staff take a more active role in the referral. Few studies focus specifically on referral to treatment (RT). Rather, RT is often examined as part of trials on the full SBIRT model (Glass, 2015; Newhouse et al., 2018). It has been noted that RT is the least developed component in SBIRT studies and is almost an afterthought, with RT procedures greatly varying between studies (Glass, 2015; Glass et al., 2015).

National survey data have suggested that alcohol screening and brief intervention increases the odds of treatment engagement (Bandara et al., 2018). However, other studies, meta-analyses, and reviews have concluded that there is limited to no support for SBIRT leading to increases in treatment utilization (Glass et al., 2015; Glass, Hamilton, et al., 2016; Kim et al., 2017; Simioni, Cottencin, & Rolland, 2015, 2016). Practically, it is easy to imagine that a patient who was opportunistically identified as part of a health care visit may not be seeking or interested in treatment at that time. There are a number of reasons patients may not seek treatment, including lack of problem awareness, ambivalence, stigma, or shame (Probst, Manthey, Martinez, & Rehm, 2015).

Several important questions have to be answered about the state of RT science. These include determining the content and procedures of a strong, effective RT protocol and whether such a protocol would be effective in increasing treatment entry. Protocols should consider the various reasons patients may not seek treatment. In addition, because patients may have to develop motivation and interest in seeking treatment, other tactics may have to be added to the RT protocol, such as ongoing contacts and other therapeutic techniques (e.g., cognitive behavior therapy) that are not typically part of SBIRT practice (Cucciare, Coleman, & Timko, 2015; Cucciare & Timko, 2015; Stecker, McGovern, & Herr, 2012). The duration, content, and best process for ongoing contacts has to be developed and tested, keeping in mind the implementation challenges for extended substance use monitoring and intervention in health care settings (Cucciare et al., 2015). For primary care, there is a need for more research to determine when a referral to specialty SUD care is necessary given recent initiatives to provide more care within primary care (McCambridge & Saitz, 2017). Finally, RT studies focus mainly on referral for AUD treatment; more focus is needed on referral for other SUDs.

SBIRT for Drug Use

Much SBIRT research in health care settings has focused on alcohol use, with studies on SBIRT for other drug use lacking (Timko, Kong, Vittorio, & Cucciare, 2016). Taken together, results do not support the idea that SBIRT is efficacious for drug use (Saitz, 2014; USPSTF, 2014; Young et al., 2014). In the 5 years since reviews were conducted, studies have continued to show that BIs do not seem to affect drug use (e.g., Bogenschutz et al., 2014; Woodruff et al., 2014), with a notable exception (Gelberg et al., 2015). The exception was relatively intensive by BI standards, including brief provider advice, a video doctor message, educational materials, and up to two 20- to 30-minute coaching sessions. Other studies on SBIRT for drug use are currently underway (Chambers et al., 2016).

Several research avenues should be pursued. First, an updated meta-analysis and review should be conducted with attention to the details of BI content, BI intensity, setting, and who is conducting the BI. Second, despite the lack of efficacy for drug use SBIRT, the practice of identifying and addressing drug use in health care settings should not be discarded. It is still important for health care practitioners to be aware of and provide services for drug use, given the severe health consequences that could occur if this is unaddressed. This notion is supported by the new USPSTF draft recommendation that primary care providers conduct screening for illicit drug use (USPSTF, 2019). However, better models of care beyond traditional SBIRT have to be developed and tested.

SBIRT by Mental Health Professionals

There is little research on how mental health professionals implement and practice SBIRT. However, mental health professionals are well-positioned to conduct SBIRT, given their training in counseling techniques and the high rates of co-occurrence between SUDs and mental health problems. In a mental health setting, providing training and clinical tools modified to respond to the needs and infrastructures of the mental health setting tended to improve clinician knowledge and confidence in addressing substance use while also increasing their identification and management of substance use problems (Heslop, Ross, Osmond, & Wynaden, 2013). However, research among direct service staff in social service and mental health settings that have implemented SBIRT highlights the need for model adaptation for different client populations and settings (e.g., mental health, homeless individuals), as well as determination of best ways to gain staff buy-in and provide training (Patterson Silver Wolf, Ramsey, & van den Berk-Clark, 2015; Satre, Leibowitz, Mertens, & Weisner, 2014).

SBIRT Implementation

Even though studies guided by implementation science have started to lead to a better understanding of practices that may increase adoption of SBIRT (Mitchell et al., 2016), and there are several guides available on how to implement SBIRT, there is still much to understand about its implementation in health care settings (Ducharme, Chandler, & Harris, 2016). One important factor is the setting in which SBIRT is being implemented. Research has suggested that the demands of SBIRT programs in ED and primary care settings may differ on the patient as well as the site level (O'Grady, Kapoor, Kwon, et al., 2019). Even less is known about implementation needs in other settings. Several studies have indicated that there may be important interactions between the patient and provider that affect SBIRT implementation

(Bachhuber et al., 2017; Hodgson et al., 2016). The patient perspective has not been well documented in SBIRT studies. Therefore, including patients will be an important future direction to inform SBIRT implementation (McNeely et al., 2018). There is a need for randomized trials in all settings that draw from implementation science models, address the multiple levels of barriers and facilitators identified in past research, and thoroughly describe and test specific implementation methods that are replicable (Newhouse et al., 2018; O'Donnell et al., 2014).

CONCLUSION

Identifying and initiating care for people with substance use problems is critical for health care settings; SBIRT is an important practice to be included in the clinical toolbox to accomplish this essential task. This chapter outlined SBIRT efficacy for EDs and primary care practices, reviewed barriers to implementation, and highlighted model innovations and research directions. Continued development and study of SBIRT model adaptations and implementation facilitators will move this clinical practice in health care settings into the future.

REFERENCES

Allen, J. D., Shelton, R. C., Emmons, K. M., & Linnan, L. A. (2017). Fidelity and its relationship to implementation effectiveness, adaptation, and dissemination. In R. C. Brownson, G. A. Golditz, & E. K. Proctor (Eds.), *Dissemination and implementation research in health: Translating science to practice* (2nd ed., pp. 267–284). New York, NY: Oxford University Press.

Álvarez-Bueno, C., Rodríguez-Martín, B., García-Ortiz, L., Gómez-Marcos, M. Á., & Martínez-Vizcaíno, V. (2015). Effectiveness of brief interventions in primary health care settings to decrease alcohol consumption by adult non-dependent drinkers: A systematic review of systematic reviews. *Preventive Medicine, 76,* S33–S38. http://dx.doi.org/10.1016/j.ypmed.2014.12.010

Anderson, P., Bendtsen, P., Spak, F., Reynolds, J., Drummond, C., Segura, L., . . . Gual, T. (2016). Improving the delivery of brief interventions for heavy drinking in primary health care: Outcome results of the Optimizing Delivery of Health Care Intervention (ODHIN) five-country cluster randomized factorial trial. *Addiction, 111,* 1935–1945. http://dx.doi.org/10.1111/add.13476

Bachhuber, M. A., O'Grady, M. A., Chung, H., Neighbors, C. J., DeLuca, J., D'Aloia, E. M., . . . Cunningham, C. O. (2017). Delivery of screening and brief intervention for unhealthy alcohol use in an urban academic Federally Qualified Health Center. *Addiction Science & Clinical Practice, 12,* 33. http://dx.doi.org/10.1186/s13722-017-0100-2

Bandara, S. N., Samples, H., Crum, R. M., & Saloner, B. (2018). Is screening and intervention associated with treatment receipt among individuals with alcohol use disorder? Evidence from a national survey. *Journal of Substance Abuse Treatment, 92,* 85–90. http://dx.doi.org/10.1016/j.jsat.2018.06.009

Barbosa, C., Cowell, A., Bray, J., & Aldridge, A. (2015). The cost-effectiveness of alcohol screening, brief intervention, and referral to treatment (SBIRT) in emergency and outpatient medical settings. *Journal of Substance Abuse Treatment, 53*, 1–8. http://dx.doi.org/10.1016/j.jsat.2015.01.003

Bernstein, S. L., & D'Onofrio, G. (2017). Screening, treatment initiation, and referral for substance use disorders. *Addiction Science & Clinical Practice, 12*, 18. http://dx.doi.org/10.1186/s13722-017-0083-z

Blow, F. C., Walton, M. A., Bohnert, A. S. B., Ignacio, R. V., Chermack, S., Cunningham, R. M., . . . Barry, K. L. (2017). A randomized controlled trial of brief interventions to reduce drug use among adults in a low-income urban emergency department: The HealthiER You study. *Addiction, 112*, 1395–1405. http://dx.doi.org/10.1111/add.13773

Bogenschutz, M. P., Donovan, D. M., Mandler, R. N., Perl, H. I., Forcehimes, A. A., Crandall, C., . . . Douaihy, A. (2014) Brief intervention for patients with problematic drug use presenting in emergency departments: A randomized clinical trial. *JAMA Internal Medicine, 174*, 1736–1745. http://dx.doi.org/10.1001/jamainternmed.2014.4052

Boudreaux, E. D., Haskins, B., Harralson, T., & Bernstein, E. (2015). The remote brief intervention and referral to treatment model: Development, functionality, acceptability, and feasibility. *Drug and Alcohol Dependence, 155*, 236–242. http://dx.doi.org/10.1016/j.drugalcdep.2015.07.014

Bradley, K. A., Bobb, J. F., Ludman, E. J., Chavez, L. J., Saxon, A. J., Merrill, J. O., . . . Kivlahan, D. R. (2018). Alcohol-related nurse care management in primary care: A randomized clinical trial. *JAMA Internal Medicine, 178*, 613–621. http://dx.doi.org/10.1001/jamainternmed.2018.0388

Bradley, K. A., DeBenedetti, A. F., Volk, R. J., Williams, E. C., Frank, D., & Kivlahan, D. R. (2007). AUDIT–C as a brief screen for alcohol misuse in primary care. *Alcoholism: Clinical and Experimental Research, 31*, 1208–1217. http://dx.doi.org/10.1111/j.1530-0277.2007.00403.x

Broderick, K. B., Kaplan, B., Martini, D., & Caruso, E. (2015). Emergency physician utilization of alcohol/substance screening, brief advice and discharge: A 10-year comparison. *The Journal of Emergency Medicine, 49*, 400–407. http://dx.doi.org/10.1016/j.jemermed.2015.05.014

Brown, R. L., Moberg, P. D., Allen, J. B., Peterson, C. T., Saunders, L. A., Croyle, M. D., . . . Caldwell, S. B. (2014). A team approach to systematic behavioral screening and intervention. *American Journal of Managed Care, 20*, e113–121. Retrieved from https://www.ajmc.com/journals/issue/2014/2014-vol20-n4/a-team-approach-to-systematic-behavioral-screening-and-intervention

Burdick, T. E., & Kessler, R. S. (2017). Development and use of a clinical decision support tool for behavioral health screening in primary care clinics. *Applied Clinical Informatics, 8*, 412–429. http://dx.doi.org/10.4338/ACI-2016-04-RA-0068

Chambers, J. E., Brooks, A. C., Medvin, R., Metzger, D. S., Lauby, J., Carpenedo, C. M., . . . Kirby, K. C. (2016). Examining multi-session brief intervention for substance use in primary care: Research methods of a randomized controlled trial. *Addiction Science & Clinical Practice, 11*, 8. http://dx.doi.org/10.1186/s13722-016-0057-6

Clemence, A. J., Balkoski, V. I., Lee, M., Poston, J., Schaefer, B. M., Maisonneuve, I. M., . . . Glick, S. D. (2016). Residents' experience of screening, brief intervention, and referral to treatment (SBIRT) as a clinical tool following practical application: A mixed-methods study. *Substance Abuse, 37*, 306–314. http://dx.doi.org/10.1080/08897077.2015.1064850

Cowell, A. J., Dowd, W. N., Mills, M. J., Hinde, J. M., & Bray, J. W. (2017). Sustaining SBIRT in the wild: Simulating revenues and costs for Screening, Brief Intervention and Referral to Treatment programs. *Addiction, 112*, 101–109. http://dx.doi.org/10.1111/add.13650

Cucciare, M. A., Coleman, E. A., & Timko, C. (2015). A conceptual model to facilitate transitions from primary care to specialty substance use disorder care: A review of the literature. *Primary Health Care Research and Development, 16,* 492–505. http://dx.doi.org/10.1017/S1463423614000164

Cucciare, M. A., & Timko, C. (2015). Bridging the gap between medical settings and specialty addiction treatment. *Addiction, 110,* 1417–1419. http://dx.doi.org/10.1111/add.12977

Damschroder, L. J., Aron, D. C., Keith, R. E., Kirsh, S. R., Alexander, J. A., & Lowery, J. C. (2009). Fostering implementation of health services research findings into practice: A consolidated framework for advancing implementation science. *Implementation Science, 4,* 50. http://dx.doi.org/10.1186/1748-5908-4-50

Del Boca, F. K., McRee, B., Vendetti, J., & Damon, D. (2017). The SBIRT program matrix: A conceptual framework for program implementation and evaluation. *Addiction, 112,* 12–22. http://dx.doi.org/10.1111/add.13656

Derges, J., Kidger, J., Fox, F., Campbell, R., Kaner, E., & Hickman, M. (2017). Alcohol screening and brief interventions for adults and young people in health and community-based settings: A qualitative systematic literature review. *BMC Public Health, 17,* 562. http://dx.doi.org/10.1186/s12889-017-4476-4

D'Onofrio, G., O'Connor, P. G., Pantalon, M. V., Chawarski, M. C., Busch, S. H., Owens, P. H., . . . Fiellin, D. A. (2015). Emergency department-initiated buprenorphine/naloxone treatment for opioid dependence: A randomized clinical trial. *JAMA, 313,* 1636–1644. http://dx.doi.org/10.1001/jama.2015.3474

D'Onofrio, G., Pantalon, M. V., Degutis, L. C., Fiellin, D. A., & O'Connor, P. G. (2005). Development and implementation of an emergency practitioner-performed brief intervention for hazardous and harmful drinkers in the emergency department. *Academic Emergency Medicine, 12,* 249–256.

Ducharme, L. J., Chandler, R. K., & Harris, A. H. (2016). Implementing effective substance abuse treatments in general medical settings: Mapping the research terrain. *Journal of Substance Abuse Treatment, 60,* 110–118. http://dx.doi.org/10.1016/j.jsat.2015.06.020

Dwinnells, R., & Misik, L. (2017). An integrative behavioral health care model using automated SBIRT and care coordination in community health care. *Journal of Primary Care & Community Health, 8,* 300–304. http://dx.doi.org/10.1177/2150131917740245

Elzerbi, C., Donoghue, K., Boniface, S., & Drummond, C. (2017). Variance in the efficacy of brief interventions to reduce hazardous and harmful alcohol consumption between injury and noninjury patients in emergency departments: A systematic review and meta-analysis of randomized controlled trials. *Annals of Emergency Medicine, 70,* 714–723.e13. http://dx.doi.org/10.1016/j.annemergmed.2017.05.004

Gelberg, L., Andersen, R. M., Afifi, A. A., Leake, B. D., Arangua, L., Vahidi, M., . . . Baumeister, S. E. (2015). Project QUIT (Quit Using Drugs Intervention Trial): A randomized controlled trial of a primary care-based multi-component brief intervention to reduce risky drug use. *Addiction, 110,* 1777–1790. http://dx.doi.org/10.1111/add.12993

Glass, J. E. (2015). Challenges ahead in developing and testing referral to treatment interventions. *Addiction, 110,* 1419–1420. http://dx.doi.org/10.1111/add.13039

Glass, J. E., Bohnert, K. M., & Brown, R. L. (2016). Alcohol screening and intervention among united states adults who attend ambulatory healthcare. *Journal of General Internal Medicine, 31,* 739–745. http://dx.doi.org/10.1007/s11606-016-3614-5

Glass, J. E., Hamilton, A. M., Powell, B. J., Perron, B. E., Brown, R. T., & Ilgen, M. A. (2015). Specialty substance use disorder services following brief alcohol intervention: A meta-analysis of randomized controlled trials. *Addiction, 110,* 1404–1415. http://dx.doi.org/10.1111/add.12950

Glass, J. E., Hamilton, A. M., Powell, B. J., Perron, B. E., Brown, R. T., & Ilgen, M. A. (2016). Revisiting our review of Screening, Brief Intervention and Referral to Treatment (SBIRT): Meta-analytical results still point to no efficacy in increasing the use of substance use disorder services. *Addiction, 111*, 181–183. http://dx.doi.org/10.1111/add.13146

Gorpland, E. M., & McPherson, T. L. (2015). *Implementation barriers and facilitators of screening brief intervention and referral to treatment (SBIRT) in federally qualified health centers*. Retrieved from https://aspe.hhs.gov/report/implementation-barriers-and-facilitators-screening-brief-intervention-referral-and-treatment-sbirt-federally-qualified-health-centers-fqhcs

Graham, H. L., Copello, A., Griffith, E., Freemantle, N., McCrone, P., Clarke, L., . . . Birchwood, M. (2016). Pilot randomised trial of a brief intervention for comorbid substance misuse in psychiatric in-patient settings. *Acta Psychiatrica Scandinavica, 133*, 298–309. http://dx.doi.org/10.1111/acps.12530

Hall, K., Staiger, P. K., Simpson, A., Best, D., & Lubman, D. I. (2016). After 30 years of dissemination, have we achieved sustained practice change in motivational interviewing? *Addiction, 111*, 1144–1150. http://dx.doi.org/10.1111/add.13014

Hargraves, D., White, C., Frederick, R., Cinibulk, M., Peters, M., Young, A., & Elder, N. (2017). Implementing SBIRT (Screening, Brief Intervention and Referral to Treatment) in primary care: Lessons learned from a multi-practice evaluation portfolio. *Public Health Reviews, 38*, 31. http://dx.doi.org/10.1186/s40985-017-0077-0

Harris, B. R., & Yu, J. (2016). Attitudes, perceptions and practice of alcohol and drug screening, brief intervention and referral to treatment: A case study of New York State primary care physicians and non-physician providers. *Public Health, 139*, 70–78. http://dx.doi.org/10.1016/j.puhe.2016.05.007

Harris, S. K., & Knight, J. R. (2014). Putting the screen in screening: Technology-based alcohol screening and brief interventions in medical settings. *Alcohol Research: Current Reviews, 36*, 63–79. https://www.ncbi.nlm.nih.gov/pmc/articles/PMC4432859/

Haskins, B. L., Davis-Martin, R., Abar, B., Baumann, B. M., Harralson, T., & Boudreaux, E. D. (2017). Health evaluation and referral assistant: A randomized controlled trial of a web-based screening, brief intervention, and referral to treatment system to reduce risky alcohol use among emergency department patients. *Journal of Medical Internet Research, 19*, e119. http://dx.doi.org/10.2196/jmir.6812

Hawk, K., & D'Onofrio, G. (2018). Emergency department screening and interventions for substance use disorders. *Addiction Science & Clinical Practice, 13*, 18. http://dx.doi.org/10.1186/s13722-018-0117-1

Heslop, K., Ross, C., Osmond, B., & Wynaden, D. (2013). The Alcohol Smoking and Substance Involvement Screening Test (ASSIST) in an acute mental health setting. *International Journal of Mental Health and Addiction, 11*, 583–600. http://dx.doi.org/10.1007/s11469-013-9428-3

Hettema, J. E., Cockrell, S. A., Reeves, A., Ingersoll, K. S., Lum, P. J., Saitz, R., . . . Carrejo, V. A. (2018). Development and differentiability of three brief interventions for risky alcohol use that include varying doses of motivational interviewing. *Addiction Science & Clinical Practice, 13*, 6. http://dx.doi.org/10.1186/s13722-017-0102-0

Hingson, R., & Compton, W. M. (2014). Screening and brief intervention and referral to treatment for drug use in primary care: Back to the drawing board. *JAMA, 312*, 488–489. http://dx.doi.org/10.1001/jama.2014.7863

Hodgson, J., Stanton, M., Atherton, W., Toriello, P., Borst, C., Moran, M., & Winter, A. M. (2016). Implementation of SBIRT: Focus group analysis of provider teams in academic and community healthcare settings. *Journal of Rehabilitation, 82*, 48–59. Retrieved from https://www.researchgate.net/publication/317774382_Implementation_of_SBIRT_Focus_group_analysis_of_provider_teams_in_academic_and_community_healthcare_settings

Johnson, J. A., Woychek, A., Vaughan, D., & Seale, J. P. (2013). Screening for at-risk alcohol use and drug use in an emergency department: Integration of screening questions into electronic triage forms achieves high screening rates. *Annals of Emergency Medicine, 62*, 262–266. http://dx.doi.org/10.1016/j.annemergmed.2013.04.011

Kaner, E. F., Beyer, F. R., Muirhead, C., Campbell, F., Pienaar, E. D., Bertholet, N., . . . Burnand, B. (2018). Effectiveness of brief alcohol interventions in primary care populations. *Cochrane Database of Systematic Reviews*. http://dx.doi.org/10.1002/14651858.CD004148.pub4

Kene, M., Miller Rosales, C., Wood, S., Rauchwerger, A. S., Vinson, D. R., & Sterling, S. A. (2018). Feasibility of expanded emergency department screening for behavioral health problems. *The American Journal of Managed Care, 24*, 585–591. https://www.ajmc.com/journals/issue/2018/2018-vol24-n12/feasibility-of-expanded-emergency-department-screening-for-behavioral-health-problems

Kim, T. W., Bernstein, J., Cheng, D. M., Lloyd-Travaglini, C., Samet, J. H., Palfai, T. P., & Saitz, R. (2017). Receipt of addiction treatment as a consequence of a brief intervention for drug use in primary care: A randomized trial. *Addiction, 112*, 818–827. http://dx.doi.org/10.1111/add.13701

Landy, M. S. H., Davey, C. J., Quintero, D., Pecora, A., & McShane, K. E. (2016). A systematic review on the effectiveness of brief interventions for alcohol misuse among adults in emergency departments. *Journal of Substance Abuse Treatment, 61*, 1–12. http://dx.doi.org/10.1016/j.jsat.2015.08.004

Levesque, D., Umanzor, C., & de Aguiar, E. (2018). Stage-based mobile intervention for substance use disorders in primary care: Development and test of acceptability. *JMIR Medical Informatics, 6*(1), e1–e1. http://dx.doi.org/10.2196/medinform.7355

McCambridge, J., & Saitz, R. (2017). Rethinking brief interventions for alcohol in general practice. *BMJ, 356*, j116. http://dx.doi.org/10.1136/bmj.j116

McKnight-Eily, L. R., Okoro, C. A., Mejia, R., Denny, C. H., Higgins-Biddle, J., Hungerford, D., . . . Sniezek, J. E. (2017). Screening for excessive alcohol use and brief counseling of adults—17 states and the District of Columbia, 2014. *Morbidity Mortality Weekly Report, 66*, 313–319. Retrieved from https://www.cdc.gov/mmwr/volumes/66/wr/mm6612a1.htm

McNeely, J., Cleland, C. M., Strauss, S. M., Palamar, J. J., Rotrosen, J., & Saitz, R. (2015). Validation of self-administered single-item screening questions (SISQs) for unhealthy alcohol and drug use in primary care patients. *Journal of General Internal Medicine, 30*, 1757–1764. http://dx.doi.org/10.1007/s11606-015-3391-6

McNeely, J., Kumar, P. C., Rieckmann, T., Sedlander, E., Farkas, S., Chollak, C., . . . Rotrosen, J. (2018). Barriers and facilitators affecting the implementation of substance use screening in primary care clinics: A qualitative study of patients, providers, and staff. *Addiction Science & Clinical Practice, 13*, 8. http://dx.doi.org/10.1186/s13722-018-0110-8

Mello, M. J., Baird, J., Lee, C., Strezsak, V., French, M. T., & Longabaugh, R. (2016). A randomized controlled trial of a telephone intervention for alcohol misuse with injured emergency department patients. *Annals of Emergency Medicine, 67*, 263–275. http://dx.doi.org/10.1016/j.annemergmed.2015.09.021

Mertens, J. R., Chi, F. W., Weisner, C. M., Satre, D. D., Ross, T. B., Allen, S., . . . Sterling, S. A. (2015). Physician versus non-physician delivery of alcohol screening, brief intervention and referral to treatment in adult primary care: The ADVISe cluster randomized controlled implementation trial. *Addiction Science & Clinical Practice, 10*, 26. http://dx.doi.org/10.1186/s13722-015-0047-0

Mitchell, S. G., Schwartz, R. P., Kirk, A. S., Dusek, K., Oros, M., Hosler, C., . . . Brown, B. S. (2016). SBIRT implementation for adolescents in urban federally qualified health centers. *Journal of Substance Abuse Treatment, 60*, 81–90. http://dx.doi.org/10.1016/j.jsat.2015.06.011

Nair, N. K., Newton, N. C., Shakeshaft, A., Wallace, P., & Teesson, M. (2015). A systematic review of digital and computer-based alcohol intervention programs in primary care. *Current Drug Abuse Reviews, 8*, 111–118. http://dx.doi.org/10.2174/1874473708666150916113538

National Council for Behavioral Health. (2018). *Implementing care for alcohol and other drug use in medical settings: An extension of SBIRT.* Retrieved from https://www.thenationalcouncil.org/wp-content/uploads/2018/03/021518_NCBH_ASPTReport-FINAL.pdf

Neff, J. A., Kelley, M. L., Walters, S. T., Cunningham, T. D., Paulson, J. F., Braitman, A. L., . . . Bolen, H. (2015). Effectiveness of a Screening and Brief Intervention protocol for heavy drinkers in dental practice: A cluster-randomized trial. *Journal of Health Psychology, 20,* 1534–1548. http://dx.doi.org/10.1177/1359105313516660

Newhouse, R., Janney, M., Gilbert, A., Agley, J., Bakoyannis, G., Ferren, M., . . . Thoele, K. (2018). Study protocol testing toolkit versus usual care for implementation of screening, brief intervention, referral to treatment in hospitals: A phased cluster randomized approach. *Addiction Science & Clinical Practice, 13,* 28. http://dx.doi.org/10.1186/s13722-018-0130-4

Nunes, A. P., Richmond, M. K., Marzano, K., Swenson, C. J., & Lockhart, J. (2017). Ten years of implementing screening, brief intervention, and referral to treatment (SBIRT): Lessons learned. *Substance Abuse, 38,* 508–512. http://dx.doi.org/10.1080/08897077.2017.1362369

O'Donnell, A., Wallace, P., & Kaner, E. (2014). From efficacy to effectiveness and beyond: What next for brief interventions in primary care? *Frontiers in Psychiatry, 5,* 113.

O'Grady, M. A., Kapoor, S., Gilmer, E., Neighbors, C. J., Conigliaro, J., Kwon, N., & Morgenstern, J. (2019). Point-of-care mobile application to guide healthcare professionals in conducting substance use screening and intervention: A mixed-methods user experience study. *ACI Open, 3,* e1–e12. http://dx.doi.org/10.1055/s-0039-1684002

O'Grady, M. A., Kapoor, S., Kwon, N., Morley, J., Auerbach, M., Neighbors, C. J., . . . Morgenstern, J. (2019). Substance use screening and brief intervention: Evaluation of patient and implementation differences between primary care and emergency department settings. *Journal of Evaluation in Clinical Practice, 25,* 441–447. http://dx.doi.org/10.1111/jep.13060

Office of the Surgeon General. (2016). *Facing addiction in America: The Surgeon General's report on alcohol, drugs, and health.* Retrieved from https://store.samhsa.gov/system/files/surgeon-generals-report.pdf

Oslin, D. W., Lynch, K. G., Maisto, S. A., Lantinga, L. J., McKay, J. R., Possemato, K., . . . Wierzbicki, M. (2014). A randomized clinical trial of alcohol care management delivered in Department of Veterans Affairs primary care clinics versus specialty addiction treatment. *Journal of General Internal Medicine, 29,* 162–168. http://dx.doi.org/10.1007/s11606-013-2625-8

Patterson Silver Wolf, D. A., Ramsey, A. T., & van den Berk-Clark, C. (2015). Implementing outside the box: Community-based social service provider experiences with using an alcohol screening and intervention. *Journal of Social Service Research, 41,* 233–245. http://dx.doi.org/10.1080/01488376.2014.980963

Probst, C., Manthey, J., Martinez, A., & Rehm, J. (2015). Alcohol use disorder severity and reported reasons not to seek treatment: A cross-sectional study in European primary care practices. *Substance Abuse Treatment, Prevention, and Policy, 10,* 32. http://dx.doi.org/10.1186/s13011-015-0028-z

Rahm, A. K., Boggs, J. M., Martin, C., Price, D. W., Beck, A., Backer, T. E., & Dearing, J. W. (2015). Facilitators and barriers to implementing screening, brief intervention, and referral to treatment (SBIRT) in primary care in integrated health care settings. *Substance Abuse, 36,* 281–288. http://dx.doi.org/10.1080/08897077.2014.951140

Reho, K., Agley, J., DeSalle, M., & Gassman, R. A. (2016). Are we there yet? A review of screening, brief intervention, and referral to treatment (SBIRT) implementation fidelity tools and proficiency checklists. *The Journal of Primary Prevention, 37,* 377–388. http://dx.doi.org/10.1007/s10935-016-0431-x

Sacks, S., Gotham, H. J., Johnson, K., Padwa, H., Murphy, D. M., & Krom, L. (2016). *Integrating substance use disorder and health care services in an era of health reform: Models, interventions, and implementation strategies.* Retrieved from https://attcnetwork.org/sites/default/files/15-ATTC_WhitePaper-final-web.pdf

Saitz, R. (2014). Screening and brief intervention for unhealthy drug use: Little or no efficacy. *Frontiers in Psychiatry, 5,* 121. http://dx.doi.org/10.3389/fpsyt.2014.00121

Satre, D. D., Delucchi, K., Lichtmacher, J., Sterling, S. A., & Weisner, C. (2013). Motivational interviewing to reduce hazardous drinking and drug use among depression patients. *Journal of Substance Abuse Treatment, 44,* 323–329. http://dx.doi.org/10.1016/j.jsat.2012.08.008

Satre, D. D., Leibowitz, A. S., Mertens, J. R., & Weisner, C. (2014). Advising depression patients to reduce alcohol and drug use: Factors associated with provider intervention in outpatient psychiatry. *The American Journal on Addictions, 23,* 570–575. http://dx.doi.org/10.1111/j.1521-0391.2014.12140.x

Satre, D. D., Ly, K., Wamsley, M., Curtis, A., & Satterfield, J. (2017). A digital tool to promote alcohol and drug use screening, brief intervention, and referral to treatment skill translation: A mobile app development and randomized controlled trial protocol. *JMIR Research Protocols, 6,* e55–e55. http://dx.doi.org/10.2196/resprot.7070

Saunders, J. B., Aasland, O. G., Babor, T. F., de la Fuente, J. R., & Grant, M. (1993). Development of the Alcohol Use Disorders Identification Test (AUDIT): WHO collaborative project on early detection of persons with harmful alcohol consumption-II. *Addiction, 88,* 791–804. http://dx.doi.org/10.1111/j.1360-0443.1993.tb02093.x

Simioni, N., Cottencin, O., & Rolland, B. (2015). Interventions for increasing subsequent alcohol treatment utilisation among patients with alcohol use disorders from somatic inpatient settings: A systematic review. *Alcohol and Alcoholism, 50,* 420–429. http://dx.doi.org/10.1093/alcalc/agv017

Simioni, N., Rolland, B., & Cottencin, O. (2016). Is there really no evidence of the efficacy of brief alcohol interventions for increasing subsequent utilization of alcohol-related services? Commentary on the paper by Glass et al. (2015). *Addiction, 111,* 180–181. http://dx.doi.org/10.1111/add.13145

Smith, P. C., Schmidt, S. M., Allensworth-Davies, D., & Saitz, R. (2010). A single-question screening test for drug use in primary care. *Archives of Internal Medicine, 170,* 1155–1160. http://dx.doi.org/10.1001/archinternmed.2010.140

Spear, S. E., Shedlin, M., Gilberti, B., Fiellin, M., & McNeely, J. (2016). Feasibility and acceptability of an audio computer-assisted self-interview version of the Alcohol, Smoking and Substance Involvement Screening Test (ASSIST) in primary care patients. *Substance Abuse, 37,* 299–305. http://dx.doi.org/10.1080/08897077.2015.1062460

Stecker, T., McGovern, M. P., & Herr, B. (2012). An intervention to increase alcohol treatment engagement: A pilot trial. *Journal of Substance Abuse Treatment, 43,* 161–167. http://dx.doi.org/10.1016/j.jsat.2011.10.028

Substance Abuse and Mental Health Services Administration. (2013). *Systems-level implementation of screening, brief intervention, and referral to treatment.* Retrieved from https://store.samhsa.gov/system/files/sma13-4741.pdf

Timko, C., Kong, C., Vittorio, L., & Cucciare, M. A. (2016). Screening and brief intervention for unhealthy substance use in patients with chronic medical conditions: A systematic review. *Journal of Clinical Nursing, 25,* 3131–3143. http://dx.doi.org/10.1111/jocn.13244

U.S. Preventive Services Task Force. (2014). *Drug use, illicit: Screening.* Retrieved from https://www.uspreventiveservicestaskforce.org/Page/Document/RecommendationStatementFinal/drug-use-illicit-screening

U.S. Preventive Services Task Force. (2018). Screening and behavioral counseling interventions to reduce unhealthy alcohol use in adolescents and adults: USPSTF Recommendation. *JAMA, 320,* 1899–1909. http://dx.doi.org/10.1001/jama.2018.16789

U.S. Preventive Services Task Force. (2019). *Illicit drug use, including nonmedical use of prescription drugs: Screening.* Retrieved from https://www.uspreventiveservices taskforce.org/Page/Document/draft-recommendation-statement/drug-use-in-adolescents-and-adults-including-pregnant-women-screening

Vendetti, J., Gmyrek, A., Damon, D., Singh, M., McRee, B., & Del Boca, F. (2017). Screening, brief intervention and referral to treatment (SBIRT): Implementation barriers, facilitators and model migration. *Addiction, 112,* 23–33. http://dx.doi.org/10.1111/add.13652

Vendetti, J. A., McRee, B. G., & Del Boca, F. K. (2017) Development of the SBIRT checklist for observation in real-time (SCORe). *Addiction, 112,* 34–42. http://dx.doi.org/10.1111/add.13657

Wallace, P., Struzzo, P., Della Vedova, R., Scafuri, F., Tersar, C., Lygidakis, C., . . . Freemantle, N. (2017). Randomised controlled non-inferiority trial of primary care-based facilitated access to an alcohol reduction website. *BMJ Open, 7*(11), e014576. http://dx.doi.org/10.1136/bmjopen-2016-014576

Wamsley, M., Satterfield, J. M., Curtis, A., Lundgren, L., & Satre, D. D. (2018). Alcohol and drug screening, brief intervention, and referral to treatment (SBIRT) training and implementation: Perspectives from 4 health professions. *Journal of Addiction Medicine, 12,* 262–272. http://dx.doi.org/10.1097/ADM.0000000000000410

Watkins, K. E., Ober, A. J., Lamp, K., Lind, M., Setodji, C., Osilla, K. C., . . . Pincus, H. A. (2017). Collaborative care for opioid and alcohol use disorders in primary care: The SUMMIT randomized clinical trial. *JAMA Internal Medicine, 177,* 1480–1488. http://dx.doi.org/10.1001/jamainternmed.2017.3947

Whiteside, L. K., Darnell, D., Jackson, K., Wang, J., Russo, J., Donovan, D. M., & Zatzick, D. F. (2017). Collaborative care from the emergency department for injured patients with prescription drug misuse: An open feasibility study. *Journal of Substance Abuse Treatment, 82,* 12–21. http://dx.doi.org/10.1016/j.jsat.2017.08.005

WHO ASSIST Working Group. (2002). The alcohol, smoking and substance involvement screening test (ASSIST): Development, reliability and feasibility. *Addiction, 97,* 1183–1194. http://dx.doi.org/10.1046/j.1360-0443.2002.00185.x

Williams, E. C., Achtmeyer, C. E., Thomas, R. M., Grossbard, J. R., Lapham, G. T., Chavez, L. J., . . . Bradley, K. A. (2015). Factors underlying quality problems with alcohol screening prompted by a clinical reminder in primary care: A multi-site qualitative study. *Journal of General Internal Medicine, 30,* 1125–1132. http://dx.doi.org/10.1007/s11606-015-3248-z

Williams, E. C., Achtmeyer, C. E., Young, J. P., Rittmueller, S. E., Ludman, E. J., Lapham, G. T., . . . Bradley, K. A. (2016). Local implementation of alcohol screening and brief intervention at five Veterans Health Administration primary care clinics: Perspectives of clinical and administrative staff. *Journal of Substance Abuse Treatment, 60,* 27–35. http://dx.doi.org/10.1016/j.jsat.2015.07.011

Wilson, G. B., Heather, N., & Kaner, E. F. S. (2011). New developments in brief interventions to treat problem drinking in nonspecialty health care settings. *Current Psychiatry Reports, 13,* 422–429. http://dx.doi.org/10.1007/s11920-011-0219-x

Woodruff, S. I., Clapp, J. D., Eisenberg, K., McCabe, C., Hohman, M., Shillington, A. M., . . . Gareri, J. (2014). Randomized clinical trial of the effects of screening and brief intervention for illicit drug use: The Life Shift/Shift Gears study. *Addiction Science & Clinical Practice, 9,* 8. http://dx.doi.org/10.1186/1940-0640-9-8

Wright, T. E., Terplan, M., Ondersma, S. J., Boyce, C., Yonkers, K., Chang, G., & Creanga, A. A. (2016). The role of screening, brief intervention, and referral to treatment in the perinatal period. *American Journal of Obstetrics and Gynecology, 215,* 539–547. http://dx.doi.org/10.1016/j.ajog.2016.06.038

Young, M. M., Stevens, A., Galipeau, J., Pirie, T., Garritty, C., Singh, K., . . . Moher, D. (2014). Effectiveness of brief interventions as part of the Screening, Brief Intervention and Referral to Treatment (SBIRT) model for reducing the nonmedical use of psychoactive substances: A systematic review. *Systematic Reviews, 3,* 50. http://dx.doi.org/10.1186/2046-4053-3-50

Zarkin, G., Bray, J., Hinde, J., & Saitz, R. (2015). Costs of screening and brief intervention for illicit drug use in primary care settings. *Journal of Studies on Alcohol and Drugs, 76,* 222–228. http://dx.doi.org/10.15288/jsad.2015.76.222

7

Screening, Brief Intervention, and Referral to Treatment in College and University Settings

Unique Challenges and Opportunities

Brianna Mintz, Mary A. Marchetti, Peter P. Ehlinger, and Jessica M. Cronce

Screening, brief intervention, and referral to treatment (SBIRT) is an evidence-based practice designed to identify those at increased risk of harmful substance-related consequences, including the development of substance use–related disorders, and to prevent or reduce these outcomes (Saitz, 2007). However, the specific ways in which screening occurs, the nature of appropriate brief interventions, and the processes and options for referral to treatment are highly contingent on the population and context in which SBIRT is implemented. The focus of this chapter is on college students in university settings.

The use of many substances increases across the transition from high school to college (Schulenberg et al., 2018), making the college years ideal for prevention and intervention. Several factors have been implicated in this increase, including a dominant cultural narrative within the United States that college is a time for substance use, especially heavy alcohol use (Osberg, Billingsley, Eggert, & Insana, 2012). Consistent with this, and contrary to patterns for cannabis, cigarettes, illicit drugs, and some prescription drugs, the prevalence of alcohol consumption (with the exception of daily use) is higher among college students than their same-aged noncollege peers, suggesting there is something particular about the college environment that promotes greater alcohol use (Schulenberg et al., 2018). Thus, much of this chapter focuses on the use of SBIRT in this population to prevent and reduce harmful alcohol use, specifically.

http://dx.doi.org/10.1037/0000199-008
Screening, Brief Intervention, and Referral to Treatment for Substance Use: A Practitioner's Guide,
M. D. Cimini and J. L. Martin (Editors)

Though challenges exist in conducting SBIRT with college students, university settings provide unique opportunities. The systems and structures in place within most universities generally allow for easier implementation of interventions relative to community settings. This being said, it is important to note that most research on college student substance use to date has focused almost exclusively on those who are ages 18 to 25 because they are the majority of full-time students attending degree-granting postsecondary institutions (National Center for Education Statistics, 2017). For example, one of the largest and longest-running studies of substance use among adolescents and young adults—Monitoring the Future (MTF)—defines *college students* as individuals "one to four years past high school who report that they [are] taking courses as full-time students in a two- or four-year undergraduate college" (Schulenberg et al., 2018, p. 372). This definition excludes those pursuing their education at non-degree-earning technical colleges, as well as undergraduates returning to college after a substantial break in their educational career, often referred to as *nontraditional* students. Moreover, even though studies such as MTF may include students attending 2-year colleges, the corpus of research on SBIRT among college students predominantly comprises studies whose participants were attending 4-year universities. Research on students attending minority-serving institutions is by far the most underrepresented within the extant research; this should be considered when generalizing the information provided in this chapter.

With these important caveats noted, we begin with an overview of substance use patterns among students and other factors that may be relevant to SBIRT. This is followed by a summary of available screening measures and methods. Next, we provide a review of evidence-based brief interventions for the most common substances used by students and a discussion of considerations when referring students to treatment. We conclude with challenges and opportunities for the future of SBIRT in college and university settings.

PATTERNS OF COLLEGE STUDENT SUBSTANCE USE

According to the most recent MTF data (Schulenberg et al., 2018), approximately three out of five college students report having consumed alcohol in the past 30 days, and just over one out of five college students report having used cannabis over the same period. The reverse pattern is true when looking at daily use, with the reported use of cannabis exceeding alcohol (4.4% vs. 2.2%, respectively). Fewer than one in 10 college students (7.9%) report inhaling nicotine by smoking cigarettes in the past month, and only 2% are daily smokers, with few (0.2%) smoking 10 or more cigarettes per day. Though smoking cigarettes is often a daily habit, the discrepancy between past-month use and daily use may be accounted for by students who also vape nicotine (i.e., 6% in the past month) or those who only or primarily smoke cigarettes when they consume alcohol (sometimes referred to as *chippers*), for whom alcohol consumption serves as a cue that produces a nicotine craving (Epstein, Sher, Young, & King, 2007). Comparatively fewer students (7%) report illicit drug use, excluding cannabis, for which the legal status of its recreational use varies by jurisdiction.

Prescription drug *misuse*—use of a therapeutic drug by an individual to whom the drug was not prescribed or for a purpose other than the one for which it was prescribed—is also important to consider in the college context. Those aged 18 to 25 show the highest rates of prescription drug misuse across three of the four most commonly misused medication classes—opioids, stimulants, and tranquilizers (Substance Abuse and Mental Health Services Administration, 2018). However, the most recent MTF data suggested that the difference in prescription drug misuse between college students and their same-age noncollege peers varies by drug type. Specifically, college students are more likely to misuse stimulants such as Adderall (amphetamine and dextroamphetamine) than their noncollege peers, whereas misuse of opioid medications is higher among those not in college. Research has indicated that prescription stimulant medications are widely available in the college environment and might be more likely to be misused by students who are experiencing academic difficulties (Arria & DuPont, 2010); these same students may also be more likely to use other substances, including cannabis and alcohol (McCabe, Knight, Teter, & Wechsler, 2005).

Patterns of substance use, in particular, alcohol consumption, are highly variable among college students across days of the week, weeks of the academic term, and time of year (e.g., Neal & Fromme, 2007; Neighbors et al., 2011) and can be tied to specific events (e.g., homecoming). Alcohol misuse also varies across group membership, with greater risk of misuse for first-year students (White, Kraus, & Swartzwelder, 2006), those in fraternities and sororities (Scott-Sheldon, Carey, & Carey, 2008), and those engaged in college athletics (Leichliter, Meilman, Presley, & Cashin, 1998). Across all college students in the MTF study, roughly one out of three reported having consumed five or more drinks in a row on at least one occasion in the past 2 weeks (i.e., engaged in a pattern of heavy episodic or binge drinking), and a comparable amount reported having been drunk in the past month. A smaller percentage reported engaging in episodes of high-intensity drinking in the past 2 weeks—consuming 10 or more or 15 or more drinks in a row (10.2% and 1.3%, respectively). However, these students may be at greatest risk of harm (Read, Beattie, Chamberlain, & Merrill, 2008), especially when an occasion of binge or high-intensity drinking is due to pregaming or participation in drinking games (Zamboanga, Schwartz, Ham, Borsari, & Van Tyne, 2010). Thus, the variability and context of college student substance use should be considered when determining appropriate points and methods for screening and intervention.

Of course, students' substance use is often not the outcome of greatest concern but rather the consequences of that substance use. Although they do not occur on every drinking occasion (Lee, Maggs, Neighbors, & Patrick, 2011) and may not always be perceived by students as negative (Mallett, Bachrach, & Turrisi, 2008), alcohol-related consequences can have profoundly damaging effects for all students (Perkins, 2002) and are exacerbated for students with mental health concerns who drink (Weitzman, 2004). According to the American College Health Association (2018), three in five students felt over-whelming anxiety, two in five students felt it was hard to function due to depression, and one in 10 students reported seriously contemplating suicide at least once in the last year. Of note, roughly half of students endorsing symp-toms of depression or anxiety engage in binge drinking (Cranford, Eisenberg, & Serras, 2009). Thus, assessment of and intervention for mental health conditions may be needed in tandem with SBIRT for substance use.

SCREENING FOR SUBSTANCE USE WITH COLLEGE STUDENTS

Screening stresses the importance of assessing a broader spectrum of use, consequences, and associated risk factors rather than solely identifying the presence of a disorder (Saitz, 2007). Implementing universal screening in health centers, college counseling centers, and other community venues where college students are likely to seek services could help identify the most students at risk of high-risk substance use. There are myriad considerations in choosing the most suitable substance use screening measure, including local patterns and prevalence of use, the objective of the screening, and human and physical resources. Our aim in this section is to simplify this selection process.

Measures

Quantity-frequency questions, which ask respondents to estimate the amount of a substance that was used over a specified period and the average frequency with which use occurs, are the most commonly used screening measures for college students. With respect to alcohol use, the National Institute on Alcohol Abuse and Alcoholism (NIAAA; 2003) recommended three questions (see Table 7.1); for practitioners with more time, NIAAA also provides four-, five-, and six-item question sets that gather additional information (NIAAA, 2003).

Items on the Alcohol Use Disorders Identification Test—Concise (AUDIT–C; Bush, Kivlahan, McDonell, Fihn, & Bradley, 1998) roughly mirror NIAAA's three-item assessment and may be more effective at detecting high-risk drinking among college students relative to the full 10-item version of the AUDIT (DeMartini & Carey, 2012). However, practitioners may still wish to use the full version (Saunders & Aasland, 1987) to detect the potential presence of a *Diagnostic and Statistical Manual of Mental Disorders* (5th ed.; *DSM–5*; American Psychiatric Association, 2013) alcohol use disorder (AUD; Hagman, 2016) or International Classification of Diseases (ver. 10; World Health Orga-nization, 2016) alcohol dependence diagnosis (Coulton et al., 2019). Although the test developers recommend a cutoff score of 8 for provision of a brief

TABLE 7.1. National Institute on Alcohol Abuse and Alcoholism Recommended Three-Question Assessment

Assessment construct	Question
Frequency	During the last 12 months, how often did you usually have any kind of drink containing alcohol?
Quantity	During the last 12 months, how many alcoholic drinks did you have on a typical day when you drank alcohol?
Heavy use	During the last 12 months, how often did you have 5 or more (males) or 4 or more (females) drinks containing any kind of alcohol within a 2-hour period?

Note. Adapted from "Recommended Alcohol Questions," by National Institute on Alcohol Abuse and Alcoholism, 2003 (https://www.niaaa.nih.gov/research/guidelines-and-resources/recommended-alcohol-questions). In the public domain.

advice intervention, others have recommended the use of lower scores for college students (i.e., 5 or 7 for women and men, respectively, DeMartini & Carey, 2012; 6 for all students, Kokotailo et al., 2004). Interested readers are referred to Larimer and Cronce (2002, 2007), who included additional screening options specifically focused on alcohol use among college students.

Screening instruments that assess quantity are more complicated for drugs other than alcohol (with the exception of tobacco cigarettes) because potency is less consistent, and the methods of use are more variable, making it impossible to quantify use in terms of a "standard" dose. Thus, screenings for other drugs often rely on frequency alone. Specific measures include variations of the AUDIT, including the 10-item Cannabis Use Disorders Identification Test (CUDIT; Adamson & Sellman, 2003) and the 11-item Drug Use Disorders Identification Test (DUDIT; Berman, Bergman, Palmstierna, & Schlyter, 2003), which frames questions around the use of any drugs, including misused prescription drugs. Though we know of no study validating the CUDIT or DUDIT with college students, they were developed for use with both adolescents and adults, suggesting they are developmentally suitable for this population. Like the DUDIT, the short form Drug Abuse Screening Test (DAST–10) includes 10 yes or no questions about drugs other than alcohol. Scores group respondents into problem categories, with students in the moderate category (with a cutoff score of 3) being likely to benefit from brief intervention (McCabe, 2008).

Finally, for practitioners who wish to gather information on alcohol and other drugs simultaneously, including drug-specific information about the frequency of use and associated problems, the Alcohol, Smoking, and Substance Involvement Screening Test (ASSIST; WHO ASSIST Working Group, 2002) may be appropriate. Moreover, the ASSIST has been successfully used as the basis for brief personalized feedback interventions (PFIs) among college students (Kypri et al., 2009; Kypri, Langley, Saunders, Cashell-Smith, & Herbison, 2008). The National Institute on Drug Abuse (2018) has developed a modified version of the ASSIST that can be implemented entirely online, allowing for a broader range of implementation options.

Time Considerations

Brief screeners (taking less than 5 minutes) are appropriate for use during check-ups at college health centers or during intakes at counseling centers. Ideally, their reach can be extended by integrating them into existing, routinely administered forms. The NIAAA three-item drinking questions, AUDIT–C, and DAST–10 fall into this category. Moderate-length screeners (5–15 minutes) include brief structured interviews such as the 10-item AUDIT, which make sense to use for short appointments in medical clinics or similar settings. Finally, extended screeners (taking more than 15 minutes), such as the ASSIST, might be used principally in the context of a counseling center intake where more time is typically available.

BRIEF INTERVENTIONS

A reliable screening process is inadequate without subsequent intervention when it is necessary. The following overview serves to elucidate which brief intervention methods have demonstrated effectiveness with college students and what they entail. Though the current focus is on individual-level strategies, we encourage administrators to evaluate how their university's policies and other environmental-level prevention practices might decrease substance use behavior (e.g., prohibiting alcohol use or sale at campus sporting events; creating coalitions with the owners of bars and restaurants near campus to restrict happy hours and price promotions that encourage heavy consumption; working with local law enforcement to increase minimum legal drinking age compliance checks, especially near campus).

Harm reduction (HR) approaches to intervention demonstrate the most success with college students (Cronce & Larimer, 2011; Larimer & Cronce, 2002, 2007). Although abstinence is the optimal HR-focused intervention goal, advocating abstinence as the only option is unlikely to be successful among college students, especially with respect to alcohol use (Neighbors, Larimer, Lostutter, & Woods, 2006). From an HR perspective, any movement along the continuum toward reduced harm is viewed as a positive outcome.

For the college population, specifically, there is considerable evidence supporting the use of brief motivational interventions (BMIs) that deliver multicomponent personalized feedback using motivational interviewing techniques (MI; Miller & Rollnick, 2012) designed to garner intrinsic motivation and elicit behavior change (Cronce & Larimer, 2011). Other similar approaches rooted in MI include brief advice and a brief negotiated interview (Fedorchak & Cimini, 2018). Finally, delivery of the feedback alone (i.e., a PFI) or portions of the feedback focused solely on correcting normative misperceptions is also effective. These approaches go hand in hand with the HR model because they grant clients autonomy in their change process.

Alcohol-Specific Interventions

The Brief Alcohol Screening and Intervention for College Students (BASICS) program is a manualized BMI targeting high-risk college drinkers (Dimeff, Baer, Kivlahan, & Marlatt, 1999). BASICS has demonstrated success in reducing drinking and alcohol-related consequences up to 4 years later (Baer, Kivlahan, Blume, McKnight, & Marlatt, 2001). As developed, BASICS includes an assessment session and a personalized feedback session delivered using MI with 2 weeks of self-monitoring of alcohol use between sessions. More recently, BMIs patterned after BASICS have conducted the assessment online, reducing face-to-face student engagement to a single session, which can be quite brief. Kulesza, Apperson, Larimer, and Copeland (2010) found that a 10-minute BMI patterned after BASICS was equally efficacious as a 50-minute version of the BMI. However, such interventions do require personnel to be trained in MI and tend to be less effective when delivered in a group format; thus, implementing BMIs may be challenging for some campuses. PFIs that deliver the same feedback as used in BASICS, without the benefit of an MI-trained facilitator, are sound alternatives. Many commercial programs exist, though campuses can create their own programs relying on extant examples (e.g., Martens, Kilmer, Beck, & Zamboanga, 2010). Because information on these programs is constantly changing, interested readers are referred to the College Alcohol Intervention Matrix (CollegeAIM; see Cronce et al., 2018).

Brief advice has been used with college students, largely within medical settings (Walters & Baer, 2006). Evidence suggests it may be as effective as formal motivational interventions (Soderstrom et al., 2007) and leads to greater reductions in alcohol use and other related outcomes among college students and young adults (Fleming et al., 2010; Grossberg, Brown, & Fleming, 2004). Five key components of brief advice interventions include a summary of the individual's drinking, a discussion of the pros and cons, a discussion of life goals, encouraging an agreement to reduce risk, and self-monitoring of alcohol use (Grossberg et al., 2010). Such interventions can be augmented through real-time behavioral supports that use technologies (e.g., text messaging) that are more palatable to young adults than in-person meetings. Such interventions have shown promise (Suffoletto et al., 2014).

Drug-Specific Interventions

As with screening instruments, formal brief interventions targeting the use of drugs (other than alcohol) among college students are lacking. As noted earlier, the ASSIST has been used as the basis for PFIs among college students (Kypri et al., 2008, 2009). Denering and Spear (2012) also examined the effectiveness of an ASSIST-linked BMI in a university counseling center and found modest effects. The manualized intervention can be delivered within 3 to 15 minutes. Other brief interventions specifically targeting high-risk cannabis use have shown some success in college settings, including one BMI patterned after BASICS, which demonstrated short-term efficacy in reducing quantity consumed (Lee et al., 2013).

In the absence of a specific evidence-based protocol, we recommend drawing on the principles highlighted in most of the aforementioned brief interventions, namely, maintaining an HR focus, using MI techniques, recommending self-monitoring of use, and helping the student to develop a personalized risk-reduction plan. To the extent possible, challenging normative misperceptions of use (when students' perceived norms exceed actual norms) is also advisable.

An Integrative Approach

College students often do not see the same campus health provider consistently, and many may continue to see a family physician at home and/or seek services in the surrounding community. The changing landscape of parental involvement and insurance instability can add further complexity. Attending to these issues and prioritizing collaboration across health care providers will ensure effectual intervention delivery. Whenever possible, collaboration in SBIRT training is an optimal starting place. Providers who are experienced in SBIRT and able to offer training will benefit their colleagues, clients, and the broader community by eliminating this initial barrier to implementation; alternatively, resources might be pooled within or across institutions to enlist outside SBIRT training.

Regular communication between providers within and—to the extent possible, within the confines of client privacy—across agencies, is also key to implementation. Providers should document screening and intervention occurrence, outcome, and referral, and they should monitor these processes to avoid missteps and promote continuity of care. Repeated screening, for example, can detect behavior changes over time (and account for variability in patterns of use), but a student who is seeing three different providers is unlikely to benefit from three screenings and interventions in immediate succession. When referring to specialized addiction treatment, early and proactive collaboration becomes especially vital to ensure that the student can access and engage with the needed care.

REFERRAL TO TREATMENT

Referral to treatment (RT), the final component of the SBIRT process, ordinarily receives the least attention. Because screening and brief intervention outcomes look different for every individual and because the contexts and resources surrounding a referral vary, RT can be difficult to discuss in an explicit manner. Yet this step plays a pivotal role in determining health outcomes and long-term success of SBIRT, especially for the individuals at greatest risk. What follows is an attempt to navigate the RT component, including why and how to refer and ways in which specialized treatment interacts with the traditional college environment.

Causes for Referral

The setting in which screening and brief intervention occurs, including the expertise and resources available within, will importantly govern when a student must receive a referral. For example, a practitioner in a student health center that uses only a three-item screener and brief advice intervention may refer out at a lower level of severity than a campus mental health facility staffed by addiction specialists and equipped to offer multisession, in-depth interventions. Each facility should assess what level of care they can competently provide within the SBIRT framework and establish a referral system for any student beyond that level (Fedorchak & Cimini, 2018). These differences notwithstanding, some causes for referral are common across divergent settings.

When screened, many college students demonstrate low-to-moderate substance use–related risk, in which case a brief intervention is usually sufficient. Some students, however, evidence high risk, including meeting diagnostic criteria for a disorder. High risk represents the most common cause for referral. For example, it is typically recommended to refer out when a student scores over 20 on the AUDIT or when a professional believes a disorder may exist (Babor, Higgins-Biddle, Saunders, & Monteiro, 2001). Caution should be used, however, as up to 50% of college students who drink could be diagnosed with AUD using *DSM–5* criteria (Hagman & Cohn, 2011). Most of these individuals may only meet criteria because they endorsed drinking more than intended and are experiencing tolerance, thus meeting criteria for mild severity AUD (Rinker & Neighbors, 2015). These students would be well-suited to a BMI, and premature RT may lead to psychological reactance, based on a mismatch between the student's experience of problems and their perceived need for assistance (Wu, Pilowsky, Schlenger, & Hasin, 2007). Additional circumstances calling for referral represent more urgent concerns (e.g., the existence of an immediate risk to safety, severe concurrent mental health condition such as psychosis), and an intervention focused on substance use may have to be deferred or subsumed within other treatment.

Strategies and Options for Referral

A sensible first step in creating a referral system is establishing partnerships with local treatment agencies. Depending on the situation, a student might benefit from inpatient, outpatient, mental health–focused or substance use–focused treatment, and disparate treatment models. Identifying a variety of agencies and providers on and around campus will ensure that referrals can be individualized to maximize the chance of finding a good fit for each student. After agency partnerships have been established, a referral process should be standardized, including criteria for selecting one referral option over another.

A misconception is that the RT process stops after an appropriate referral has been made. In reality, successful RT is an ongoing process that involves following up with students to make sure they are receiving the help they need, often through a "warm hand-off" between clinicians to increase the likelihood of follow-through. One investigation of off-campus referrals by a university counseling center found that 42% of students receiving a referral were unsuccessful in connecting with the outside provider (Owen, Devdas, & Rodolfa, 2007), highlighting the need for follow-up. As part of routine practice, providers check in with students to determine whether a referral was successful and, if not, explore alternative options.

Recovery on Campus

Developing a thorough RT system is important, but it is similarly important to acknowledge that college students will not always accept a referral. Abstinence-based treatment programs like Alcoholics Anonymous (AA) may present a developmental and motivational mismatch with college populations. Indeed, Buscemi and colleagues (2010) found that less than 3% of students indicated that they would attend an AA meeting. College students reported a preference for informal help seeking (e.g., talking with friends and family) over formal resources. In response to the unique college environment and the need for treatment options in which students will actually engage, collegiate recovery programs (CRPs) have emerged.

CRPs are campus-based, peer-driven support programs that typically involve substance-free student housing, ongoing support meetings, and counseling resources offered by a small group of staff. Students may find CRPs a better fit than outside support groups, which tend to be geared toward adults who are experiencing different obstacles and stages of recovery and more strictly adhere to an abstinence-only model. CRPs offer a promising model for preventing relapse and achieving academic success in an environment where alcohol and other drug use are prevalent, and substance-free support networks are often lacking (Laudet, Harris, Kimball, Winters, & Moberg, 2016). Institutions interested in developing CRPs may benefit from collaborations with other educational institutions who have already created CRPs and from an open dialogue with student representatives or student groups on their campuses (Laudet et al., 2016).

VENUES FOR SBIRT WITH COLLEGE STUDENTS

Student contact with teaching faculty, academic advisors, and resident advisors can be initiated for reasons completely unrelated to substance use (which is most common; Walters & Baer, 2006) or in direct response to the violation of a campus substance use policy. Thus, training in MI for this personnel can be beneficial (Tollison et al., 2008). Depending on the individual's job duties, implementing an impromptu screening and delivering a brief intervention (if needed) may be appropriate. Interventions that have been found to be effective with students who are mandated to receive an alcohol intervention are detailed in the CollegeAIM (Cronce et al., 2018). However, for many personnel, engaging in SBIRT directly could create problematic multiple-role relationships, so these individuals (e.g., faculty) should be trained on how to provide a supportive referral to the appropriate person or center for screening and possible intervention. Such venues include college health centers, counseling centers, or—if the situation is urgent—emergency departments.

College Health Centers

Because students who are seen at college health centers might be more likely to have experienced substance use consequences, SBIRT in this venue is likely to be particularly effective. Screening for substance use can be easily added to existing batteries administered at routine care appointments. Despite this, in many cases, unhealthy or risky substance use goes unrecognized (Fedorchak & Cimini, 2018). Health center care providers often avoid asking questions about substance use, or if they do, they fail to use evidence-based techniques such as MI to intervene. Training health care staff to use evidence-based SBIRT techniques with confidence could be an important step in improving implementation (Fedorchak & Cimini, 2018).

College Counseling Centers

Providers in college counseling centers are ideally suited to implement SBIRT. First, college counselors have typically received training in the use of MI and related micro-skills. Moreover, the format of individual therapy lends itself to both brief and longer forms of intervention. College counselors can assess for substance use, provide feedback to students about their use, provide psychoeducation that supports skill building (e.g., use of protective behavioral strategies), and challenge unhelpful substance-related beliefs, all using an MI approach (Larimer, Cronce, Lee, & Kilmer, 2004). College counseling centers also typically offer both individual and group intervention formats and, therefore, may reach a large number of students.

Emergency Departments

Emergency department (ED) personnel are likely to encounter college students who are being seen for overdoses or injuries caused by substance use. Approximately 10.5% of college students between the ages of 18 and 25 are injured each year under the influence of alcohol (Hingson, Zha, & Weitzman, 2009), and data suggest acute alcohol-related ED visits are increasing annually at a rate that far surpasses population-level changes in alcohol consumption (e.g., 51.5% vs. < 2%, respectively; White, Slater, Ng, Hingson, & Breslow, 2018). For these reasons, EDs are a promising venue for SBIRT for college students (Bernstein, Bernstein, Stein, & Saitz, 2009). The practitioners who will most likely be using SBIRT in the ED setting include medical doctors, physicians' assistants, nurse practitioners, and nurses, though trauma centers often employ psychiatrists and psychologists who can conduct brief bedside interventions.

CONCLUSION

Several challenges exist with respect to implementing SBIRT among college students. For example, students may not pay attention to their level of consumption, leading to false negatives on screening assessments (Presley, Meilman, & Leichliter, 2002). As noted earlier, students' patterns of drinking are highly variable, thus a screening of past-month drinking completed in December (encompassing final exams) may look dramatically different than one completed in April (encompassing spring break). Moreover, knowing the total number of drinks a student consumed on their peak drinking occasion tells one little about the period over which that drinking occurred, which can have significant implications for the harms that would likely be experienced (e.g., five drinks over 2 hours is very different from five drinks over 7 hours). Similarly, when only the frequency of drug use can be assessed, it may obscure the true risk of harm. For example, the legalization of recreational use of cannabis in some states has led to increases in average potency and greater availability of high-potency concentrates, the use of which has been associated with acute psychosis (Carlini, Garrett, & Harwick, 2017). Thus, the impact of smoking dried cannabis buds or flowers may be very different than using edibles or dabbing, even if the reported frequency of use is the same. Currently available screening measures do not assess this.

Also, as noted earlier, students rarely perceive their substance use as concerning or in need of formal assistance (Wu et al., 2007). This can hinder participation in brief interventions and derail engagement in treatment referrals. Moreover, few studies have assessed the effects of SBIRT for young adults with marginalized identities, including sexual and gender minority students who may experience elevated levels of high-risk substance use and associated disorders as sequelae of minority stress (Hatzenbuehler, 2009; Hendricks & Testa, 2012). Systematic evaluation of screening accuracy and brief intervention efficacy with students with marginalized identities is needed, given that methods that work for one group cannot always be generalized or may be iatrogenic to others.

Despite these challenges, university settings create opportunities for reaching a large segment (i.e., approximately 70%) of the young adult population (National Center for Education Statistics, n.d.). Interventions to reduce or prevent substance use among college students may promote long-term well-being in addition to reducing immediate harm (Perkins, 2002). In particular, substance use is associated with college attrition (Martinez, Sher, & Wood, 2008), and dropping out of college can have profound impacts on individuals' economic prospects (Carnevale, Rose, & Cheah, 2013).

From a broader perspective, screening instruments and brief interventions may be more easily developed and evaluated using college students as participants and then adapted for use with other populations because students are accustomed to participation in research and in need of substance use prevention and intervention services. For example, many brief interventions administered via employee assistance programs draw on principles and practices that were first developed among college students (e.g., Broome & Bennett, 2011; Walters & Woodall, 2003). Thus, continued exploration of optimizing SBIRT in college populations and university settings may ultimately enhance the implementation of SBIRT for other young adult and adult populations.

Finally, as noted earlier, much research is needed on how to best conduct SBIRT with subpopulations of young adults. In particular, more research into the best approaches for screening and brief intervention for those at risk of elevated substance use and health disparities due to minority stress is warranted. Most of this research is stymied by small sample sizes; however, collaborative partnerships across colleges and universities could be harnessed to complete this important work.

REFERENCES

Adamson, S. J., & Sellman, J. D. (2003). A prototype screening instrument for cannabis use disorder: The Cannabis Use Disorders Identification Test (CUDIT) in an alcohol-dependent clinical sample. *Drug and Alcohol Review, 22*, 309–315. http://dx.doi.org/10.1080/0959523031000154454

American College Health Association. (2018, December 28). *American College Health Association-National College Health Assessment II—Fall 2018 Reference Group Data Report.* Retrieved from https://www.acha.org/documents/ncha/NCHA-II_Fall_2018_Reference_Group_Data_Report.pdf

American Psychiatric Association. (2013). *Diagnostic and statistical manual of mental disorders* (5th ed.). Washington, DC: Author.

Arria, A. M., & DuPont, R. L. (2010). Nonmedical prescription stimulant use among college students: Why we need to do something and what we need to do. *Journal of Addictive Diseases, 29*, 417–426. http://dx.doi.org/10.1080/10550887.2010.509273

Babor, T. F., Higgins-Biddle, J. C., Saunders, J. B., & Monteiro, M. G. (2001). *AUDIT The Alcohol Use Disorders Identification Test: Guidelines for use in primary health* (2nd ed.). Geneva, Switzerland: World Health Organization. Retrieved from https://apps.who.int/iris/handle/10665/67205

Baer, J. S., Kivlahan, D. R., Blume, A. W., McKnight, P., & Marlatt, G. A. (2001). Brief intervention for heavy-drinking college students: 4-year follow-up and natural history. *American Journal of Public Health, 91*, 1310–1316. http://dx.doi.org/10.2105/AJPH.91.8.1310

Berman, A. H., Bergman, H., Palmstierna, T., & Schlyter, F. (2003). *DUDIT manual: The Drug Use Disorders Identification Test, Version 1.0.* Retrieved from https://paihdelinkki.fi/sites/default/files/duditmanual.pdf

Bernstein, E., Bernstein, J. A., Stein, J. B., & Saitz, R. (2009). SBIRT in emergency care settings: Are we ready to take it to scale? *Academic Emergency Medicine, 16*, 1072–1077. http://dx.doi.org/10.1111/j.1553-2712.2009.00549.x

Broome, K. M., & Bennett, J. B. (2011). Reducing heavy alcohol consumption in young restaurant workers. *Journal of Studies on Alcohol and Drugs, 72*, 117–124. http://dx.doi.org/10.15288/jsad.2011.72.117

Buscemi, J., Murphy, J. G., Martens, M. P., McDevitt-Murphy, M. E., Dennhardt, A. A., & Skidmore, J. R. (2010). Help-seeking for alcohol-related problems in college students: Correlates and preferred resources. *Psychology of Addictive Behaviors, 24*, 571–580. http://dx.doi.org/10.1037/a0021122

Bush, K., Kivlahan, D. R., McDonell, M. B., Fihn, S. D., & Bradley, K. A. (1998). The AUDIT alcohol consumption questions (AUDIT–C): An effective brief screening test for problem drinking. *Archives of Internal Medicine, 158*, 1789–1795. http://dx.doi.org/10.1001/archinte.158.16.1789

Carlini, B. H., Garrett, S. B., & Harwick, R. M. (2017). Beyond joints and brownies: Marijuana concentrates in the legal landscape of WA State. *International Journal of Drug Policy, 42*, 26–29. http://dx.doi.org/10.1016/j.drugpo.2017.01.004

Carnevale, A. P., Rose, S. J., & Cheah, B. (2013). *The college payoff: Education, occupations, lifetime earnings*. Retrieved from https://cew.georgetown.edu/cew-reports/the-college-payoff/

Coulton, S., Alam, M. F., Boniface, S., Deluca, P., Donoghue, K., Gilvarry, E., . . . Drummond, C. (2019). Opportunistic screening for alcohol use problems in adolescents attending emergency departments: An evaluation of screening tools. *Journal of Public Health, 41*, e53–e60. http://dx.doi.org/10.1093/pubmed/fdy049

Cranford, J. A., Eisenberg, D., & Serras, A. M. (2009). Substance use behaviors, mental health problems, and use of mental health services in a probability sample of college students. *Addictive Behaviors, 34*, 134–145. http://dx.doi.org/10.1016/j.addbeh.2008.09.004

Cronce, J. M., & Larimer, M. E. (2011). Individual-focused approaches to the prevention of college student drinking. *Alcohol Research & Health, 34*, 210–221.

Cronce, J. M., Toomey, T. L., Lenk, K., Nelson, T. F., Kilmer, J. R., & Larimer, M. E. (2018). NIAAA's College Alcohol Intervention Matrix. *Alcohol Research: Current Reviews, 39*, 43–47.

DeMartini, K. S., & Carey, K. B. (2012). Optimizing the use of the AUDIT for alcohol screening in college students. *Psychological Assessment, 24*, 954–963. http://dx.doi.org/10.1037/a0028519

Denering, L. L., & Spear, S. E. (2012). Routine use of screening and brief intervention for college students in a university counseling center. *Journal of Psychoactive Drugs, 44*, 318–324. http://dx.doi.org/10.1080/02791072.2012.718647

Dimeff, L. A., Baer, J. S., Kivlahan, D. R., & Marlatt, G. A. (1999). *Brief Alcohol Screening and Intervention for College Students (BASICS): A harm reduction approach*. New York, NY: Guilford Press.

Epstein, A. M., Sher, T. G., Young, M. A., & King, A. C. (2007). Tobacco chippers show robust increases in smoking urge after alcohol consumption. *Psychopharmacology, 190*, 321–329. http://dx.doi.org/10.1007/s00213-006-0438-8

Fedorchak, D., & Cimini, M. D. (2018). Implementing screening, brief intervention, and referral to treatment in college student behavioral health settings. In M. D. Cimini & E. M. Rivero (Eds.), *Promoting behavioral health and reducing risk among college students* (pp. 139–148). New York, NY: Routledge. http://dx.doi.org/10.4324/9781315175799-7

Fleming, M. F., Balousek, S. L., Grossberg, P. M., Mundt, M. P., Brown, D., Wiegel, J. R., . . . Saewyc, E. M. (2010). Brief physician advice for heavy drinking college students: A randomized controlled trial in college health clinics. *Journal of Studies on Alcohol and Drugs, 71*, 23–31. http://dx.doi.org/10.15288/jsad.2010.71.23

Grossberg, P. M., Brown, D. D., & Fleming, M. F. (2004). Brief physician advice for high-risk drinking among young adults. *Annals of Family Medicine, 2*, 474–480. http://dx.doi.org/10.1370/afm.122

Grossberg, P., Halperin, A., Mackenzie, S., Gisslow, M., Brown, D., & Fleming, M. (2010). Inside the physician's black bag: Critical ingredients of brief alcohol interventions. *Substance Abuse, 31,* 240–250. http://dx.doi.org/10.1080/08897077. 2010.514242

Hagman, B. T. (2016). Performance of the AUDIT in detecting *DSM–5* alcohol use disorders in college students. *Substance Use & Misuse, 51,* 1521–1528. http://dx.doi.org/10.1080/10826084.2016.1188949

Hagman, B. T., & Cohn, A. M. (2011). Toward *DSM–V*: Mapping the alcohol use disorder continuum in college students. *Drug and Alcohol Dependence, 118,* 202–208. http://dx.doi.org/10.1016/j.drugalcdep.2011.03.021

Hatzenbuehler, M. L. (2009). How does sexual minority stigma "get under the skin"? A psychological mediation framework. *Psychological Bulletin, 135,* 707–730. http://dx.doi.org/10.1037/a0016441

Hendricks, M. L., & Testa, R. J. (2012). A conceptual framework for clinical work with transgender and gender nonconforming clients: An adaptation of the minority stress model. *Professional Psychology: Research and Practice, 43,* 460–467. http://dx.doi.org/10.1037/a0029597

Hingson, R. W., Zha, W., & Weitzman, E. R. (2009). Magnitude of and trends in alcohol-related mortality and morbidity among U.S. college students ages 18–24, 1998–2005. *Journal of Studies on Alcohol and Drugs, s16,* 12–20. http://dx.doi.org/10.15288/jsads.2009.s16.12

Kokotailo, P. K., Egan, J., Gangnon, R., Brown, D., Mundt, M., & Fleming, M. (2004). Validity of the Alcohol Use Disorders Identification Test in college students. *Alcoholism: Clinical and Experimental Research, 28,* 914–920. http://dx.doi.org/10.1097/01.ALC. 0000128239.87611.F5

Kulesza, M., Apperson, M., Larimer, M. E., & Copeland, A. L. (2010). Brief alcohol intervention for college drinkers: How brief is? *Addictive Behaviors, 35,* 730–733. http://dx.doi.org/10.1016/j.addbeh.2010.03.011

Kypri, K., Hallett, J., Howat, P., McManus, A., Maycock, B., Bowe, S., & Horton, N. J. (2009). Randomized controlled trial of proactive web-based alcohol screening and brief intervention for university students. *Archives of Internal Medicine, 169,* 1508–1514. http://dx.doi.org/10.1001/archinternmed.2009.249

Kypri, K., Langley, J. D., Saunders, J. B., Cashell-Smith, M. L., & Herbison, P. (2008). Randomized controlled trial of web-based alcohol screening and brief intervention in primary care. *Archives of Internal Medicine, 168,* 530–536. http://dx.doi.org/10.1001/archinternmed.2007.109

Larimer, M. E., & Cronce, J. M. (2002). Identification, prevention and treatment: A review of individual-focused strategies to reduce problematic alcohol consumption by college students. *Journal of Studies on Alcohol, s14,* 148–163. http://dx.doi.org/10.15288/jsas.2002.s14.148

Larimer, M. E., & Cronce, J. M. (2007). Identification, prevention, and treatment revisited: Individual-focused college drinking prevention strategies 1999–2006. *Addictive Behaviors, 32,* 2439–2468. http://dx.doi.org/10.1016/j.addbeh.2007.05.006

Larimer, M. E., Cronce, J. M., Lee, C. M., & Kilmer, J. R. (2004). Brief intervention in college settings. *Alcohol Research & Health, 28,* 94–104.

Laudet, A. B., Harris, K., Kimball, T., Winters, K. C., & Moberg, D. P. (2016). In college and in recovery: Reasons for joining a Collegiate Recovery Program. *Journal of American College Health, 64,* 238–246. http://dx.doi.org/10.1080/07448481.2015. 1117464

Lee, C. M., Kilmer, J. R., Neighbors, C., Atkins, D. C., Zheng, C., Walker, D. D., & Larimer, M. E. (2013). Indicated prevention for college student marijuana use: A randomized controlled trial. *Journal of Consulting and Clinical Psychology, 81,* 702–709. http://dx.doi.org/10.1037/a0033285

Lee, C. M., Maggs, J. L., Neighbors, C., & Patrick, M. E. (2011). Positive and negative alcohol-related consequences: Associations with past drinking. *Journal of Adolescence, 34*, 87–94. http://dx.doi.org/10.1016/j.adolescence.2010.01.009

Leichliter, J. S., Meilman, P. W., Presley, C. A., & Cashin, J. R. (1998). Alcohol use and related consequences among students with varying levels of involvement in college athletics. *Journal of American College Health, 46*, 257–262. http://dx.doi.org/10.1080/07448489809596001

Mallett, K. A., Bachrach, R. L., & Turrisi, R. (2008). Are all negative consequences truly negative? Assessing variations among college students' perceptions of alcohol related consequences. *Addictive Behaviors, 33*, 1375–1381. http://dx.doi.org/10.1016/j.addbeh.2008.06.014

Martens, M. P., Kilmer, J. R., Beck, N. C., & Zamboanga, B. L. (2010). The efficacy of a targeted personalized drinking feedback intervention among intercollegiate athletes: A randomized controlled trial. *Psychology of Addictive Behaviors, 24*, 660–669. http://dx.doi.org/10.1037/a0020299

Martinez, J. A., Sher, K. J., & Wood, P. K. (2008). Is heavy drinking really associated with attrition from college? The alcohol–attrition paradox. *Psychology of Addictive Behaviors, 22*, 450–456. http://dx.doi.org/10.1037/0893-164X.22.3.450

McCabe, S. E. (2008). Screening for drug abuse among medical and nonmedical users of prescription drugs in a probability sample of college students. *Archives of Pediatrics & Adolescent Medicine, 162*, 225–231. http://dx.doi.org/10.1001/archpediatrics.2007.41

McCabe, S. E., Knight, J. R., Teter, C. J., & Wechsler, H. (2005). Non-medical use of prescription stimulants among US college students: Prevalence and correlates from a national survey. *Addiction, 100*, 96–106. http://dx.doi.org/10.1111/j.1360-0443.2005.00944.x

Miller, W. R., & Rollnick, S. (2012). *Motivational interviewing: Helping people change.* New York, NY: Guilford Press.

National Center for Education Statistics. (n.d.). *Back to school statistics.* Retrieved from https://nces.ed.gov/fastfacts/display.asp?id=372

National Center for Education Statistics. (2017). *Total fall enrollment in degree-granting post-secondary institutions, by attendance status, sex, and age: Selected years, 1970 through 2026.* Retrieved from https://nces.ed.gov/programs/digest/d16/tables/dt16_303.40.asp?current=yes

National Institute on Alcohol Abuse and Alcoholism. (2003). *Recommended alcohol questions.* Retrieved from https://www.niaaa.nih.gov/research/guidelines-and-resources/recommended-alcohol-questions

National Institute on Drug Abuse. (2018). *Screening tools and prevention.* Retrieved from https://www.drugabuse.gov/nidamed-medical-health-professionals/tool-resources-your-practice/additional-screening-resources

Neal, D. J., & Fromme, K. (2007). Hook 'em horns and heavy drinking: Alcohol use and collegiate sports. *Addictive Behaviors, 32*, 2681–2693. http://dx.doi.org/10.1016/j.addbeh.2007.06.020

Neighbors, C., Atkins, D. C., Lewis, M. A., Lee, C. M., Kaysen, D., Mittmann, A., . . . Rodriguez, L. M. (2011). Event-specific drinking among college students. *Psychology of Addictive Behaviors, 25*, 702–707. http://dx.doi.org/10.1037/a0024051

Neighbors, C., Larimer, M. E., Lostutter, T. W., & Woods, B. A. (2006). Harm reduction and individually focused alcohol prevention. *International Journal of Drug Policy, 17*, 304–309. http://dx.doi.org/10.1016/j.drugpo.2006.05.004

Osberg, T. M., Billingsley, K., Eggert, M., & Insana, M. (2012). From *Animal House* to *Old School*: A multiple mediation analysis of the association between college drinking movie exposure and freshman drinking and its consequences. *Addictive Behaviors, 37*, 922–930. http://dx.doi.org/10.1016/j.addbeh.2012.03.030

Owen, J., Devdas, L., & Rodolfa, E. (2007). University counseling center off-campus referrals: An exploratory investigation. *Journal of College Student Psychotherapy, 22,* 13–29. http://dx.doi.org/10.1300/J035v22n02_03

Perkins, H. W. (2002). Surveying the damage: A review of research on consequences of alcohol misuse in college populations. *Journal of Studies on Alcohol, s14,* 91–100. http://dx.doi.org/10.15288/jsas.2002.s14.91

Presley, C. A., Meilman, P. W., & Leichliter, J. S. (2002). College factors that influence drinking. *Journal of Studies on Alcohol, s14,* 82–90. http://dx.doi.org/10.15288/jsas.2002.s14.82

Read, J. P., Beattie, M., Chamberlain, R., & Merrill, J. E. (2008). Beyond the "binge" threshold: Heavy drinking patterns and their association with alcohol involvement indices in college students. *Addictive Behaviors, 33,* 225–234. http://dx.doi.org/10.1016/j.addbeh.2007.09.001

Rinker, D. V., & Neighbors, C. (2015). Latent class analysis of *DSM–5* alcohol use disorder criteria among heavy-drinking college students. *Journal of Substance Abuse Treatment, 57,* 81–88. http://dx.doi.org/10.1016/j.jsat.2015.05.006

Saitz, R. (2007). Screening and brief intervention enter their 5th decade. *Substance Abuse, 28*(3), 3–6. http://dx.doi.org/10.1300/J465v28n03_02

Saunders, J. B., & Aasland, O. G. (1987). *WHO collaborative project on the identification and treatment of persons with harmful alcohol consumption. Report on phase I: The development of a screening instrument.* Retrieved from https://apps.who.int/iris/handle/10665/62031

Schulenberg, J. E., Johnston, L. D., O'Malley, P. M., Bachman, J. G., Miech, R. A., & Patrick, M. E. (2018). *Monitoring the future: National survey results on drug use, 1975–2017. Volume II. College students and adults ages 19–55.* Retrieved from http://monitoringthefuture.org/pubs/monographs/mtf-vol2_2017.pdf

Scott-Sheldon, L. A., Carey, K. B., & Carey, M. P. (2008). Health behavior and college students: Does Greek affiliation matter? *Journal of Behavioral Medicine, 31,* 61–70. http://dx.doi.org/10.1007/s10865-007-9136-1

Soderstrom, C. A., DiClemente, C. C., Dischinger, P. C., Hebel, J. R., McDuff, D. R., Auman, K. M., & Kufera, J. A. (2007). A controlled trial of brief intervention versus brief advice for at-risk drinking trauma center patients. *The Journal of Trauma, 62,* 1102–1112. http://dx.doi.org/10.1097/TA.0b013e31804bdb26

Substance Abuse and Mental Health Services Administration. (2018). *Key substance use and mental health indicators in the United States: Results from the 2017 National Survey on Drug Use and Health* (HHS Publication No. SMA 18-5068, NSDUH Series H-53). Retrieved from https://www.samhsa.gov/data/sites/default/files/cbhsq-reports/NSDUHFFR2017/NSDUHFFR2017.htm

Suffoletto, B., Kristan, J., Callaway, C., Kim, K. H., Chung, T., Monti, P. M., & Clark, D. B. (2014). A text message alcohol intervention for young adult emergency department patients: A randomized clinical trial. *Annals of Emergency Medicine, 64,* 664–72.e4. http://dx.doi.org/10.1016/j.annemergmed.2014.06.010

Tollison, S. J., Lee, C. M., Neighbors, C., Neil, T. A., Olson, N. D., & Larimer, M. E. (2008). Questions and reflections: The use of motivational interviewing microskills in a peer-led brief alcohol intervention for college students. *Behavior Therapy, 39,* 183–194. http://dx.doi.org/10.1016/j.beth.2007.07.001

Walters, S. T., & Baer, J. S. (2006). *Talking with college students about alcohol: Motivational strategies for reducing abuse.* New York, NY: Guilford Press.

Walters, S. T., & Woodall, W. G. (2003). Mailed feedback reduces consumption among moderate drinkers who are employed. *Prevention Science, 4,* 287–294. http://dx.doi.org/10.1023/A:1026024400450

Weitzman, E. R. (2004). Poor mental health, depression, and associations with alcohol consumption, harm, and abuse in a national sample of young adults in college. *Journal of Nervous and Mental Disease, 192,* 269–277. http://dx.doi.org/10.1097/01.nmd.0000120885.17362.94

White, A. M., Kraus, C. L., & Swartzwelder, H. (2006). Many college freshmen drink at levels far beyond the binge threshold. *Alcoholism: Clinical and Experimental Research, 30*, 1006–1010. http://dx.doi.org/10.1111/j.1530-0277.2006.00122.x

White, A. M., Slater, M. E., Ng, G., Hingson, R., & Breslow, R. (2018). Trends in alcohol-related emergency department visits in the United States: Results from the Nationwide Emergency Department Sample, 2006 to 2014. *Alcoholism, Clinical and Experimental Research, 42*, 352–359. http://dx.doi.org/10.1111/acer.13559

WHO ASSIST Working Group. (2002). The Alcohol, Smoking and Substance Involvement Screening Test (ASSIST): Development, reliability and feasibility. *Addiction, 97*, 1183–1194. http://dx.doi.org/10.1046/j.1360-0443.2002.00185.x

World Health Organization. (2016). *International classification of diseases* (ver. 10). Retrieved from https://www.who.int/classifications/icd/icdonlineversions/en/

Wu, L. T., Pilowsky, D. J., Schlenger, W. E., & Hasin, D. (2007). Alcohol use disorders and the use of treatment services among college-age young adults. *Psychiatric Services, 58*, 192–200. http://dx.doi.org/10.1176/ps.2007.58.2.192

Zamboanga, B. L., Schwartz, S. J., Ham, L. S., Borsari, B., & Van Tyne, K. (2010). Alcohol expectancies, pregaming, drinking games, and hazardous alcohol use in a multiethnic sample of college students. *Cognitive Therapy and Research, 34*, 124–133. http://dx.doi.org/10.1007/s10608-009-9234-1

8

Screening, Brief Intervention, and Referral to Treatment With Adolescents

Strategies, Opportunities, and Challenges

Miriam A. Schizer, Sharon Levy, and Elissa R. Weitzman

Adolescent substance use is a significant public health problem associated with substantial morbidity and mortality. As more is understood about the nuances of adolescent brain development, a clear picture has emerged of adolescents' unique vulnerabilities to substance use and attendant disorders. Young persons who initiate substance use early in life are more likely to experience serious use–related consequences than are those who initiate use later in life (Hingson & Zha, 2009). However, screening and intervention can ameliorate harms. In a 2016 policy statement, the American Academy of Pediatrics issued a mandate for universal screening for substance use by adolescents, given the potential to make a positive impact with an intrinsically simple intervention (Levy & Williams, 2016).

This chapter begins with a review of the current understanding of adolescent brain development and its complex links to substance use initiation and progression. The epidemiology of adolescent substance use and co-occurring mental health disorders is also reviewed, with special attention given to recent trends in the use of various substances favored by adolescents. The remainder of the chapter focuses on the intricacies of screening, brief intervention, and referral to treatment (SBIRT) in adolescents, highlighting various validated screening tools and general guidelines for effective brief interventions. Treatment options of varying intensities for adolescents who screen positive for substance use are also considered. Finally, the chapter provides an update regarding the current status of adolescent SBIRT in general medical and school-based settings.

http://dx.doi.org/10.1037/0000199-009
Screening, Brief Intervention, and Referral to Treatment for Substance Use: A Practitioner's Guide,
M. D. Cimini and J. L. Martin (Editors)

ADOLESCENT BRAIN DEVELOPMENT

Adolescence is a key period for both initiating substance use and developing substance use disorders. The nucleus accumbens, often referred to as the brain's "reward center," matures rapidly during the school-age years and into early adolescence (Arain et al., 2013). This maturation is important for the progression of goal-directed behavior that is associated with this developmental stage as children begin to discriminate consequential from insignificant rewards (Galvan, 2010). Maturation of the prefrontal cortex, the region of the brain associated with executive functions such as self-monitoring, error correction, and impulse control, lags behind and is not complete until the middle of the third decade of life (Arain et al., 2013).

During adolescence, the drive toward large neurological reward is relatively unrestrained, resulting in the teenage propensity for engaging in extreme and exciting behaviors. Psychoactive substance use delivers large neurological rewards by increasing dopamine release in the nucleus accumbens, thus "hijacking" the neurological reward system. Thus, substance use effectively satisfies the adolescent developmental drive for large neurological reward. The peak ages of substance use initiation occur during adolescence and early adulthood and fall dramatically by the mid-20s when brain development is complete (Lipari, Kroutil, & Pemberton, 2015).

Addiction is a medical disorder that results from neurological changes in the nucleus accumbens (Volkow, Koob, & McLellan, 2016). The prefrontal cortex appears to play a role in protecting the brain from developing these changes. Thus, immaturity of the prefrontal cortex places adolescents at increased risk of developing the neurological changes associated with the clinical disorder of addiction. Indeed, the risk of developing a substance use disorder is inversely correlated with age of initiation regardless of the choice of substance; children who experience alcohol intoxication (Hingson & Zha, 2009), marijuana use (Le Strat, Dubertret, & Le Foll, 2015), or nonmedical use of opioids (McCabe, West, Morales, Cranford, & Boyd, 2007) during early adolescence are 3 to 5 times more likely to develop a substance use disorder compared with individuals who initiate in early adulthood.

EPIDEMIOLOGY AND CO-OCCURRING DISORDERS

Alcohol is the substance most widely used by adolescents in the United States—nearly two thirds (62%) of teenagers report annual use, and nearly one quarter (23%) report annual use by eighth grade. Intoxication is common and increases markedly once youth enter high school. In 2017, 9% of eighth-grade youth reported having been drunk at least once in their lives, whereas 45% of 12th-grade students report this (Miech et al., 2018).

The prevalence of any alcohol use among adolescents has declined over the past 2-plus decades (Esser, Clayton, Demissie, Kanny, & Brewer, 2017), as has the prevalence of drinking at a binge level (i.e., ≥ 5 per occasion in the past 2 weeks). However, binge drinking remains high, with more than one out of five high school students reporting binge drinking (Esser et al., 2017). Furthermore, high-intensity alcohol use (i.e., ≥ 10 drinks per occasion in the past 2 weeks) is increasingly common. In 2011, high-intensity use was reported by 10.5% of 12th-grade youth surveyed in the national Monitoring the Future study (Patrick et al., 2013). Among high school youth surveyed in the national Youth Risk Behavior Survey in 2015, a majority (57.8%) of those who reported drinking alcohol in the past 30 days reported doing so at a binge level, with nearly half (43.8%) reporting they consumed in excess of eight drinks on at least one occasion in that time (Esser et al., 2017). Drinking patterns vary by race, ethnicity, and gender—overall, being non-Hispanic White or Hispanic (compared with non-Hispanic Black) and male and having college-educated parents are risk factors for current and binge alcohol use among adolescents, as is rural compared with urban residence (Patrick et al., 2013).

The prevalence of any illicit drug use among adolescents is substantial and rises precipitously over the high school years. Nationally, 23%, 37%, and 50% of eighth, 10th, and 12th graders, respectively, report ever using any illicit drug (Miech et al., 2018). In 2017, cannabis was the most common drug used by adolescents after alcohol, with annual (past month) prevalence levels of 10.5% (5.6%), 27.5% (16.7%), and 35.9% (22.2%) for youth in Grades 8, 10, and 12, respectively. Among 12th graders, daily use was reported by 5.9% (Miech et al., 2018). Excluding marijuana and looking across grades nationally in 2017, 14% of high school youth reported ever using cocaine, inhalants, heroin, methamphetamines, hallucinogens, or ecstasy (Centers for Disease Control and Prevention [CDC], 2018).

Tobacco use has declined from the peak levels of the mid-1990s. As of 2017, lifetime use of cigarettes ranged from 9% among eighth-graders to 27% of 12th-graders (Johnston et al., 2018). Adolescents' risks for using cigarettes and cannabis have reversed in rank over the past decades. In 1997, among 12th-graders, the prevalence levels of past-month cigarette and marijuana use were 36.5% and 23.7%, respectively, compared with 9.7% and 22.9% in 2017 (Johnston et al., 2018).

Along with changes in use, the mode of administration of these substances is changing. Currently, large percentages of youth are using commercially available battery-powered electronic cigarettes to inhale vapors (i.e., "vaping") of these substances. More than one sixth (16.6%) of 12th-grade youth reported past-month vaping of any substance in 2017, and the level of use of nicotine vapes in 2018 approximately doubled from 2017 levels (Miech et al., 2018), with increases observed among youth in the eighth and 10th grade, too (Miech et al., 2018). It is unclear whether the promotion and availability of e-cigarette devices will reverse the downward trends in cigarette and nicotine use of the past decades and further drive uptake of cannabis use by youth.

Nonmedical use of prescription medications represents a serious concern for youth and young adults. Rates of misuse of prescription medications peak during adolescence (McCabe, Kloska, Veliz, Jager, & Schulenberg, 2016). In 2017, lifetime misuse of prescription opioids was reported by 14% of adolescents (CDC, 2018). It is estimated that one third of youth continue this behavior into young adulthood. (McCabe, Schulenberg, O'Malley, Patrick, & Kloska, 2014).

Other substance use is trending downward overall. However, among recent national studies, nontrivial minorities of youth report lifetime use of a range of substances, including inhalants, which are favored by younger youth; amphetamines, favored by older youth; tranquilizers and nonheroin narcotics; semisynthetic narcotics such as OxyContin (oxycodone) and Vicodin (hydrocodone and acetaminophen); hallucinogens; and other substances. Lifetime prevalence of the aforementioned substances ranges between 1% and 8% of older youth, depending on the substance (Johnston et al., 2018). Moreover, using multiple substances, or polysubstance use, is common among youth, with the most common pattern being simultaneous use of alcohol and marijuana, reported by 20% of high school seniors (Patrick, Veliz, & Terry-McElrath, 2017). High-intensity alcohol use and daily use of marijuana both predict heightened risk of simultaneous use of alcohol and marijuana, whereas high-intensity alcohol use predicts nonmedical use of prescription drugs (McCabe, Veliz, & Patrick, 2017).

Several data sources, the findings of which are freely available, provide information about patterns of substance use among adolescents that are especially helpful for monitoring shifting trends. These include the Monitoring the Future survey (supported by the National Institute on Drug Abuse), the National Survey on Drug Use and Health (supported by the Substance Abuse and Mental Health Services Administration [SAMHSA]), and the Youth Risk Behavior Surveillance System (supported by the Centers for Disease Control and Prevention [CDC]). These surveys provide estimates of the prevalence of alcohol and other substance use behaviors among school-based and house-hold samples using a range of measures and methods (CDC, 2014; Monitoring the Future, n.d.; National Survey on Drug Use and Health, 2018). In-depth national surveys of alcohol use have also been conducted to characterize prevalence, comorbidities, and treatment patterns for persons who use alcohol and have alcohol use disorders (Grant et al., 2015, 2017). Robust SBIRT programs that use thoughtful screening tools should be able to discern patient-level substance use behaviors for clinical response. Awareness of ambient patterns of substance use and shifting trends may also help inform clinical awareness.

CO-OCCURRING SUBSTANCE USE AND
MENTAL HEALTH DISORDERS AMONG ADOLESCENTS

Substance use is common among youth with a mental health problem. Youth who experience both sets of problems are often referred to as having a "dual-disorder" or "co-occurring problems." From a life-course perspective, adolescence and young adulthood are periods of peak prevalence of substance use; these periods are often when use escalates or intensifies into disorders. Older adolescence/young adulthood is also a period of peak onset for many mental health problems.

Among adolescents and young adults diagnosed with either a mental illness or substance use disorder, there are high percentages diagnosed with the other condition: Among adolescents with a past year substance use disorder, 29.1% had a past year major depressive episode; whereas among adolescents with a past year major depressive episode, 11.6% had a past year substance use disorder. In parallel, the percentage of young adults with any mental illness in the past year who have a substance use disorder is 38.7%; whereas 27.2% of young adults ages 18 to 25 years with any mental illness in the past year have a co-occurring substance use disorder (Center for Behavioral Health Statistics and Quality, 2016).

These patterns are suggestive of several influential mechanisms, including underlying within-person vulnerabilities that are associated with both outcomes (i.e., poor coping abilities), interdependencies related to timing or course of conditions (i.e., the experience of mental illness as a consequence of substance use, or substance use to alleviate symptoms of mental illness), and exposure to environmental triggers that may influence risk of mental health and substance use concerns (i.e., each problem may be influenced by stress or trauma). The scientific literature on these topics is advancing with the benefit of national surveys (Kessler et al., 2009; Merikangas, Avenevoli, Costello, Koretz, & Kessler, 2009), and researchers are using tools of genetic and psychiatric epidemiology, psychology, and sociology to understand dual vulnerabilities and disorder patterns. Regardless of the causal mechanisms underlying dual disorders, they require comprehensive evaluation for clinicians to tailor a response appropriately. Treatment for mental health and substance use concerns among youth with co-occurring problems is rare. In 2015, only 3.8% and 5.4% of dually disordered adolescents and young adults, respectively, received services for both problems (Center for Behavioral Health Statistics and Quality, 2016).

SBIRT WITH ADOLESCENTS: CORE PRINCIPLES

SBIRT is a key strategy developed to identify and respond to substance use problems and disorders. Initially developed for use in medical settings to reduce "risky" drinking in adults seeking medical care, there has been substantial investment in recent years to increase its scope and broaden its purview. Adolescent SBIRT appears to be gaining traction in clinical settings (Levy et al., 2017) and, more recently, has been expanded broadly in school and other settings (Mitchell, Gryczynski, Gonzales, et al., 2012).

Screening

Screening to identify substance use creates an opportunity for health care professionals to bring up the topic and focus subsequent counseling

(Lunstead et al., 2019). Asking the right questions to identify substance use risk and the likelihood of substance use disorders is important for guiding interventions. Using general impressions, a strategy that typically relies on the recognition of advanced symptoms of substance use disorders, has poor sensitivity for identifying regular use, early problems, and even a mild disorder (Hassan et al., 2009; Wilson, Sherritt, Gates, & Knight, 2004). Recommended adolescent SBIRT models encourage the use of validated screening tools that can accurately identify an adolescent's substance use experience, from *none* to *severe substance use disorder* to tailor guidance rather than simply categorizing a substance use disorder as present or absent (Massachusetts Department of Public Health Bureau of Substance Abuse Services, 2009). This strategy emphasizes the benefit of preventing, delaying, or modifying the trajectory of substance use during adolescence.

The ideal screening tool is quick and easy to administer and interpret and accurately identifies regular substance use and substance use disorders. Several screening tools have been validated for use with adolescents; these tools fall into two broad categories. Problem-based screens categorize adolescents into "low" versus "high" risk of substance use disorder based on the number of problems endorsed, whereas frequency-based screens determine the risk of a substance use disorder based on the reported frequency of use.

The CRAFFT tool is a problem-based screening instrument that has been validated for identifying high-risk substance use in adolescents (Knight, Sherritt, Shrier, Harris, & Chang, 2002; Knight et al., 1999). Although it remains popular, it is insufficient as a stand-alone tool for substance use identification. The questions combine the consequences from the use of multiple substances, which limits information for targeting specific behaviors. Thus, the CRAFFT may be better suited as an assessment guide rather than a screening tool.

Two newer tools, Screening to Brief Intervention (S2BI; Levy et al., 2014) and Brief Screen for Tobacco, Alcohol, and Other Drugs (BSTAD; Kelly et al., 2014), use past-year frequency-of-use questions to identify substance use regularity and assess the risk of a substance use disorder. These brief and efficient tools generate separate substance use disorder risk levels for alcohol, tobacco, and marijuana.

The BSTAD is an open-ended questionnaire that asks three separate questions: "In the past year, have you smoked cigarettes or used other tobacco products/had more than a few sips of beer, wine, or any drink containing alcohol/sniffed or 'huffed' anything; taken illegal drugs like marijuana (weed, blunts), cocaine, etc.; taken prescription medications that were not prescribed for you; or taken prescription or over-the-counter medications and took more than you were supposed to take?" Optimal cutoff points for identifying a substance use disorder were ≥ 6 days of tobacco use (sensitivity = 0.95; specificity = 0.97); ≥ 2 days of alcohol use (sensitivity = 0.96; specificity = 0.85); and ≥ 2 days of marijuana use (sensitivity = 0.80; specificity = 0.93; Kelly et al., 2014).

The S2BI asks, "In the past year, how many times did you use alcohol/ marijuana/tobacco" as three separate questions and provides categorical response items (none, once or twice, monthly, weekly, or more). This tool has high sensitivity and specificity for discriminating between no use, sporadic use, and substance use disorders (Levy et al., 2014). Both S2BI and BSTAD are available in an electronic format through the NIDAMED website (http:// www.drugabuse.gov/nidamed-medical-health-professionals).

Although several tools have been established as sensitive and specific for identifying adolescents with substance use disorders in research trials, results have not directly translated into clinical (Gryczynski et al., 2019) or school-based settings (Chadi, Levy, Wisk, & Weitzman, 2018). Implementation strategies that allow adolescents to self-report substance use, either on paper or electronically, may support more disclosure than interview-administered screens (Levy et al., 2017). Yet, such strategies also pose a number of challenges. For example, screening results must be delivered to the appropriate provider while protecting confidentiality. During health care appointments, asking screening questions appears to trigger counseling. Thus, self-administered screens may reduce the incidence of follow-up conversations if not explicitly built into the infrastructure of health maintenance activities. Implementation strategies that best support effective SBIRT practices have to be further delineated as behavioral health integration progresses.

Substance Use Guidance and Counseling

Because the risk of substance use initiation and escalation increases with age throughout adolescence, general goals of guidance and counseling with this group are to prevent, delay, cease, or reduce use. For individuals that report no use or sporadic use in the past year, adolescent SBIRT guidelines recommend brief advice that emphasizes nonuse as a means for preserving health and maximizing potential. There is evidence that brief advice delivered by health care professionals may delay initiation and promote cessation (Knight et al., 1999), and it is important for the caring adults around them to give teens consistent messages promoting abstinence.

For individuals for whom substance use has become regular, brief interventions are recommended. *Brief intervention* refers to a conversation that explicitly encourages behavior change, such as a reduction or cessation of substance use or reduction of associated risk, such as driving while impaired. For adolescents that have developed substance use disorders and associated problems, brief intervention may be used to encourage engagement in more substantial counseling or other treatment.

Brief Intervention Models for Adolescents

Two brief intervention models have been tested with adolescents: the Brief Negotiated Interview (BNI; Fuster et al., 2016) and the 5 A's (Friedman et al., 2017). Both have shown promise for reducing substance use with this age group. The BNI is a motivational interview–based structured intervention composed of five steps: establishing rapport, raising the subject of substance use, assessing readiness to change, providing feedback, and offering further support. Among a group of youth aged 14 to 21 with heavy marijuana use or marijuana-related problems, those who received a BNI intervention were nearly three times more likely to report abstinence 12 months after the intervention compared with a control group that received usual treatment (E. Bernstein et al., 2009). In a separate study looking at youth aged 14 to 21 screened at a pediatric emergency department, implementing an SBIRT protocol using the BNI led to high rates of referral for both substance use treatment and other health services (J. Bernstein et al., 2017).

The 5 A's model is a structured brief intervention that was initially developed to encourage and support tobacco cessation. Each step begins with a key word that starts with the letter *A*: ask to identify use; advise cessation in a clear, strong, and personalized manner; assess willingness to make a quit attempt; assist by direction to resources to support quitting; and arrange for follow-up shortly after the quit date. In a cluster-randomized trial of high school smokers, those who received the 5 A's intervention were more likely to be abstinent 6 months after the intervention, though the effect was gone by 12 months (Pbert et al., 2008). Likewise, nonsmokers who received a preventive intervention were less likely to initiate tobacco use up to 12 months after the intervention (Pbert et al., 2008).

Referral to Treatment for Adolescents

Referral describes a facilitative process through which adolescents identified as having substance use disorders or associated problems are encouraged and supported to access appropriate treatment services. This activity is composed of two distinct activities: working with the adolescent to accept a referral and be willing to engage in treatment, and facilitating the referral process to connect the teen to appropriate services. There is surprisingly little research on the topic of the referral to treatment portion of SBIRT (Levy et al., 2017; Mitchell, Gryczynski, O'Grady, & Schwartz, 2012; Ozechowski, Becker, & Hogue, 2016). However, existing evidence suggests the referral process is most promising for programs that integrate substance use counselors into primary care settings (Levy, Mountain-Ray, Reynolds, Mendes, & Bromberg, 2018). A study in California found that adolescent primary care patients who received a brief intervention from a behavioral health specialist in primary care were more likely to initiate treatment compared with those who received a brief intervention directly from their primary care provider (Sterling et al., 2017). Another small study found high levels of engagement in substance use treatment in a setting in which an integrated substance use treatment specialist provided services on site (Levy et al., 2018). Innovative service delivery models are worth exploring to surmount common barriers.

Deciding where to refer an adolescent for substance use disorder treatment is complicated by limited treatment availability, insurance coverage complexities, and patient preference. In most cases, health care providers and school staff refer adolescent patients to a mental health specialist to conduct an assessment and then either provide treatment or refer to a program that can deliver the appropriate level of care, ranging from outpatient counseling to long-term residential treatment programs. Co-occurring mental health problems should be assessed and, if present, treated simultaneously. Because mental health problems, such as mood and anxiety disorders, may be a driving factor for substance use for some individuals, exploring mental health concerns may be a key component of brief intervention. Pinpointing mental health problems can serve as a "hook" for making an acceptable referral. For example, it may be more palatable for an adolescent to consider addressing both anxiety and marijuana use or depression and alcohol use than simply addressing cannabis or alcohol use alone.

SBIRT WITH ADOLESCENTS IN THE GENERAL MEDICAL SETTING

In a 2016 policy statement, the American Academy of Pediatrics (AAP) recommended that pediatricians "become familiar with adolescent SBIRT practices and their potential for incorporation into universal screening and comprehensive care of adolescents in the medical home" (Levy & Williams, 2016, p. 1907). Citing the unique longitudinal role pediatricians play in the lives of adolescents, the AAP urged providers to adhere to SBIRT guidelines and increase their capacity to identify and address substance use (Levy & Williams, 2016).

Screening for a variety of conditions and providing relevant anticipatory guidance have long been considered within the purview of the pediatric well-visit. Given the significant morbidity and mortality associated with adolescent substance use and its potential impact on health, it is reasonable to expect SBIRT to be performed at each adolescent annual well-visit in the primary care setting. The consensus is that providers should start screening their young patients for substance use starting the first time the patient is seen without a parent present (Levy & Williams, 2016). Alcohol-based screens have been promoted by the National Institute on Alcohol Abuse and Alcoholism for use with children as young as 9 years old when appropriate.

Because adolescents with more severe substance use disorders might not present for routine well-visits, it is important to screen for substance use in urgent care situations as well, particularly if the visit might be related to underlying substance use. Potential examples include visits for sexually transmitted infections or accidental injuries. Whereas this section focuses on SBIRT in the primary care setting, there is also a growing body of literature supporting the efficacy of performing adolescent SBIRT in the emergency department (Barata et al., 2017; Hawk & D'Onofrio, 2018).

Confidentiality

AAP policy recommends that health care providers explain how information is managed before screening adolescents for substance use in the general medical setting (Levy & Williams, 2016). It is recommended that they preface the interaction by explaining that information shared in this context remains private between patient and provider unless the safety of the patient or a third party is at imminent risk. This policy can be explained to the adolescent in a clear and developmentally appropriate manner. Moreover, if the patient is given a screening tool in the waiting room before the visit, the patient and parent should understand beforehand that the information requested is personal and confidential.

Adolescent substance use is intrinsically high risk and often linked to other high-risk behaviors. Health care providers engaging in SBIRT often face challenges in determining what information shared by the adolescent can be considered confidential and not shared with parents. As part of this determination, providers should be familiar with their state laws regarding confidentiality and adolescent substance use. The benefit of not sharing information with parents is the preservation of the therapeutic alliance, thus increasing the likelihood that the adolescent will continue to share sensitive information in the future. However, certain substance-related behaviors should be considered sufficiently dangerous that an automatic breach of confidentiality is warranted. These include injection drug use; mixing sedatives such as opioids, alcohol, and benzodiazepines; consuming life-threatening quantities of alcohol; and driving while impaired. Patient age is also a factor; a 17-year-old reporting certain use-related behaviors might merit privacy, whereas a 14-year-old engaging in similar behaviors would not. Other personal characteristics also impact risk level. For example, even small amounts of alcohol use may be particularly dangerous for an adolescent with Type 1 diabetes.

If an adolescent shares information with the health care provider that warrants breach of confidentiality, the clinician should first assess whether there is a risk to the adolescent in sharing this information with parents. It is recommended that the health care provider determine whether there is domestic violence in the home or whether either parent has an active mental health or substance use disorder. In those specific contexts, sharing information with the parent might put the adolescent at further risk of harm and should be avoided in favor of other options, such as involving a child protection team. Cultural factors should also be considered; certain cultures might have more extreme views toward substance use and mental health issues, potentially placing the adolescent at heightened risk following a disclosure.

Once the health care provider has determined the overall safety of sharing information with parents, he or she should explain the concerns to the patient, providing a clear rationale for the need to breach confidentiality. The clinician should reassure the patient that only limited information will be shared, and he or she can practice the wording beforehand with the adolescent. For example, an adolescent who is using heroin might prefer that the term *opioids* be used instead of *heroin*.

Engaging Parents in SBIRT

Although the initial conversation with adolescents about their substance use should take place privately, one of the clinician's goals in addressing the teen's substance use should be parental involvement, particularly if a referral to treatment is indicated. Parents are better able to schedule appointments, navigate insurance-related issues, and provide transportation for their children to requisite appointments. Abundant evidence suggests that treatment of adolescent substance use and substance use disorders is more effective if parents are involved (Baldwin, Christian, Berkeljon, & Shadish, 2012).

Clinicians skilled at performing SBIRT with their adolescent patients frequently combine motivational interviewing (MI) techniques with psycho-education and clear advice that abstinence is the healthiest choice in order to influence their patients' substance-related behaviors. Just as MI can be used to motivate an adolescent to stop or cut back on their use or accept a referral to treatment, it can also be used to motivate adolescents to assent to parental involvement, particularly in instances in which breach of confidentiality is not automatically warranted. For adolescents who initially refuse to allow the clinician to share concerns with parents, clinicians can create a management plan that includes follow-up and parental involvement as a treatment goal, if appropriate.

For adolescents with regular heavy substance use, it is commonplace for parents to have some knowledge of this already. In many instances, there is subsequent tension between the adolescent and his or her parents, which may manifest as frequent fighting. The pediatrician can offer to step in as a mediator, advocating for the adolescent and their willingness to engage in substance use treatment. The hook for adolescents is that open discussion of their use with their health care provider in a controlled manner, with emphasis on their willingness to consider treatment, could alleviate stress in the home. Treatment that includes parents may also be appealing to adolescents who feel that their parents are too strict, too worried, or simply do not understand the situation.

Managing Referrals

Adolescents who screen positive for problems related to substance use or meet criteria for a substance use disorder should be referred immediately for additional treatment as part of the SBIRT intervention. Therefore, it is important for health care providers to have a broad working knowledge of substance use treatment options in their community. Consideration of the nuances of the individual patient's presentation when making a referral is also important. Adolescent patients should receive treatment in programs tailored to their specific ages and developmental stages and should not receive treatment in primarily adult programs. Providers should also consider the phenomenon of contagion, in which patients with substance use disorders are grouped with more severely affected patients and might actually worsen behaviorally as a result of the interaction (Dishion & Dodge, 2005; Valente et al., 2007). Peer contagion was hypothesized with regard to substance use in teens (Dishion & Dodge, 2005) and observed in the reversal of the beneficial effects of a curriculum designed to decrease alcohol and drug use through peer influence when the peers reported substance use (Valente et al., 2007).

Ideally, patients could be referred to a specialty program caring for adolescents with substance use and substance use disorders that could design an optimal and individualized treatment program for the adolescent. Unfortunately, there are few such programs. Alternatively, referral to a behavioral counselor in the community is recommended, particularly one specializing in treating substance use disorders, who can further assess and determine the appropriate level of care.

Adolescent patients with mild substance use disorders often benefit from one-on-one counseling with a behavioral health clinician. Because not all therapists evidence comparable comfort levels caring for patients with substance use disorders, it is important for primary care practices to be able to identify appropriate community therapists for referral. For patients with severe substance use disorders, more intensive treatment, including programs such as intensive outpatient programs and partial hospital programs that include several hours a day of substance use disorder treatment, is recommended. Patients in crisis, particularly those with unstable co-occurring mental health disorders, might require acute stabilization in a short-term residential program, typically referred to as acute residential treatment. SAMHSA has a national helpline that providers can use to familiarize themselves with resources in their area.

Challenges to SBIRT in the General Medical Setting

As increasing attention is paid to the importance of screening adolescents for substance use in primary care, it is important to acknowledge the most frequently reported obstacles. The most common reasons given by primary care physicians for not screening are insufficient time and inadequate time alone with the adolescent (Levy et al., 2017). Barriers to the follow-up and referral process include the adolescent being unwilling to return for follow-up and issues relating to confidentiality. Self-administered screening is recommended and can shorten the length of time required for SBIRT. Skilled use of MI and facility with hooks to engage the adolescent make the process of arranging follow-up less daunting and more likely to be successful.

As more providers receive training in the use of SBIRT and become comfortable with how to screen, what to do if the screen is positive, and how to manage confidentiality, rates of screening, brief intervention, and referral to treatment for substance use in primary care should improve. The medical home is an optimal context for the identification of problematic substance use and substance use disorders in adolescents and a natural nexus for successful follow-up and treatment of this potentially life-threatening condition.

SBIRT IN THE SCHOOLS

Schools may be ideal settings for delivering SBIRT (Benningfield, Riggs, & Stephan, 2015). There is potential for efficiently accessing large populations and overcoming basic access barriers that may operate for youth who are not connected to primary care. School settings may enable confidential conversations about substance use while maintaining privacy and supporting the autonomy of the maturing child. Infrastructure supports include the physical space and potential engagement of trained staff, including guidance counselors, faculty, and nurses.

Delivery of SBIRT in school settings is a frontier area of public health intervention. Initial reports show a high willingness of school staff to engage in this role but also the need for training and support for the delivery of SBIRT services (Lunstead, Weitzman, Kaye, & Levy, 2017). There is considerable need to advance the evidence base for the acceptability and efficacy of reaching youth in school settings, as well as to train more school staff in SBIRT. Potential challenges include access to resources and guaranteeing the availability and willingness of appropriately trained staff, providing adequate space, scheduling, gaining permissions of parents or legal guardians to undertake SBIRT, ensuring adequate referral networks and clinical resources for youth who need more intensive support services and treatment, and developing policies and practices that suitably address the need for privacy and confidentiality protections.

CONCLUSION

Developmentally appropriate and evidence-based adolescent SBIRT programs provide an important strategy for addressing adolescents' unique vulnerabilities to substance use and associated disorders. Consideration of a range of factors is vital, including appreciation for the age, life stage, and circumstances of each youth, substance use patterns, problems and comorbidities, and their need for and availability of helping resources. Although it is not a panacea, adolescent SBIRT provides an approach for bringing into clinical and community settings scalable tools and practices from the continually developing sciences of assessment, prevention, and treatment to address significant adolescent health concerns.

REFERENCES

Arain, M., Haque, M., Johal, L., Mathur, P., Nel, W., Rais, A., . . . Sharma, S. (2013). Maturation of the adolescent brain. *Neuropsychiatric Disease and Treatment, 9,* 449–461. http://dx.doi.org/10.2147/NDT.S39776

Baldwin, S. A., Christian, S., Berkeljon, A., & Shadish, W. R. (2012). The effects of family therapies for adolescent delinquency and substance abuse: A meta-analysis. *Journal of Marital and Family Therapy, 38,* 281–304. http://dx.doi.org/10.1111/j.1752-0606.2011.00248.x

Barata, I., Shandro, J., Montgomery, M., Polansky, R., Sachs, C., Duber, H., . . . Macias-Konstantopoulos, W. (2017). Effectiveness of SBIRT for alcohol use disorders in the emergency department: A systematic review. *Western Journal of Emergency Medicine, 18,* 1143–1152. http://dx.doi.org/10.5811/westjem.2017.7.34373

Benningfield, M. M., Riggs, P., & Stephan, S. H. (2015). The role of schools in substance use prevention and intervention. *Child and Adolescent Psychiatric Clinics of North America, 24,* 291–303. http://dx.doi.org/10.1016/j.chc.2014.12.004

Bernstein, E., Edwards, E., Dorfman, D., Heeren, T., Bliss, C., & Bernstein, J. (2009). Screening and brief intervention to reduce marijuana use among youth and young adults in a pediatric emergency department. *Academic Emergency Medicine, 16,* 1174–1185. http://dx.doi.org/10.1111/j.1553-2712.2009.00490.x

Bernstein, J., Dorfman, D., Lunstead, J., Topp, D., Mamata, H., Jaffer, S., & Bernstein, E. (2017). Reaching adolescents for prevention: The role of pediatric emergency department health promotion advocates. *Pediatric Emergency Care, 33,* 223–229. http://dx.doi.org/10.1097/PEC.0000000000000662

Center for Behavioral Health Statistics and Quality. (2016). *Key substance use and mental health indicators in the United States: Results from the 2015 National Survey on Drug Use and Health.* Retrieved from http://www.samhsa.gov/data/sites/default/files/NSDUH-FFR1-2015/NSDUH-FFR1-2015/NSDUH-FFR1-2015.pdf

Centers for Disease Control and Prevention. (2014). *Behavioral risk factor surveillance system.* Retrieved from https://www.cdc.gov/brfss/about/index.htm

Centers for Disease Control and Prevention. (2018). *Youth risk behavior survey: Data summary & trends report 2007–2017.* Retrieved from https://www.cdc.gov/healthyyouth/data/yrbs/pdf/trendsreport.pdf

Chadi, N., Levy, S., Wisk, L., & Weitzman, E. (2018). *Experience of school SBIRT in a sample of middle and high school students in Massachusetts.* Paper presented at the meeting of the Pediatric Academic Societies, Toronto, Canada.

Dishion, T. J., & Dodge, K. A. (2005). Peer contagion in interventions for children and adolescents: Moving towards an understanding of the ecology and dynamics of change. *Journal of Abnormal Child Psychology, 33,* 395–400. http://dx.doi.org/10.1007/s10802-005-3579-z

Esser, M. B., Clayton, H., Demissie, Z., Kanny, D., & Brewer, R. D. (2017). Current and binge drinking among high school students—United States, 1991–2015. *Morbidity and Mortality Weekly Report, 66,* 474–478. http://dx.doi.org/10.15585/mmwr.mm6618a4

Friedman, J. L., Lyna, P., Sendak, M. D., Viera, A. J., Silberberg, M., & Pollak, K. I. (2017). Use of the 5 As for teen alcohol use. *Clinical Pediatrics, 56,* 419–426. http://dx.doi.org/10.1177/0009922816655884

Fuster, D., Cheng, D. M., Wang, N., Bernstein, J. A., Palfai, T. P., Alford, D. P., . . . Saitz, R. (2016). Brief intervention for daily marijuana users identified by screening in primary care: A subgroup analysis of the ASPIRE randomized clinical trial. *Substance Abuse, 37,* 336–342. http://dx.doi.org/10.1080/08897077.2015.1075932

Galvan, A. (2010). Adolescent development of the reward system. *Frontiers in Human Neuroscience, 4,* 1–9. http://dx.doi.org/10.3389/NEURO.09.006.2010

Grant, B. F., Chou, S. P., Saha, T. D., Pickering, R. P., Kerridge, B. T., Ruan, W. J., . . . Hasin, D. S. (2017). Prevalence of 12-month alcohol use, high-risk drinking, and

DSM–IV alcohol use disorder in the United States, 2001–2002 to 2012–2013: Results from the National Epidemiologic Survey on Alcohol and Related Conditions. *JAMA Psychiatry, 74*, 911–923. http://dx.doi.org/10.1001/jamapsychiatry.2017.2161

Grant, B. F., Goldstein, R. B., Saha, T. D., Chou, S. P., Jung, J., Zhang, H., . . . Hasin, D. S. (2015). Epidemiology of *DSM–5* alcohol use disorder results from the national epidemiologic survey on alcohol and related conditions III. *JAMA Psychiatry, 72*, 757–766. http://dx.doi.org/10.1001/jamapsychiatry.2015.0584

Gryczynski, J., Mitchell, S. G., Schwartz, R. P., Kelly, S. M., Dušek, K., Monico, L., . . . Hosler, C. (2019). Disclosure of adolescent substance use in primary care: Comparison of routine clinical screening and anonymous research interviews. *Journal of Adolescent Health, 64*, 541–543. http://dx.doi.org/10.1016/j.jadohealth.2018.10.009

Hassan, A., Harris, S. K., Sherritt, L., Van Hook, S., Brooks, T., Carey, P., . . . Knight, J. R. (2009). Primary care follow-up plans for adolescents with substance use problems. *Pediatrics, 124*, 144–150. http://dx.doi.org/10.1542/peds.2008-2979

Hawk, K., & D'Onofrio, G. (2018). Emergency department screening and interventions for substance use disorders. *Addiction Science & Clinical Practice, 13*, 18. http://dx.doi.org/10.1186/s13722-018-0117-1

Hingson, R. W., & Zha, W. (2009). Age of drinking onset, alcohol use disorders, frequent heavy drinking, and unintentionally injuring oneself and others after drinking. *Pediatrics, 123*, 1477–1484. http://dx.doi.org/10.1542/peds.2008-2176

Johnston, L. D., Miech, R. A., O'Malley, P. M., Bachman, J. G., Schulenberg, J. E., & Patrick, M. E. (2018). *2017 Overview: Key findings on adolescent drug use*. Retrieved from https://deepblue.lib.umich.edu/bitstream/handle/2027.42/142406/Overview2017FINAL.pdf?sequence=1&isAllowed=y

Kelly, S. M., Gryczynski, J., Mitchell, S. G., Kirk, A., O'Grady, K. E., & Schwartz, R. P. (2014). Validity of brief screening instrument for adolescent tobacco, alcohol, and drug use. *Pediatrics, 133*, 819–826. http://dx.doi.org/10.1542/peds.2013-2346

Kessler, R. C., Avenevoli, S., Costello, E. J., Green, J. G., Gruber, M. J., Heeringa, S., . . . Zaslavsky, A. M. (2009). National comorbidity survey replication adolescent supplement (NCS-A): II. Overview and design. *Journal of the American Academy of Child and Adolescent Psychiatry, 48*, 380–385. http://dx.doi.org/10.1097/CHI.0b013e3181999705

Knight, J. R., Sherritt, L., Shrier, L. A., Harris, S. K., & Chang, G. (2002). Validity of the CRAFFT substance abuse screening test among adolescent clinic patients. *Archives of Pediatrics & Adolescent Medicine, 156*, 607–614. http://dx.doi.org/10.1001/archpedi.156.6.607

Knight, J. R., Shrier, L. A., Bravender, T. D., Farrell, M., Vander Bilt, J., & Shaffer, H. J. (1999). A new brief screen for adolescent substance abuse. *Archives of Pediatrics & Adolescent Medicine, 153*, 591–596. http://dx.doi.org/10.1001/archpedi.153.6.591

Le Strat, Y., Dubertret, C., & Le Foll, B. (2015). Impact of age at onset of cannabis use on cannabis dependence and driving under the influence in the United States. *Accident Analysis & Prevention, 76*, 1–5. http://dx.doi.org/10.1016/J.AAP.2014.12.015

Levy, S., Mountain-Ray, S., Reynolds, J., Mendes, S. J., & Bromberg, J. (2018). A novel approach to treating adolescents with opioid use disorder in pediatric primary care. *Substance Abuse, 39*, 173–181. http://dx.doi.org/10.1080/08897077.2018.1455165

Levy, S., Weiss, R., Sherritt, L., Ziemnik, R., Spalding, A., Van Hook, S., & Shrier, L. A. (2014). An electronic screen for triaging adolescent substance use by risk levels. *JAMA Pediatrics, 168*, 822–828. http://dx.doi.org/10.1001/jamapediatrics.2014.774

Levy, S. J., & Williams, J. F. (2016). Substance use screening, brief intervention, and referral to treatment. *Pediatrics, 138*, e20161211. http://dx.doi.org/10.1542/peds.2016-1211

Levy, S., Ziemnik, R. E., Harris, S. K., Rabinow, L., Breen, L., Fluet, C., . . . Straus, J. H. (2017). Screening adolescents for alcohol use: Tracking practice trends of Massachusetts pediatricians. *Journal of Addiction Medicine, 11*, 427–434. http://dx.doi.org/10.1097/ADM.0000000000000340

Lipari, R., Kroutil, L. A., & Pemberton, M. R. (2015). *Risk and protective factors and initiation of substance use: Results from the 2014 National Survey on Drug Use and Health.* Retrieved from https://www.samhsa.gov/data/sites/default/files/NSDUH-DR-FRR4-2014rev/ NSDUH-DR-FRR4-2014.pdf

Lunstead, J., Weitzman, E. R., Harstad, E., Dedeoglu, F., Gaffin, J. M., Garvey, K. C., . . . Levy, S. (2019). Screening and counseling for alcohol use in adolescents with chronic medical conditions in the ambulatory setting. *Journal of Adolescent Health, 64,* 804–806. http://dx.doi.org/10.1016/J.JADOHEALTH.2019.02.011

Lunstead, J., Weitzman, E. R., Kaye, D., & Levy, S. (2017). Screening and brief intervention in high schools: School nurses' practices and attitudes in Massachusetts. *Substance Abuse, 38,* 257–260. http://dx.doi.org/10.1080/08897077.2016.1275926

Massachusetts Department of Public Health Bureau of Substance Abuse Services. (2009). *Provider guide: Adolescent screening, brief intervention, and referral to treatment— Using the CRAFFT screening tool.* Boston, MA: Massachusetts Department of Public Health.

McCabe, S. E., Kloska, D. D., Veliz, P., Jager, J., & Schulenberg, J. E. (2016). Developmental course of non-medical use of prescription drugs from adolescence to adulthood in the United States: National longitudinal data. *Addiction, 111,* 2166–2176. http://dx.doi.org/10.1111/add.13504

McCabe, S. E., Schulenberg, J., O'Malley, P., Patrick, M., & Kloska, D. (2014). Nonmedical use of prescription opioids during the transition to adulthood: A multi-cohort national longitudinal study. *Addiction, 109,* 102–110. http://dx.doi.org/10.1111/add.12347

McCabe, S. E., Veliz, P., & Patrick, M. E. (2017). High-intensity drinking and nonmedical use of prescription drugs: Results from a national survey of 12th grade students. *Drug and Alcohol Dependence, 178,* 372–379. http://dx.doi.org/10.1016/j.drugalcdep.2017.05.038

McCabe, S. E., West, B. T., Morales, M., Cranford, J. A., & Boyd, C. J. (2007). Does early onset of non-medical use of prescription drugs predict subsequent prescription drug abuse and dependence? Results from a national study. *Addiction, 102,* 1920–1930. http://dx.doi.org/10.1111/j.1360-0443.2007.02015.x

Merikangas, K. R., Avenevoli, S., Costello, E. J., Koretz, D., & Kessler, R. C. (2009). National comorbidity survey replication adolescent supplement (NCS-A): I. Background and measures. *Journal of the American Academy of Child & Adolescent Psychiatry, 48,* 367–379. http://dx.doi.org/10.1097/CHI.0b013e31819996f1

Miech, R. A., Johnston, L. D., O'Malley, P. M., Bachman, J. G., Schulenberg, J. E., & Patrick, M. E. (2018). *Monitoring the Future national survey results on drug use, 1975–2017: Vol. I. Secondary school students.* Ann Arbor: Institute for Social Research, The University of Michigan.

Mitchell, S. G., Gryczynski, J., Gonzales, A., Moseley, A., Peterson, T., O'Grady, K. E., & Schwartz, R. P. (2012). Screening, Brief Intervention, and Referral to Treatment (SBIRT) for substance use in a school-based program: Services and outcomes. *The American Journal on Addictions, 21,* S5–S13. http://dx.doi.org/10.1111/j.1521-0391.2012.00299.x

Mitchell, S. G., Gryczynski, J., O'Grady, K. E., & Schwartz, R. P. (2012). SBIRT for adolescent drug and alcohol use: Current status and future directions. *Journal of Substance Abuse Treatment, 44,* 463–472. http://dx.doi.org/10.1016/j.jsat.2012.11.005

Monitoring the Future. (n.d.). *Purpose and design.* Retrieved from http://www.monitoringthefuture.org/purpose.html

National Survey on Drug Use and Health. (2018). *About the survey.* Retrieved from https://nsduhweb.rti.org/respweb/about_nsduh.html

Ozechowski, T. J., Becker, S. J., & Hogue, A. (2016). SBIRT-A: Adapting SBIRT to maximize developmental fit for adolescents in primary care. *Journal of Substance Abuse Treatment, 62,* 28–37. http://dx.doi.org/10.1016/j.jsat.2015.10.006

Patrick, M. E., Schulenberg, J. E., Martz, M. E., Maggs, J. L., O'Malley, P. M., & Johnston, L. D. (2013). Extreme binge drinking among 12th-grade students in the United States: Prevalence and predictors. *JAMA Pediatrics, 167,* 1019–1025. http://dx.doi.org/10.1001/jamapediatrics.2013.2392

Patrick, M. E., Veliz, P. T., & Terry-McElrath, Y. M. (2017). High-intensity and simultaneous alcohol and marijuana use among high school seniors in the United States. *Substance Abuse, 38,* 498–503. http://dx.doi.org/10.1080/08897077.2017.1356421

Pbert, L., Flint, A. J., Fletcher, K. E., Young, M. H., Druker, S., & DiFranza, J. R. (2008). Effect of a pediatric practice-based smoking prevention and cessation intervention for adolescents: A randomized, controlled trial. *Pediatrics, 121,* e738–e747. http://dx.doi.org/10.1542/peds.2007-1029

Sterling, S., Kline-Simon, A. H., Jones, A., Sartre, D. D., Parthasarathy, S., & Weisner, C. (2017). Specialty addiction and psychiatry treatment initiation and engagement: Results from an SBIRT randomized trial in pediatrics. *Journal of Substance Abuse Treatment, 82,* 48–54. http://dx.doi.org/10.1016/j.jsat.2017.09.005

Valente, T. W., Ritt-Olson, A., Stacy, A., Unger, J. B., Okamoto, J., & Sussman, S. (2007). Peer acceleration: Effects of a social network tailored substance abuse prevention program among high-risk adolescents. *Addiction, 102,* 1804–1815. http://dx.doi.org/10.1111/j.1360-0443.2007.01992.x

Volkow, N. D., Koob, G. F., & McLellan, A. T. (2016). Neurobiologic advances from the brain disease model of addiction. *The New England Journal of Medicine, 374,* 363–371. http://dx.doi.org/10.1056/NEJMra1511480

Wilson, C. R., Sherritt, L., Gates, E., & Knight, J. R. (2004). Are clinical impressions of adolescent substance use accurate? *Pediatrics, 114,* e536–e540. http://dx.doi.org/10.1542/peds.2004-0098

Screening, Brief Intervention, and Referral to Treatment for Racial and Ethnic Minority Populations

State of the Science and Implications for Adaptation

Jason J. Burrow-Sánchez and Marjean Nielsen

creening, brief intervention, and referral to treatment (SBIRT) is a public health approach to identifying individuals who may be at risk of developing a substance use disorder (Babor et al., 2007). Like public health screening for other diseases (e.g., hypertension, diabetes), SBIRT provides health care practitioners with ways to assess the risk of substance use disorder and if warranted, provide a brief intervention or referral to treatment. To date, SBIRT has been used in a range of health (e.g., primary care clinics, dental offices) and educational settings (e.g., secondary schools) following a public health approach (Agerwala & McCance-Katz, 2012; Babor, Del Boca, & Bray, 2017; Curtis, McLellan, & Gabellini, 2014; Neff et al., 2015). SBIRT has been examined with adult and adolescent populations; reviews in these areas can be found in other chapters in this volume. This chapter focuses on understanding SBIRT with racial and ethnic minority adult populations. Our original intention for the chapter was to cover diverse adult populations, using the term *diverse* broadly to include age, gender, socioeconomic status, ethnicity, and other categories; however, the reader will see that our use of the term was defined by the existing research, which largely focuses on differences between racial and ethnic minority subgroups.

http://dx.doi.org/10.1037/0000199-010
Screening, Brief Intervention, and Referral to Treatment for Substance Use: A Practitioner's Guide,
M. D. Cimini and J. L. Martin (Editors)

Of the more than 320 million people in the United States, 61.5% are non-Hispanic White, 17.6% Hispanic, 12.3% African American, 5.3% Asian American, and 0.7% American Indian,[1] with the total adult population consisting of more than 247 million individuals (U.S. Census Bureau, 2017). In the 1990s, approximately one in five individuals in the United States identified as other than White; this number increased to one in four individuals in the 2000s (Hobbs & Stoops, 2002). By 2060, approximately one in three individuals in the United States are projected to identify as other than non-Hispanic White (Vespa, Medina, & Armstrong, 2018). For example, the non-Hispanic White population is expected to decrease from 61% in 2016 to 44% by 2060, whereas the Hispanic population will grow from 17% in 2016 to 27%; individuals from two or more races are expected to grow the fastest (i.e., by almost 200%) in the coming 3 decades. According to the 2060 projections, non-Hispanic Whites will cease to be the numerical majority in the United States (Vespa et al., 2018). These changing national demographics necessitate our understanding of how substance use trends differ across racial and ethnic groups and how to provide culturally competent services.

SUBSTANCE USE, TREATMENT UTILIZATION, INJURY, AND MORTALITY TRENDS

Data from the National Survey on Drug Use and Health (Substance Abuse and Mental Health Services Administration [SAMHSA], 2018b) frequently underscore that prevalence rates in substance use vary across racial and ethnic groups in the United States. In 2017, an estimated 56% percent of the adult population were current[2] users of alcohol, with differences in prevalence rates across racial and ethnic groups as follows: 60.5% non-Hispanic White, 50.1% Hispanic, 47.3% African American, 44.6% American Indian, and 41.5%, Asian (SAMHSA, 2018a). The proportions of Hispanic and African Americans considered current users of alcohol were roughly 10% lower compared with non-Hispanic Whites. For illicit[3] substances, 11.5% of U.S. adults were estimated current users, with the following differences in proportions by racial

---

[1]The terms *African American*, *American Indian*, *Asian American*, and *Hispanic* are used throughout the chapter and reflect the terms used in SAMHSA surveys. We recognize, however, that different terms may be used in the literature.

[2]*Current use* is defined as substance use that occurred in the past 30 days by the National Survey on Drug Use and Health (NSDUH; https://www.samhsa.gov/data/data-we-collect/nsduh-national-survey-drug-use-and-health). NSDUH is conducted annually by the Substance Abuse and Mental Health Services Administration (SAMHSA) and is a frequently cited source for national prevalence rates for substance use and other mental health behaviors.

[3]The National Survey on Drug Use and Health (https://www.samhsa.gov/data/data-we-collect/nsduh-national-survey-drug-use-and-health) includes 10 substances in the illicit drug category: (a) marijuana, (b) cocaine (including crack), (c) heroin, (d) hallucinogens, (e) inhalants, (f) methamphetamines, (g) tranquilizers, (h) stimulants, (i) sedatives, and (j) prescription pain meds.

and ethnic background: 17.9% American Indian, 13.7% African American, 11.8% non-Hispanic White, 10.3% Hispanic, and 4.6% Asian American. The most frequently used illicit substance is marijuana[4] and, as in the use of illicit substances, American Indian and African American individuals reported the highest rates of marijuana use, 15.6% and 12.2%, respectively, followed by 10.1% non-Hispanic Whites, 8.5% Hispanics, and 3.8% Asian Americans.

Although the use of opioid-based substances receives significant attention in the media, overall prevalence rates for these substances are lower compared with alcohol and marijuana. Specifically, 1.3% of U.S. adults were estimated to have misused[5] opioids in the past month, and prevalence rates were similar across racial and ethnic groups, with the exception of Asian Americans: 1.7% American Indian, 1.5% non-Hispanic White, 1.3% Hispanic, 1.1% African American, and 0.4% Asian American (SAMHSA, 2018a).

Not all individuals who use substances will go on to develop a substance use disorder (SUD). A person with an SUD meets clinical diagnostic criteria found in the *Diagnostic and Statistical Manual of Mental Disorders* (5th ed.; *DSM–5*; American Psychiatric Association, 2013) for one or more substances. In 2017, 7.6% of the adult population met criteria[6] for an SUD, and the differences across racial and ethnic groups were as follows: 13.7% American Indian, 8.0% non-Hispanic White, 7.2% African American, 6.9% Hispanic, and 3.9% Asian American (SAMHSA, 2018a). Meeting *DSM* diagnostic criteria is one indicator used to determine whether an individual is in need of treatment.

In 2017, 8% of the adult population was in need of treatment[7] for an SUD (SAMHSA, 2018a). Only 12.4% of those who needed treatment actually received it. The percentages of African Americans (15.1%) and non-Hispanic White (12.6%) Americans who needed treatment and received it were higher compared with their Hispanic (9.6%) and Asian American (2.3%) counterparts. A study by Lo and Cheng (2011) found that African American and Asian American individuals (with the exception of Hispanics) were less likely than non-Hispanic White individuals to access treatment for SUDs through specialty facilities.[8] In general, the most frequently cited reasons individuals do not receive treatment for an SUD are not being ready to stop using and the prohibitive cost of treatment (i.e., lack of health coverage or inability to afford out-of-pocket costs; SAMHSA, 2018b).

---

[4]Certain states have legalized medical or recreational marijuana, but at the time of this writing it is illegal at the federal level.

[5]The misuse of opioids includes taking prescription-based medication for nonmedical purposes.

[6]The 2017 National Survey on Drug Use and Health (https://www.samhsa.gov/data/data-we-collect/nsduh-national-survey-drug-use-and-health) used the *DSM–IV* diagnostic criteria.

[7]Met criteria for a substance use disorder or received treatment at specialty facility for a substance.

[8]The Substance Abuse and Mental Health Services Administration defines *specialty facilities* as an inpatient or outpatient drug and alcohol rehabilitation facility, inpatient hospital, or mental health center.

Completion rates of treatment also vary by race and ethnicity. For example, a study by Saloner and Lê Cook (2013) analyzed SAMHSA's treatment episode data for discharges with a sample of over 1 million individuals. They found that Asian Americans were more likely to complete treatment regardless of the substance[9] compared with non-Hispanic Whites. However, African American and Hispanic individuals were less likely to complete treatment compared with their non-Hispanic White counterparts across all substances, with the exception of opiates. The treatment completion rates for African American and Hispanic individuals were also lower across all settings (i.e., outpatient, intensive outpatient, residential) compared with non-Hispanic Whites and higher for Asian Americans.

Race and ethnicity differences in substance use patterns extend to injury and mortality rates. Racial and ethnic disparities in injury, social consequences, and mortality attributable to alcohol use have received increased attention in the literature, due in part to alcohol being the most commonly used substance in the nation (SAMHSA, 2018b). Caetano (2003) reported that the rates of death from cirrhosis attributable to alcohol use was higher for Hispanic men compared with African American or non-Hispanic White men; in addition, the rates of cirrhosis were higher for African American men compared with non-Hispanic Whites. Another study by Mulia, Ye, Greenfield, and Zemore (2009) analyzed national survey data on alcohol use and found that African American and Hispanic individuals were more likely to experience social consequences (e.g., arguments or fights, accidents, health problems) related to drinking compared with non-Hispanic Whites. Furthermore, Witbrodt, Mulia, Zemore, and Kerr (2014) analyzed data from two administrations of a national alcohol survey and found that African Americans and Hispanic men reported higher rates of accidents, injuries, and social problems (e.g., arguments with others) compared with their non-Hispanic White counterparts. Taken together, findings suggest that even though non-Hispanic Whites have the highest rates of alcohol use (SAMHSA, 2018b), individuals from other racial and ethnic groups are at greater risk of injury, social consequences, and mortality related to alcohol use. A public health approach to early identification and treatment of high-risk substance use and SUDs, such as SBIRT, may help to identify and mitigate racial and ethnic health-related disparities.

RELEVANCE OF SBIRT FOR DECREASING RACIAL AND ETHNIC DISPARITIES

SBIRT provides a useful framework to decrease racial and ethnic disparities in substance use treatment. For instance, screening individuals for problems with substance use in general medical settings, such as primary care

---

[9]Saloner and Lê Cook (2013) included the following substances in their analysis: alcohol, cocaine, marijuana, heroin, opiates, and methamphetamine.

doctor visits or dental clinics, can increase the identification of people from all racial and ethnic backgrounds at risk of substance use problems or SUDs who may otherwise go undetected. Early detection of risk for an SUD may make it more likely that the substance use behaviors are amenable to change through a brief intervention, thereby reducing the potential of experiencing future harm attributable to substance use. Moreover, individuals screened in nonspecialty settings (i.e., outpatient primary care) can be referred to specialty settings for assessment and treatment, providing greater continuity of care between settings. Early identification and risk reduction for SUDs is especially important for individuals from racial and ethnic minority backgrounds because of the disproportionate number of negative health, interpersonal, and social consequences they experience as a result of substance use.

Selecting Screening Measures

The use of a screening tool is the first component of the SBIRT process. A positive screen (i.e., moderate to high-risk substance use is present) provides an opportunity for a brief intervention and referral to treatment for those at severe risk or with an SUD. A number of screening measures have been used in the context of SBIRT, and we review their use with individuals from racial and ethnic groups. We recommend that any screening measure chosen for SBIRT have adequate psychometric properties and, ultimately, serve the screening needs of the participants and setting. There are three areas to consider when selecting screening instruments: (a) reliability, (b) validity, and (c) prior use with particular samples. First, *reliability* refers to the instrument providing similar results across different occasions of measurement for the same person. Second, *validity* refers to the extent to which an instrument measures what it is purported to measure. Third, not all screening measures have been psychometrically tested or validated for use with individuals from all racial and ethnic backgrounds. Thus, it cannot be assumed that all screening measures work equally well with individuals from all racial and ethnic minority backgrounds without prior validation. In the context of SBIRT, the goal of any screening measure is to assist in identifying the individual's level of risk for substance use. The score is used to determine the level of risk along a continuum ranging from no risk, potential risk, harmful use, to potential dependency. Screening measures are not designed to provide a definitive diagnosis. Establishing the presence of an SUD diagnosis and the need for subsequent treatment is accomplished via a more comprehensive assessment. The following is a description of some of the most commonly used screening instruments associated with SBIRT, with a focus on their use with individuals from racial and ethnic minority groups. The discussion of the properties of the measures is minimal because they are reviewed more fully elsewhere in the volume. An overview of the measures is provided in Table 9.1.

TABLE 9.1. Validated SBIRT Screening Tools for Racial and Ethnic Minority Populations

Screener name (acronym)	Substances covered	Age	Items/scoring/admin time	Initial validation and additional samples tested
Alcohol Use Disorders Identification Test (AUDIT)	Alcohol	Adults	10 items scored on a scale of 0–40; a score of ≥8 indicates harmful and hazardous drinking, a score of ≥ 13 for women and ≥ 15 for men indicates alcohol use disorder; takes 5–10 minutes to administer	Initial sample (Babor & Grant, 1989); non-Hispanic White, African American and Hispanic patients (Cherpitel & Bazargan, 2003); Northern Plains American Indians (Leonardson et al., 2005)
Alcohol Use Disorder Identification Test—C (AUDIT-C)	Alcohol	Adults	Three items scored on a scale of 0–12; a score of ≥ 3 for women and ≥ 4 for men indicates harmful and hazardous drinking and probable alcohol use disorder; takes 1–5 minutes to administer	Initial sample (Bush, Kivlahan, McDonell, Fihn, & Bradley, 1998); non-Hispanic White, African American, and Hispanic primary care patients (Frank et al., 2008)
Alcohol, Smoking, and Substance Involvement Screening Test (ASSIST)	Tobacco, alcohol, cannabis, cocaine, amphetamine, inhalants, sedatives or sleeping pills, hallucinogens, opioids	Adults and adolescents	Eight items scored on a scale of 0–39; a score of 3 indicates low risk, 4–26 moderate risk, and ≥ 27 is probable of severe-level use; takes 5–10 minutes to administer	International sample of participants from Australia, Brazil, Ireland, India, Israel, the Palestinian territories, Puerto Rico, the United Kingdom, and Zimbabwe (WHO ASSIST Working Group, 2002)
CAGE Questionnaire (CAGE)	Alcohol	Adults	Four items scored on a scale of 0–4; a score of ≥ 1 calls for further evaluation and ≥ 2 is probable harmful and hazardous drinking; takes 1–5 minutes to administer	Initial sample (Ewing, 1984); non-Hispanic White, African American, and Hispanic individuals (Cherpitel, 1999)

CAGE-AID Questionnaire (CAGE-AID)	Alcohol and other drugs	Adults	Four items scored on a scale of 0–4; a score of ≥ 1 calls for further evaluation and ≥ 2 is probable harmful and hazardous alcohol and/or drug use; takes 1–5 minutes to administer	Initial sample (Brown & Rounds, 1995); Northern Plains American Indians (Leonardson et al., 2005)
Drug Abuse Screening Test (DAST-10)	Drugs	Adults	10 items scored on a scale of 0–10; a score of 1–2 indicates low level use, 3–5 moderate level use, 6–8 substantial level use, and 9–10 severe level use; takes 5–10 minutes to administer	Initial sample (Skinner, 1982); Hispanic individuals (Bedregal, Sobell, Sobell, & Simco, 2006)
National Institute on Alcohol Abuse and Alcoholism Single-Item Screener (NIAAA-SIS)	Alcohol	Adults and adolescents	Single-item question; score of 1 calls for further evaluation; takes 1–2 minutes to administer	Initial sample non-Hispanic White, African American, and Hispanic primary care patients (Smith, Schmidt, Allensworth-Davies, & Saitz, 2009)
National Institute on Drug Abuse Single Item Screener (NIDA-SIS)	Drugs and nonmedical prescriptions	Adults and adolescents	Single-item question; score of 1 calls for further evaluation; takes 1–2 minutes to administer	Initial sample non-Hispanic White, African American, and Hispanic primary care patients (Smith, Schmidt, Allensworth-Davies, & Saitz, 2010)
Additional Adolescent Validated Screening Tools (details not covered in this chapter)				
Car, Relax, Alone, Forget, Friends, Trouble (CRAFFT)	Alcohol, cannabis, and other drugs	Adolescents	Nine items scored on a scale of 0–9; a score of ≥ 2 indicates high-risk use; takes 1–5 minutes to administer	Initial sample (Knight et al., 1999); 32% non-Hispanic White, 19% Hispanic, and 36% African American
Drug Abuse Screening Test for Adolescents (DAST-A)	Drugs	Adolescents	27 items scored on a scale of 0–27; a score of ≥ 6 indicated a substance use problem (abuse or dependence); takes 5–10 minutes to administer	Initial sample (Martino, Grilo, & Fehon, 2000); 84% non-Hispanic White, 9% African American, and 7% Hispanic

Alcohol Use Disorders Identification Test

The 10-item Alcohol Use Disorders Identification Test (AUDIT; Babor & Grant, 1989) screens for harmful and hazardous drinking and includes questions on the amount and frequency of drinking, alcohol dependence symptoms, and personal and social problems associated with alcohol misuse. The measure was initially validated for alcohol use, demonstrating high sensitivity (.92)[10] and specificity (.98). Early studies examining the role of ethnicity on the validity of the AUDIT conducted in a Level 1 trauma center found no difference in the validity of scores between African American and White patients (Allen, Litten, Fertig, & Babor, 1997; Cherpitel, 1995a, b). Since then, the AUDIT has been tested for use with individuals from different racial and ethnic groups, including a sample of 50 Northern Plains American Indians (Leonardson et al., 2005), and translated into many languages, such as Spanish, Hindi, Japanese, Thai, Chinese, Arabic, and Korean (Almarri, Oei, & Amir, 2009; Kim, Gulick, Nam, & Kim, 2008). Studies have demonstrated higher sensitivity for alcohol dependence than for harmful drinking at .95 compared with .54 in a sample of 1,511 emergency room patients who self-identified as Mexican American and .87 compared with .79 in a sample of 395 male and female African American and Hispanic patients recruited from emergency rooms (Cherpitel & Bazargan, 2003; Cherpitel & Borges, 2000). The AUDIT has also been examined as a screening tool in Chinese language populations living in the United States and globally (Manuel et al., 2015; Volk, Steinbauer, Cantor, & Holzer, 1997). Li, Babor, Hao, and Chen (2011) conducted a systematic review of the AUDIT in Chinese language populations published in English ($n = 10$) and Chinese ($n = 11$). The measure demonstrated good levels of sensitivity (.88–.99) and specificity (.79–93) for alcohol dependence across study samples, with the exception of a sample of Min-Nan Taiwanese (specificity = .58).

Alcohol Use Disorders Identification Test—Concise

The three-item Alcohol Use Disorders Identification Test—Concise (AUDIT–C; Bush, Kivlahan, McDonell, Fihn, & Bradley, 1998) contains the first three questions of the AUDIT related to the amount and frequency of drinking. The measure was initially validated with 447 Veterans Affairs patients (data on ethnicity was missing for 34% of participants, 89% were non-Hispanic White), with high sensitivity for hazardous drinking (.98) and alcohol dependency (.90; Bush et al., 1998). The AUDIT–C has also been evaluated in a sample of 1,292 African American, Hispanic, and non-Hispanic White primary care patients (Frank et al., 2008). Findings indicated that among women, the measure demonstrated higher sensitivity for detecting alcohol misuse in Hispanic (.85) than in African American (.67) or White (.70) patients. Among men, the measure demonstrated higher sensitivity for detecting alcohol misuse in

---

[10]*Sensitivity* refers to the ability of a measure to indicate that a condition exists, whereas *specificity* is the ability to indicate that it does not. Scores closer to one are better.

White (.95) and Hispanic (.85) patients compared with African American (.76) patients.

Alcohol, Smoking, and Substance Involvement Screening Test

The 10-item Alcohol, Smoking, and Substance Involvement Screening Test (ASSIST; WHO ASSIST Working Group, 2002) screens for alcohol, tobacco, and other drugs (e.g., cannabis, stimulants, hallucinogens) during an individual's lifetime or the past 3 months. The measure was initially validated with a sample of adults recruited across multiple sites (i.e., alcohol and drug treatment facilities, general medical settings, psychiatric facilities) and countries (i.e., Australia, Brazil, Ireland, India, Israel, Palestinian Territories, Puerto Rico, United Kingdom, Zimbabwe); the validation sample consisted of 236 individuals, the majority male and of an average age of 34 years. The ASSIST demonstrated test–retest reliability ranging from 0.58 to 0.90 for questions on the past use of substances and concerns for using specific substances.

Cutting Down, Annoyance, Guilty Feeling, Eye-Openers

The four-item Cutting Down, Annoyance, Guilty Feeling, Eye-Openers (CAGE; Ewing, 1984) screens for alcohol problems and was originally developed in the late 1960s with samples of patients from a general medical hospital ($N = 130$) and an alcohol rehabilitation center ($N = 160$). The four questions of the CAGE are: (a) "Have you ever felt you should *cut down* on your drinking?" (b) "Have people *annoyed* you by criticizing your drinking?" (c) "Have you ever felt bad or *guilty* about your drinking?" and (d) "Have you ever had a drink first thing in the morning to steady your nerves or to get rid of a hangover (*eye-opener*)?" The CAGE has been evaluated in more recent studies, such as one by Cherpitel (1999) that included a sample of 1,004 White or other, 797 African American, and 642 Hispanic individuals (52% women). The results indicated no differences in sensitivity or specificity by gender or race or ethnicity for current drinkers in the sample.

CAGE Adapted to Include Drugs

The CAGE (Ewing, 1984) was adapted to include drugs (CAGE-AID; Brown & Rounds, 1995) and validated in an initial study of 124 primary care patients. The CAGE-AID consists of the same four questions described for the CAGE, with the addition of the words *drug use* (Questions 1 to 3) or *used drugs* (Question 4). In a study of 50 Northern Plains American Indians with diabetes, the CAGE-AID demonstrated good reliability as well as reasonable concurrent and divergent reliability with other psychosocial measures (Leonardson et al., 2005).

Drug Abuse Screening Test

The 28-item Drug Abuse Screening Test (DAST; Skinner, 1982) and the 10-item version of the measure (DAST–10) ask respondents about the use of and consequences of using substances in the past 12-month period. A Spanish language version of the DAST–10 was examined in a sample of 222 adults (66% male) recruited from communities in South Florida. Results suggested good convergent and discriminant validity (Bedregal, Sobell, Sobell, & Simco, 2006).

National Institute on Alcohol Abuse and Alcoholism Single-Item Screener

The National Institute on Alcohol Abuse and Alcoholism Single-Item Screener (NIAAA-SIS) is a single item measure that asks about alcohol use in the past year. The measure asks respondents, "How many times in the past year have you had X or more drinks in a day?" (X = four drinks for women and five drinks for men). Any response greater than one is considered a positive screen. The measure was initially validated in a sample ($N = 286$) of primary care patients (56% female) recruited from waiting room clinics in an urban hospital who identified as African American (63%), non-Hispanic White (17%), and Hispanic (16%). The measure was sensitive at .82/.88 and specific at .79/.67 for unhealthy alcohol use or current alcohol use disorder, respectively (Smith, Schmidt, Allensworth-Davies, & Saitz, 2009).

National Institute on Drug Abuse Single Item Screener

The National Institute on Drug Abuse Single Item Screener (NIDA–SIS) is a single item screener that asks respondents, "How many times in the past year have you used an illegal drug or used a prescription medication for nonmedical reasons?" Any response of one or higher is considered positive and recommended to be followed up with additional screening questions. The measure was validated in the same sample as the NIAAA–SIS measure described previously (i.e., Smith et al., 2009) but reported in a later paper (Smith, Schmidt, Allensworth-Davies, & Saitz, 2010). The NIDA–SIS measure was sensitive at .93/.10 and specific at .94/.74 for current drug use or a current drug use disorder, respectively.

Brief Interventions

Brief intervention (BI) refers to a counseling interaction between a professional provider (e.g., doctor, psychologist, counselor) and an individual at risk of harmful substance use. In general, the goal of a BI is to increase the individual's awareness of the level of risk of their substance use, discuss the potential for harm if the behavior continues, and create a plan for behavior change to decrease substance use, if the client is ready to do so. There are many models of BIs in the literature; however, most of them contain elements of motivational interviewing (MI), with the goal of increasing the individual's motivation to change their behavior from the status quo (Babor et al., 2017). A meta-analytic study by Hettema, Steele, and Miller (2005) found that the use of MI was related to positive effects for racial and ethnic minority individuals across a range of substances.

The effectiveness of brief motivational interviewing (BMI) versus standard care was evaluated in a study of English- and Spanish-speaking participants in a trauma care setting (Field & Caetano, 2010). The sample comprised 667 non-Hispanic White, 539 Hispanic, and 287 African American individuals. The results showed significant reductions in alcohol use for Hispanic patients in the BMI condition but not for non-Hispanic Whites or African Americans (Field, Cochran, & Caetano, 2013). Field and colleagues (Field & Caetano, 2010; Field, Cochran, & Caetano, 2013) thought that cultural adaptation in treatment might have occurred accidentally when Hispanic participants were matched with Hispanic providers. Increasing the cultural congruence between patient and provider may be an important consideration for effectively using BMI with individuals from diverse racial and ethnic backgrounds. Relatedly, Ornelas, Allen, Vaughan, Williams, and Negi (2015) interviewed Hispanic male day labor workers and also found they preferred interactions with health providers whom they could trust and who spoke Spanish.

Another BI model is termed brief treatment (BT). It involves an increased level of interaction between provider and client compared with BI; however, BT is meant to offer more flexibility, accessibility, and convenience compared with traditional inpatient or outpatient treatment services (Babor et al., 2017). However, participation in BT does not preclude the individual from being referred to traditional therapies. BT often includes components of cognitive behavior therapy or motivational enhancement therapy (Aldridge, Linford, & Bray, 2017). Findings from a large cross-site evaluation of SBIRT involving a total of 3,218 patients (32% were women, 32% non-Hispanic White, 24% African American, 23% Hispanic, and 21% other) indicated that, overall, BT demonstrated better outcomes compared with BI for reducing illicit drug use but not for reductions in alcohol use (Aldridge et al., 2017; Babor et al., 2017; Bray, Del Boca, McRee, Hayashi, & Babor, 2017).

Culturally Adapting SBIRT for Diverse Populations

In our review of the literature, we did not find any studies that tested cultural adaptations of SBIRT as a complete model; rather, we found components of the SBIRT model (i.e., screening measures, BIs) that had been tested or adapted for use with diverse samples, as described previously. We did locate two papers that described the methodology for a cultural adaption of SBIRT (Ornelas et al., 2015) and a BI (Field et al., 2015), but the outcomes of these studies have yet to be reported in the literature. Ornelas et al. (2015) indicated that barriers to engaging in screening and BI might be reduced for Hispanic day laborers by receiving services in Spanish from trusted providers in community settings. We also located a study by Lee and colleagues (2013) who tested culturally adapted motivational interviewing (CAMI) against a nonadapted version with a sample of adult Hispanic drinkers. The researchers found reductions in drinking levels for participants in both interventions, but greater reductions were noted for participants in the CAMI condition at 2- and 6-month follow-up time points. Modifications to the CAMI intervention included decreasing barriers to access to intervention, such as the provision of child care and transportation, scheduling appointments after hours, and integrating relevant cultural and contextual issues to increase the cultural congruence between participants and the intervention (Lee et al., 2013).

Ideally, a culturally adapted version of SBIRT is tested against its standard version counterpart because this type of design allows one to assess whether culturally adapted versions of interventions provide benefit above and beyond standard versions of interventions (Burrow-Sánchez, Martinez, Hops, & Wrona, 2011; Huey, Tilley, Jones, & Smith, 2014). No such studies could be located. Instead, we found reports from several cross-site evaluations of SBIRT funded by SAMHSA that tested a standard version of SBIRT with samples of participants from diverse racial and ethnic backgrounds (Aldridge et al., 2017; Babor et al., 2017; Bray et al., 2017). The first of these cross-site evaluations was funded in 2004, followed by two others funded in 2009 and 2013,[11] with the goal of examining SAMHSA grantee SBIRT programs on a large scale (Bray et al., 2017). Over 1 million patients were screened in the first two cross-site SBIRT evaluations, and on average, 17% of participants screened positively for a substance. The majority of participants were non-Hispanic White (57%), in their mid-40s (average age = 44), and female (56%; Babor et al., 2017; Bray et al., 2017). About 25% of participants across both evaluations were African American, whereas almost 30% in the first evaluation were Hispanic. Alcohol was the most commonly screened substance (77%), followed by illicit substances (44%), with almost one third reporting the use of both alcohol and illicit substances (Babor et al., 2017).

Aldridge and colleagues (2017) examined data from the first cross-site evaluation study with a sample of 17, 575 patients who screened positive for substance use (71% alcohol, 40% illicit substances). The sample of adults were non-Hispanic Whites (53%), African American (25%), and Hispanic (14%), and a higher percentage were male. The researchers compared substance use levels before being referred for an SBIRT intervention (i.e., BI, BT, referral to treatment) and 6 months after receiving SBIRT services; they found post-SBIRT decreases in alcohol use by 36% and 76% for illicit substances. It was not clear whether differences in outcomes were due to race or ethnicity because these variables were controlled for in the analysis. It will be important for future research to be conducted to determine whether outcomes for SBIRT are equally beneficial for individuals across racial and ethnic backgrounds, which will help determine the need for culturally adapting SBIRT.

---

[11]Only data from the first two evaluations have been reported in the literature at the time of this writing.

RECOMMENDATIONS FOR ADAPTING SBIRT FOR DIVERSE POPULATIONS

Our recommendations for adapting SBIRT for diverse populations focus on three general areas. First, we suggest that practitioners use screening instruments that are relevant and appropriate for the patient population. Second, we suggest that practitioners use BI and BT strategies that are culturally relevant and sensitive for the patient population. Finally, we suggest that practitioners increase their cultural competence in working with individuals from diverse backgrounds and consider the importance of the provider–patient relationship in the delivery of SBIRT. In the section that follows, we briefly consider each of these suggestions.

Our review of the literature earlier in this chapter indicates that a number of screening measures exist for use with SBIRT that have relevance for individuals from diverse racial and ethnic backgrounds (see Table 9.1 for a review). We suggest that practitioners choose measures that meet the clinical and cultural needs of the patients with whom they work. Some issues to consider when selecting an appropriate screening measure are the validity of the measure with patients from different cultural backgrounds, availability of the measure in a language other than English, and utility of the measure for appropriately assessing the level of substance use risk for diverse populations. We understand that practitioners will have to rely on their knowledge, clinical expertise, and cultural competence when selecting appropriate screening measures in their settings for use with diverse patient populations.

The review of the literature on BIs earlier in this chapter indicates that they can be effective, with and without adaptations, for individuals from diverse racial and ethnic backgrounds. We suggest, however, that the practitioner consider the efficacy of BIs in relation to the interaction and cultural context of the provider and patient. In particular, the provider should consider how the interpersonal interaction between provider and patient and understanding of cultural nuances may enhance the efficacy of BIs (Field & Caetano, 2010; Ornelas et al., 2015).

The patient–provider relationship is foundational and essential to enhancing patient engagement in and the efficacy of SBIRT. Typically, researchers suggest some level of cultural tailoring of an intervention to enhance its effectiveness. However, the most important aspects of an intervention are the interactions between the practitioner and patient based on the principles of MI, which include listening to the patient, understanding the patient's concerns, and developing trust. Key cultural adaptations in the delivery of SBIRT include practitioner–patient language congruence, understanding of patient-specific cultural norms and values, and the use of cultural-specific scripts to assist the effectiveness of the intervention. However, without the foundation of a positive patient–provider relationship, culturally adapted interventions will likely have less effect on the outcomes of the SBIRT intervention.

CONCLUSION

The use of SBIRT is relevant for individuals from diverse racial and ethnic backgrounds in the United States. The growing number of racially and ethnically diverse individuals in the nation, the prevalence of substance use, and the existence of health disparities all provide support for the use of SBIRT. Practitioners can increase their effectiveness in the delivery of SBIRT with diverse populations by selecting validated screening tools, providing BI based on the principles of MI, implementing culturally relevant adaptations, and improving the quality of provider–patient interactions. Finally, there is a need for research testing cultural adaptations of SBIRT, as a complete model, compared with its standard version counterpart with diverse populations.

REFERENCES

Agerwala, S. M., & McCance-Katz, E. F. (2012). Integrating screening, brief intervention, and referral to treatment (SBIRT) into clinical practice settings: A brief review. *Journal of Psychoactive Drugs, 44*, 307–317. http://dx.doi.org/10.1080/02791072.2012.720169

Aldridge, A., Linford, R., & Bray, J. (2017). Substance use outcomes of patients served by a large US implementation of Screening, Brief Intervention and Referral to Treatment (SBIRT). *Addiction, 112*, 43–53. http://dx.doi.org/10.1111/add.13651

Allen, J. P., Litten, R. Z., Fertig, J. B., & Babor, T. (1997). A review of research on the Alcohol Use Disorders Identification Test (AUDIT). *Alcoholism: Clinical and Experimental Research, 21*, 613–619. http://dx.doi.org/10.1111/j.1530-0277.1997.tb03811.x

Almarri, T. S. K., Oei, T. P. S., & Amir, T. (2009). Validation of the alcohol use identification test in a prison sample living in the Arabian Gulf region. *Substance Use & Misuse, 44*, 2001–2013. http://dx.doi.org/10.3109/10826080902848533

American Psychiatric Association. (2013). *Diagnostic and statistical manual of mental disorders* (5th ed.). Washington, DC: Author.

Babor, T. F., Del Boca, F., & Bray, J. W. (2017). Screening, Brief Intervention and Referral to Treatment: Implications of SAMHSA's SBIRT initiative for substance abuse policy and practice. *Addiction, 112*, 110–117. http://dx.doi.org/10.1111/add.13675

Babor, T. F., & Grant, M. (1989). From clinical research to secondary prevention: International collaboration in the development of the Alcohol Disorders Identification Test (AUDIT). *Alcohol Health and Research World, 13*, 371–374.

Babor, T. F., McRee, B. G., Kassebaum, P. A., Grimaldi, P. L., Ahmed, K., & Bray, J. (2007). Screening, Brief Intervention, and Referral to Treatment (SBIRT): Toward a public health approach to the management of substance abuse. *Substance Abuse, 28*, 7–30. http://dx.doi.org/10.1300/J465v28n03_03

Bedregal, L. E., Sobell, L. C., Sobell, M. B., & Simco, E. (2006). Psychometric characteristics of a Spanish version of the DAST–10 and the RAGS. *Addictive Behaviors, 31*, 309–319. http://dx.doi.org/10.1016/j.addbeh.2005.05.012

Bray, J. W., Del Boca, F. K., McRee, B. G., Hayashi, S. W., & Babor, T. F. (2017). Screening, Brief Intervention and Referral to Treatment (SBIRT): Rationale, program overview and cross-site evaluation. *Addiction, 112*, 3–11. http://dx.doi.org/10.1111/add.13676

Brown, R. L., & Rounds, L. A. (1995). Conjoint screening questionnaires for alcohol and other drug abuse: Criterion validity in a primary care practice. *Wisconsin Medical Journal, 94*, 135–140.

Burrow-Sánchez, J. J., Martinez, C. R., Jr., Hops, H., & Wrona, M. (2011). Cultural accommodation of substance abuse treatment for Latino adolescents. *Journal of Ethnicity in Substance Abuse, 10*, 202–225. http://dx.doi.org/10.1080/15332640.2011.600194

Bush, K., Kivlahan, D. R., McDonell, M. B., Fihn, S. D., & Bradley, K. A. (1998). The AUDIT alcohol consumption questions (AUDIT–C): An effective brief screening test for problem drinking. *Archives of Internal Medicine, 158,* 1789–1795. http://dx.doi.org/10.1001/archinte.158.16.1789

Caetano, R. (2003). Alcohol-related health disparities and treatment-related epidemiological findings among Whites, Blacks, and Hispanics in the United States. *Alcoholism: Clinical and Experimental Research, 27,* 1337–1339. http://dx.doi.org/10.1097/01.ALC.0000080342.05229.86

Cherpitel, C. J. (1995a). Analysis of cut points for screening instruments for alcohol problems in the emergency room. *Journal of Studies on Alcohol, 56,* 695–700. http://dx.doi.org/10.15288/jsa.1995.56.695

Cherpitel, C. J. (1995b). Screening for alcohol problems in the emergency department. *Annals of Emergency Medicine, 26,* 158–166. http://dx.doi.org/10.1016/S0196-0644(95)70146-X

Cherpitel, C. J. (1999). Screening for alcohol problems in the U.S. general population: A comparison of the CAGE and TWEAK by gender, ethnicity, and services utilization. *Journal of Studies on Alcohol, 60,* 705–711. http://dx.doi.org/10.15288/jsa.1999.60.705

Cherpitel, C. J., & Bazargan, S. (2003). Screening for alcohol problems: Comparison of the audit, RAPS4 and RAPS4-QF among African American and Hispanic patients in an inner city emergency department. *Drug and Alcohol Dependence, 71,* 275–280. http://dx.doi.org/10.1016/S0376-8716(03)00140-6

Cherpitel, C. J., & Borges, G. (2000). Performance of screening instruments for alcohol problems in the ER: A comparison of Mexican-Americans and Mexicans in Mexico. *The American Journal of Drug and Alcohol Abuse, 26,* 683–702. http://dx.doi.org/10.1081/ADA-100101902

Curtis, B. L., McLellan, A. T., & Gabellini, B. N. (2014). Translating SBIRT to public school settings: An initial test of feasibility. *Journal of Substance Abuse Treatment, 46,* 15–21. http://dx.doi.org/10.1016/j.jsat.2013.08.001

Ewing, J. A. (1984). Detecting alcoholism: The CAGE questionnaire. *JAMA, 252,* 1905–1907. http://dx.doi.org/10.1001/jama.1984.03350140051025

Field, C., & Caetano, R. (2010). The role of ethnic matching between patient and provider on the effectiveness of brief alcohol interventions with Hispanics. *Alcoholism: Clinical and Experimental Research, 34,* 262–271. http://dx.doi.org/10.1111/j.1530-0277.2009.01089.x

Field, C. A., Cabriales, J. A., Woolard, R. H., Tyroch, A. H., Caetano, R., & Castro, Y. (2015). Cultural adaptation of a brief motivational intervention for heavy drinking among Hispanics in a medical setting. *BMC Public Health, 15,* 724. http://dx.doi.org/10.1186/s12889-015-1984-y

Field, C. A., Cochran, G., & Caetano, R. (2013). Treatment utilization and unmet treatment need among Hispanics following brief intervention. *Alcoholism: Clinical and Experimental Research, 37,* 300–307. http://dx.doi.org/10.1111/j.1530-0277.2012.01878.x

Frank, D., DeBenedetti, A. F., Volk, R. J., Williams, E. C., Kivlahan, D. R., & Bradley, K. A. (2008). Effectiveness of the AUDIT-C as a screening test for alcohol misuse in three race/ethnic groups. *Journal of General Internal Medicine, 23,* 781–787. http://dx.doi.org/10.1007/s11606-008-0594-0

Hettema, J., Steele, J., & Miller, W. R. (2005). Motivational interviewing. *Annual Review of Clinical Psychology, 1,* 91–111. http://dx.doi.org/10.1146/annurev.clinpsy.1.102803.143833

Hobbs, F., & Stoops, N. (2002). *Demographic trends in the 20th Century.* Retrieved from https://www.census.gov/prod/2002pubs/censr-4.pdf

Huey, S. J., Jr., Tilley, J. L., Jones, E. O., & Smith, C. A. (2014). The contribution of cultural competence to evidence-based care for ethnically diverse populations.

Annual Review of Clinical Psychology, 10, 305–338. http://dx.doi.org/10.1146/annurev-clinpsy-032813-153729

Kim, S. S., Gulick, E. E., Nam, K. A., & Kim, S.-H. (2008). Psychometric properties of the Alcohol Use Disorders Identification Test: A Korean version. *Archives of Psychiatric Nursing, 22*, 190–199. http://dx.doi.org/10.1016/j.apnu.2007.07.005

Knight, J. R., Shrier, L. A., Bravender, T. D., Farrell, M., Vander Bilt, J., & Shaffer, H. J. (1999). A new brief screen for adolescent substance abuse. *Archives of Pediatrics & Adolescent Medicine, 153*, 591–596. http://dx.doi.org/10.1001/archpedi.153.6.591

Lee, C. S., López, S. R., Colby, S. M., Rohsenow, D., Hernández, L., Borrelli, B., & Caetano, R. (2013). Culturally adapted motivational interviewing for Latino heavy drinkers: Results from a randomized clinical trial. *Journal of Ethnicity in Substance Abuse, 12*, 356 373. http://dx.doi.org/10.1080/15332640.2013.836730

Leonardson, G. R., Kemper, E., Ness, F. K., Koplin, B. A., Daniels, M. C., & Leonardson, G. A. (2005). Validity and reliability of the audit and CAGE-AID in Northern Plains American Indians. *Psychological Reports, 97*, 161–166. http://dx.doi.org/10.2466/PR0.97.5.161-166

Li, Q., Babor, T. F., Hao, W., & Chen, X. (2011). The Chinese translations of Alcohol Use Disorders Identification Test (AUDIT) in China: A systematic review. *Alcohol and Alcoholism, 46*, 416–423. http://dx.doi.org/10.1093/alcalc/agr012

Lo, C. C., & Cheng, T. C. (2011). Racial/ethnic differences in access to substance abuse treatment. *Journal of Health Care for the Poor and Underserved, 22*, 621–637. http://dx.doi.org/10.1353/hpu.2011.0054

Manuel, J. K., Satre, D. D., Tsoh, J., Moreno-John, G., Ramos, J. S., McCance-Katz, E. F., & Satterfield, J. M. (2015). Adapting screening, brief intervention, and referral to treatment for alcohol and drugs to culturally diverse clinical populations. *Journal of Addiction Medicine, 9*, 343–351. http://dx.doi.org/10.1097/ADM.0000000000000150

Martino, S., Grilo, C. M., & Fehon, D. C. (2000). Development of the Drug Abuse Screening Test for Adolescents (DAST–A). *Addictive Behaviors, 25*, 57–70. http://dx.doi.org/10.1016/S0306-4603(99)00030-1

Mulia, N., Ye, Y., Greenfield, T. K., & Zemore, S. E. (2009). Disparities in alcohol-related problems among White, Black, and Hispanic Americans. *Alcoholism: Clinical and Experimental Research, 33*, 654–662. http://dx.doi.org/10.1111/j.1530-0277.2008.00880.x

Neff, J. A., Kelley, M. L., Walters, S. T., Cunningham, T. D., Paulson, J. F., Braitman, A. L., . . . Bolen, H. (2015). Effectiveness of a screening and brief intervention protocol for heavy drinkers in dental practice: A cluster-randomized trial. *Journal of Health Psychology, 20*, 1534–1548. http://dx.doi.org/10.1177/1359105313516660

Ornelas, I. J., Allen, C., Vaughan, C., Williams, E. C., & Negi, N. (2015). Vida PURA: A cultural adaptation of screening and brief intervention to reduce unhealthy drinking among Latino day laborers. *Substance Abuse, 36*, 264–271. http://dx.doi.org/10.1080/08897077.2014.955900

Saloner, B., & Lê Cook, B. (2013). Blacks and Hispanics are less likely than whites to complete addiction treatment, largely due to socioeconomic factors. *Health Affairs, 32*, 135–145. http://dx.doi.org/10.1377/hlthaff.2011.0983

Skinner, H. A. (1982). The Drug Abuse Screening Test. *Addictive Behaviors, 7*, 363–371. http://dx.doi.org/10.1016/0306-4603(82)90005-3

Smith, P. C., Schmidt, S. M., Allensworth-Davies, D., & Saitz, R. (2010). A single-question screening test for drug use in primary care. *Archives of Internal Medicine, 170*, 1155–1160. http://dx.doi.org/10.1001/archinternmed.2010.140

Smith, P. C., Schmidt, S. M., Allensworth-Davies, D., & Saitz, R. (2009). Primary care validation of a single-question alcohol screening test. *Journal of General Internal Medicine, 24*, 783–788. http://dx.doi.org/10.1007/s11606-009-0928-6

Substance Abuse and Mental Health Services Administration. (2018a). *2017 National Survey on Drug Use and Health: Detailed Tables*. Rockville, MD: Center for Behavioral

Health Statistics and Quality, Substance Abuse and Mental Health Services Administration.

Substance Abuse and Mental Health Services Administration. (2018b). *Key substance use and mental health indicators in the United States: Results from the 2017 National Survey on Drug Use and Health* (HHS Publication No. SMA 18-5068, NSDUH Series H-53). Rockville, MD: Center for Behavioral Health Statistics and Quality, Substance Abuse and Mental Health Services Administration.

U.S. Census Bureau. (2017). *2013–2017 American community survey 5-year estimates.* Retrieved from https://factfinder.census.gov/faces/tableservices/jsf/pages/product view.xhtml?src=bkmk

Vespa, J., Medina, L., & Armstrong, D. M. (2018). *Demographic turning points for the United States: Population projections for 2020 to 2060* (Current Population Reports, No. P25-1144). Retrieved from U.S. Census Bureau website: https://www.census. gov/content/dam/Census/library/publications/2020/demo/p25-1144.pdf

Volk, R. J., Steinbauer, J. R., Cantor, S. B., & Holzer, C. E., III. (1997). The Alcohol Use Disorders Identification Test (AUDIT) as a screen for at-risk drinking in primary care patients of different racial/ethnic backgrounds. *Addiction, 92,* 197–206. http:// dx.doi.org/10.1111/j.1360-0443.1997.tb03652.x

WHO ASSIST Working Group. (2002). The Alcohol, Smoking and Substance Involvement Screening Test (ASSIST): Development, reliability and feasibility. *Addiction, 97,* 1183–1194. http://dx.doi.org/10.1046/j.1360-0443.2002.00185.x

Witbrodt, J., Mulia, N., Zemore, S. E., & Kerr, W. C. (2014). Racial/ethnic disparities in alcohol-related problems: Differences by gender and level of heavy drinking. *Alcoholism: Clinical and Experimental Research, 38,* 1662–1670. http://dx.doi.org/ 10.1111/acer.12398

10

Screening, Brief Intervention, and Referral to Treatment for Older Adults

Lessons Learned From the Florida BRITE Project

Lawrence Schonfeld

Older adults who misuse substances have been underserved by substance abuse treatment systems. This chapter describes the extent of the problem and the advantages and challenges of implementing screening, brief intervention, and referral to treatment (SBIRT) with this population based on studies conducted in Florida. Florida's aging population is considered a bellwether for other states. Its total population ranks third in the United States, with 21 million residents, more than 20% of whom are age 65 and older (65+). Our experience in Florida with older adults who misuse substances began with elder-specific group treatment programs but has evolved with SBIRT to address problems on a larger scale. This chapter presents the lessons learned from the implementation of the Florida BRITE Project (http://BRITE.fmhi.usf.edu) and the challenges facing clinicians.

EXTENT OF THE PROBLEM

Older adults represent a small segment of people admitted to substance abuse treatment. However, the baby boom generation is projected to lead to increased admissions, straining service and treatment systems (Gfroerer, Penne, Pemberton, & Folsom, 2003). In the United States, total substance abuse treatment admissions decreased from 1,957,460 in 2006 to 1,696,648 in 2016. However, over that span, admissions for people ages 50+ increased

http://dx.doi.org/10.1037/0000199-011
Screening, Brief Intervention, and Referral to Treatment for Substance Use: A Practitioner's Guide,
M. D. Cimini and J. L. Martin (Editors)

179

dramatically, with the largest increases among people ages 60 to 69, almost doubling in numbers from 26,993 to 53,265 (Substance Abuse and Mental Health Services Administration [SAMHSA], 2018b).

In addition to the increases in older adult admissions, "risky use" of alcohol is also increasing. A comparison of the National Epidemiologic Survey on Alcohol and Related Conditions data from 2001–2002 ($N = 43,093$), with data from 2012–2013 ($N = 36,309$), showed that high-risk drinking and alcohol use disorders increased across all age groups. However, the largest increase in 12-month alcohol use was among those ages 65 and older, increasing from 45% to 55% (Grant et al., 2017).

EARLY STUDIES OF OLDER ADULTS

When we began research on substance misuse among older adults at the Florida Mental Health Institute (FMHI), they were a vastly underserved population. The few older individuals identified in publicly funded treatment programs were mostly long-term, "early-onset" drinkers whose problems began decades earlier. These people experienced significant medical impairments, alienation from families, legal problems, and financial difficulties. Far fewer were "late-life onset" alcohol abusers, whose drinking problems began at age 50 or later.

In the late 1970s, we developed the Gerontology Alcohol Project (GAP) at FMHI, a day treatment program specifically for people 55+ and whose alcohol abuse began after age 50 (Dupree, Broskowski, & Schonfeld, 1984). At admission to GAP, each client was interviewed using a drinking profile, in which we applied an "A–B–C" approach (i.e., antecedents–behavior–consequences) to identify the drinking behavior chain. Each person's chain consisted of antecedents that preceded drinking (i.e., situations or places, thoughts, feelings, cues, and urges preceding the first drink), the behavior (i.e., the first drink), and consequences that were either short-term reinforcers (e.g., feeling happier, social, less lonely, less tense), short-term negative consequences (e.g., feeling guilty, arguing with a spouse), or longer term negative consequences (e.g., medical problems, alienation of family). Clients were taught to recognize their A–B–C chain and taught cognitive behavioral and self-management skills necessary to prevent relapse. Success was demonstrated by a reduction in alcohol consumption, fewer lapses, decreased depression, increased life satisfaction, and increased social support (Dupree et al., 1984). Key findings were that, before admissions, most drank in response to feelings of depression, loneliness, and boredom (i.e., "intrapersonal" events not involving other people). We found that indicators commonly used to identify younger alcohol abusers (e.g., marital, work, legal, social indicators) did not hold for older individuals who tended to live alone (often widowed or divorced), lived far from family, were retired, and did not drive as much. Our subsequent studies revealed similar findings, even among early-onset substance users (Schonfeld & Dupree, 1991).

Discussions in the published literature at that time seemed to "lump" together medication-related problems among older adults irrespective of the causes. Although medication misuse among younger treatment admissions was demonstrated by those who obtained pills illegally and used them for non-medical reasons, among older treatment admissions, such behavior was rare. Our studies indicated that older adults often unintentionally mismanaged medications, such as when they used more medication than prescribed to overcome persistent pain, stopped taking medication due to side effects or prohibitive costs, or forgot to take pills due to memory impairments.

As we assisted other states in replicating our approaches (Outlaw et al., 2012; Schonfeld et al., 2000), similar high-risk situations among older adults in those states were observed. Hence, we developed a relapse prevention curriculum published by SAMHSA (Center for Substance Abuse Treatment, 2005) and incorporated experiences from which others might benefit. Results from these early efforts helped shape our initial SBIRT approaches for addressing the misuse of alcohol, medications, and illicit drugs among older adults. To summarize, we emphasized that for older adults

- early-onset abuse was associated with significant medical problems concomitant with, or caused by, years of substance use that had to be addressed;

- screening should be conducted for depressive symptoms even at subclinical levels because depression and loneliness were common antecedents for drinking;

- assessing for suicide risk is recommended because research demonstrated the highest rates of suicide were among middle-aged women and older adult men;

- cognitive behavioral skills were effective in preventing relapse as long as the content and exercises related to older adults' experiences;

- diminished social support related to substance abuse, whether caused by alienation of family or due to age-related losses, was a factor;

- in retirement communities and clubs social activities often encouraged excessive drinking; and

- assessments of prescription and over-the-counter medications, including prescribing practices and patients' abilities, are needed, especially for women who receive more prescriptions than men.

FLORIDA BRITE PROJECT

In the late 1990s, the state of Florida Department of Children and Families (DCF) identified improving behavioral health services delivery to older adults as a high-priority goal in its strategic plans. In 2002, I partnered with the lead staff of the DCF Substance Abuse Program Office to design an SBIRT program for older adults. In 2003, our team applied to SAMHSA for its first wave of state cooperative agreement SBIRT grants. When Florida was not selected to be in the first cohort of four states, DCF provided pilot funding to implement SBIRT for adults ages 60+.

In developing the pilot project, we relied on the SAMHSA Treatment Improvement Protocol (TIP) Series 34 (Center for Substance Abuse Treatment, 1999) and implemented SBIRT in four counties. DCF awarded contracts to one behavioral health provider agency in each county to conduct SBIRT. These agencies were selected on the basis of their experience working with older adults and links to aging services. For marketing purposes, the pilot was branded as the "Florida BRITE Project": BRief Intervention and Treatment for Elders (Schonfeld et al., 2010). BRITE targeted alcohol, medications (prescription and over-the-counter), illicit drugs, depression, and suicide risk. Age-appropriate assessments were selected and administered at initial screening and follow-ups for those who screened positive and were provided brief interventions. BRITE staff entered clients' responses into a web-based program that provided instantaneous feedback on the level of risk of substance use, depression, and suicide.

A total of 3,497 screenings were conducted from 2004 to 2007. Among positive screenings, 26.4% were for medication misuse, 9.7% for alcohol use, and 1.2% for illicit drug use. Reassessed at follow-up, those who had screened positive and provided brief interventions demonstrated significant reductions in drinking, drug use, medication misuse, and depression.

Brief interventions were conducted using the scripted Health Promotion Workbook modified from the TIP 34 version to address medication misuse. Using the workbook served to maintain consistency across providers.

In late 2006, our team applied for, and SAMHSA awarded, a 5-year, $14-million state cooperative agreement grant among the second cohort of grant recipients. The funding was used to expand BRITE beyond the four counties in the pilot, with full implementation in 2007 (Schonfeld et al., 2015). Florida's grant was unique because it was the only state focusing solely on older adults and including depression screening.

All SAMHSA's state grantees were expected to reach certain goals for the number of people screened. In other states where SBIRT was implemented across all ages, goals of 100,000 screenings were attained by screening within one or two "high-volume" hospital emergency departments. Florida's goal was set by SAMHSA at 66,000 for people ages 55+. Given the age restriction, this required expansion of BRITE across numerous counties and provider agencies.

Over the 5 years of the SAMHSA grant, a total of 30 agencies in 18 counties were awarded contracts. Each agency hired BRITE counselors to implement the protocol. Our training manager, a clinical psychologist who previously directed an SBIRT project in another state, provided training at each agency on prescreening; administration of the Alcohol, Smoking and Substance Involvement Screening Test (ASSIST; WHO ASSIST Working Group, 2002);

brief interventions; and data entry. Together, we posted all instruments in English and Spanish on the BRITE website (see Resources section). Providers collected data using specialized software on laptops, with data to be uploaded later to SAMHSA's Government Performance and Results Act (GPRA) data system, as required by the agency. Collectively, the 30 agencies screened 85,001 adults of ages 55 and older in over 70 different settings, thus exceeding the goal set by SAMHSA.

CHALLENGES FOR CONDUCTING SBIRT WITH OLDER ADULTS

Perhaps the biggest challenge for conducting SBIRT with older populations is the difficulty in identifying problem substance use or abuse. Older adults are often labeled as "hidden abusers" and not easily identified in community settings. The behavior often goes unnoticed unless events occur, such as falls, car crashes, or self-neglect, that come to the attention of family or protective services. Over time, our team has learned that, for better access to SBIRT for older adults, updates to many commonly used screening tools are needed; likewise, social outreach and health care services in retirement communities have to address individuals' levels of social support. In addition to these issues, other barriers to the effective delivery of SBIRT include ageism, cognitive impairments, and failure to identify illicit substance use and nonprescription use of prescription drugs.

IDENTIFICATION OF OLDER ADULTS USING SUBSTANCES

Identification of older adults within community settings required significant case-finding efforts and community education. As noted earlier, indicators commonly used to identify substance abuse in younger people were not useful for older adults in most community settings. Clinicians should understand that many of the *Diagnostic and Statistical Manual of Mental Disorders* criteria may not apply to older adults. For example,

- drinking more or drinking over a longer period do not apply because many consumed fewer drinks than in their youth due to changes in metabolism;

- changes in social, occupational, or recreational activities often do not apply to "late-onset" drinkers whose losses occurred late in life, before the onset of drinking problems; and

- failure to fulfill role obligations (e.g., work, school, or home), experiencing social or interpersonal problems, or giving up various activities rarely applies to older adults whose roles have already changed (e.g., retirement, widowhood, moving away from family).

SBIRT screening does not aim to identify diagnostic criteria. Instead, it focuses on identifying individuals at moderate to high risk for negative consequences resulting from their substance use. For older adults, some instruments might require lowering the threshold for defining risky drinking or changing how we conceptualize medication misuse and mismanagement when illicit activity is not involved.

Changes in pharmacodynamics and pharmacokinetics contribute to side effects and increased concentrations or "half-lives" of alcohol and drugs, especially among the most medically impaired (Moore, Whiteman, & Ward, 2007). As a result, older adults may become intoxicated even when consuming less alcohol than they did years ago. Also, because they consume more medications than other age groups, they are likely to experience more alcohol–drug interactions. As a result, clinicians should be aware that relatively small quantities of alcohol may adversely affect older adults even if they drink below recommended limits for their age group.

For people living in large, planned retirement communities, social activities seem to revolve around drinking. In central Florida, one 55+ community with over 100,000 residents participated in a health survey conducted by our university. We found many drank beyond recommended limits but did not experience symptoms of depression (Fishleder, Schonfeld, Corvin, Tyler, & VandeWeerd, 2016). Two urgent care clinics in this retirement community were included in BRITE. Despite stories of excessive drinking, the clinics did not find many patients who screened positive in comparison with aging and other services (Schonfeld et al., 2015), perhaps because the retirees who visit the clinics pay more attention to health and do not drink to excess.

Continuing care retirement communities (CCRCs) differ from such large retirement communities. CCRCs provide a continuum of care, including independent living, assisted living, and skilled nursing, so residents can "age in place" as functionality changes. In a study of 71 CCRC residents (average age of 80, about two thirds women), brief screenings conducted via telephone interviews revealed that nearly half were drinking at hazardous levels and often alone (e.g., in their apartment; Sacco et al., 2015). Thus, in both types of communities, brief screening could be incorporated to promote a healthy lifestyle.

Aging services are excellent additions to SBIRT to identify older adults with substance use problems who may not be visiting health care facilities. Their case managers are trained to conduct home visits often triggered by referrals by family, neighbors, or adult protective services investigators based on elders showing self-neglect or declining function. Aging services case managers often assess support systems, a key for SBIRT, because social isolation is a major antecedent for drinking. They are accustomed to working with people grieving the loss of a loved one and those lacking social support.

Clinicians treating older people for mood disorders should routinely screen for substance use. As noted in a study of 154 older patients being treated at a clinic for depression, more than half consumed alcohol, often beyond recommend limits, and use of cannabis was associated with higher depression scores (Satre, Sterling, Mackin, & Weisner, 2011).

Finally, the identification of substance misuse can be enhanced using technology. In a recent study, clients interested in reducing alcohol intake learned to use smartphones to complete daily diaries of substance use, resulting in the finding that older adults increased drinking due to increased levels of boredom (Kuerbis et al., 2018). The use of such technology to conduct brief screening should resonate well with baby boomers and subsequent cohorts of older adults who readily use the Internet and online communication with health care providers.

Ageism

Ageism describes the bias and stereotyping of older people based on age (Butler, 1969). Health care professionals' ageism can lead to misdiagnosis, errors in prescribing, and misassumptions about physical and mental decline (T. R. Skinner, Scott, & Martin, 2016). Clinicians must be aware of their biases to avoid such problems. Ageism can also be exhibited by family and the older adults themselves. Myths about getting old can lead to self-fulfilling prophecies about physical and mental decline being inevitable and irreversible, when, in fact, drinking or medication use may be the cause. SBIRT neutralizes such assumptions by providing universal screening for all and screening for risky use, as well as severe risk. SBIRT brief interventions are nonconfrontational, avoid labels, and eschew pre-assumptions, all of which maintain a person's self-esteem.

Cognitive Impairment

Memory problems can affect recall and comprehension during SBIRT. Severity can range from mild cognitive impairment (MCI) that is sometimes reversible when drinking or drug use ceases, to severe and irreversible impairment caused by long-term substance abuse, such as Wernicke's encephalopathy and Korsakoff's syndrome. Such cases should be referred for complete assessment (e.g., neuropsychological, magnetic resonance imaging) to a memory disorder clinic or specialist to determine the severity and type of impairment.

About 15% to 20% of people 65+ have MCI affecting recall that may not necessarily interfere with the person's daily activities (Alzheimer's Association, 2019). People with MCI are at higher risk of developing Alzheimer's disease and related dementias (ADRDs). By 2060, it is projected there will be 13.9 million with ADRDs (Matthews et al., 2019). Heavy drinkers are at increased risk for ADRDs (Becker, Schaffert, LoBue, Adinoff, & Cullum, 2018), as are long-term users of benzodiazepines (Billioti de Gage et al., 2014; Crowe & Stranks, 2018).

Clinicians implementing SBIRT may be concerned about the reliability of a client's self-report due to memory problems. They might ask multiple questions about quantity, frequency, and type of substances to look for consistency in clients' answers and, if permitted, interview a family member for corroboration.

Multiple and longer sessions may be necessary when implementing SBIRT in community settings. In hospitals, where one brief intervention session of about 15 minutes is the norm, multiple sessions are unlikely scenarios. In community settings, if longer and follow-up sessions are possible, brief intervention can be reinforced by repetition and perhaps by providing "homework" or activities, such as completing a daily log of substance use.

Use of Illicit Substances and Nonmedical Use of Prescription Drugs

Prevalence of illicit drug use in older adults is relatively low but may increase with aging baby boomers and new laws on the use of marijuana. Data from the National Survey on Drug Use and Health (NSDUH) indicated that by 2020, past-year marijuana use in people ages 50+ will increase to 2.9% (about 3.3 million), use of illicit drugs will increase to 3.1% (3.5 million), and nonmedical use of psychotherapeutic drugs will increase to 2.4% (2.7 million; Colliver, Compton, Gfroerer, & Condon, 2006).

Illicit medication use, or nonmedical use of prescription medications, may occur via theft, obtaining prescriptions under false pretenses, or "doctor shopping" (Drug Enforcement Administration, 2018). This does not appear to be the case for older medication misusers. A study aimed at estimating doctor shopping for opioids analyzed data from 146.1 million prescriptions for buprenorphine, codeine/dihydrocodeine, fentanyl, hydrocodone, methadone, oxycodone, oxymorphone, propoxyphene, or tramadol dispensed during 2008 by 37,000 pharmacies (McDonald & Carlson, 2013). Patients were divided into three groups based on the number of physicians prescribing opioids: single prescriber, two to three, or 10 or more prescribers. The good news is that less than 2% of all patients, irrespective of age, fell into the last group (10 or more prescribers), and more important, trends in doctor shopping decreased for people 60+, irrespective of the number of prescribers.

Older adults did not escape the opioid crisis that began in the late 1990s. A study of data from the Poison Centers Program identified 184,136 calls reporting abuse, misuse, or use with suicidal intent relating to prescription opioids for two groups: adults ages 20 to 59 and ages 60 and older during the period from 2006 to 2013 (West, Severtson, Green, & Dart, 2015). The 60+ group totaled 13,628 or 7.4% of calls and had a lower rate of abuse, yet higher rates of misuse and use with suicidal intent. Last, a study of NSDUH data found that lifetime prevalence rates of older adults' nonmedical opioid use continued to increase, rising from 5.6% in 2002 to 8% in 2013.

Prescriptions for benzodiazepines are of great concern for older adults. A national study of outpatient medical visits from 2003 through 2015 showed increases for all age groups in benzodiazepine-related overdose mortality, falls, fractures, automobile crashes, and cognitive impairment, especially when combined with alcohol, opioids, or other medications (Agarwal & Landon, 2019). That study showed that older adults' benzodiazepine-related visits increased from 7 million to 19.4 million visits. In general, primary care physicians were responsible for about half of the benzodiazepine prescriptions and increases in benzodiazepines coprescribed with opioids, other sedative-hypnotics, muscle relaxants, and antipsychotics. Coprescribing medications for older adults mostly reflects their increasing health problems but increases the risk of adverse drug events and potential alcohol–medication interactions.

Adverse drug events (ADEs) constitute a significant health problem for the older population. Older adults experience the highest rates of ADEs and are seven times more likely than younger people to have an ADE leading to hospital admission. Older adults' ADEs are often caused by the most common medications and are considered preventable issues (U.S. Department of Health and Human Services, 2014). ADEs were involved in about one third of all ages' hospital adverse events, 280,000 hospital admissions (53% of which were for people age 65+), more than 3.5 million physician office visits, and 1 million emergency department visits (U.S. Department of Health and Human Services, 2014). Contributing to ADEs is polypharmacy (i.e., simultaneous use of multiple medications). The National Health and Nutrition Examination Survey indicated that 9% of people 65+ consumed five or more prescription medications (Kantor, Rehm, Haas, Chan, & Giovannucci, 2015).

Medications may present challenges for SBIRT screening. Assessments such as the ASSIST can help staff to identify the level of risk of nonmedical use of prescription medications. However, when BRITE providers entered ASSIST information into SAMHSA's GPRA data system, medication problems could only be classified as illicit drug use in GPRA, a flaw we reported to SAMHSA (Schonfeld et al., 2015). Aging services case managers often conduct a "brown bag" review in which the client is asked ahead of time to collect all medications in a bag to review his or her knowledge about the medications and how they are used. Once a misuse is identified, SBIRT staff should begin immediate education about using medications as prescribed, the risks of not doing so, methods for maintaining a correct medication schedule, and encouragement of good communication between the client and prescribing physician about side effects or interactions. For those who intentionally misuse medications, SBIRT includes educating them about the need to stop such behavior, the repercussions of not doing so, and what to do to avoid relapses.

RECOMMENDATIONS FOR SBIRT FOR OLDER ADULTS

There are many "upsides" to incorporating SBIRT into clinical practice. Screening can easily be built into the intake process, brief advice and preprinted education materials can be offered in a short amount of time, and clinicians eligible to bill for Medicare-covered services can be reimbursed for delivering SBIRT. There is one rate for screening and brief intervention services from 15 to 30 minutes and a higher rate for screening and brief intervention services greater than 30 minutes (Center for Medicare and Medicaid Services, 2017).

In this section, I share recommendations for implementing SBIRT with older adults, based on the BRITE Project experience, with particular attention to "elder-friendly" practices and screener tools, as well as ethical issues such as maintaining patient privacy and referring to treatment programs that meet older adults' needs.

Implementation in Community Settings by Health Educators

SBIRT was originally designed for implementation in health care settings, such as hospital emergency departments, primary care, and community health centers, recognizing that (a) most people visit a primary care physician or emergency room at some time, (b) physicians have a great deal of influence on patients when suggesting changes in lifestyle, and (c) universal screening for substance use can easily be incorporated into the health care intake process. However, because older adults with substance use problems are often "hidden abusers," we designed the Florida BRITE Project to include additional community sites and included in-home visits.

Agencies awarded contracts by DCF were required to have a plan for implementing BRITE in their communities in a variety of settings where older adults congregated or lived, such as senior centers, congregate meal sites, retirement communities, and older adults' homes. They were also required to have a formal agreement with at least one local hospital or medical clinic to conduct SBIRT. BRITE agencies not affiliated with a hospital had to obtain a formal agreement with that hospital to conduct screenings and brief interventions with patients. Typically, these BRITE staff introduced themselves as "health educators" and described their role. This working title of "health educator" was used to make patients feel comfortable because the approach was positive, health-oriented, and less threatening than to present the introduction solely as a substance use screening.

When first approaching participants, a short prescreen is the easiest way to rule out those who do not use any substances or who are at low risk. Prescreens are often abbreviated versions of longer validated assessments that can be administered easily by any staff member in less than 1 minute. If the outcome of the prescreen is positive, the staff member can immediately administer a more in-depth assessment, such as the ASSIST, to determine the severity of the problem. For older adults in the Florida BRITE Project, we aimed for an "elder-friendly" SBIRT screening approach that included questions about high-risk situations common to older adults. We found this type of screening instrument was readily accepted by the older adults, as well as by the interviewer.

Screening for Risky Use of Alcohol

In the BRITE pilot, a prescreen began with two screening questions: "Have you ever, in your entire life, consumed any alcohol, such as wine, beer, or liquor?" If a client responded yes, we asked: "Have you had any alcohol in the past 5 years?" A positive response led to the administration of the three-item AUDIT–C (Bush, Kivlahan, McDonell, Fihn, & Bradley, 1998) and the Short Michigan Alcoholism Screening Test-Geriatric Version (SMAST-G; Blow, Gillespie, Barry, Mudd, & Hill, 1998).

In the larger, SAMHSA-funded BRITE project, we used the National Institute of Alcohol Abuse and Alcoholism (2005) three-item screen as the prescreen. The first two questions asked about the number of days per week the person drank and the number of drinks on a typical day. Risk could be determined by multiplying the numbers from the client's responses, and if the score were greater than seven, the person would be administered the ASSIST to determine the level of severity. The third question in the AUDIT–C asked about the maximum number of drinks on any given day in the past month, and if the response more than three, that could also trigger the administration of the ASSIST for a more comprehensive screening of risk.

The CAGE (Mayfield, McLeod, & Hall, 1974) is another brief instrument recommended by SAMHSA for SBIRT that is useful because of its brevity. The questionnaire's name is an acronym derived from its four questions (based on the words in upper case), for which a "yes" response to at least two questions is considered a positive screen for adults. The four questions are as follows:

1. Have you ever felt you should CUT down on your drinking?
2. Have people ANNOYED you by criticizing your drinking?
3. Have you ever felt bad or GUILTY about your drinking?
4. Have you ever had a drink first thing in the morning to steady your nerves or to get rid of a hangover (EYE-opener)?

The CAGE does not provide a time frame for these four questions. Older adults considered to be early-onset alcohol abusers may be responding to the items based on experiences that occurred years before, rather than recent times, which could result in a false-positive screen. Because SBIRT is best suited for current use, additional questions about the time frame for any positive response would be helpful. Furthermore, there are questions about the sensitivity of the CAGE when used with older adults. Moore, Seeman, Morgenstern, Beck, and Reuben (2002) compared the CAGE and SMAST-G in a study of 1,889 adults ages 55 to 103 (Moore et al., 2002). Fewer than half of all participants who screened positive on either instrument screened positive on both measures. Those screening positive on the SMAST-G drank less than persons screening positive on the CAGE, and males screened positive more often on the CAGE than the SMAST-G.

A study conducted on a sample of 602 randomly selected Spanish-speaking patients in two health care centers compared patients less than 65 years old with those age 65 and older using the full AUDIT, the AUDIT–C, and the CAGE (Gómez et al., 2006). They found that for the older patients, the sensitivity for detecting hazardous drinking was 100% using the AUDIT–C, 67% for the AUDIT, and 39% for the CAGE. These results suggest the AUDIT–C is better for identifying drinking problems in the older population.

Screening for Nonmedical Use of Prescription Drugs

Having brief screening instruments for older adults' use of prescription and over-the-counter (OTC) medications would be helpful, but brief prescreens that are often recommended focus on using medication as if it were an illicit drug. For example, SAMHSA has suggested using the Drug Abuse Screening Test (DAST; H. A. Skinner, 1982). The various versions (28, 20, and 10 items) of the DAST ask about the consequences of abuse (e.g., blackouts, withdrawal symptoms, memory loss, inability to stop using) and may address the non-medical use of medications, but they do not address older adults who commit medication errors or experience adverse drug interactions.

Because we conceptualized mismanagement and adverse drug reactions in the BRITE pilot project, we decided to use several steps: a brown bag review followed by the interviewer's impressions based on yes or no to each of the following four observations of the client:

1. Cannot correctly recall the purpose of one or more medications.
2. Reports the wrong dose/amount of one or more medications.
3. Takes one or more medications for the wrong reasons or symptoms.
4. Needs education and/or assistance on proper medication use.

For any yes response, the interviewer completed a checklist we developed for BRITE, consisting of 17 items (requiring yes or no responses) about medication use, adverse drug reactions, and errors. These items, derived from the research literature and our experience, were as follows:

1. Do you take more than one type of prescribed medication each day?
2. Is it difficult to remember how many medications you are supposed to take?
3. Do you receive prescription medications from two or more doctors?
4. Have you ever felt worse soon after taking medications?
5. Are you taking medications to help you sleep?
6. Do you use up your medications faster than your doctor prescribes?
7. Are you prescribed any pills for nervousness or anxiety?
8. Has a doctor or nurse ever said they were worried or concerned about your use of medications?
9. Do you take medication to relieve pain?
10. When you feel lonely or sad, do you ever take pills to deal with it?
11. Do you save old medications for future use?
12. Do you often have to choose between the cost of your prescriptions and other necessary expenses?
13. Does a family member or someone else often remind you to take your pills?
14. Do you use a pill dispenser or other method to help remind you when to take your pills?
15. Are there any medications you are supposed to take but do not?
16. Do you ever borrow or use someone else's prescription medications?
17. Do you ever feel groggy after taking certain medications?

We developed eight additional items about the use of OTC medications (e.g., use of analgesics, sleeping aids, herbal remedies, and other nonprescription medications). After recording the client's answers, the interviewer would answer the question, Is there any indication this person is misusing OTC medications and requires further education? Positive answers to the medication questions then triggered a discussion about proper medication compliance using the Health Promotion Workbook mentioned earlier to guide the conversation.

In the larger, SAMHSA-funded BRITE Project, we used a prescreen that included two questions similar in theme to other screenings:

1. In the last year, have you tried to cut down on the drugs (including tobacco) or medication that you use?
2. In the last year, have you used prescription or other drugs more than you meant to?

A positive response to either question would trigger the administration of the ASSIST.

SBIRT professionals should be aware of the American Geriatric Society Beers Criteria (see the Resources section), which are updated every 3 years and address "potentially inappropriate medication" (PIM) use in older adults that is best avoided by older adults and their prescribing health care professionals. SBIRT counselors, with the client's permission, might provide the prescribing physician with information on medication misuse for potential changes in the regimen.

Screening for the Use of Illicit Substances

In the BRITE pilot project, recognizing that most older adults rarely use illicit drugs, we developed a simple prescreen. The items simply asked whether, in the past year, the client used marijuana, cocaine, crack, heroin, hallucinogens (e.g., LSD, PCP), or "substances you sniff or inhale to get high or escape from reality." A positive response to any of these would be flagged for brief intervention.

In the larger SAMHSA SBIRT grant, we again relied on the two-item prescreen mentioned earlier (i.e., tried to cut down, used more than meant to). A positive response related to illicit drugs triggered the administration of the ASSIST.

Screening for Depressive Symptoms

Given the strong association between depressive symptoms and substance use, in the BRITE pilot project, we used the Geriatric Depression Scale—Short Form (GDS–SF; Yesavage & Sheikh, 1986), a 15-item, empirically supported instrument for rating symptoms as none to mild, moderate, or severe. For the larger SAMHSA-funded project, we included a prescreen for depression: the Patient Health Questionnaire-2, a two-item screen that has been used previously for older adults (Li, Friedman, Conwell, & Fiscella, 2007). Any client responding yes to either of the questions would be administered the GDS–SF and, if necessary, referred for mental health services as appropriate.

Brief Interventions

The principles for conducting brief intervention are well established and described throughout the chapters in this edited book. In short, the goals are to increase the client's awareness regarding substance use and increase one's motivation toward behavioral change. Motivational interviewing (Miller & Rollnick, 2002) relies on four principles: (a) expressing empathy and avoiding arguing, (b) developing discrepancy, (c) rolling with resistance, and (d) supporting self-efficacy.

These principles have always been applied in our treatment programs for older adults beginning in the late 1970s through the Florida BRITE Project, as well as in the SAMHSA Treatment Improvement Protocol on Substance Abuse and Older Adults (TIP 26; Center for Substance Abuse Treatment, 1998). The emphasis on using nonconfrontational approaches, providing advice and education, and reinforcing what is learned are key components in working with older adults who may be the least likely subgroup of the population to enter traditional treatment programs.

In the BRITE pilot project, we recognized that BRITE counselors were not physicians and varied in their previous training, education, and professional field. As such, we elected to use the Health Promotion Workbook (from the Florida BRITE Project) so that we had a standardized dialogue and approach. This helps to eliminate personal biases that might influence the outcome.

In the SAMHSA grant-funded version of BRITE, the health educators met the high volume of screenings required for the grant by providing much shorter sessions that could be considered brief advice. The training manager ensured all health educators were trained in motivational interviewing and the use of educational materials available from SAMHSA and the National Institute on Drug Abuse.

Ethical Issues

One ethical issue in the application of SBIRT with older adults is the privacy of the screening and brief intervention and whether others, such as spouses or adult sons or daughters, should be involved. All health care and social services providers are mandated to protect personally identifiable information and adhere to Health Insurance Portability and Accountability Act of 1996 (HIPAA) patient privacy regulations. Clients must first consent to participate, read, and sign HIPAA and confidentiality forms. This process not only addresses the protection of their personal health information but also can request the name of a family member or other person with whom staff can share information. During brief interventions, there may be discussions about family members and how an older adult's substance use affects their family. However,

SBIRT is not family therapy, and it is usually conducted one-on-one. The brief intervention focuses on how to educate and motivate the person toward behavior change. For isolated older adults, others may not be aware of the problem. Yet, for SBIRTs conducted during home visits, a spouse, an adult son or daughter, or a caregiver may participate in the visit or may be within earshot. In such situations, the interviewer should be aware of the sensitive nature of the questions and ask permission to speak with the client alone. In situations when cognitive impairment is also present, a judgment about the presence of a family member will have to be made.

Another ethical issue relates to referral to treatment for those classified as being at severe risk. Treatment programs must be made aware of the needs, medical issues, and cognitive capabilities of the older person who misuses substances. A concomitant referral should be made to the local Area Agency on Aging to ensure that other needs are addressed. Referring to a substance abuse program that specializes in the treatment of older adults is ideal but often not an available option, resulting in a default decision to refer to a program that treats younger people as well. According to the 2017 National Survey of Substance Abuse Treatment Services (SAMHSA, 2018a), of the 13,857 facilities representing 89% of all treatment facilities in the United States, only 2,669 (or about 19%) reported having some form of special program or group for treating older adults. Also, only 35% of facilities accept Medicare. By comparison, 90% of treatment programs require self-payment, 70% will accept private insurance, and 64% accept Medicaid. These payments may thwart the follow-through on a recommendation for admission to treatment.

CONCLUSION

This chapter focused on the implementation of SBIRT with older adults on the basis of several decades of experience in implementing evidence-based practices with older adults in Florida and other states. The SBIRT initiative is advantageous, given that older adults with substance use problems have been underidentified and underrepresented in formal treatment programs, and SBIRT screening can identify risky use of alcohol, medications, and illicit drugs that might be otherwise overlooked. SBIRT is also advantageous in that providers who serve the older population can conduct SBIRT in older adults' homes, at senior centers, within retirement communities, and in other settings that the older person is likely to be found.

SBIRT has been effective in reducing the risk and harm of older adults' misuse of alcohol, medications, and illicit substances (Schonfeld et al., 2010, 2015). For optimal success, clinicians should consider how best to meet the needs of this age group, recognizing that older adults who misuse substances

- are more likely than younger adults to engage in risky use of alcohol or other substances following feelings of depression, loneliness, and boredom;

- in retirement communities may drink beyond recommended limits as part of the social environment and activities;

- may not meet diagnostic criteria for substance use disorders;

- are underrepresented in traditional treatment programs;

- may refuse treatment programs for reasons such as cost or lack of elder-specific programs; and

- may be victims of overmedication and ADEs due to prescribing practices and increased sensitivity to substances rather than intentionally seeking substances for recreational or nonmedical purposes.

Substance use in the older population is a growing concern that has to be addressed. The number of older adults engaged in the risky use of alcohol and illicit drugs is increasing, and issues about medication misuse and abuse will have to be studied further. Implementation of SBIRT will be a valuable addition to the systems and providers who serve the older adult population.

WEB-BASED RESOURCES

- The Florida BRITE Project website (http://BRITE.fmhi.usf.edu) provides descriptions of BRITE, prescreen and screening assessments, the Health Promotion Workbook, and educational materials for older adults. Documents are also available in Spanish.

- The SAMHSA-HRSA Center for Integrated Health Solutions website (https://www.integration.samhsa.gov/clinical-practice/sbirt) provides links for materials on screening, motivational interviewing, and brief interventions.

- The American Geriatrics Society website (https://www.americangeriatrics. org/publications-tools) is updated every 3 years to educate professionals about PIM use in older adults, the use of which are best avoided by older adults and their prescribing health care professionals.

REFERENCES

Agarwal, S. D., & Landon, B. E. (2019). Patterns in outpatient benzodiazepine prescribing in the United States. *JAMA Network Open, 2*, e187399–e187399. http://dx.doi.org/10.1001/jamanetworkopen.2018.7399

Alzheimer's Association. (2019). *Mild cognitive impairment (MCI)*. Retrieved from https://www.alz.org/alzheimers-dementia/what-is-dementia/related_conditions/mild-cognitive-impairment

Becker, J., Schaffert, J., LoBue, C., Adinoff, B., & Cullum, C. (2018). Aging and dementia—1: History of alcohol misuse is associated with an earlier onset of Alzheimer's disease. *Archives of Clinical Neuropsychology, 33*, 692–702. http://dx.doi.org/10.1093/arclin/acy060.01

Billioti de Gage, S., Moride, Y., Ducruet, T., Kurth, T., Verdoux, H., Tournier, M., . . . Bégaud, B. (2014). Benzodiazepine use and risk of Alzheimer's disease: Case-control study. *BMJ, 349*, g5205. http://dx.doi.org/10.1136/bmj.g5205

Blow, F., Gillespie, B., Barry, K., Mudd, S., & Hill, E. (1998). Brief screening for alcohol problems in elderly populations using the Short Michigan Alcoholism Screening Test-Geriatric Version (SMAST-G). *Alcoholism: Clinical and Experimental Research, 22,* 131.

Bush, K., Kivlahan, D. R., McDonell, M. B., Fihn, S. D., & Bradley, K. A. (1998). The AUDIT alcohol consumption questions (AUDIT–C): An effective brief screening test for problem drinking. *Archives of Internal Medicine, 158,* 1789–1795. http://dx.doi.org/ 10.1001/archinte.158.16.1789

Butler, R. N. (1969). Age-ism: Another form of bigotry. *The Gerontologist, 9,* 243–246. http://dx.doi.org/10.1093/geront/9.4_Part_1.243

Center for Medicare and Medicaid Services. (2017). *Screening, Brief Intervention, and Referral to Treatment (SBIRT) services.* Retrieved from https://www.cms.gov/Outreach-and-Education/Medicare-Learning-Network-MLN/MLNProducts/Downloads/SBIRT_Factsheet_ICN904084.pdf

Center for Substance Abuse Treatment. (1998). *Substance abuse among older adults* (HHS Publication No. (SMA) 12-3918). Retrieved from http://www.ncbi.nlm.nih.gov/ books/NBK64419/pdf/TOC.pdf

Center for Substance Abuse Treatment. (1999). *Brief interventions and brief therapies for substance abuse: Treatment improvement protocol (TIP) Series 34* (DHHS Publication No. (SMA) 99-3353). Retrieved from https://store.samhsa.gov/system/files/sma12-3952.pdf

Center for Substance Abuse Treatment. (2005). *Substance abuse relapse prevention for older adults: A group treatment approach.* Rockville, MD: Substance Abuse and Mental Health Services Administration.

Colliver, J. D., Compton, W. M., Gfroerer, J. C., & Condon, T. (2006). Projecting drug use among aging baby boomers in 2020. *Annals of Epidemiology, 16,* 257–265. http://dx.doi.org/10.1016/j.annepidem.2005.08.003

Crowe, S. F., & Stranks, E. K. (2018). The residual medium and long-term cognitive effects of benzodiazepine use: An updated meta-analysis. *Archives of Clinical Neuropsychology, 33,* 901–911. http://dx.doi.org/10.1093/arclin/acx120

Drug Enforcement Administration. (2018). *2017 National drug threat assessment.* Retrieved from https://safemedsonline.org/wp-content/uploads/2017/12/DEA-National-Drug-Threat-Assessment-Oct.-2017.pdf

Dupree, L. W., Broskowski, H., & Schonfeld, L. (1984). The gerontology alcohol project: A behavioral treatment program for elderly alcohol abusers. *The Gerontologist, 24,* 510–516. http://dx.doi.org/10.1093/geront/24.5.510

Fishleder, S., Schonfeld, L., Corvin, J., Tyler, S., & VandeWeerd, C. (2016). Drinking behavior among older adults in a planned retirement community: Results from The Villages survey. *International Journal of Geriatric Psychiatry, 31,* 536–543. http:// dx.doi.org/10.1002/gps.4359

Gfroerer, J., Penne, M., Pemberton, M., & Folsom, R. (2003). Substance abuse treatment need among older adults in 2020: The impact of the aging baby-boom cohort. *Drug and Alcohol Dependence, 69,* 127–135. http://dx.doi.org/10.1016/S0376-8716(02)00307-1

Gómez, A., Conde, A., Santana, J. M., Jorrín, A., Serrano, I. M., & Medina, R. (2006). The diagnostic usefulness of AUDIT and AUDIT–C for detecting hazardous drinkers in the elderly. *Aging & Mental Health, 10,* 558–561. http://dx.doi.org/10.1080/ 13607860600637729

Grant, B. F., Chou, S. P., Saha, T. D., Pickering, R. P., Kerridge, B. T., Ruan, W. J., . . . Hasin, D. S. (2017). Prevalence of 12-month alcohol use, high-risk drinking, and *DSM–IV* alcohol use disorder in the United States, 2001–2002 to 2012–2013: Results from the National Epidemiologic Survey on Alcohol and Related Conditions. *JAMA Psychiatry, 74,* 911–923. http://dx.doi.org/10.1001/jamapsychiatry.2017.2161

The Health Insurance Portability and Accountability Act of 1996, P.L. No. 104-191, 110 Stat. 1938 (1996).

Kantor, E. D., Rehm, C. D., Haas, J. S., Chan, A. T., & Giovannucci, E. L. (2015). Trends in prescription drug use among adults in the United States from 1999–2012. *JAMA, 314*, 1818–1831. http://dx.doi.org/10.1001/jama.2015.13766

Kuerbis, A., Treloar Padovano, H., Shao, S., Houser, J., Muench, F. J., & Morgenstern, J. (2018). Comparing daily drivers of problem drinking among older and younger adults: An electronic daily diary study using smartphones. *Drug and Alcohol Dependence, 183*, 240–246. http://dx.doi.org/10.1016/j.drugalcdep.2017.11.012

Li, C., Friedman, B., Conwell, Y., & Fiscella, K. (2007). Validity of the Patient Health Questionnaire 2 (PHQ-2) in identifying major depression in older people. *Journal of the American Geriatrics Society, 55*, 596–602. http://dx.doi.org/10.1111/j.1532-5415.2007.01103.x

Matthews, K. A., Xu, W., Gaglioti, A. H., Holt, J. B., Croft, J. B., Mack, D., & McGuire, L. C. (2019). Racial and ethnic estimates of Alzheimer's disease and related dementias in the United States (2015–2060) in adults aged ≥65 years. *Alzheimer's & Dementia, 15*, 17–24. http://dx.doi.org/10.1016/j.jalz.2018.06.3063

Mayfield, D., McLeod, G., & Hall, P. (1974). The CAGE questionnaire: Validation of a new alcoholism screening instrument. *The American Journal of Psychiatry, 131*, 1121–1123.

McDonald, D. C., & Carlson, K. E. (2013). Estimating the prevalence of opioid diversion by "doctor shoppers" in the United States. *PLoS ONE, 8*, e69241. http://dx.doi.org/10.1371/journal.pone.0069241

Miller, W. R., & Rollnick, S. (2002). *Motivational interviewing: Preparing people for change* (2nd ed.). New York, NY: Guilford Press.

Moore, A. A., Seeman, T., Morgenstern, H., Beck, J. C., & Reuben, D. B. (2002). Are there differences between older persons who screen positive on the CAGE questionnaire and the Short Michigan Alcoholism Screening Test-Geriatric Version? *Journal of the American Geriatrics Society, 50*, 858–862. http://dx.doi.org/10.1046/j.1532-5415.2002.50211.x

Moore, A. A., Whiteman, E. J., & Ward, K. T. (2007). Risks of combined alcohol/medication use in older adults. *American Journal of Geriatric Pharmacotherapy, 5*, 64–74. http://dx.doi.org/10.1016/j.amjopharm.2007.03.006

National Institute of Alcohol Abuse and Alcoholism. (2005). *The pocket guide for alcohol screening and brief intervention.* Retrieved from http://pubs.niaaa.nih.gov/publications/Practitioner/PocketGuide/pocket_guide.htm

Outlaw, F. H., Marquart, J. M., Roy, A., Luellen, J. K., Moran, M., Willis, A., & Doub, T. (2012). Treatment outcomes for older adults who abuse substances. *Journal of Applied Gerontology, 31*, 78–100. http://dx.doi.org/10.1177/0733464810382906

Sacco, P., Burruss, K., Smith, C. A., Kuerbis, A., Harrington, D., Moore, A. A., & Resnick, B. (2015). Drinking behavior among older adults at a continuing care retirement community: Affective and motivational influences. *Aging & Mental Health, 19*, 279–289. http://dx.doi.org/10.1080/13607863.2014.933307

Satre, D. D., Sterling, S. A., Mackin, R. S., & Weisner, C. (2011). Patterns of alcohol and drug use among depressed older adults seeking outpatient psychiatric services. *The American Journal of Geriatric Psychiatry, 19*, 695–703. http://dx.doi.org/10.1097/JGP.0b013e3181f17f0a

Schonfeld, L., & Dupree, L. W. (1991). Antecedents of drinking for early- and late-onset elderly alcohol abusers. *Journal of Studies on Alcohol, 52*, 587–592. http://dx.doi.org/10.15288/jsa.1991.52.587

Schonfeld, L., Dupree, L. W., Dickson-Fuhrmann, E., Royer, C. M., McDermott, C. H., Rosansky, J. S., . . . Jarvik, L. F. (2000). Cognitive-behavioral treatment of older veterans with substance abuse problems. *Journal of Geriatric Psychiatry and Neurology, 13*, 124–129. http://dx.doi.org/10.1177/089198870001300305

Schonfeld, L., Hazlett, R. W., Hedgecock, D. K., Duchene, D. M., Burns, L. V., & Gum, A. M. (2015). Screening, brief intervention, and referral to treatment for older adults with substance misuse. *American Journal of Public Health*, *105*, 205–211. http://dx.doi.org/10.2105/AJPH.2013.301859

Schonfeld, L., King-Kallimanis, B. L., Duchene, D. M., Etheridge, R. L., Herrera, J. R., Barry, K. L., & Lynn, N. (2010). Screening and brief intervention for substance misuse among older adults: The Florida BRITE project. *American Journal of Public Health*, *100*, 108–114. http://dx.doi.org/10.2105/AJPH.2008.149534

Skinner, H. A. (1982). The Drug Abuse Screening Test. *Addictive Behaviors*, *7*, 363–371. http://dx.doi.org/10.1016/0306-4603(82)90005-3

Skinner, T. R., Scott, I. A., & Martin, J. H. (2016). Diagnostic errors in older patients: A systematic review of incidence and potential causes in seven prevalent diseases. *International Journal of General Medicine*, *9*, 137–146. http://dx.doi.org/10.2147/IJGM.S96741

Substance Abuse and Mental Health Services Administration. (2018a). *National Survey of Substance Abuse Treatment Services (N-SSATS): 2017 data on substance abuse treatment facilities.* Retrieved from https://www.samhsa.gov/data/sites/default/files/cbhsq-reports/2017_NSSATS.pdf

Substance Abuse and Mental Health Services Administration. (2018b). *Treatment Episode Data Set (TEDS) 2016: Admissions to and discharges from publicly funded substance use treatment.* Retrieved from https://www.samhsa.gov/data/sites/default/files/2016_Treatment_Episode_Data_Set_Annual.pdf

U.S. Department of Health and Human Services. (2014). *National action plan for adverse drug event prevention.* Retrieved from https://health.gov/hcq/pdfs/ADE-Action-Plan-508c.pdf

West, N. A., Severtson, S. G., Green, J. L., & Dart, R. C. (2015). Trends in abuse and misuse of prescription opioids among older adults. *Drug and Alcohol Dependence*, *149*, 117–121. http://dx.doi.org/10.1016/j.drugalcdep.2015.01.027

WHO ASSIST Working Group. (2002). The Alcohol, Smoking and Substance Involvement Screening Test (ASSIST): Development, reliability and feasibility. *Addiction*, *97*, 1183–1194. http://dx.doi.org/10.1046/j.1360-0443.2002.00185.x

Yesavage, J. A., & Sheikh, J. I. (1986). 9/Geriatric Depression Scale (GDS): Recent evidence and development of a shorter version. *Clinical Gerontologist*, *5*, 165–173. http://dx.doi.org/10.1300/J018v05n01_09

III

NEW FRONTIERS IN SCREENING, BRIEF INTERVENTION, AND REFERRAL TO TREATMENT

11

Using Technology for Training in and the Delivery of Screening, Brief Intervention, and Referral to Treatment

Michael V. Pantalon and Heather J. Gotham

Originally, the joke "There's an app for that" was meant to convey light-hearted awe at the fast-growing popularity of mobile applications (apps) designed to help users access driving directions, chat with friends, or check social media sites. In 2010, at the height of this joke's popularity, the Apple iPhone boasted 250,000 apps (Gross, 2010). In 2018, Google Play (the app store for Android smartphones) and Apple combined had roughly 5 million apps (Clement, 2019). Now, there literally is an app for almost everything.

Psychologists from a variety of specialties are using technology to advance the mission of the American Psychological Association (APA), namely, the "advancement, communication, and application of psychological knowledge to benefit society and improve people's lives" (APA, n.d., p. 5). We have myriad opportunities to integrate technology into our work, particularly for training and service delivery, and indeed, we recommend that all psychologists embrace technology for its potential to advance scientific findings and promote health more widely. In this chapter, we discuss how tech-enabled screening, brief intervention, and referral to treatment (SBIRT) can be delivered to clients and how clinicians can use technology platforms to receive training in SBIRT.

Dr. Pantalon has a financial interest and affiliation with http://www.recoverypad.com, one of the products discussed in this chapter; he is the co-owner of the Center for Progressive Recovery, LLC, the makers of that web application.

Dr. Gotham has no disclosures.

The authors wish to thank Madeleine Wood, BS, for her indispensable assistance in preparing this manuscript.

http://dx.doi.org/10.1037/0000199-012
Screening, Brief Intervention, and Referral to Treatment for Substance Use: A Practitioner's Guide,
M. D. Cimini and J. L. Martin (Editors)

SBIRT has demonstrated efficacy across multiple settings and populations and has been recommended or mandated by groups including the U.S. Preventive Services Task Force (screening and brief intervention for alcohol misuse in adults, U.S. Preventive Services Task Force, 2018; screening for drug use in adults, U.S. Preventive Services Task Force, 2019). Although the implementation of SBIRT across health care settings has been slow, SBIRT is ripe for the type of positive disruption that technology would allow. Its brief, manualized nature lends itself to dissemination via web-based or mobile applications. Moreover, given SBIRT's application as a primary, secondary, and tertiary prevention tool, it stands out as an important approach to disseminate more widely.

It is beyond the scope of this chapter to provide an exhaustive review of technology-based brief intervention programs and their efficacy. We instead highlight technology-enabled SBIRT tools designed for psychologists and allied health professionals working with diverse clients across settings. The reader will gain competence in identifying the following as they relate to the delivery of technology-enabled SBIRT: intended audience, substances addressed, types of technologies, modes of engagement, SBIRT components covered, level of scientific evidence for applications or programs, program availability, and a clear plan for implementing the programs that best fit psychologists' needs. These concepts and highlighted programs are presented in two tables that summarize technology-enabled programs for providing SBIRT (see Table 11.1) and for training and education in SBIRT (see Table 11.2).

WHY SHOULD I CARE? THE BENEFITS OF TECHNOLOGY-ENABLED SBIRT

There are a number of benefits of using technology to provide SBIRT services to clients and to train psychologists and allied health professionals to deliver SBIRT (e.g., via client-facing computerized screening and brief intervention, clinician-facing apps to facilitate standardized screening, online SBIRT training). Some of those benefits are as follows:

- It increases provider awareness of SBIRT and facilitates its implementation.

- It provides greater access to treatment and support on demand through 24/7 web-based SBIRT.

- It improves workforce competence by providing training to students and health professionals (e.g., only 46% of clinical psychology training programs provided specialty training in addiction in 2014; Dimoff, Sayette, & Norcross, 2017).

- It improves client outcomes (e.g., Tansil et al., 2016; White et al., 2010) and garners more accurate screening results (e.g., Lotfipour et al., 2013b), especially for adolescents (e.g., Ozechowski, Becker, & Hogue, 2016; Turner et al., 1998).

- It reduces cost through decreasing expensive clinician time (McCormack, 2017), expands revenue by increasing the number of clients receiving services, and maximizes billing by accurately documenting SBIRT in the electronic health record.

- It tailors services to the postmillennial generation that is more likely to seek out health care information on the Internet and be accepting of health care technologies (e.g., Hollis et al., 2017).

Now that we have reviewed why we think you should care about using technology-enabled SBIRT, let us do a "readiness ruler" exercise (common in SBIRT) to see what your reasons for caring might be. On a scale from 1 to 10, where 1 is *not at all ready* and 10 is *totally ready*, how ready are you to use technology-enabled SBIRT? When you have answered that question, ask yourself another question. Why are you at that number and not a lower one? You should have responded with the reasons you care about using technology-enabled SBIRT. Keep these in mind as we proceed.

PUTTING TECHNOLOGY-ENABLED SBIRT TO GOOD USE

Before you begin selecting apps or other tools, you have to consider your audience and goals and the availability of technology, as well as its primary functions, costs, privacy protections, and usability. Likewise, you have to know details about how the user interface works and the level of scientific evidence for the tool's effectiveness.

Know Your Audience

As with clinical work, teaching, and research, your SBIRT approach will change based on who you are trying to motivate and toward what target goal. Whether you are training psychology interns, medical residents, or staff or targeting clients, their support system, or the broader community, first decide who your audience is and begin contemplating which aspects of technology-enabled programs might most appeal to and work for them.

Know Your Goals

Next, what is your goal for the technology-enabled program? What would you like it to do for its user? Both technology-enabled SBIRT delivery and training programs can address a variety of (a) substances or substance-related consequences, (b) screening goals (e.g., level of risk vs. substance use disorder), and (c) brief intervention goals (e.g., reduced use, reduced negative consequences, cessation of use, treatment engagement). Given the large number of apps available, it is helpful to operationally define goals for the technology-enabled program before beginning your search. The goals may also relate to the specific setting in which you practice; SBIRT is needed across settings, including private practice, schools, health care, and mental health agencies and hospitals.

TABLE 11.1. Technology-Enabled SBIRT Delivery Programs

Program	Developer	Target audience	Target substance	Technology type[a]
Check Your Drinking (CYD) and Check Your Drinking U (CYDU)[e]	Evolution Health Systems Inc.	Adults (CYD), college students (CYDU)	Alcohol	Web-based (2)
The Drinker's Check Up (DCU; now CheckUp & Choices)[f] and College Drinker's Check Up (CDCU)[g]	Behavior Therapy Associates	Adults, college students	Alcohol	Web based (2)
Moderate Drinking (now CheckUp & Choices)[h]	CheckUp & Choices, LLC	Adults	Alcohol	Web-based (1)
Oregon SBIRT app	OHSU	Adults, adolescents	All classes	Web-based (2)
Computerized Alcohol Screening and Intervention (CASI)[i], Bilingual CASI[j]	UC Irvine	Adults	Alcohol	Non-web-based tablet
Motivational Alcohol Treatments to Enhance Roadway Safety (MATTERS)[k]	Neurobehavioral Research Laboratory and Clinic	Adults charged with driving while intoxicated	Alcohol	Non-web-based tablet
eCheckup to Go[l]	San Diego State University	Adolescents, young adults	Alcohol, tobacco, marijuana	Web-based
Interactive Voice Response–Brief Alcohol Intervention (IVR-BI)[m]	University of Vermont	Adult PC patients	Alcohol	Interactive voice response
Caring TXT[n]	Health Stratica	Young adults (18–25 years)	Alcohol	Interactive text messaging
Text Messaging to Reduce Adolescent Alcohol and Marijuana Use	Yale School of Medicine	Adolescents	Alcohol, marijuana	Interactive text messaging
SafERteens[o]	University of Michigan	Adolescents	Alcohol	Non-web-based, computer or tablet
Cannabis Computerized Brief Intervention (CBI)[p]	University of Michigan	Adolescents	Cannabis, illicit substances	Non-web-based computer or tablet
HealthiER[q]	University of Michigan	Adults	Illicit substances	Non-web-based tablet or computer assisted
Computer-delivered Screening and Brief Intervention (e-SBI)[r]	Wayne State University/ Interva, Inc.	Adult pregnant and postpartum women	All classes	Non-web-based computer
Screening and Brief Intervention (SBI) embedded into personal health record MyHERO[s]	University of California, San Francisco	HIV positive adults	Illicit substances	Web-based computer

Mode of engagement	Goal	SBIRT components[b]	Evidence-based score[c]	Availability Score[d]	Link
Algorithm, synchronous	Reduction	S, F	4	2	https://screen.evolutionhealth.care/cyd
Algorithm, synchronous	Reduction	S, BI	4	4 (DCU), 7 (CDCU)	https://drinkerscheckup.com
Algorithm, synchronous	Reduction	BMI, P	5	4	https://checkupandchoices.com/moderate-drinking/
Algorithm, synchronous	Reduction	S, R	3	7	https://sbirtapp.org/intro
Algorithm and provider, synchronous	Reduction, treatment engagement	S, BI	3	2	http://www.ctipr.uci.edu/programs.asp
Algorithm (screener) and provider (BI with assistance of computer report), synchronous	Reduction and referral to treatment	S, F	3	3	http://nrlc-group.net/treatment-and-research/treatment-and-research
Algorithm, synchronous	Reduction	BI	6	2	http://www.echeckuptogo.com/
Algorithm, synchronous	Reduction	S, BI	4	1	None
Chatbot, asynchronous	Reduction	BMI, P	4	2	https://www.healthstratica.com/
Chatbot, asynchronous	Reduction	SBIRT	3	1	None
Avatar, synchronous	Reduction	S, BI	4	1	None
Avatar, synchronous	Primary and secondary prevention, reduction	BI	4	1	None
Avatar, synchronous	Reduction	BI	4	1	None
Algorithm and video, synchronous	Reduction, cessation	BI	3	1	None
Algorithm, synchronous	Reduction	SBIRT	6	1	None

(continues)

TABLE 11.1. Technology-Enabled SBIRT Delivery Programs (*Continued*)

Program	Developer	Target audience	Target substance	Technology type[a]
Motivational Computer Intervention (MAPIT)[t]	University of North Texas Science Center	Adult probationers	All classes	Web-based computer
Health Evaluation and Referral Assistant (HERA)[u]	Polaris Health Directions	Adult ED patients	Alcohol, tobacco	Non-web-based tablet
Automated Bilingual Computerized Alcohol Screening and Intervention (AB-CASI) Yale[v]	Yale School of Medicine	Adult ED patients	Alcohol	Non-web-based tablet assisted
Remote Brief Intervention and Referral to Treatment (R-BIRT)[w]	Polaris Health Directions	Adult ED patients	Alcohol	Telehealth
Computerized Brief Intervention (CBI)[x]	Friends Research Institute	Adult PC patients	All classes	Non-web-based computer
Computer-facilitated Screening and Brief Advice system (cSBA)[y]	Harvard University	Adolescents (in PC)	Cannabis, alcohol	Non-web-based computer
RecoveryPad	Center for Progressive Recovery, LLC	Substance using adults, concerned significant others	All classes	Web app (3)
Project U-Connect[z]	University of Michigan	Adolescents, young adults	Alcohol	Non-web-based tablet
Alcohol Use and Misuse[aa]	Sachin Patel	Firefighters	Alcohol	Native app
Audio Computer Assisted Self-Interview (CASI) of the Alcohol, Smoking and Substance Involvement Screening Test (ASSIST)[bb]	New York University	Adult PC patients	All classes	Non-web-based computer or tablet

Note. References are to efficacy evaluations and not the original development of the program. ED = emergency department; PC = primary care.
[a]Mobile readiness: 1 = visible; 2 = ready; 3 = friendly; 4 = optimized/mobile app; blank = not applicable. [b]BI = all components of the BI (i.e., F, BMI, P); BMI = brief motivational interview; F = feedback; P = plans for change; R = results; RT = referral to treatment; S = screening; SBIRT = all components of screening, brief intervention, and referral to treatment. [c]1 = no studies; 2 = any study; 3 = positive results with no control or based on evidence-based SBIRT approach; 4 = randomized controlled trial (RCT) showing superiority compared with lower intensity control; 5 = RCT showing superiority compared to an equal intensity control (not human delivered); 6 = RCT showing no difference between technology versus human-delivered intervention; 7 = RCT showing superiority compared to human-delivered intervention. [d]1 = not available; 2 = available only to clients in participating institutions; 3 = available and free but requires client and provider to use together; 4 = available for clients to use on their own for a fee; 5 = available and free for clients to use on their own; 6 = available and free for clients to use on their own with mobile device access; 7 = available and free for clients to use on their own with all devices. [e]Cunningham, Wild, Cordingley, van Mierlo, and Humphreys (2009); Doumas, McKinley, and Book (2009). [f]Hester, Squires, and Delaney (2005). [g]Hester, Delaney, and Campbell (2012). [h]Hester, Delaney, and Campbell (2011). [i]Vaca, Winn, Anderson, Kim, and Arcila (2011). [j]Lotfipour et al. (2013a, 2013b). [k]Mullen, Ryan, Mathias, and Dougherty (2015). [l]Alfonso, Hall, and Dunn (2013). [m]Rose et al. (2017). [n]Suffoletto et al. (2015). [o]Walton et al. (2010). [p]Walton et al. (2013, 2014). [q]Blow et al. (2017). [r]Ondersma et al. (2015). [s]Dawson-Rose et al. (2017). [t]Lerch, Walters, Tang, and Taxman (2017). [u]Haskins et al. (2017). [v]Abujarad and Vaca (2015). [w]Boudreaux, Haskins, Harralson, and Bernstein (2015). [x]Schwartz et al. (2014). [y]Harris et al. (2012). [z]Cunningham et al. (2015). [aa]Mitchell et al. (2018). [bb]McNeely, Strauss, Rotrosen, Ramautar, and Gourevitch (2016).

Mode of engagement	Goal	SBIRT components[b]	Evidence-based score[c]	Availability Score[d]	Link
Algorithm, synchronous and asynchronous (via smartphone)	Treatment engagement, reduction	BMI, P	4	1	None
Algorithm	Treatment engagement	S, F, BMI, RT	5	1	None
Algorithm, synchronous	Reduction, treatment engagement	SBIRT	3	2	None
Provider, synchronous	Treatment engagement	SBIRT	3	1	None
Interactive avatar, synchronous	Reduction, cessation, harm reduction	BI	7	1	None
Algorithm, synchronous	Cessation, prevention	S, R	3	1	None
Person-to-person text, asynchronous	Reduction, cessation, treatment engagement, education for concerned significant others	SBIRT	3	4	https://recoverypad.com
Avatar, synchronous	Reduction	BMI	4	1	None
Algorithm	Reduction, cessation, treatment engagement	S, F, RT	3	2	Apple App Store
Algorithm, synchronous	Identifying risk	S	6	1	None

TABLE 11.2. Technology-Enabled SBIRT Training Programs

Program	Developer	Target trainee audience	Target patient audience	Target substance	Technology type[a]
Coach Vicky[e]	Yale School of Medicine	ED providers	Adult ED patients	Alcohol	Web-based application
Kognito[f]	Kognito, LLC	Healthcare providers, educators, health professionals, college students	Adolescent and adult ED and PC patients, college students	All classes	Web-based application
SIMmersion[g]	SIMmersion LLC	Healthcare providers	Adult PC patients	Alcohol	Web-based application
Northwell Health SBIRT	Northwell Health	Healthcare providers	Adults	All classes	Native app (4)
Open Health Network SBIRT[h]	University of California at San Francisco	Healthcare providers	Adults	All classes	Native app (4)
Baylor SBIRT	Baylor School of Medicine	Healthcare providers	Adults	All classes	Native app (4)
SBIRT for Health and Behavioral Health Professionals	University of Missouri– Kansas City	Health, oral health, and behavioral health students and providers	Adults	All classes	Web-based application (3)
Catalyst Screening and Brief Intervention	Catalyst Learning Center, University of Missouri– Columbia	Healthcare providers	Adults	Alcohol	Web-based application (3)
Alcohol Screening and Brief Intervention[i]	University of Pittsburgh School of Nursing, Johns Hopkins School of Nursing	Nursing students, registered nurses, and advanced practice nurses	Adults	Alcohol	Web-based application (3)
Clinical Decision Support	New York University	Primary care providers	Adults	Illicit substances	Non-web-based tablet
Alcohol Use and Misuse for Providers	Sachin Patel	SBIRT providers	Firefighters	Alcohol	Native app (4)

Note. ED = emergency department; PC = primary care. [a]Mobile readiness: 1 = visible; 2 = ready; 3 = friendly; 4 = optimized; blank = not applicable. [b]BI = all components of the BI (i.e., F, BMI, and P); BMI = brief motivational interview; F = feedback; P = plans for change; R = results; RT = referral to treatment; S = screening; SBIRT = all components of screening, brief intervention, and referral to treatment. [c]1 = no studies; 2 = any study; 3 = positive results with no control or based on evidence-based SBIRT approach; 4 = randomized controlled trial (RCT) showing superiority compared to lower intensity control; 5 = RCT showing superiority compared to an equal intensity control (not human delivered); 6 = RCT showing no difference between technology versus human-delivered intervention. [d]1 = not available; 2 = available only to clinicians in participating institutions; 3 = available and free; 4 = available for clinicians to use on their own for a fee; 5 = available and free for clinicians to use on their own; 6 = available and free for clinicians to use on their own with mobile device access. [e]Magerko, Dean, Idnani, Pantalon, and D'Onofrio (2011); Pantalon et al. (2019). [f]Albright, Adam, Serri, Bleeker, and Goldman (2016). [g]Fleming et al. (2009). [h]Satre, Ly, Wamsley, Curtis, and Satterfield (2017). [i]Mitchell et al. (2018).

Mode of engagement	Goal	SBIRT components[b]	Evidence-based score[c]	Availability score[d]	Link
Adaptive avatar	Reduction, cessation	BI	6	5	https://em-bni.med.yale.edu/sbirtClient/login.jsp
Adaptive avatar	Reduction, cessation, treatment engagement	SBIRT	3	2	https://kognito.com/products
Adaptive avatar	Reduction, cessation	SBIRT	4	4	https://www.simmersion.com/products/view.html?ID=3bfd1b92-fbe2-4746-a1e9-8b4ba3af1fa3
Algorithm	Reduction, cessation, treatment engagement	SBIRT	3	6	Apple App Store
Algorithm	Reduction, cessation, treatment engagement	SBIRT	3	1	Apple App Store
Algorithm	Reduction, cessation, treatment engagement	SBIRT	3	1	None
Interactive	Reduction, cessation, treatment engagement	SBIRT	3	5	https://sbirt.care/training.aspx
Interactive avatar	Reduction, cessation	SBI	3	2	https://catalystlearningcenter.com
Interactive avatar	Reduction, cessation	SBI	3	4	https://learn.nursing.jhu.edu/instruments-interventions/alcohol-screening/index.html
Algorithm	Reduction	BI	3	1	None
Algorithm	Reduction, cessation, treatment engagement, education	SBIRT	3	2	Apple App Store

Know Your Technology

Become familiar with the different types of technology and their strengths and limitations. Consider also the potential for each of these programs. That is, consider what may become possible with technological advances. For example, an existing text-based program sending daily reminders to drink within low-risk levels could be modified in the near future to include different content or to be sent with differing frequencies. Next, we summarize various types of technology-enabled SBIRT (see also Tables 11.1 and 11.2).

Interactive voice response is a relatively low-cost, low-tech method that uses a prerecorded interview and/or statements to which the caller responds using the phone keys.

Text messaging interventions can be facilitated by human providers or preprogrammed (similar to interactive voice response). Preprogrammed interventions deliver questions to the client on a set schedule and provide tailored feedback depending on the response (e.g., asking college students about planned alcohol use on typical drinking nights and providing texts to help set drinking limits; Suffoletto et al., 2015).

Telephone or video chat used in telehealth or telemedicine are closest to standard face-to-face SBIRT implementation. They can decrease costs and increase client access because they are often provided by bachelor's or master's level care providers to clients with limited transportation or those in rural areas.

Non-web-based computer or tablet programs (in situ) include those delivered via a preinstalled program on a provider's computer or tablet or in the electronic health record. The key is that they are not connected to or dependent on the Internet. Most often, these are standardized screeners. For example, McNeely, Strauss, Rotrosen, Ramautar, and Gourevitch (2016) developed a computerized version of a standard screener that was as reliable as the staff administered version, with a high rate of patient preference for the computer-assisted version. Advantages of computerized screeners include completion in the waiting room; eliciting more honest, accurate responses; automatic scoring; and bundling with other screeners (e.g., Johnson, Woychek, Vaughan, & Seale, 2013). A step beyond screening are programs that also provide tailored feedback about the consequences of substance use, the level of risk, or local treatment and recovery services. Programs may also provide a brief intervention (Abujarad & Vaca, 2015) or guide a provider through delivering the brief intervention (HealthiER; Blow et al., 2017). These programs vary in level of interactivity and sophistication of graphics, from simple text presentation to audio and/or video recordings of a character or avatar coach.

Web-based applications are accessed via a hyperlink (e.g., https://www.recoverypad.com) and use the Internet's functionality to provide individually tailored interactions. However, just because a web app can be accessed on a mobile device, it does not necessarily mean that it is a "mobile app" per se. In Tables 11.1 and 11.2, the following ranking system designates ease of use of a web app on a mobile device: *mobile visible* means that the website can be viewed on a smartphone or tablet, but information or clickable content may be lost due to incompatible formatting; *mobile ready* indicates an app in which all information is viewable, but the formatting may make it difficult to navigate; *mobile friendly* means that all the content is visible and its formatting has minimal problems; *mobile optimized* (a true mobile app, otherwise known as a *native application*) indicates that all content is visible and formatted with the smartphone and tablet in mind, and it is optimized to leverage the features of a mobile device (e.g., swiping; integrating with other mobile apps, such as social media and calendars).

The levels of interactivity of web-based programs can be (a) *minimally interactive*, which allows the user to view material and answer questions through a series of prompts—although the material within such programs can be tailored, it is not fully interactive because each user will be asked the same questions; (b) *moderately interactive* for programs whose materials and questions are based on each of the user's responses; or (c) *adaptive*, which means the applications rely on the Internet and artificial intelligence (AI), machine learning (ML), and/or natural language processing (NLP) to customize training components to the user's needs and level of competency while interacting with virtual or simulated standardized patients. The pace of the simulation can be slowed or quickened and made more or less difficult based on the program learning about the user.

Know Your Mode of Engagement

Mode of engagement refers to with whom and when your target audience will engage with the program. With regard to whom, the possibilities are (a) *algorithm*, such as by a non-web-based computer program or a web-based computer program of minimal interactivity; (b) *interactive*, as with a moderately interactive program; or (c) *adaptive*, such as with a program that uses AI, ML, and/or NLP. When adaptive programs are offered in the form of SMS text only, they are usually referred to as *chatbots*. Users can be guided through web-based interactive programs by *avatars*, which are video or animated human-like characters. For example, Coach Vicky (Magerko, Dean, Idnani, Pantalon, & D'Onofrio, 2011; Pantalon et al., 2019) uses images such as the ones in Figure 11.1. Finally, some technology-enabled programs have a person-to-person component that requires a human clinician, coach, or technician on both ends, for at least some of the time, such as a provider texting with a client to implement a brief intervention (e.g., https://www.recoverypad.com).

The when is the timing of interactions. In *synchronous* interactions, clients or trainees input the answers to a program's questions as they receive them and then receive an immediate response from the program. The conversation unfolds in synchrony. If the person leaves the program or exceeds its idle time requirement (i.e., times out), the program will not interact until they sign back in. A program is *asynchronous* when the bidirectional interaction between

FIGURE 11.1. Sample Avatars From Coach Vicky

Note. From *"Coach Vicky": A Web-Based, Self-Directed Brief Intervention Training Program*, by M. V. Pantalon, F. Abujarad, J. Tetrault, J. Butner, S. Martel, C. Anderson, . . . G. D'Onofrio, 2019. Manuscript submitted for publication. Copyright 2019 by Yale University. Reprinted with permission.

the program and client is separated by time (e.g., a chatbot texts a screening question at a predetermined time, and a client replies at a later point).

Know the Scientific Evidence for the Selected Applications

Much like you would not choose an intervention for posttraumatic stress disorder that did not have sufficient empirical evidence of efficacy, you should not select a technology-enabled program that is of unknown efficacy or known ineffectiveness or potential harmfulness. That said, the nascent efficacy literature on technology-enabled SBIRT programs is far from conclusive. We carefully surveyed over 100 existing studies on technology-enabled programs and summarized the level of evidence for a representative sampling (see Tables 11.1 and 11.2). The variability in studies across participants, technologies, and research designs makes it difficult to draw robust conclusions regarding the empirical support for a given program. Instead, we describe the quality of each program's current evidence base.

TECHNOLOGY-ENABLED SBIRT DELIVERY

Overall, extant evidence suggests that technology-enabled SBIRT programs are generally effective (see Tables 11.1 and 11.2), with 13 of 25 programs demonstrating superiority over control conditions that offered a less intensive level of intervention (e.g., screening or information only). However, when compared with an intervention delivered by a human, less than a handful programs were either not statistically significantly different (eCheckup to Go for adolescent marijuana use, Alfonso, Hall, & Dunn, 2013; MyHERO for patients who are HIV positive and use illicit substances, Dawson-Rose et al., 2017; audio-guided, computer-assisted self-interview Alcohol, Smoking and Substance Involvement Screening Test [ACASI ASSIST], McNeely et al., 2016) or superior (Computerized Brief Intervention [CBI] for primary care patient alcohol and drug use, Schwartz et al., 2014). However, of these four programs (i.e., eCheckup to Go, MyHERO, CBI, ACASI ASSIST), only eCheckup to Go is available to the general public, but one has to be affiliated with an institution that offers it. Thus, a psychologist wanting to use these three programs—the ones we judge as having the most robust evidence supporting their efficacy—would have a difficult time finding them. However, two of the three (CBI and ACASI ASSIST) are broadly applicable (considering audience and substance) for psychologists in practice. The AB-CASI-Yale (Abujarad & Vaca, 2015), which was found to be superior to an equal intensity control (but not implemented by a human), was similarly unavailable. However, many programs with lower rankings of supporting evidence are readily available.

Two programs at the highest ranking of availability (i.e., Check Your Drinking U, Doumas, McKinley, & Book, 2009; College Drinker's Check-Up, Hester, Delaney, & Campbell, 2012) both focus on college students and demonstrated superior efficacy when compared with a less intensive control. The remainder of the most widely available programs use evidence-based SBIRT approaches (i.e., Oregon SBIRT [https://www.sbirtoregon.org/] and Alcohol Use and Misuse [https://itunes.apple.com/us/app/alcohol-use-and-misuse/id1334710200?mt=8]). Of the three non-free programs, Moderate Drinking (now CheckUp & Choices; Hester, Delaney, & Campbell, 2011; $24.95/month) was superior to an equal intensity control that was not implemented by a human. Drinker's Checkup (Hester, Squires, & Delaney, 2005), designed for cutting down or quitting drinking, was free for the assessment and $29 for the rest of the program (i.e., one-time feedback, motivational interview, and change plan). This tool was superior to a lesser intensity control. Finally, RecoveryPad (https://www.recoverypad.com), which is free for the first 2 days and then $100/month for person-to-person asynchronous texting, uses evidence-based SBIRT strategies (e.g., brief negotiation interview; D'Onofrio et al., 2012).

Notably, only two programs were native apps (i.e., Alcohol Use and Misuse: Mitchell et al., 2018, and University of California, San Francisco [UCSF] SBIRT: Satre, Ly, Wamsley, Curtis, & Satterfield, 2017), which are considered the most accessible and user-friendly type of technology and, hence, the technology hypothesized to have the greatest sustainable population health impact. Only UCSF SBIRT (Satre et al., 2017) offers all the components of SBIRT (i.e., screening, brief intervention, and referral to treatment). Finally, there was only one web app (i.e., RecoveryPad), a program that is just below native app status in terms of being mobile friendly. RecoveryPad was also the only program that offered person-to-person SBIRT via technology (text). Interestingly, a recent study suggested that without some person-to-person component, patients do not sustain engagement in technology-enabled health behavior change efforts (Lie, Karlsen, Oord, Graue, & Oftedal, 2017).

Given the similarity of telephone and video conference to face-to-face SBIRT models, one would think that their effectiveness would be similar. Yet, only one extant study examined a telephone model, and the authors found no differences between the telephone brief intervention and a no-intervention control group on alcohol consumption (Rose et al., 2017).

TECHNOLOGY-ENABLED SBIRT TRAINING

Evidence for technology-enabled SBIRT training programs is limited. Although Pantalon and colleagues (2019) found no significant differences between technology and human-delivered SBIRT training ("Coach Vicky"; see Figure 11.1), all remaining programs either (a) failed to include a control group or (b) were not empirically tested whatsoever. In terms of availability, only the Northwell SBIRT app (https://itunes.apple.com/us/app/sbirt-for-health-professionals/id1352895522?mt=8) was available, easily accessible, and free for providers to use on their own with mobile device access. Only Coach Vicky (Pantalon et al., 2019) and the University of Missouri-Kansas City (UMKC) SBIRT (http://www.sbirt.care/) were available, easily accessible, and free for providers to use on their nonmobile devices (i.e., computers). SIMmersion (Fleming et al., 2009) is available for a fee (see https://www.simmersion.com/products/forsale/index.html).

Finally, it should be noted that most programs we reviewed are focused on either medical patients or medical providers, even if many of them were either developed and/or researched by psychologists. This is another limitation of the field of technology-enabled SBIRT interventions. For technology-enabled SBIRT to be integrated into psychologists' clinical, research, training, and policy work, more of the programs should focus on the contexts in which psychologists and allied professionals work and the types of clients they treat.

WHAT DO I HAVE TO DO? SELECTING A PROGRAM FOR YOUR DELIVERY AND TRAINING NEEDS

Now that you are knowledgeable about the important aspects of technology-enabled SBIRT, you can start selecting and trying programs. Let us first consider SBIRT delivery programs. After reviewing your needs based on your intended audience, substance, technology type, and goal, we suggest making a list and comparing what you need to what is available. Let us imagine, for example, you are a psychologist in a college counseling center and are charged with finding a free program for heavy drinkers. Your clients are impatient with your current online questionnaires that cannot be accessed by smartphone, and they want a plan for how to cut down or stop drinking (i.e., a complete SBIRT package). Which program might you choose? There is no right or wrong answer. You may choose the College Drinker's Check-Up (Hester et al., 2012) for its focus on college students, efficacy, availability, mobile readiness, and no-cost option. However, if you work with adults who have the same profile but are willing to pay a small fee and do not care that much about mobile readiness (they prefer to use their laptops), you might choose the Drinker's Checkup (Hester et al., 2005) or Moderate Drinking (Hester et al., 2011).

Another important issue to consider when recommending an SBIRT delivery app is data privacy. Although protected health information can and should also be kept secure within an app and its servers, breaches to databases are not unheard of. Therefore, users of these apps should be mindful of that possibility and always be aware that even if their sensitive health data is anonymized, it is often stored on remote servers outside of the app and mined for insights to better help customers in the future. One way users can mitigate the risks of potential sensitive information leakage is to ensure that the apps they use are Health Insurance Portability and Accountability Act (HIPAA) compliant (e.g., RecoveryPad). Other programs do not collect identifying information within their screener or feedback components (e.g., Oregon SBIRT app) and, therefore, have an inherently lower risk of privacy breaches, though appropriate precautions should be taken if e-mailing results or otherwise documenting them.

For those looking to train others in SBIRT, the choices are fewer, and only one program has shown superiority to a human-delivered training in a randomized controlled trial (i.e., Coach Vicky; Pantalon et al., 2019). However, programs that use evidence-based SBIRT training approaches (all programs in Table 11.2) may be just as effective and simply currently lack evidence. If your trainees want a more immersive, realistic experience, you may choose Kognito (Albright, Adam, Serri, Bleeker, & Goldman, 2016) or SIMmersion (Fleming et al., 2009). If your trainees want something accessible by smartphone, the best choices may be the UCSF SBIRT (Satre et al., 2017) or Northwell SBIRT native apps. Alternatively, you may choose Catalyst (https://catalystlearning center.com/courses/alcohol-sbi-training-for-the-healthcare-professional/) or Alcohol Screening and Brief Intervention (Mitchell et al., 2018), if your institution participated with them or had funds available for training.

IMPLEMENTING YOUR CHOSEN PROGRAMS INTO YOUR WORK SETTING

Once you have decided on the technology-enabled SBIRT program you would like to use, plan how to implement it. The following are some tips for implementing technology-enabled SBIRT programs into clinical practice, training, and research.

Tips for Implementing Technology-Enabled SBIRT Into Clinical Practice

- Use only programs that are either evidence-based practices (EBPs) themselves (best) or based on EBPs (acceptable).

- Use a client-centered approach to selecting a program.

- Use a scientific approach to evaluating the helpfulness of programs (i.e., pre- posttest design; do not make other major changes at the same time).

- Follow guidelines established for integrating self-help books into clinical practice (Pantalon, Lubetkin, & Fishman, 1995), such as

  - Inform the client that there are no empirically established guidelines for the selection process or how technology-enabled SBIRT is to be used in or in conjunction with therapy, nor any conclusive evidence for their efficacy.

  - Use a client-centered approach to set reasonable expectations for the level of investment and return.

  - Use the considerations described in this chapter (e.g., audience, target, goal, evidence) to help the client make their selection.

  - Manage resistance to suggested or assigned programs with EBPs (e.g., brief motivational interviewing, gradual approximations of change, revisiting agreements about the use of the app).

Tips for Implementing Technology-Enabled SBIRT Into Training

- Embed SBIRT education throughout the curriculum, not just as a one-time training. This is a great opportunity to consider what addiction-related content is already in the program.

- Provide education and training across the continuum from knowledge and attitudes, through practice with peers or standardized patients, to provision of SBIRT with clients and how to implement SBIRT in clinical practice.

- Ensure faculty are well-trained, not just in the basics of SBIRT, but in providing brief interventions and supervision for their use, and train all faculty in case of turnover.

- Consider the technology already used in the curriculum. Are there technology-enabled SBIRT options that fit current pedagogy? If courses use a flipped classroom style, have students complete an online SBIRT course, and then conduct role-plays with peers. Are you looking to increase technology use in the program? If your program has not used mobile apps yet, try the technology.

Tips for Implementing Technology-Enabled SBIRT Into Research

- Focus on programs that already have preliminary data or test programs that are based on EBPs.

- Develop programs that focus on psychologists and their particular contexts and clients.

- Develop and pilot test programs in "untapped technologies," especially those with broader appeal and greater accessibility (native apps).

- Consider the full arc of an innovation from the beginning of its development, including how the technology can be implemented, sustained, and commercialized for broad accessibility.

- Include community stakeholders at the outset of development and testing so that effectiveness and dissemination and implementation trials are more likely and successful.

- Propose hybrid effectiveness-implementation research designs (Curran, Bauer, Mittman, Pyne, & Stetler, 2012) that study the effect of the innovation, as well as how it can best be implemented (including cost-effectiveness) to accelerate the use of the technology in the practice of psychology.

CONCLUSION

In summary, the aims and scope of this chapter were to provide a high-level view of where we are as a field with regard to technology-enabled SBIRT delivery and training. Furthermore, we aimed to describe a process by which psychologists can select and use a given type of program that matches their audience, substances involved, technology needs, modes of engagement, goals, empirical evidence, and availability. Although we have attempted to be practical, this is currently the "wild west" of our field, and as such, there are no hard and fast rules. We have endeavored to keep up with what our clients and society wants, lest we and our helpful treatments lose relevance.

Technology-enabled SBIRT programs are beginning to be developed in a few "untapped technologies." Social media captures the attention of many across the world; it is a natural type of technology to harness for positive health changes, including SBIRT. This might be especially true and relevant for adolescents and young adults (e.g., Moreno, D'Angelo, & Whitehill, 2016).

In *virtual reality* programs, people interact with a computer-generated, three-dimensional reality with audio, visual, and tactile aspects through a helmet and hand sensors. One feasibility study explored the use of virtual reality in coping skills training for nicotine dependence (Bordnick, Traylor, Carter, & Graap, 2012). SBIRT seems a natural next step for this technology.

As in video games, *gamification* means using game-like elements in nongame situations to increase motivation and engagement to complete a task. Gamification has been added to a plethora of health behavior change technologies, such as apps that allow you to earn points and electronic badges for exercise targets. However, none have been developed using SBIRT for substance use.

Artificial intelligence in SBIRT is only barely being addressed (See Coach Vicky: Magerko et al., 2011; Pantalon et al., 2019, and Kognito: Albright et al., 2016). However, it is a technology that is ripe for the picking in SBIRT because it could adapt both technology-enhanced interventions and training to the highly unique needs, characteristics, contexts, and even moods of its users or trainees.

Another future trend concerns the seeking and granting of U.S. Food and Drug Administration (FDA) approval for SBIRT apps, which can be thought of as "psychological devices," similar to the way a hearing aid is considered a medical device (Weir, 2018). At present, two apps are FDA-approved for the treatment of substance use disorders (U.S. FDA, 2017, 2018). One benefit of obtaining FDA approval is safety because programs will have to pass rigorous effectiveness standards (e.g., multiple randomized controlled trials demonstrating efficacy). FDA approval could also pave the way for insurance reimbursement; however, this is not guaranteed. Conversely, requiring a physician prescription for a psychological treatment takes treatment out of psychologists' hands, further medicalizing psychological treatment. Another possible downside would be that FDA-approved programs would be seen as more legitimate than other programs that may be as effective but have not been submitted for approval. This could have serious ramifications for the practice of psychology.

Finally, native apps that provide text-based psychotherapy (e.g., https://www.TalkSpace.com, https://www.BetterHelp.com) are amassing millions of users (McHugh, 2020), but their efficacy is not well established. Therapists for those programs are also not required to use evidence-based therapies. Without similar entrepreneurial efforts on the part of clinical, research, training, and technology-focused psychologists, we may not be able to keep pace with promoting evidence-based SBIRT and other interventions to our clients via technology, or otherwise. That said, and on a more optimistic note, given that psychologists have been at the center of the development of SBIRT since its inception, no other field is better equipped to achieve the goal of universally (i.e., technologically) available, evidence-based SBIRT delivery and training.

REFERENCES

Abujarad, F., & Vaca, F. E. (2015). mHealth tool for alcohol use disorders among Latinos in emergency department. *Proceedings of the International Symposium of Human Factors and Ergonomics in Healthcare. International Symposium of Human Factors and Ergonomics in Healthcare, 4*, 12–19. http://dx.doi.org/10.1177/2327857915041005

Albright, G., Adam, C., Serri, D., Bleeker, S., & Goldman, R. (2016). Harnessing the power of conversations with virtual humans to change health behaviors. *mHealth, 2*, 44–56. http://dx.doi.org/10.21037/mhealth.2016.11.02

Alfonso, J., Hall, T. V., & Dunn, M. E. (2013). Feedback-based alcohol interventions for mandated students: An effectiveness study of three modalities. *Clinical Psychology & Psychotherapy, 20*, 411–423.

American Psychological Association. (n.d.). *Impact: APA and APA Strategic Services, Inc. strategic plan.* Retrieved from https://www.apa.org/about/apa/strategic-plan/impact-apa-strategic-plan.pdf

Blow, F. C., Walton, M. A., Bohnert, A. S. B., Ignacio, R. V., Chermack, S., Cunningham, R. M., . . . Barry, K. L. (2017). A randomized controlled trial of brief interventions to reduce drug use among adults in a low-income urban emergency department:

The HealthiER You study. *Addiction, 112*, 1395–1405. http://dx.doi.org/10.1111/add.13773

Bordnick, P. S., Traylor, A. C., Carter, B. L., & Graap, K. M. (2012). A feasibility study of virtual reality-based coping skills training for nicotine dependence. *Research on Social Work Practice, 22*, 293–300. http://dx.doi.org/10.1177/1049731511426880

Boudreaux, E. D., Haskins, B., Harralson, T., & Bernstein, E. (2015). The remote brief intervention and referral to treatment model: Development, functionality, acceptability, and feasibility. *Drug and Alcohol Dependence, 155*, 236–242. http://dx.doi.org/10.1016/j.drugalcdep.2015.07.014

Clement, J. (2019, August 1). *Mobile app usage—Statistics and facts.* Retrieved from https://www.statista.com/topics/1002/mobile-app-usage/

Cunningham, J. A., Wild, T. C., Cordingley, J., van Mierlo, T., & Humphreys, K. (2009). A randomized controlled trial of an internet-based intervention for alcohol abusers. *Addiction, 104*, 2023–2032. http://dx.doi.org/10.1111/j.1360-0443.2009.02726.x

Cunningham, R. M., Chermack, S. T., Ehrlich, P. F., Carter, P. M., Booth, B. M., Blow, F. C., . . . Walton, M. A. (2015). Alcohol interventions among underage drinkers in the ED: A randomized controlled trial. *Pediatrics, 136*, e783–e793. http://dx.doi.org/10.1542/peds.2015-1260

Curran, G. M., Bauer, M., Mittman, B., Pyne, J. M., & Stetler, C. (2012). Effectiveness-implementation hybrid designs: Combining elements of clinical effectiveness and implementation research to enhance public health impact. *Medical Care, 50*, 217–226. http://dx.doi.org/10.1097/MLR.0b013e3182408812

Dawson-Rose, C., Draughon, J. E., Cuca, Y., Zepf, R., Huang, E., Cooper, B. A., & Lum, P. J. (2017). Changes in Specific Substance Involvement Scores among SBIRT recipients in an HIV primary care setting. *Addiction Science & Clinical Practice, 12*, 34. http://dx.doi.org/10.1186/s13722-017-0101-1

Dimoff, J. D., Sayette, M. A., & Norcross, J. C. (2017). Addiction training in clinical psychology: Are we keeping up with the rising epidemic? *American Psychologist, 72*, 689–695. http://dx.doi.org/10.1037/amp0000140

D'Onofrio, G., Fiellin, D. A., Pantalon, M. V., Chawarski, M. C., Owens, P. H., Degutis, L. C., . . . O'Connor, P. G. (2012). A brief intervention reduces hazardous and harmful drinking in emergency department patients. *Annals of Emergency Medicine, 60*, 181–192. http://dx.doi.org/10.1016/j.annemergmed.2012.02.006

Doumas, D. M., McKinley, L. L., & Book, P. (2009). Evaluation of two web-based alcohol interventions for mandated college students. *Journal of Substance Abuse Treatment, 36*, 65–74. http://dx.doi.org/10.1016/j.jsat.2008.05.009

Fleming, M., Olsen, D., Stathes, H., Boteler, L., Grossberg, P., Pfeifer, J., . . . Skochelak, S. (2009). Virtual reality skills training for health care professionals in alcohol screening and brief intervention. *Journal of the American Board of Family Medicine, 22*, 387–398. http://dx.doi.org/10.3122/jabfm.2009.04.080208

Gross, D. (2010, October 12). *Apple trademarks 'There's an app for that.'* Retrieved from https://www.cnn.com/2010/TECH/mobile/10/12/app.for.that/index.html

Harris, S. K., Csémy, L., Sherritt, L., Starostova, O., Van Hook, S., Johnson, J., . . . Knight, J. R. (2012). Computer-facilitated substance use screening and brief advice for teens in primary care: An international trial. *Pediatrics, 129*, 1072–1082. http://dx.doi.org/10.1542/peds.2011-1624

Haskins, B. L., Davis-Martin, R., Abar, B., Baumann, B. M., Harralson, T., & Boudreaux, E. D. (2017). Health evaluation and referral assistant: A randomized controlled trial of a web-based screening, brief intervention, and referral to treatment system to reduce risky alcohol use among emergency department patients. *Journal of Medical Internet Research, 19*, e119. http://dx.doi.org/10.2196/jmir.6812

Hester, R. K., Delaney, H. D., & Campbell, W. (2011). ModerateDrinking.com and moderation management: Outcomes of a randomized clinical trial with non-dependent problem drinkers. *Journal of Consulting and Clinical Psychology, 79*, 215–224. http://dx.doi.org/10.1037/a0022487

Hester, R. K., Delaney, H. D., & Campbell, W. (2012). The College Drinker's Check-Up: Outcomes of two randomized clinical trials of a computer-delivered intervention. *Psychology of Addictive Behaviors, 26*, 1–12. http://dx.doi.org/10.1037/a0024753

Hester, R. K., Squires, D. D., & Delaney, H. D. (2005). The Drinker's Check-up: 12-month outcomes of a controlled clinical trial of a stand-alone software program for problem drinkers. *Journal of Substance Abuse Treatment, 28*, 159–169. http://dx.doi.org/10.1016/j.jsat.2004.12.002

Hollis, C., Falconer, C. J., Martin, J. L., Whittington, C., Stockton, S., Glazebrook, C., & Davies, E. B. (2017). Annual research review: Digital health interventions for children and young people with mental health problems—A systematic and meta-review. *Journal of Child Psychology and Psychiatry, 58*, 474–503. http://dx.doi.org/10.1111/jcpp.12663

Johnson, J. A., Woychek, A., Vaughan, D., & Seale, J. P. (2013). Screening for at-risk alcohol use and drug use in an emergency department: Integration of screening questions into electronic triage forms achieves high screening rates. *Annals of Emergency Medicine, 62*, 262–266. http://dx.doi.org/10.1016/j.annemergmed.2013.04.011

Lerch, J., Walters, S. T., Tang, L., & Taxman, F. S. (2017). Effectiveness of a computerized motivational intervention on treatment initiation and substance use: Results from a randomized trial. *Journal of Substance Abuse Treatment, 80*, 59–66. http://dx.doi.org/10.1016/j.jsat.2017.07.002

Lie, S. S., Karlsen, B., Oord, E. R., Graue, M., & Oftedal, B. (2017). Dropout from an ehealth intervention for adults with type 2 diabetes: A qualitative study. *Journal of Medical Internet Research, 19*, e187. http://dx.doi.org/10.2196/jmir.7479

Lotfipour, S., Cisneros, V., Anderson, C. L., Roumani, S., Hoonpongsimanont, W., Weiss, J., . . . Vaca, F. (2013a). Assessment of alcohol use patterns among Spanish-speaking patients. *Substance Abuse, 34*, 155–161. http://dx.doi.org/10.1080/08897077.2012.728990

Lotfipour, S., Howard, J., Roumani, S., Hoonpongsimanont, W., Chakravarthy, B., Anderson, C. L., . . . Dykzeul, B. (2013b). Increased detection of alcohol consumption and at-risk drinking with computerized alcohol screening. *The Journal of Emergency Medicine, 44*, 861–866. http://dx.doi.org/10.1016/j.jemermed.2012.09.038

Magerko, B., Dean, J., Idnani, A., Pantalon, M., & D'Onofrio, G. (2011). Dr. Vicky: A virtual coach for learning brief negotiated interview techniques for treating emergency room patients. *Artificial Intelligence & Health Communication, 11*, 1–8.

McCormack, R. P. (2017). Commentary on Blow et al. (2017): Leveraging technology may boost the effectiveness and adoption of interventions for drug use in emergency departments. *Addiction, 112*, 1406–1407. http://dx.doi.org/10.1111/add.13872

McHugh, S. V. (2020, January 6). *The best online therapy services of 2020 compared.* Retrieved from https://www.e-counseling.com/online-therapy/

McNeely, J., Strauss, S. M., Rotrosen, J., Ramautar, A., & Gourevitch, M. N. (2016). Validation of an audio computer-assisted self-interview (ACASI) version of the alcohol, smoking and substance involvement screening test (ASSIST) in primary care patients. *Addiction, 111*, 233–244. http://dx.doi.org/10.1111/add.13165

Mitchell, A. M., Finnell, D. S., Kane, I., Halge, H., Puskar, K., & Savage, C. L. (2018). Time-conscious alcohol screening and brief intervention for students, nurses, and nurse leaders. *The Journal of Continuing Education in Nursing, 49*, 467–473. http://dx.doi.org/10.3928/00220124-20180918-07

Moreno, M. A., D'Angelo, J., & Whitehill, J. (2016). Social media and alcohol: Summary of research, intervention ideas and future study directions. *Media and Communication, 4*, 50–59. http://dx.doi.org/10.17645/mac.v4i3.529

Mullen, J., Ryan, S. R., Mathias, C. W., & Dougherty, D. M. (2015). Feasibility of a computer-assisted alcohol screening, brief intervention and referral to treatment program for DWI offenders. *Addiction Science & Clinical Practice, 10*, 25. http://dx.doi.org/10.1186/s13722-015-0046-1

Ondersma, S. J., Beatty, J. R., Svikis, D. S., Strickler, R. C., Tzilos, G. K., Chang, G., . . . Sokol, R. J. (2015). Computer-delivered screening and brief intervention for alcohol use in pregnancy: A pilot randomized trial. *Alcoholism: Clinical and Experimental Research, 39,* 1219–1226. Doi.org/10.1111/acer.12747. http://dx.doi.org/10.1111/acer.12747

Ozechowski, T. J., Becker, S. J., & Hogue, A. (2016). SBIRT-A: Adapting SBIRT to maximize developmental fit for adolescents in primary care. *Journal of Substance Abuse Treatment, 62,* 28–37. http://dx.doi.org/10.1016/j.jsat.2015.10.006

Pantalon, M. V., Abujarad, F., Tetrault, J., Butner, J., Martel, S., Anderson, C., . . . D'Onofrio, G. (2019). *"Coach Vicky": A web-based, self-directed brief intervention training program.* Manuscript submitted for publication.

Pantalon, M. V., Lubetkin, B. S., & Fishman, S. T. (1995). Use and effectiveness of self-help books in the practice of cognitive and behavioral therapy. *Cognitive and Behavioral Practice, 2,* 213–228. http://dx.doi.org/10.1016/S1077-7229(05)80011-2

Rose, G. L., Badger, G. J., Skelly, J. M., MacLean, C. D., Ferraro, T. A., & Helzer, J. E. (2017). A randomized controlled trial of brief intervention by interactive voice response. *Alcohol and Alcoholism, 52,* 335–343. http://dx.doi.org/10.1093/alcalc/agw102

Satre, D. D., Ly, K., Wamsley, M., Curtis, A., & Satterfield, J. (2017). A digital tool to promote alcohol and drug use screening, brief intervention, and referral to treatment skill translation: A mobile app development and randomized controlled trial protocol. *JMIR Research Protocols, 6,* e55. http://dx.doi.org/10.2196/resprot.7070

Schwartz, R. P., Gryczynski, J., Mitchell, S. G., Gonzales, A., Moseley, A., Peterson, T. R., . . . O'Grady, K. E. (2014). Computerized versus in-person brief intervention for drug misuse: A randomized clinical trial. *Addiction, 109,* 1091–1098. http://dx.doi.org/10.1111/add.12502

Suffoletto, B., Kristan, J., Chung, T., Jeong, K., Fabio, A., Monti, P., & Clark, D. B. (2015). An interactive text message intervention to reduce binge drinking in young adults: A randomized controlled trial with 9-month outcomes. *PloS ONE, 10,* e0142877. http://dx.doi.org/10.1371/journal.pone.0142877

Tansil, K. A., Esser, M. B., Sandhu, P., Reynolds, J. A., Elder, R. W., Williamson, R. S., . . . Fielding, J. E. (2016). Alcohol electronic screening and brief intervention: Recommendation of the community preventive services task force. *American Journal of Preventive Medicine, 51,* 801–811. http://dx.doi.org/10.1016/j.amepre.2016.04.013

Turner, C. F., Ku, L., Rogers, S. M., Lindberg, L. D., Pleck, J. H., & Sonenstein, F. L. (1998). Adolescent sexual behavior, drug use, and violence: Increased reporting with computer survey technology. *Science, 280,* 867–873. http://dx.doi.org/10.1126/science.280.5365.867

U.S. Food and Drug Administration. (2017, September 14). *FDA permits marketing of mobile medical application for substance use disorder.* Retrieved from https://www.fda.gov/news-events/press-announcements/fda-permits-marketing-mobile-medical-application-substance-use-disorder

U.S. Food and Drug Administration. (2018, December 10). *FDA clears mobile medical app to help those with opioid use disorder stay in recovery programs.* Retrieved from https://www.fda.gov/NewsEvents/Newsroom/PressAnnouncements/ucm628091.htm

U.S. Preventive Services Task Force. (2018). Screening and behavioral counseling interventions to reduce unhealthy alcohol use in adolescents and adults: U.S. Preventive Services Task Force recommendation statement. *JAMA, 320,* 1899–1909. http://dx.doi.org/10.1001/jama.2018.16789

U.S. Preventive Services Task Force. (2019, August). *Draft Recommendation Statement. Illicit Drug Use, Including Nonmedical Use of Prescription Drugs: Screening.* Retrieved from https://www.uspreventiveservicestaskforce.org/Page/Document/draft-recommendation-statement/drug-use-in-adolescents-and-adults-including-pregnant-women-screening

Vaca, F. E., Winn, D., Anderson, C. L., Kim, D., & Arcila, M. (2011). Six-month follow-up of computerized alcohol screening, brief intervention, and referral to treatment in the emergency department. *Substance Abuse, 32,* 144–52. http://dx.doi.org/10.1080/08897077.2011.562743

Walton, M. A., Bohnert, K., Resko, S., Barry, K. L., Chermack, S. T., Zucker, R. A., . . . Blow, F. C. (2013). Computer and therapist based brief interventions among cannabis-using adolescents presenting to primary care: One year outcomes. *Drug and Alcohol Dependence, 132,* 646–653. http://dx.doi.org/10.1016/j.drugalcdep.2013.04.020

Walton, M. A., Chermack, S. T., Shope, J. T., Bingham, C. R., Zimmerman, M. A., Blow, F. C., & Cunningham, R. M. (2010). Effects of a brief intervention for reducing violence and alcohol misuse among adolescents: A randomized controlled trial. *JAMA, 304,* 527–535. http://dx.doi.org/10.1001/jama.2010.1066

Walton, M. A., Resko, S., Barry, K. L., Chermack, S. T., Zucker, R. A., Zimmerman, M. A., . . . Blow, F. C. (2014). A randomized controlled trial testing the efficacy of a brief cannabis universal prevention program among adolescents in primary care. *Addiction, 109,* 786–797. http://dx.doi.org/10.1111/add.12469

Weir, K. (2018). The ascent of digital therapies. *Monitor on Psychology, 49,* 80.

White, A., Kavanagh, D., Stallman, H., Klein, B., Kay-Lambkin, F., Proudfoot, J., . . . Young, R. (2010). Online alcohol interventions: A systematic review. *Journal of Medical Internet Research, 12,* e62. http://dx.doi.org/10.2196/jmir.1479

12

SBIRT for Cannabis Use

Improving Clinical Competencies for a Changing Cultural Landscape

Win Turner, Joseph Hyde, Jody Kamon, and Gregory R. Hancock

Health care providers need new clinical strategies to address cannabis use in the United States. An estimated 128 million Americans have tried cannabis, 24 million of whom are current (i.e., past-month) users, making cannabis the fourth most commonly used mind-altering substance, after caffeine, nicotine, and alcohol, among those age 12 and older (Substance Abuse and Mental Health Services Administration [SAMHSA], 2018). One in six cannabis users qualifies for a diagnosis of cannabis use disorder (CUD), representing 4 million people in the United States (SAMHSA, 2018). The 2018 Monitoring the Future survey found that only 18% of teens discontinued use over time, the lowest rate of any substance in 22 years. This fact suggests that trends toward continued use are increasing, in particular when there is adolescent onset (Struble, Ellis, & Lundahl, 2019). ⊀ *Increase continue use of start as teen*

Similar to individuals who meet criteria for other substance use disorders (SUDs), most individuals who meet criteria for a CUD do not seek treatment. The many reasons cited include not being ready to stop, embarrassment regarding their use, financial costs of treatment, and stigma and negative attitude toward treatment. In addition, treatment is often perceived as designed for those already committed to change and perhaps not for the many who are ambivalent (Hill, 2015; Roffman & Stephens, 2006). As with other SUDs, only a relatively small number of people needing treatment enter specialty treatment settings. Furthermore, many people who qualify for a diagnosis of CUD do not believe they need treatment (Hill, 2015). These data underline

http://dx.doi.org/10.1037/0000199-013

Screening, Brief Intervention, and Referral to Treatment for Substance Use: A Practitioner's Guide, M. D. Cimini and J. L. Martin (Editors) the importance of reexamining our current understanding of cannabis use and our approaches to addressing risky cannabis use.

In this chapter we cannot address all of the topics needed to fully inform providers with sufficient cannabis clinical competencies; instead, we focus on topics that influence providers' clinical stance when trying to identify cannabis risk and engage cannabis users in health-based conversations.

GAPS IN CLINICAL UNDERSTANDING OF CANNABIS

Recent decades have seen a dramatic change in our cultural relationship with cannabis. In 2015, for the first time, a majority of Americans said they support legalization of cannabis (Jones, 2015). This trend has continued unabated. The most recent Gallup poll (2017) found that 64% of U.S. citizens approve legalization (Reinhart, 2018). In addition, although in a large 2016 Monitoring the Future survey (Schulenberg et al., 2017) respondents stated they do not approve of regular cannabis use, these same respondents also did not see cannabis use as harmful. The terms *legal, approve, harmful,* and *regular use* have many meanings, which are in continual flux, so careful interpretations are warranted. This new reality has spurred scattershot state-level efforts to change cannabis laws, including decriminalization, legalized medical use of cannabis, and legalization of recreational consumption. As of this writing, 11 states and the District of Columbia allow recreational use, and 34 states have either decriminalized or allow medical cannabis use (DISA Global Solutions, 2019).

Cannabis is now easier to obtain, cheaper to buy, and stronger in potency than at any time since it was criminalized (Hill, 2015). Delta-9-tetrahydrocannabinol (THC) is the primary psychoactive ingredient found in cannabis. The term *cannabis* is used throughout this chapter as opposed to other culturally popular nonscientific terms such as *pot, marijuana,* or *weed,* which can not only lead to confusion but also have negative connotations. *Cannabis* refers to the taxonomenclature of the plant genus that contains three psychoactive species with a long history of domestication, and this term is now being used by most researchers, medical producers, dispensaries, and federal agencies (Pollio, 2016). Cannabis potency is measured by the amount of THC present in the dried plant. Cannabis potency has increased by between 4 and 12 times in the past 30 years. Today, on average, the cannabis found on the street contains 13% THC, whereas recreational cannabis sold in dispensaries in Colorado has an average of 17% THC (Marijuana Policy Group, 2015).

Our clinical science and research understanding have not kept pace with changes in cannabis potency and availability; thus, our historical conceptions of how cannabis affects users may or may not be relevant as we examine and update our clinical practices. In fact, most cannabis studies supported by the National Institute on Drug Abuse (NIDA) are based on 3% THC potency, with a few as high as 8% THC. However, the scientific study of cannabis is rapidly increasing. The number of PubMed citations published in 2020 totaled 31,923 (based on a PubMed keyword search for "marijuana"), representing a four-fold increase from the 8,168 citations published in 2000. Cannabidiol (CBD), the second primary component of cannabis, is now getting as much attention as THC because it is thought to be the main medicinal chemical in the cannabis plant. In fact, the CBD:THC ratio is one way of qualifying cannabis strains and their potential "benefits." Around the globe, CBD research is taking off in attempts to demonstrate its potential health impact.

Tectonic changes in our cultural relationship with cannabis, followed by new policies and breeding practices, have created a landscape in which clinicians find themselves in need of better information and techniques for engaging clients in conversations about cannabis. Many clinicians lack the necessary information and clinical tools to work effectively with clients who use cannabis (Barnett et al., 2013; Budney et al., 2011). Interventionists interacting with users need cannabis clinical competencies because of the changing landscape in cannabis strains, potency, method of use, legality, perception of harm, and positive and negative effects of use. The dynamic world of cannabis use demands a heightened awareness of and mindful approach toward understanding the complexities of cannabis science, our cultural interpretations of use and the risks involved and, most important, clients' expressions of their own biopsychosocial experience.

A BRIEF REVIEW OF DIVERGENT CONCLUSIONS IN CANNABIS RESEARCH

Examples of divergent findings include highway safety, enduring cognitive impairment, schizophrenia, and prevention science (i.e., reduced perception of harm leading to increased substance use). As we summarize shortly, one study raises the specter of potential catastrophic risks in a given domain, whereas another study refutes those findings. This confusion can detract from our appreciation of known adverse psychosocial consequences of cannabis use, and this phenomenon illustrates there is much still to be learned. Any definitive understanding gleaned from past and current cannabis research needs careful interpretation based on the specifics of the population of study (e.g., age, gender, whether the subject is a polysubstance user); the specifics of cannabis, including but not limited to potency, methods of use, and frequency of use; and the empirical methods and design of the study itself. In general, because cannabis is a Schedule 1 substance, the allowed potency of approved cannabis strains in U.S. research studies is substantially lower than most users currently experience. Increased THC and decreased CBD in the new cannabis strains as well as newer methods (e.g., dabs, edibles, and vapes) and types of use (e.g., concentrates, resins) are hypothesized to create the most negative impacts across a wide array of domains, including mental health symptoms, cognitive performance, executive function, inhibitory motor control, and increased desires for continued use (Mashhoon, Sagar, & Gruber, 2019). Acute symptoms associated with overconsumption of high-potency cannabis (e.g., edibles, concentrates) can include rapid heart rate, irritability, panic, nausea, drowsiness, confusion, short-term psychosis, or vomiting (Struble et al., 2019).

Clearest from the most current findings is that most studies are unclear as to the benefits of cannabis use, and only a limited number of published results have demonstrated any significant improvements with medical or nonmedical cannabis. A comprehensive review from the National Academies of Sciences, Engineering, and Medicine (2017) on the science to date, including the health impact of medical and recreational cannabis use, reported few significant positive benefits. In addition, there is a strong medical consensus that no cannabis use should occur during vulnerable periods of human development, including before, during, and after pregnancy and throughout childhood, adolescence, and into young adulthood. However, clients often convincingly report that they feel better across a wide range of physical and mental health symptoms. The answers as to why they feel this way are slowly emerging as we learn more about the endocannabinoid system, but there are vast inconsistencies in findings, amplifying the need to further understand clients through the use of refined cannabis-specific screeners.

Pregnancy

As legal access to cannabis expands, there has been a growing concern about the effects of prenatal cannabis exposure (Committee on Obstetric Practice, 2017). Self-report data from the National Survey on Drug Use and Health show a significant increase in the recent prevalence of reported prenatal exposure to cannabis in the United States (Volkow, Han, Compton, & McCance-Katz, 2019). Between 2002 and 2017, past-month cannabis use increased from 3.4% to 7.0% among pregnant women overall and from 5.7% to 12.1% during the first trimester (Volkow et al., 2019). Percentages for use are higher for younger women, and of lower socioeconomic status, and those living in urban environments (Committee on Obstetric Practice, 2017). Recent studies in the United States that have used toxicology screening suggest that the incidence may be larger than these data suggest. Many women choose not to disclose prenatal cannabis use to providers, suggesting that the actual rate of use among pregnant women is higher (Rodriguez et al., 2019; Young-Wolff et al., 2019). Given this new extent of use, providers and the public need to be aware of the known potentials for harm.

Concerns arising from repeated findings in more recent meta-analyses fall into several primary areas, including anemia in pregnant mothers; decreased birth weight; increased need for neonatal intensive care; and a number of potential neurological, neurocognitive, and neurodevelopmental impacts for newborns that can persist into adolescence. Recent data and meta-analyses suggest effects on fetal developmental trajectories whereby prenatal exposure leads to higher rates of preterm birth and a greater need for intervention

(Conner et al., 2016; Gunn et al., 2016). In a recent example, Corsi and colleagues (2019) studied a large matched sample of Canadian women and found a modest increase in the likelihood of several developmental markers— including preterm birth, being small for gestational age, placental abruption, and an increased need for neonatal intensive care—among women who used cannabis during pregnancy. The findings published for newborns and youth listed a variety of symptoms: tremors, altered sleep patterns, lower memory scores, attention problems and, in adolescence, a greater likelihood of emotional and behavioral problems (El Marroun et al., 2018; Gunn et al., 2016). The authors stated that the results of these studies "suggest that the endocannabinoid system plays an essential role in the ontogeny of the nervous system during fetal brain development and that early gestational exposure to cannabis is able to induce lasting but subtle neurodevelopmental alterations" (El Marroun et al., 2018, p. 2). Of note is that other published meta-analyses have not found the extent of consequences listed above. Methodological limitations in this field of research include a lack of well-controlled studies; confounds such as polysubstance use, tobacco use, and socioeconomic status; and a lack of longitudinal data (Metz & Borgelt, 2018). Still, all emerging data suggest the need for caution. Because of the known and potential concerns with any cannabis use regardless of method, the Committee on Obstetric Practice (2017) strongly recommends that all providers advise their patients to stop using before, during, and after pregnancy.

Highway Safety

Driving under the influence of any substance is a behavior that has received decades of fear-driven national public attention. Although certainly no practitioner would ever endorse driving while high on cannabis, the evidence for cannabis impairment while driving is equivocal. The March 2013 report "Cannabis Effects on Driving Skills" (Hartman & Huestis, 2013) stated that certain driver skills, such as reaction times, divided-attention tasks, and lane-position variability, showed cannabis-induced impairment. A newer study, from the National Highway Traffic Safety Administration, found that drivers who used cannabis were at a significantly lower risk for a crash than drivers who used alcohol (Berning, Compton, & Wochinger, 2015). After adjustments were made for age, gender, race, and alcohol use, drivers who tested positive for cannabis were no more likely to crash than those who had not used any drugs or alcohol before driving. The authors concluded that "specific drug concentration levels cannot be reliably equated with a specific degree of driver impairment" (Berning et al., 2015). Last, a study released in February 2019 by the Society for the Study of Addiction looked at cannabis-related traffic fatalities in cannabis-legal states such as Colorado and Washington. Lane and Hall (2019) documented an increase in cannabis-associated traffic fatalities in the year following legalization at a rate of increase of 1.08 traffic fatalities per 1 million residents in the first year (2014), followed by a trend reduction of −0.06 per month in the year following (2015).

Cognitive Impairment

It is generally accepted that cannabis has a broad array of short-term neuro-cognitive effects, including detriments in learning and memory, executive function, and motor control (National Academies of Sciences, Engineering, & Medicine, 2017). Furthermore, several studies have found a correlation between regular adolescent use of cannabis and an increased likelihood of negative outcomes, such as lower academic attainment and employment instability (Meier et al., 2012; Silins et al., 2014). However, whether the relationship is causal remains controversial given that social determinants and genetic factors may play a disproportionately influential role in one's life trajectory. Until recently, a study conducted by Zalesky et al. (2012) was cited as evidence of enduring cognitive decline due to cannabis use; however, in the past year a large cross-sectional study of associations between cannabis use and the cognitive function of adolescents and young adults (Scott et al., 2018) indicated that abstinence of longer than 72 hours diminished most of the cognitive deficits associated with cannabis use. The study's results indicated that previous studies of cannabis in youth may have overstated the magnitude and persistence of cognitive deficits associated with use (Scott et al., 2018).

Schizophrenia

A growing body of literature supports a correlation between cannabis use and early onset of psychotic illness (Davis, Compton, Wang, Levin, & Blanco, 2013). Psychotic illnesses are relatively rare: Approximately 3% of people develop one of the psychotic illnesses (e.g., schizophrenia, bipolar disorder, schizoaffective disorder; Perälä et al., 2007) in their lifetime. The use of cannabis has been viewed as a risk factor for early expression of a psychotic illness (Radhakrishnan, Wilkinson, & D'Souza, 2014), and risk may increase as the potency of cannabis increases (Di Forti et al., 2015; Large, Sharma, Compton, Slade, & Nielssen, 2011). Research has not determined, however, whether cannabis use is a direct contributor to increased risk for a psychotic illness, as opposed to genetic and environmental factors (Shakoor et al., 2015).

The authors of a recent genome-wide association study confirmed a "significant genetic correlation" between cannabis use and schizophrenia (Pasman et al., 2018). Instead of cannabis causing the early emergence of schizophrenia, the authors found causation moving in the opposite direction; the emergence of schizophrenia led to a greater probability of cannabis use. One theory suggested that people struggling with early signs of schizophrenia may try to calm their brain and alleviate other symptoms by consuming cannabis. The authors stated, "Our findings may indicate that individuals at risk for developing schizophrenia may experience prodromal symptoms"—in other words, early signs of the condition—"or negative affect that make[s] them more likely to start using cannabis to cope or self-medicate" (Pasman et al., 2018, pp. 1169–1170).

Perception of Risk and Harm

The pillar of prevention theory asserts that perception of risk and harm has a causal link to increases or decreases in substance use (Hawkins, Catalano, & Miller, 1992; Lipari, 2013). People who perceive low risk or harm associated with cannabis use, for example, should theoretically engage in increased use. This theory has generally proven to be accurate with tobacco and alcohol, and it also holds true for cannabis. According to the National Survey on Drug Use and Health, perceptions of the harm of weekly cannabis use were lower in 2018 compared with earlier years, whereas past-year cannabis use was higher than the percentages from 2002 through 2017 (SAMHSA, 2019). The most recent data from the longitudinal Monitoring the Future Study demonstrated that, across all age groups, rates of past-month, past-year, and lifetime use of marijuana have remained steady (NIDA, 2019); however, daily use—defined as using at least 20 of the past 30 days—significantly increased among eighth and 10th graders, but not 12th graders. In general, the percentages of youth who perceive cannabis use as risky have been on a downward trend since the mid-2000s (NIDA, 2019). In addition, after cannabis was decriminalized in California the perceived risk decreased while use increased in eighth and 10th graders; a similar pattern was observed in Washington State after legalization.

Evidence has demonstrated both the potential benefits and harms of cannabis. Although recent research has noted that some of the feared catastrophic consequences may be less likely than earlier reports claimed, researchers agree there are other known psychosocial impacts for some users. Thus, given the state of confusion in the current research, we recommend that providers (a) increase their awareness of their own beliefs and attitudes about cannabis use and how it may affect their practice, (b) always listen to their clients' experience of use before emphasizing preconceived ideas about cannabis use and associated consequences (e.g., impaired driving, cognitive impairment, and mental health concerns), and (c) use refined screening and assessment tools specifically developed for cannabis users.

As state and national efforts for legalization continue, practitioners need to be more cognizant of the impacts of cannabis use. We need to build our skills to have thoughtful, nonjudgmental, non–fear-based conversations with our clients regarding their cannabis use so that they might make better decisions regarding their psychosocial, emotional, and physical health. We practitioners must also urge clients to be discerning consumers of cannabis-related science.

METHODS FOR EFFECTIVE SCREENING

Medical settings that implement the Screening, Brief Intervention, and Referral to Treatment (SBIRT) protocol adopt a broad range of universal screening questions to identify patients with social, environmental, mental health, and substance use risk. Essential lessons learned from several large-scale SBIRT projects suggest that universal screening, and framing the entire SBIRT process as a "wellness project aimed at reducing the risks of preventable disease and injury," helps ameliorate patient concerns (Substance Abuse and Mental Health Services Administration–Health Resources & Services Administration, 2015). For example, the 2012 SAMHSA-funded SBIRT Tennessee project discovered a 14% increase in screening adherence when they included a statement emphasizing that because they cared about *all* of their patients' health concerns, all patients were being screened for general wellness as part of a new public health approach. In effect, "these types of introductory messages help to normalize the screening process and ease patient concerns they are not being singled out," said Tennessee SBIRT Project Director Angela McKinney-Jones (JBS International, 2017).

The lesson learned from Tennessee's SBIRT grant initiative, and adopted in 2013 by Vermont's SBIRT project, is the importance of first asking "disarming" questions that are nonintrusive and lacking in significant stigma relative to substance use (JBS International, 2017). These questions commonly address other health risk topics, such as seat belt use, flu shots, or distracted driving. From a population-based risk reduction perspective, this strategy increases opportunities to reduce other health risk behaviors while also serving as a rapport builder and a screening induction method. This wellness-induction approach helps minimize patient discomfort at the start of the screening process and allows an opportunity for affirming healthy lifestyle choices.

As with any SBIRT screening protocol, patients who endorse risk for any of the wellness questions, such as seat belt nonuse or distracted driving, receive a brief motivational interaction or written psychoeducational information. After responding to these introductory questions, patients are asked about tobacco, alcohol, substance use, and mood. SBIRT programs typically adopt very brief single drug or alcohol questions for assessing use in the past year. Questions about substance use often include a single or several yes/no–type drug screen questions about cannabis, opiates, other illegal drug misuse, as well as three alcohol consumption questions (e.g., AUDIT–C: frequency, quantity, and binge; see https://www.mdcalc.com/audit-c-alcohol-use) and a tobacco use question. Common secondary screening tools used in SBIRT include the Alcohol Use Disorders Identification Test (AUDIT; Babor, Higgins-Biddle, Saunders, & Monteiro, 2011) and the Drug Abuse Screening Test 10 (DAST; Skinner, 1982).

Regardless of the administration method or approach, there are several primary goals of effective, efficient, and valid substance use screening tools used in population health projects such as SBIRT. Initial brief questions triage patients with risk from those unlikely to have risk. Secondary questions asked of patients needing further screening attempt to elicit any negative or concerning consequences of use that map onto the *Diagnostic and Statistical Manual of Mental Disorders* (5th ed.; *DSM–5*; American Psychiatric Association, 2013) criteria and allow providers a jump start toward exploration and engagement in motivating discussions with patients. These tools result in screening scores that can be stratified on the basis of the degree of risk that corresponds to a recommended level of intervention (i.e., brief intervention, brief treatment, or treatment referral); hence, the endorsed responses to secondary screening questions become an essential component of the same-day or immediate interventions that are most often delivered as reflective feedback sessions.

A well-researched, potent, and common brief intervention model used in SBIRT is the Brief Negotiated Interview (D'Onofrio, Bernstein, & Rollnick, 1996), which is structured on the basis of the four phases of motivational interviewing interventions: (a) engage, (b) focus, (c) evoke, and (d) plan (Miller & Rollnick, 2013). Screening risk scores and both positive- and negative-consequence items correspond with the phases of the structured intervention. The endorsed responses create the topics of personal consequence (i.e., possible reasons for change) and help focus provider feedback discussions. Thus, screening tools, combined with Motivational Interviewing, may help providers develop patient discrepancies and activate patient motivation to reduce risk. Using an SBIRT approach driven by use of motivational interviewing propelled us to develop a cannabis-specific screening tool.

NEED FOR A NEW TOOL FOR CANNABIS SCREENING

In 2013, as our statewide SBIRT project began, the prevalence of risky cannabis use for Vermonters and those elsewhere was concerning. In a sample of 34,819 Vermont adult medical patients, 21% reported using cannabis in the past year. Past-year use varied by age, with 41% of persons ages 18 to 24, 25% of persons ages 25 to 44, 17% of persons ages 45 to 54, 11% of persons ages 55 to 64, and 3% of persons age 65 and older endorsing past-year cannabis use. Use was most prevalent for young adults ages 18 through 24, an age group vulnerable to developmental sensitivities, as compared with older adults. Vermont's patients' frequency of use is that of the bimodal curve (see Figure 12.1), illustrating that the greatest percentages of individuals reporting cannabis use fall in either very infrequent or very frequent (i.e., near-daily) use groupings.

When our SBIRT project began, there was no universally accepted frequency measure for triaging cannabis use. In fact, the most common question used by clinical practitioners was the NIDA single-item question: a yes/no inquiry about use of illegal drugs in the past year (NIDA, 2012). On the basis of recent increases in the prevalence of cannabis use and the shifting cultural landscape in which patients may not identify cannabis as "illegal," our health care system stakeholders (e.g., medical champions) encouraged us to develop an initial frequency measure for cannabis use. Such a frequency measure would allow for a more comprehensive understanding of how Vermont's population used cannabis and assist with triage of our patients determined by frequency of use.

FIGURE 12.1. Frequency of Marijuana Use Among Those Endorsing Any Use in the Past Year (*N* = 7,281)

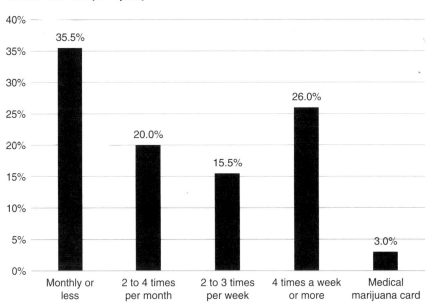

Vermont medical champions based their recommendations for an initial "risk" versus "no risk" frequency cutoff of twice weekly or greater use on the following two factors: (a) Their high-demand emergency department work-flow could not be interrupted by "prevention" interventions, and (b) the extant literature demonstrated little to no impact for infrequent cannabis use in adults. In addition, medical champions also elected to screen out patients who endorsed cannabis use by means of a cannabis medical card, again because of concern regarding the emergency department workflow. We quickly learned that by using this new cannabis frequency measure in conjunction with a specific cannabis secondary screen we could begin to better understand how frequency of use was associated with the reported effects of use. Many agencies and SBIRT program directors across the United States have now adopted our initial cannabis frequency question (see first question in Figure 12.2).

Health care providers consistently voice their concerns about and frustrations with their perceived inability to intervene meaningfully for patients who use cannabis. Patients often do not verbalize reasons to change their use and, in fact, state they feel cannabis is helpful for a variety of mental health and physical symptoms, including those for which there is no evidence base. In our SBIRT project, interventionists' concerns were validated by the lack of patient-endorsed consequences (items) on the DAST. Out of a possible nine secondary DAST[1] items, patients engaging in regular cannabis use, defined as

---

[1]Although the Drug Abuse Screening Test has 10 items, the first item is answered as part of the initial screening. Thus, in the secondary screening respondents are asked to complete the remaining nine items.

FIGURE 12.2. Cannabis Intervention Screener (CIS; Including Initial and Secondary Screening Questions)

Question	Never	Monthly or less	Several days per month	Weekly	Several days per week (2–4 days)	Daily or almost daily (5–7 days)
How often have you used marijuana **in the past year?** (including smoking, vaping, dabbing, or edibles)	☐	☐	☐	☐	☐	☐

If you chose **"Never"** please **STOP HERE**. Otherwise, go to the next question.

	One	Two	Three	Four or more
When you use marijuana, how many *times per day* do you typically use?	☐	☐	☐	☐

	Smoke (joints, bong, pipe, etc.)	Vape (inhaling plant/ herb or liquid vapor via electronic device)	Dab (inhaling intensely heated hash oil/resin)	Edibles (brownies, candy, etc.)
How do you use marijuana? (check all that apply)	☐	☐	☐	☐

	Yes	No
A. Have you used marijuana for personal enjoyment and/or recreational reasons?	☐	☐
B. Have you used marijuana for medical or physical health reasons such as pain, cancer, or epilepsy?		☐
C. Have you used marijuana for mental health reasons such as trouble focusing, worries or anxiety, stress, negative or sad emotions?		☐
D. Do you have a medical marijuana card?	☐	☐

(continues)

FIGURE 12.2. Cannabis Intervention Screener (CIS; Including Initial and Secondary Screening Questions) (*Continued*)

Different things happen to people when they are using marijuana, or as a result of their marijuana use. Read each statement below carefully and check "Yes" if it happened to you in the past year. Check "No" if it never happened to you in the past year.

In relation to your marijuana use in the past year . . .	Yes	No
Have you tried to **control** your marijuana use by smoking only at certain times of the day or certain places?	☐	☐
Have you worried about the amount of **money** you've been spending on marijuana?	☐	☐
Have you gone to **work** or **school** high or stoned?	☐	☐
Has your family, friends, or a health provider expressed **concern** about your marijuana use?	☐	☐
Have you **driven** a car or other vehicle, including a bicycle, after using marijuana, on more than a few occasions (at least three)?	☐	☐
Have you noticed the **amount** or **frequency** of your marijuana use has increased over time?	☐	☐
Have you noticed that your **memory** is not as good as it used to be?	☐	☐
Have you **continued** to smoke marijuana when you promised yourself you would not?	☐	☐
[☐ *Not applicable: I've not promised myself that I would not use marijuana*]		
When you have **stopped using marijuana** for a period of time (even several days), have you experienced any of the following: irritability, restlessness, anxiety, depression, loss of appetite, sleep problems, pain, or headaches?	☐	☐
[☐ *Not applicable: I've not tried to stop using marijuana*]		

In relation to your lifetime marijuana use . . .	Yes	No
Have you ever seen a counselor or other professional as a result of your own concerns, or concerns that someone else has had, about your marijuana use?	☐	☐

Note. On the basis of postanalyses clinician feedback, we added a question on recreational use to the "reasons for using" section (questions A–D). Initial screening: cannabis use frequency item (initial triage question). Cutoff = weekly use or greater. If cutoff is endorsed, action = administer secondary screening (full screen). Secondary screening: The full CIS is administered to those who endorse using cannabis weekly or more often. CIS stratifications are based on the number of endorsed items (out of 10).

twice weekly or greater (with no other substance use reported), endorsed an average of 1.3 items ($SD = 1.7$, range: 0–9). Such low endorsement of consequences limited the "potential reasons for change" content focus of brief interventions.

The low endorsement of cannabis-related consequences presented an important question that needed to be addressed. For patients with risky cannabis use, would the addition of a short cannabis-specific secondary screening tool increase the number of items patients endorse, consequently increasing the potential for the brief intervention to have greater potency and meaning? Phrased in more precise terms, if patients are presented with items more specific to potential impacts of cannabis use versus general drug use, will they identify with, and consequently endorse, more items? In doing so, will their interest in discussing the item content increase? If the substance and quality of the patient and provider discussions increase, will this lead to more opportunities for the interventionist to develop discrepancies and elicit change talk? From a Motivational Interviewing perspective, increased change talk has been shown to equal a greater chance that patients will take actual steps toward change (Miller & Rollnick, 2013).

DEVELOPMENT OF THE CANNABIS INTERVENTION SCREENER

The Vermont SBIRT team found six validated cannabis screeners in their review of the literature and selected several specific tools from which to guide the development of the new instrument. It is important to note that a primary challenge with all existing tools reviewed was the length of the screeners. In medical settings, providers needed a screener that was brief, easy to administer, and easy to score. Decisions were made on the basis of which tools were most helpful based on content, brevity, and distinction from the DAST (Adamson et al., 2010; Alexander & Leung, 2004; Bashford, 2009; Bashford, Flett, & Copeland, 2010; Hodgins & Stea, 2018; Martin, Copeland, Gilmour, Gates, & Swift, 2006). On the basis of validated screening tool items, and our SBIRT providers' recommendations as well as needs, we created a pool of 21 possible cannabis-specific consequence items. We also added one additional question about driving after using cannabis because this is a topic of heightened public concern. On the basis of pilot findings and provider feedback, we created the 10-item Cannabis Intervention Screener (CIS; Turner, Hyde, Selig, & Kamon, 2018; see Figure 12.2).

Vermont's SBIRT interventionists administered the standard SBIRT tools (initial screening questions, AUDIT, and DAST), including the initial frequency screening question for cannabis use and the newly created CIS. The initial pilot study included 215 patients and demonstrated that patients who endorsed using cannabis twice weekly or more also endorsed significantly more total items on the CIS versus the DAST (CIS = 449 items, DAST = 225 items; $t = 2.3$, $p < .05$). The CIS led to further delineation for patients with more significant cannabis use. We found that a significantly greater number of patients who used cannabis more often (four or more times a week as compared with two to three times a week) reported driving after cannabis use ($\chi^2 = 3.3$, $p < .05$), worrying about the cost of cannabis ($\chi^2 = 6.8$, $p < .01$), experiencing memory loss ($\chi^2 = 4.5$, $p < .05$), and continuing to use cannabis after promising themselves they would stop ($\chi^2 = 7.6$, $p < .01$).

To understand whether this cannabis-specific screening facilitated more meaningful (potent) conversations aimed at generating change talk, we asked SBIRT clinicians after each intervention to answer a set of questions rating their impression of the cannabis brief intervention, how meaningful they felt the discussion was for the patient, discrepancies developed, and ease of discussing risks and eliciting change talk. We also surveyed providers to record highlights of the discussion content. Forty-two percent of providers indicated the discussion was somewhat to a great deal more potent, and the interventionists endorsed being able to engage in more meaningful discussions about cannabis and its effect on the person's life. When asked whether the CIS allowed them to develop discrepancies between the patient's ongoing use and that patient's goals, 32% reported somewhat to a great deal, and another 39% reported a little bit. In 63% of the brief interventions, providers indicated that they agreed or strongly agreed that the CIS made it easier to discuss the risks associated with the patient's cannabis use.

Further examination of the qualitative responses elicited from providers highlighted additional benefits of CIS screening. Providers reported increased patient dialogue and stated that motivational interventions were effective. Patients' reported use of cannabis to help them cope with a range of physical and emotional problems included sleep, worry, ability to focus, painful or traumatic emotions, and physical pain. In addition, patients verbalized the following factors as possible reasons why they might consider changing their cannabis use: cost, trouble with memory and cognition, managing anxiety, managing pain, health, and concerns about driving under the influence.

After pilot testing in Vermont, our team partnered with SBIRT implementation efforts in Washington and Iowa to conduct an initial validation evaluation of the CIS. These three states represent different landscapes of cannabis public access and policy. Participating sites included diverse practice settings such as community health centers, emergency departments, college health services, and routine primary-care practices. Additional data regarding patients' risky alcohol use (AUDIT) and mood (Patient Health Questionnaire–9; see https://www.mdcalc.com/phq-9-patient-health-questionnaire-9) were collected in all three states. The final sample size was 651 adult patients (18 and older) across the three states and various medical settings (Vermont: $n = 128$, Iowa: $n = 228$, Washington: $n = 295$).

As part of the process for validating the CIS, multiple analyses were conducted, including predictive and concurrent construct validity; classification tree analysis using chi-square automatic interaction detection; and significance tests analyzing frequency of use, method of use (i.e., smoke, vape, dab, or edibles), and reasons for use (i.e., physical vs. mental health) in relation to the number of items endorsed on the CIS scale of 10 items measuring consequences of cannabis use.

FINDINGS AND RECOMMENDATIONS FOR USING THE CANNABIS INTERVENTION SCREENER

Only patients who endorsed more frequent cannabis use were given the full CIS in Vermont. As such, Figure 12.3 reflects only frequency data from Washington and Iowa ($n = 523$) because this reflects a total population of cannabis users, including those who used less frequently. Figure 12.3 illustrates that 34% of patients endorsed using cannabis less than weekly, whereas 66% endorsed using it weekly or more often, and, of those who used it weekly or more often, 41% endorsed daily or almost-daily use. Patients who endorsed weekly or greater use had a significantly elevated CIS impact score.

Methods of cannabis use were compared using the full sample. It is important to note that patients were asked to identify all methods of cannabis use versus their single preferred method; thus, some patients selected more than one method. The primary method of use among this sample was smoking (93.2%), followed by edibles (21.4%), dabbing (13.4%), and vaping (12.9%). Seventy-three percent of patients reported having only one method of use, with the majority of those (92%) endorsing smoking as their sole method. More frequent use was equated to engaging in multiple methods of use. Patients who endorsed using at least several days a week or more had a significantly elevated chance of also vaping or consuming edibles. Also, if patients endorsed using weekly or more often, there was an elevated chance of dabbing.

The CIS elicits concerns an individual may experience as a result of using cannabis (see Figure 12.4). The concerns elicited by the CIS items support the

FIGURE 12.3. Frequency of Cannabis Use ($N = 523$)

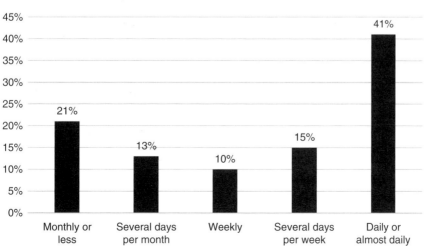

FIGURE 12.4. Endorsement Frequency of Cannabis Intervention Screener "Concern" or "Impact" Items

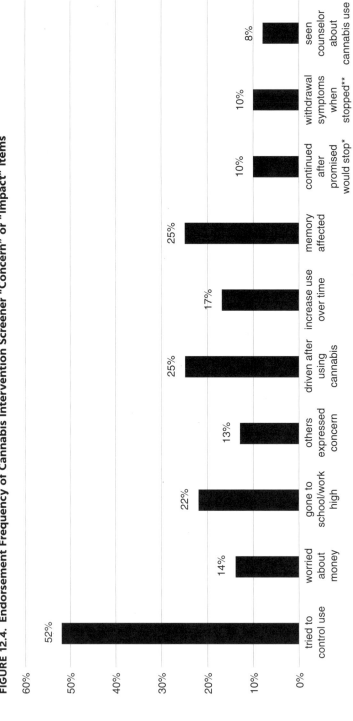

Note. Two items had substantial amounts of missing data as respondents could indicate if they felt the item was not applicable to them. *38% missing data. **17% missing data.

measure's internal consistency and reliability, as measured by Cronbach's alpha ($\alpha = .75$). In past year, users most frequently reported attempts to control use (52%), followed by endorsement of use while driving (25%), experience of memory impairment (25%), and use at school and work (22%). This information is essential for focusing the brief cannabis-specific intervention and understanding how to best interact with cannabis users.

Within the screening and brief intervention process, stratification to differentiate risk levels (low, moderate, high) is critical. This enables providers to match risk level with the appropriate intervention. The following CIS scale scores (see Table 12.1) and associated suggested risk levels reflect the number of consequences endorsed while capturing the prevalence rates and risk levels defined in the *DSM–5* for CUD ($n = 523$). The risk levels correspond with *DSM–5* categorizations of low, moderate, and severe CUD. Thus, a score of 0 would indicate that the patient did not endorse any of the CIS items numbered 7 through 16, whereas a score of 10 would indicate the patient endorsed all items.

There was a strong correlation between the frequency of use and the number of negative consequences endorsed, not dissimilar to findings in alcohol screening (AUDIT; Centers for Disease Control and Prevention, 2014). For individuals who reported using cannabis more than weekly, or multiple times per day, there was a significantly greater chance they had tried to control their use. Similarly, patients who endorsed using multiple times per day (two to three times) endorsed all CIS impacts at significantly greater levels (i.e., money spent, others expressing concern, increasing use over time, using after promising not to, experiencing symptoms after stopping, seeing a counselor, driving, memory impairment, and using at work/school). Figure 12.5 illustrates the difference in CIS risk by frequency of use. Among patients who used less frequently (less than weekly), 17% fell in the moderate to high CIS risk levels, whereas 45% of those who used more frequently (weekly or greater) were in the moderate to high CIS risk levels, $\chi^2(3) = 69.9$, $p < .001$. Our results suggest that health care providers pay special attention to users who report daily or more than daily use.

It is interesting to note that patients who endorsed using cannabis for mental health reasons were significantly more likely to have moderate to high levels of CIS risk, $\chi^2(9) = 61.4$, $p < .001$. Perhaps individuals who use cannabis to cope with mental health symptoms are also more likely to endorse negative impacts related to their cannabis use. This is not viewed as a causal

TABLE 12.1. Cannabis Intervention Screener Impact Scale Scores

Risk level (cutoff score)	% of patients
None (0–1)	48
Low (2–3)	32
Moderate (4–5)	14
Severe (6+)	6

FIGURE 12.5. Cannabis Intervention Screener Risk by Frequency of Use

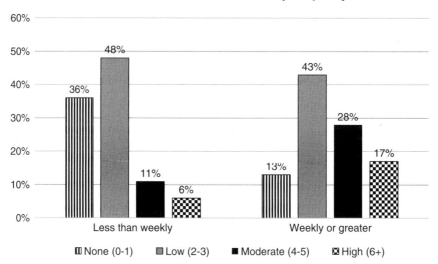

relationship. Individuals with mental health problems who also use cannabis may have a different outlook on their cannabis use compared with those who use it for physical or solely recreational reasons and thus perceive the impact differently. It may also be true that although individuals are instructed to endorse items only in relation to their cannabis use, their endorsement of items may reflect a consequence they are experiencing related to additional factors. Further research is needed to draw any causal conclusions.

CONCLUSIONS AND FUTURE DIRECTIONS FOR SCREENING AND INTERVENING WITH CANNABIS USE

The CIS pilot and validation study across multiple medical settings and in multiple states with differing legal environments yielded several significant findings that are helpful in advancing our clinical effectiveness when working with those who use cannabis. Using a single-item frequency-of-use triage question resulted in a clear delineation of who will later endorse impact of use and who likely will not. The CIS reasons-for-use and methods-of-use questions enable a more refined understanding of current cannabis use trends and how those trends associate with risk. The 10 impact questions stratify users into low, moderate, and severe risk categories, allowing for a matched intervention approach, a hallmark of SBIRT. In addition, providers skilled in Motivational Interviewing the strategies and tools for increasing change, and the brief negotiated intervention (D'Onofrio et al., 1996) can incorporate the CIS concern scale results into individual feedback sessions.

There are several limitations to the CIS studies we have described. A major limitation of the initial validation study is that the data were self-report and collected concurrently (i.e., a cross-sectional design). Second, the pilot and validation studies occurred in naturalistic medical settings, and SBIRT delivery and cutoff rates used varied by setting. As mentioned earlier, medical providers in Vermont did not want to intervene with patients who had obtained a medical registration card, which we also see as a limitation based on a need to further understand the impact of use regardless of the patient's obtaining a "prescription." Another limitation concerns our inability to use comparison tools such as the *DSM* Structured Clinical Interview tool for CUD (First, Williams, Karg, & Spitzer, 2016), or other cannabis screeners (e.g., Multidimensional Prognostic Index [Pilotto et al., 2008], Cannabis Use Disorder Identification Test—Revised [Adamson et al., 2010], Cannabis Abuse Screening Test [Legleye, Kraus, Piontek, Phan, & Jouanne, 2012]) for increased psychometric validity. Because of the naturalistic implementation of our study protocol, the study settings were already taxed with using standard SBIRT tools and unable to screen patients further.

We realize the CIS reasons-for-use questions are limited to either physical or mental health and that, as such, the results fail to capture individuals who are using for the pleasure or the "high" associated with cannabis use. However, it is important to note that respondents may have selected "no" for both reasons-for-use items. To better capture this motive, one of the authors suggested changing the tool to include the following item: "Have you used marijuana for personal enjoyment and/or recreational reasons?" The CIS also currently does not assess quantity (milligrams) and type of cannabis (THC and CBD percentages) used. Future iterations of the CIS should screen for this information, and then a simple formula can be used to try and ascertain the typical dose of THC (CBD). Similarly, future research should include items that assess for the impact of cannabis on sleep and on effective communication. These concerns were not included in the CIS validation study yet have been mentioned in web-based discussion groups as affecting individuals with increased frequency (i.e., daily or more) and duration of use (i.e., more than 2 years; "Marijuana Enthusiasts!," 2019).

The landscape of cannabis use is ever changing in regard to prevalence and methods of cannabis use, dose, and impact, and hence new tools are needed to assist health care providers in identifying patients at risk for negative consequences. SBIRT as a population health strategy including effective universal cannabis screening enables access to cannabis users never before realized in U.S. health care settings. The timely development of the CIS is a marked improvement from current SBIRT tools to address risky cannabis use in a motivational manner. Looking to the future, we would like to further our investigation of cannabis-specific screening and interventions that help providers and patients with the tectonic change in methods of use such as new technologies like vaping.

The CIS validation study demonstrated that the initial frequency prescreen, and the weekly use cutoff, is successful at triaging those negatively affected by cannabis use and those with no or few negative impacts of use. This larger validation study confirmed the opinions of Vermont's medical champions: that patients who use cannabis infrequently (less than weekly) endorse little or no negative impacts associated with use, whereas patients who use it multiple times daily (cannabis binge use) report the highest CIS impact scores. An examination of the concerns endorsed revealed that there were no significant differences between those who used cannabis for physical or mental health reasons. Trying to control use was a significant indicator of those with more chronic use and a good starting place for a discussion in the context of a brief intervention. Other identified concerns reported among those who used more frequently include driving under the influence, memory loss, and using during work/school.

Our initial multistate trial across several different types of SBIRT-infused medical settings and the adoption of the tool by many agencies now suggests that a brief cannabis-specific screening tool (the CIS) is not only acceptable by providers but also eases their integration effort to address patients' cannabis risk. However, additional validation of the CIS is needed. Attention to differences in age, multiple time points, a larger sample, and comparisons with other cannabis-specific screening tools (i.e., to establish concurrent validity) will be helpful. In addition, evaluation of how the CIS influences population health initiatives such as SBIRT is needed. Studies that examine the impact of the CIS on the efficacy of brief interventions for cannabis risk will help health care providers and their patients and will advance our field during this critical period of rapid change in cannabis culture and research.

HELPFUL RESOURCES

- Turner, W., Hyde, J., Selig, A., & Kamon, J. (2018). *A practitioner's guide to cannabis intervention.* Montpelier, VT: Center for Behavioral Health Integration.

- Visit https://www.c4bhi.com to see videos related to SBIRT, cannabis intervention, and the Cannabis Intervention Screener.

REFERENCES

Adamson, S. J., Kay-Lambkin, F. J., Baker, A. L., Lewin, T. J., Thornton, L., Kelly, B. J., & Sellman, J. D. (2010). An improved brief measure of cannabis misuse: The Cannabis Use Disorders Identification Test—Revised (CUDIT–R). *Drug and Alcohol Dependence, 110*, 137–143. http://dx.doi.org/10.1016/j.drugalcdep.2010.02.017

Alexander, D. E., & Leung, P. (2004). The Marijuana Screening Inventory (MSI–X): Reliability, factor structure, and scoring criteria with a clinical sample. *The American Journal of Drug and Alcohol Abuse, 30*, 321–351. http://dx.doi.org/10.1081/ADA-120037381

American Psychiatric Association. (2013). *Diagnostic and statistical manual of mental disorders* (5th ed.). Washington, DC: Author.

Babor, T. F., Higgins-Biddle, J. C., Saunders, J. B., & Monteiro, M. G. (2011). *AUDIT: The Alcohol Use Disorders Identification Test: Guidelines for use in primary healthcare.* Geneva, Switzerland: World Health Organization.

Barnett, E., Moyers, T. B., Sussman, S., Smith, C., Rohrbach, L. A., Sun, P., & Spruijt-Metz, D. (2013). From counselor skill to decreased marijuana use: Does change talk matter? *Journal of Substance Abuse Treatment, 46*, P498–P505. http://dx.doi.org/10.1016/j.jsat.2013.11.004

Bashford, J. (2009). *Screening and assessment for cannabis use disorders.* Sydney, New South Wales, Australia: National Cannabis Prevention and Information Centre. Retrieved from https://pdfs.semanticscholar.org/dd6e/338543f2fa49bb6cdf9e29cd917419b8d7cc.pdf

Bashford, J., Flett, R., & Copeland, J. (2010). The Cannabis Use Problems Identification Test (CUPIT): Development, reliability, concurrent and predictive validity among adolescents and adults. *Addiction, 105*, 615–625. http://dx.doi.org/10.1111/j.1360-0443.2009.02859.x

Berning, A., Compton, R., & Wochinger, K. (2015, February). *Results of the 2013–2014 National Roadside Survey of alcohol and drug use by drivers* [Traffic Safety Facts Research Note; Report No. DOT HS 112 118]. Washington, DC: National Highway Traffic Safety Administration. Retrieved from https://www.nhtsa.gov/sites/nhtsa.dot.gov/files/812118-roadside_survey_2014.pdf

Budney, A. J., Fearer, S., Walker, D. D., Stanger, C., Thostenson, J., Grabinski, M., & Bickel, W. K. (2011). An initial trial of a computerized behavioral intervention for cannabis use disorder. *Drug and Alcohol Dependence, 115*, 74–79. http://dx.doi.org/10.1016/j.drugalcdep.2010.10.014

Centers for Disease Control and Prevention. (2014). *Planning and implementing screening and brief intervention for risky alcohol use: A step-by-step guide for primary care practices.* Atlanta, GA: Author.

Committee on Obstetric Practice. (2017). Committee Opinion No. 722: Marijuana use during pregnancy and lactation. *Obstetrics and Gynecology, 130*, e205–e209. http://dx.doi.org/10.1097/AOG.0000000000002354

Conner, S. N., Bedell, V., Lipsey, K., Macones, G. A., Cahill, A. G., & Tuuli, M. G. (2016). Maternal marijuana use and adverse neonatal outcomes: A systematic review and meta analysis. *Obstetrics and Gynecology, 128*, 713–723. http://dx.doi.org/10.1097/AOG.0000000000001649

Corsi, D. J., Walsh, L., Weiss, D., Hsu, H., El-Chaar, D., Hawken, S., . . . Walker, M. (2019). Association between self-reported prenatal cannabis use and maternal, perinatal, and neonatal outcomes. *JAMA, 322*, 145–152. http://dx.doi.org/10.1001/jama.2019.8734

Davis, G. P., Compton, M. T., Wang, S., Levin, F. R., & Blanco, C. (2013). Association between cannabis use, psychosis, and schizotypal personality disorder: Findings from the National Epidemiologic Survey on Alcohol and Related Conditions. *Schizophrenia Research, 151*, 197–202. http://dx.doi.org/10.1016/j.schres.2013.10.018

Di Forti, M., Marconi, A., Carra, E., Fraietta, S., Trotta, A., Bonomo, M., . . . Murray, R. M. (2015). Proportion of patients in south London with first-episode psychosis attributable to use of high potency cannabis: A case-control study. *The Lancet Psychiatry, 2*, 233–238. http://dx.doi.org/10.1016/S2215-0366(14)00117-5

DISA Global Solutions. (2019, November). *Wondering what the law is in your state?* Houston, TX: Author. Retrieved from https://disa.com/map-of-marijuana-legality-by-state

D'Onofrio, G., Bernstein, E., & Rollnick, S. (1996). Motivating patients for change: A brief strategy for negotiation. In E. Bernstein & J. Bernstein (Eds.), *Case studies in emergency medicine and the health of the public* (pp. 295–303). Burlington, MA: Jones & Bartlett Learning.

El Marroun, H., Brown, Q. L., Lund, I. O., Coleman-Cowger, V. H., Loree, A. M., Chawla, D., & Washio, Y. (2018). An epidemiological, developmental and clinical overview of cannabis use during pregnancy. *Preventive Medicine, 116*, 1–5. http://dx.doi.org/10.1016/j.ypmed.2018.08.036

First, M. B., Williams, J. B. W., Karg, R. S., & Spitzer, R. L. (2016). Structured Clinical Interview for *DSM–5* Disorders, clinician version (SCID–5–CV). Arlington, VA: American Psychiatric Association.

Gunn, J. K. L., Rosales, C. B., Center, K. E., Nuñez, A., Gibson, S. J., Christ, C., & Ehiri, J. E. (2016). Prenatal exposure to cannabis and maternal and child health outcomes: A systematic review and meta-analysis. *BMJ Open, 6*(4), e009986. http://dx.doi.org/10.1136/bmjopen-2015-009986

Hartman, R. L., & Huestis, M. A. (2013). Cannabis effects on driving skills. *Clinical Chemistry, 59*, 478–492. http://dx.doi.org/10.1373/clinchem.2012.194381

Hawkins, J. D., Catalano, R. F., & Miller, J. Y. (1992). Risk and protective factors for alcohol and other drug problems in adolescence and early adulthood: Implications for substance abuse prevention. *Psychological Bulletin, 112,* 64–105. http://dx.doi.org/10.1037/0033-2909.112.1.64

Hill, K. (2015). Medical marijuana does not increase adolescent marijuana use. *The Lancet Psychiatry, 2*, 572–573. http://dx.doi.org/10.1016/S2215-0366(15)00267-9

Hodgins, D. C., & Stea, J. N. (2018). Psychometric evaluation of a lifetime version of the Marijuana Problems Scale. *Addictive Behaviors Reports, 8*, 21–24. http://dx.doi.org/10.1016/j.abrep.2018.05.001

JBS International. (2017). *Teaching SBIRT: SAMHSA's SBIRT core curriculum. Module 2: Screening patients for substance use in your practice setting.* Rockville, MD: Author.

Jones, J. M. (2015, October 15). In U.S., 58% back legal marijuana use. *Gallup News.* Retrieved from https://news.gallup.com/poll/186260/back-legal-marijuana.aspx

Lane, T. J., & Hall, W. (2019). Traffic fatalities within U.S. states that have legalized recreational cannabis sales and their neighbours. *Addiction, 114*, 847–856. http://dx.doi.org/10.1111/add.14536

Large, M., Sharma, S., Compton, M. T., Slade, T., & Nielssen, O. (2011). Cannabis use and earlier onset of psychosis: A systematic meta-analysis. *Archives of General Psychiatry, 68*, 555–561. http://dx.doi.org/10.1001/archgenpsychiatry.2011.5

Legleye, S., Kraus, L., Piontek, D., Phan, O., & Jouanne, C. (2012). Validation of the Cannabis Abuse Screening Test in a sample of cannabis inpatients. *European Addiction Research, 18*, 193–200.

Lipari, R. N. (2013). *Trends in adolescent substance use and perception of risk from substance use.* Rockville, MD: Center for Behavioral Health Statistics and Quality, Substance Abuse and Mental Health Services Administration.

Marijuana enthusiasts! (2019). [Online forum]. https://www.reddit.com/r/marijuana enthusiasts/

Marijuana Policy Group. (2015). *Marijuana equivalency in portion and dosage.* Denver, CO: Author.

Martin, G., Copeland, J., Gilmour, S., Gates, P., & Swift, W. (2006). The Adolescent Cannabis Problems Questionnaire (CPQ–A): Psychometric properties. *Addictive Behaviors, 31*, 2238–2248. http://dx.doi.org/10.1016/j.addbeh.2006.03.001

Mashhoon, Y., Sagar, K. A., & Gruber, S. A. (2019). Cannabis use and consequences. *Pediatric Clinics of North America, 66*, 1075–1086. http://dx.doi.org/10.1016/j.pcl.2019.08.004

Meier, M. H., Caspi, A., Ambler, A., Harrington, H., Houts, R., Keefe, R. S., . . . Moffitt, T. E. (2012). Persistent cannabis users show neuropsychological decline from childhood to midlife. *Proceedings of the National Academy of Sciences of the United States of America, 109*, e2657–e2664. http://dx.doi.org/10.1073/pnas.1206820109

Metz, T. D., & Borgelt, L. M. (2018). Marijuana use in pregnancy and while breastfeeding. *Obstetrics and Gynecology, 132*, 1198–1210. http://dx.doi.org/10.1097/AOG.0000000000002878

Miller, W. R., & Rollnick, S. (2013). *Motivational Interviewing: Helping people change* (3rd ed.). New York, NY: Guilford Press.

National Academies of Sciences, Engineering, and Medicine. (2017). *The health effects of cannabis and cannabinoids: The current state of evidence and recommendations for research.* Washington, DC: National Academies Press. http://dx.doi.org/10.17226/24625

National Academy of Sciences. (2017). *The health effects of cannabis and cannabinoids: The current state of evidence and recommendations for research.* Washington, DC: National Academies Press.

National Institute on Drug Abuse. (2012, March). *Resource guide: Screening for drug use in general medical settings.* Retrieved from https://www.drugabuse.gov/publications/resource-guide-screening-drug-use-in-general-medical-settings

National Institute on Drug Abuse. (2019). *Monitoring the Future survey: High school and youth trends.* Retrieved from https://www.drugabuse.gov/publications/drugfacts/monitoring-future-survey-high-school-youth-trends

Pasman, J. A., Verweij, K. J. H., Gerring, Z., Stringer, S., Sanchez-Roige, S., Treur, J. L., . . . The International Cannabis Consortium. (2018). GWAS of lifetime cannabis use reveals new risk loci, genetic overlap with psychiatric traits, and a causal effect of schizophrenia liability. *Nature Neuroscience, 21,* 1161–1170. http://dx.doi.org/10.1038/s41593-018-0206-1

Perälä, J., Suvisaari, J., Saarni, S. I., Kuoppasalmi, K., Isometsä, E., Pirkola, S., . . . Lönnqvist, J. (2007). Lifetime prevalence of psychotic and bipolar I disorders in a general population. *Archives of General Psychiatry, 64,* 19–28. http://dx.doi.org/10.1001/archpsyc.64.1.19

Pilotto, A., Ferrucci, L., Franceschi, M., D'Ambrosio, L. P., Scarcelli, C., Cascavilla, L., . . . Leandro, G. (2008). Development and validation of a multidimensional prognostic index for one-year mortality from comprehensive geriatric assessment in hospitalized older patients. *Rejuvenation Research, 11,* 151–161.

Pollio, A. (2016). The name of *cannabis*: A short guide for nonbotanists. *Cannabis and Cannabinoid Research, 1,* 234–238. http://dx.doi.org/10.1089/can.2016.0027

Radhakrishnan, R., Wilkinson, S. T., & D'Souza, D. C. (2014). Gone to pot—A review of the association between cannabis and psychosis. *Frontiers in Psychiatry, 5,* 54. http://dx.doi.org/10.3389/fpsyt.2014.00054

Reinhart, R. (2018, January 4). In the news: Marijuana legalization. *Gallup News.* Retrieved from https://news.gallup.com/poll/225017/news-marijuana-legalization.aspx

Rodriguez, C. E., Sheeder, J., Allshouse, A. A., Scott, S., Wymore, E., Hopfer, C., . . . Metz, T. D. (2019). Marijuana use in young mothers and adverse pregnancy outcomes: A retrospective cohort study. *BJOG, 126,* 1491–1497. http://dx.doi.org/10.1111/1471-0528.15885

Roffman, R., & Stephens, R. (2006). *Cannabis dependence: Its nature, consequences and treatment.* Cambridge, England: Cambridge University Press.

Schulenberg, J. E., Johnston, L. D., O'Malley, P. M., Bachman, J. G., Miech, R. A., & Patrick, M. E. (2017). *Monitoring the Future national survey results on drug use, 1975–2016: Volume II. College students and adults ages 19–55.* Ann Arbor: Institute for Social Research, The University of Michigan.

Scott, J. C., Slomiak, S. T., Jones, J. D., Rosen, A. F. G., Moore, T. M., & Gur, R. C. (2018). Association of cannabis with cognitive functioning in adolescents and young adults: A systematic review and meta-analysis. *JAMA Psychiatry, 75,* 585–595. http://dx.doi.org/10.1001/jamapsychiatry.2018.0335

Shakoor, S., Zavos, H. M., McGuire, P., Cardno, A. G., Freeman, D., & Ronald, A. (2015). Psychotic experiences are linked to cannabis use in adolescents in the community because of common underlying environmental risk factors. *Psychiatry Research, 227,* 144–151. http://dx.doi.org/10.1016/j.psychres.2015.03.041

Silins, E., Horwood, L. J., Patton, G. C., Fergusson, D. M., Olsson, C. A., Hutchinson, D. M., . . . Mattick, R. P. (2014). Young adult sequelae of adolescent cannabis use: An integrative analysis. *The Lancet Psychiatry, 1,* 286–293. http://dx.doi.org/10.1016/S2215-0366(14)70307-4

Skinner, H. A. (1982). *The Drug Abuse Screening Test–10 item version*. Toronto, Ontario, Canada: Centre for Addiction and Mental Health.

Struble, C. A., Ellis, J. D., & Lundahl, L. H. (2019). Beyond the bud: Emerging methods of cannabis consumption for youth. *Pediatrics Clinics of North America, 66*, 1087–1097. http://dx.doi.org/10.1016/j.pcl.2019.08.012

Substance Abuse and Mental Health Services Administration. (2018). *Results from the National Survey on Drug Use and Health 2016: Detailed tables*. Retrieved from https://www.samhsa.gov/data/sites/default/files/NSDUH-DetTabs-2016/NSDUH-DetTabs-2016.pdf

Substance Abuse and Mental Health Services Administration. (2019). *Key substance use and mental health indicators in the United States: Results from the 2018 National Survey on Drug Use and Health* (DHHS Publication No. PEP19-5068). Rockville, MD: Center for Behavioral Health Statistics and Quality, Substance Abuse and Mental Health Services Administration.

Substance Abuse and Mental Health Services Administration–Health Resources & Services Administration. (2015). *Culture of wellness organizational self-assessment (COW–OSA)*. Retrieved from https://www.integration.samhsa.gov/Culture_of_Wellness_Self-Assessment_-COW-OSA-_Summer_2015.pdf

Turner, W., Hyde, J., Selig, A., & Kamon, J. (2018). *A practitioner's guide for cannabis intervention*. Montpelier, VT: Center for Behavioral Health Integration.

Volkow, N. D., Han, B., Compton, W. M., & McCance-Katz, E. F. (2019). Self-reported medical and nonmedical cannabis use among pregnant women in the United States. *JAMA, 322*, 167–169. http://dx.doi.org/10.1001/jama.2019.7982

Young-Wolff, K. C., Sarovar, V., Tucker, L.-Y., Conway, A., Alexeeff, S., Weisner, C., . . . Goler, N. (2019). Self-reported daily, weekly, and monthly cannabis use among women before and during pregnancy. *JAMA Network Open, 2*, e196471. http://dx.doi.org/10.1001/jamanetworkopen.2019.6471

Zalesky, A., Solowij, N., Yücel, M., Lubman, D. I., Takagi, M., Harding, I. H., . . . Seal, M. (2012). Effect of long-term cannabis use on axonal fibre connectivity. *Brain, 135*, 2245–2255. http://dx.doi.org/10.1093/brain/aws136

13

Integrating SBIRT Training Into Graduate Programs for Mental Health Service Providers

Jessica L. Martin and M. Dolores Cimini

Alcohol and substance use (i.e., use of illicit drugs, as well as misuse of prescription medications) are well-known public health problems in the United States. The Substance Abuse and Mental Health Services Administration (SAMHSA; 2019) estimated that in 2018 in the United States approximately 67.1 million people had engaged in risky alcohol use and 14.8 million people met diagnostic criteria for an alcohol use disorder in the past year Also in 2018, approximately 53.2 million people age 12 or older reported illicit drug use, including 1.7 million who reported misuse of prescription pain medication, and an estimated 8.1 million Americans met criteria for an illicit drug use disorder (SAMHSA, 2019). In 2018, 9.2 million people, or 3.7% of those surveyed who were age 18 or older, had a diagnosable substance use and mental health disorder (SAMHSA, 2019). Roughly 30% to 35% of individuals with a mental health disorder reported heavy alcohol use, use of cannabis, and use of illicit drugs (SAMHSA, 2019).

According to SAMHSA's Center for Behavioral Health Statistics and Quality (2019), 15% of all individuals age 12 and older who were served in state mental health treatment settings in 2017 had co-occurring mental health and substance use disorders (SUDs). Depressive disorders and trauma- and stressor-related disorders were the most common diagnoses co-occurring with SUDs across men and women.

A study that comprised a representative sample of practitioners in six mental health professions (psychiatrists, psychologists, professional counselors,

http://dx.doi.org/10.1037/0000199-014
Screening, Brief Intervention, and Referral to Treatment for Substance Use: A Practitioner's Guide,
M. D. Cimini and J. L. Martin (Editors)

social workers, marriage and family therapists, and substance abuse counselors) working in private practice and organizational settings indicated that one in five clients seen in private practice had an SUD, with somewhat higher rates (38%) in organized mental health treatment settings (Harwood, Kowalski, & Ameen, 2004). These figures demonstrate the large proportion of clients who need substance use interventions or treatment. The results of a recent national survey suggest that only a small proportion of those who need substance use treatment actually receive it. In 2018, 21.2 million people age 12 or older (or one in 13 people) needed substance use treatment, but only 11.1% of those people received it (SAMHSA, 2019).

IMPACT OF PROVIDER TRAINING ON TREATMENT SEEKING AND ENGAGEMENT

There are several reasons why people do not engage in treatment when needed; among them are perceived lack of need for treatment and stigma (SAMHSA, 2005). Many individuals with substance use problems, instead of seeking specialized substance use treatment, often turn first to primary care, mental health care services, or both (Denering & Spear, 2012; Edlund, Booth, & Han, 2012). This means that mental health practitioners who routinely screen their clients for substance use have the opportunity to intervene with a population that might otherwise not be identified as in need of substance use services. Regrettably, most health care providers, including mental health practitioners, do not screen for substance use (Broderick, Kaplan, Martini, & Caruso, 2015; Martin, Cimini, Longo, Sawyer, & Ertl, in press), resulting in a great deal of missed opportunities for identifying individuals who may benefit from prevention or intervention efforts. Universal substance use screening (i.e., screening every person who presents for services regardless of their stated presenting concern) done as part of the screening, brief intervention, and referral to treatment (SBIRT) model, can identify not only clients in need of specialty substance use treatment but also those engaging in risky substance use who may benefit from a brief motivational intervention to help them reduce their use to low risk levels and prevent escalation to an SUD (SAMHSA, 2011). In fact, assessment of substance use alone can cause people to modify their behavior (e.g., Borsari et al., 2016).

Responding to the need for a coordinated effort to promote the widespread adoption of SBIRT in the United States to address the above gaps in assessment and referral, SAMHSA's Center for Substance Abuse Treatment initiated the SBIRT program in 2003 with cooperative agreements to its first cohort of grant recipients: six states (California, Illinois, New Mexico, Pennsylvania, Texas, and Washington) and one tribal council (based in Anchorage, Alaska). SAMHSA awarded 5-year grants to promote the adoption and sustained implementation of SBIRT in a variety of medical settings. The goals were (a) to expand the continuum of care for all SUDs and (b) to integrate substance abuse treatment and early intervention into the traditional medical care system (Babor, Del Boca, & Bray, 2017).

After SBIRT practices became part of the national landscape with the support of SAMHSA, it became clear that training mental health providers to engage in universal substance use screening as part of SBIRT's public health treatment approach had the potential to affect millions of people who would otherwise be unaware of or avoid discussing their need for substance use treatment services. The motivational interviewing skills taught as the framework within which to deliver SBIRT are key to helping clients engage in treatment. Mental health providers, and psychologists in particular, already possess clinical skills (e.g., training in Motivational Interviewing and other clinical interventions, case conceptualization and assessment skills) that should facilitate their learning and delivery of SBIRT (Wamsley, Satterfield, Curtis, Lundgren, & Satre, 2018).

In addition to equipping mental health service providers with additional tools they may need to engage clients in services, SBIRT training can also reduce providers' negative attitudes about people who use substances (i.e., stigma), which serves as a barrier to treatment. Although many people are aware that stigma about substance use exists among the general public (Lang & Rosenberg, 2017), fewer recognize that, unfortunately, stigma also exists among health care providers (van Boekel, Brouwers, van Weeghel, & Garretsen, 2013). Patients who fear stigma on the part of their providers report being less likely to disclose the use of substances (McNeely et al., 2018). Furthermore, patients who perceived stigma about their drug use from their provider rated their provider less favorably (Brener, von Hippel, & Kippax, 2007), which could negatively influence the treatment process and outcome. In one study, clients who perceived discrimination from their health care providers were less likely to complete treatment (Brener, von Hippel, Kippax, & Preacher, 2010).

It has been hypothesized that a lack of education and training, resulting in low levels of self-reported knowledge about substance use and the skills to treat those who use substances, contributes to the stigma reported by health care professionals in various physical and mental health specialty areas (van Boekel et al., 2013). Indeed, the majority of social workers, mental health counselors, and psychologists receive no training in substance use or its treatment (Dimoff, Sayette, & Norcross, 2017; Madson, Bethea, Daniel, & Necaise, 2008; Wilkey, Lundgren, & Amodeo, 2013). As a result, most mental health providers feel inadequately trained and in fact do lack the competency needed to treat this population (Burrow-Sánchez, Call, Adolphson, & Hawken, 2009; Cardoso, Pruett, Chan, & Tansey, 2006; Madson et al., 2008). The results of a study of clients seeking outpatient services for depression who also reported hazardous drinking or drug use underscored the low frequency with which mental health providers intervene with substance use (Satre, Leibowitz, Mertens, & Weisner, 2014). The researchers found that 70% of clients reported that their usual care providers did not suggest they reduce their alcohol or drug use (only 30% received a recommendation to reduce substance use), despite screening results suggesting drug use, hazardous alcohol use, or both; clients with higher depression and substance use severity were more likely to receive the recommendation (Satre et al., 2014).

Stigma, as well as a lack of knowledge and skills, is associated with less involvement in identifying and treating SUDs. For example, a study of general internists found that, in comparison with those who felt more prepared, those who felt less prepared to diagnose and treat patients with SUDs were less likely to report involvement in the following five activities: (a) diagnosing SUDs, (b) providing a brief intervention, (c) determining a patient's readiness to change, (d) offering help based on readiness level, and (e) referring patients to treatment (Wakeman, Pham-Kanter, & Donelan, 2016). In contrast, Harris, Shaw, Sherman, and Lawson (2016) found that, among school-based health center providers (program directors, physician assistants, nurses, and social workers), role responsibility, self-efficacy, and perceived effectiveness were all significantly, positively associated with self-reported provision of screening, brief intervention, and referral to treatment for substance use. In sum, provider stigma prevents clients from discussing substance use with their health care providers and seeking treatment when necessary, and it keeps providers from screening for substance use and engaging in prevention and intervention practices, thereby perpetuating the problem of low engagement in substance use treatment for those who need it.

Fortunately, research suggests that training in SBIRT can improve providers' attitudes toward clients who use substances (Putney, O'Brien, Collin, & Levine, 2017; Senreich, Ogden, & Greenberg, 2017). In addition, training in SBIRT increases providers' self-reported knowledge and self-efficacy to treat patients who use substances (Martin et al., in press; Putney et al., 2017; Stoner, Mikko, & Carpenter, 2014; Tanner, Wilhelm, Rossie, & Metcalf, 2012). In turn, increased knowledge and self-efficacy are associated with conducting more substance use screenings (Agley et al., 2016; Bernstein et al., 2007). Hence, training more mental health practitioners in SBIRT should not only decrease stigma among providers but also improve their ability to identify patients at risk for SUDs and effectively intervene to reduce risk and prevent future problems.

HISTORY OF SBIRT TRAINING FOR MENTAL HEALTH PROVIDERS

Over the past 10 years, SAMHSA began to focus its grant-making efforts more toward the training of health care professionals through its Screening, Brief Intervention, and Referral to Treatment Health Professions Student Training Grant Program. The purpose of this program was to develop and implement training programs to teach students in health professions (physician assistants, dentists, psychologists, pharmacists, nurses, social workers, counselors, and medical students and residents) the skills necessary to provide evidence-based screening and brief intervention and refer persons who are at risk for an SUD to appropriate treatment. A second aim was to develop the leadership skills needed to champion the implementation of SBIRT throughout the U.S. health care system with the ultimate goal of helping clients avoid SUDs. SAMHSA stated clearly its expectation that SBIRT was to be a component of the education curriculum for the identified programs in each academic year for the duration of the grant and an ongoing element of the academic curriculum postgrant award. This program aimed to address workforce development by increasing the number of health care professionals who can address the needs of persons at risk for SUDs; it also promoted the emphasis from the Patient Protection and Affordable Care Act (2010) of a multidisciplinary team approach to the integration of behavioral health into medical health care systems. Finally, the SBIRT Health Professions Student Training Grant Program sought to address behavioral health disparities among racial, ethnic, sexual, and gender minorities by encouraging the implementation of strategies to decrease the differences in access, service use, and outcomes among those served.

SBIRT TRAINING MODELS

Varied training models and modalities have been used to teach SBIRT to health and mental health providers. For example, some programs have used a one-shot approach whereby students or professionals are provided SBIRT training during one lecture or workshop lasting anywhere between 1 and 8 hours (e.g., Tetrault et al., 2012). Others have provided one in-person or online training and followed it with a booster training held sometime afterward in an attempt to increase or maintain the impact of the training on providers' knowledge, self-efficacy, and use of SBIRT skills. Still others have embedded SBIRT training into core courses within professional training curricula (e.g., Putney et al., 2017; Senreich et al., 2017). Several programs have trained supervisors and other instructors in SBIRT along with the target student population to enhance the likelihood that students would implement SBIRT and foster sustainability of the use of SBIRT in practice (e.g., Putney et al., 2017; Senreich et al., 2017; Tetrault et al., 2012). In the paragraphs that follow, we review various aspects of SBIRT training approaches.

Training Schedule and Structure

A limitation of much of the literature on SBIRT training is that few details are provided about when and how often trainings are offered. Hence, we do not know at what point in students' curriculum SBIRT training will be most effective (e.g., first semester, third year), or the optimal training schedule (e.g., three trainings over the course of 2 weeks or five trainings over the course of 2 months). Decisions about how and when to offer trainings may be best made after conducting a needs assessment among key stakeholders and the population for which the training is intended, subsequent to a literature review focused on the effectiveness of various training approaches that have been used for the target population (for an example, see Tetrault et al., 2012). Furthermore, it is necessary to consider the unique schedules of the trainees. For example, medical residents will require a training schedule that fits with their distinct arrangement of rotations and other educational requirements, and psychologists will require a different training arrangement and timeline (for examples of SBIRT training implementation considerations in various specialty training programs, see Tetrault et al., 2012). Mental health counseling trainees ideally will receive SBIRT training after they have been introduced to basic helping skills in other coursework but before they see clients in a practicum setting (Ogden, Vinjamuri, & Kahn, 2016). Under these ideal circumstances, mental health practitioners will have in place the basic ethical, professional, and counseling foundations and core competencies and will be immediately ready to implement SBIRT skills and receive guidance and feedback from supervisors while doing so.

Training Components

Almost all approaches to teaching SBIRT include a combination of didactic training, interactive live or video demonstrations, and experiential skills practice and evaluation of proficiency through role plays or the use of standardized patients. The practice component of trainings in which personalized feedback and coaching is provided is essential, as research suggests that information-only training strategies alone do not lead to adoption of a new clinical skill in practice settings (Forsetlund et al., 2009; Oxman, Thomson, Davis, & Haynes, 1995). Furthermore, supervised practice with feedback is recommended to increase use of a new skill and enhance clinicians' proficiency using the new skill (Hall, Staiger, Simpson, Best, & Lubman, 2016; Miller, Yahne, Moyers, Martinez, & Pirritano, 2004).

The didactic portion of SBIRT training is focused on motivational interviewing as a framework within which to deliver SBIRT (see Chapter 4, this volume) and includes information on SBIRT as a public health approach to prevention and intervention, approaches to screening and validated screening tools (see Chapters 2 and 3), one or more approaches to providing a brief intervention (see Chapter 5), and best practices for referring to specialty treatment clients who present with SUDs (Babor et al., 2007). Most trainings are tailored to the professional specialty area of the student population (for a detailed description of an SBIRT training program tailored to pediatric medical residents and its evaluation, see Bray et al., 2014).

To evaluate trainees' proficiency in delivering SBIRT, some programs have made use of standardized patient simulations (e.g., Satterfield et al., 2012; Whittle, Buckelew, Satterfield, Lum, & O'Sullivan, 2015). Others have used online mobile apps or online simulations with adaptive avatars (e.g., "Coach Vicky"; Pantalon et al., 2015) to evaluate trainees' SBIRT skills (see Chapter 11, this volume, for a review of technology-enabled SBIRT training and delivery options). For example, one social work program created a 15-hour stand-alone SBIRT course that used videotaped standardized patient sessions before and at the end of a course to evaluate students' proficiency in delivering SBIRT (Sacco et al., 2017). Sacco et al. (2017) found that after completion of the SBIRT course, objective SBIRT knowledge scores increased significantly, as did self-reported SBIRT confidence and use of SBIRT behaviors. Furthermore, measures of SBIRT adherence when working with a standardized patient revealed that students displayed an increase of approximately three SBIRT behaviors after the training. Hence, objective measures of SBIRT behaviors corroborated students' self-report. When assessing training programs it is important to assess not only self-reported use of SBIRT skills but also competency in delivering SBIRT because clinician adherence to key aspects of an evidence-based practice is associated with greater effectiveness (Miller, Benefield, & Tonigan, 1993).

Training Modalities

SBIRT training modalities include face-to-face (e.g., Sacco et al., 2017), online (e.g., Tanner et al., 2012), and blended (e.g., Clemence et al., 2016; Scott et al., 2012) approaches. In all of the studies we have reviewed, regardless of the modality or training approach, the overwhelming majority of training participants reported they were satisfied with the training experience and found it helpful to their careers. In general, face-to-face and online training programs have both demonstrated efficacy in increasing SBIRT knowledge, self-efficacy, and use of SBIRT skills in clinical practice (Bray et al., 2014; Sacco et al., 2017; Stoner et al., 2014; Tanner et al., 2012) and increasing the use of SBIRT in practice (e.g., Bray et al., 2014; Tetrault et al., 2012). In a study of baccalaureate nursing students, Knopf-Amelung et al. (2018) evaluated three didactic instruction methods for teaching students about SBIRT: (a) in-person, (b) asynchronous narrated slides, and (c) interactive online instruction. All three of the aforementioned groups of students practiced SBIRT skills through role plays with peers and practiced with two standardized patients, receiving live feedback after the first practice standardized patient session and written feedback after the second. The results indicated that all three approaches were effective in enhancing students' competency; however, the two approaches that involved active learning (i.e., delivery of information in person and by means of an interactive online course) were more effective in changing students' attitudes about their role in working with clients who use drugs, and students in those two groups reported a better working knowledge of substance use and related problems. These results are consistent with findings reported in a critique of the literature on training therapists in evidence-based practice that stated that change in therapist behaviors and client outcomes occurred only when training interventions included active learning (Beidas & Kendall, 2010).

Summary of Training Models and Outcomes

SBIRT trainings delivered online, face-to face, and in blended formats appear similarly effective in providing health and mental health professionals the knowledge, self-efficacy, and skills they need to implement SBIRT with their patients and clients. No known study has directly compared an online versus face-to-face or blended SBIRT training to determine the superiority of one modality over the other. Research on this is needed, as is research on the optimal duration of training to produce desired outcomes and not pose a burden to the trainees or faculty involved. In at least one study (Martin et al., in press), a booster training was effective in increasing SBIRT knowledge, self-efficacy to deliver the intervention, and increasing use of SBIRT in practice settings. Because research on training practitioners in Motivational Interviewing and other evidence-based practices has found that booster training sessions significantly increase practice behavior above and beyond the impact of the initial training (Lopez, Osterberg, Jensen-Doss, & Rae, 2011; Miller et al., 2004), and that continued monitoring of practice with coaching and feedback enhance clinicians' skill proficiency (Hall et al., 2016), more SBIRT training models should incorporate booster trainings and posttraining supervised practice. Regardless of the discipline being trained, or the training modality or model, if SBIRT is to be incorporated into practice with clients, it is critical to incorporate opportunities for active learning and supervised practice of SBIRT with personalized feedback. More research on the use of online mobile app simulations with adaptive avatars to evaluate trainees' proficiency in delivering SBIRT is needed.

PUTTING OUR KNOWLEDGE INTO PRACTICE: AN SBIRT TRAINING PROGRAM FOR PSYCHOLOGISTS AND MENTAL HEALTH COUNSELORS

In the following subsections, we briefly describe our own experience in the design and implementation of an SBIRT training program for students in professional psychology graduate degree programs. We describe a bit about our training program and the results of the outcome study. Our goal is not to reproduce the published findings (see Martin et al., in press); instead, we aim to shed light on how we selected the training modality and approach to training and describe how well it worked for our population of trainees. In addition, we share with readers some of the facilitators and barriers we encountered in designing, implementing, and sustaining the training program.

Overview of the Training Project

With funding from SAMHSA for a 3-year SBIRT Health Professions Training Grant (TI 025946), we sought to fill the addictions training gap for trainees in five professional psychology training programs at the University at Albany,

State University of New York, by creating, implementing, and evaluating a two-part SBIRT training program. Part I of the training consisted of a face-to-face workshop that incorporated didactic and experiential learning and practice opportunities. Part II involved an online booster training that took place 9 months after the initial face-to-face training experience. Trainees were full-time students pursuing the following degrees: master's degree in mental health counseling; certificate of advance study in school counseling; and doctoral degrees in clinical, counseling, and school psychology. Most of the student trainees (82%) had never completed a course on substance use, 53% had never attended any lectures or workshops devoted to substance use, and 51% had no prior training in Motivational Interviewing. We should also note that at the time of the first training, 56% of trainees were not yet seeing clients, and at the time of the second training 9 months later 37% were still not yet seeing clients. These trainees were therefore unable to practice the SBIRT skills they learned with real clients, which is a clear limitation of our approach to training and study design.

The goals of our project were to evaluate students' satisfaction with the training, the impact of the training on students' knowledge of Motivational Interviewing and SBIRT, and students' perceived self-efficacy to implement SBIRT. Because we know that use of booster trainings after a training workshop can enhance learning and promote behavior change beyond what is accomplished by a single workshop, we implemented a second (i.e., booster) training. Our aim was to assess whether completion of the booster training would result in increases in Motivational Interviewing—and SBIRT-related knowledge, self-efficacy, and self-reported clinical practices beyond gains observed from the initial training. Our ultimate goal was to increase the frequency with which students used SBIRT in their work with clients at their field training sites. Hence, we assessed their self-reported use of SBIRT in clinical practice after each training. Our training programs and the outcome study (Martin et al., in press) are the first to focus exclusively on professional psychology trainees.

Our results indicated that the majority of trainees were satisfied or very satisfied with their overall training experience, agreed that the face-to-face and booster trainings enhanced their SBIRT skills, and found both trainings to be relevant and useful to their careers and clinical work. As a result of the face-to-face training, trainees experienced an increase in knowledge of motivational interviewing and SBIRT that was sustained through at least the 30-day follow-up period. Trainees' Motivational Interviewing knowledge remained significantly greater than it was before the initial training when surveyed just prior to completion of the booster training 9 months later. The results indicated that the booster training further enhanced Motivational Interviewing knowledge. SBIRT knowledge also increased as a result of the booster training. Comparisons of SBIRT knowledge could not be made across the two trainings because the content of each training was different, thus requiring unique SBIRT knowledge measures for each training.

In regard to the impact of trainings on SBIRT self-efficacy, trainees reported greater confidence in their ability to deliver SBIRT immediately after the face-to-face training and 30 days after the training. Self-efficacy remained stable during the 9-month period between the face-to-face and booster trainings and increased further after the booster training. Additional gains in self-efficacy also were maintained 30 days after the booster training.

Finally, the results indicated that we achieved our ultimate goal of increasing the frequency with which psychology and mental health professional trainees used SBIRT with their clients in practice settings. It was in this area that we saw the greatest effect of the booster training. Whereas approximately 20% to 28% of trainees screened clients for various substances "some of the time or more often," 62% to 78% reported doing so after the booster training. We saw a similar increase in the frequency of providing brief interventions for alcohol use after the booster training (44%) as opposed to the face-to-face training (14%).

Designing the Training Program: Lessons Learned

Given that we aimed to train approximately 100 students across five programs of study who were all in different stages of their graduate training (i.e., first year through fifth year of studies as well as predoctoral interns), we chose a one-time training approach in which we delivered the entire SBIRT curriculum (didactics and experiential learning and practice) in one 8-hour period. Benefits of this approach included standardization of the training content and instructors as well as the timing of the data collection for evaluation purposes. We observed several drawbacks to this standardized approach to training as well. First and foremost among these was the large proportion of students who were not yet working with clients in a practicum or internship and therefore could not implement SBIRT immediately after the training. Some students did not see their first clients until the following semester. To maintain gains in self-efficacy and SBIRT skills, students should ideally be able to implement the approach immediately and receive timely and responsive supervision and feedback on their performance. In addition, qualitative results of the training satisfaction survey indicated that some trainees felt that too much information was presented at once; hence, splitting the 8-hour training into several shorter segments, each with a practical component, may be ideal.

Positive results supported our decision to include a booster training session 9 months after the initial training session. The booster training enhanced knowledge, skills, self-efficacy, and use of SBIRT in practice; however, we did see some decline in the aforementioned areas during the 9-month period between the two trainings. Also, there was a steep decline in the number of students who participated in the booster training as compared with the initial training (participation in each was optional). We reasoned that if the booster training had been held closer in time to the initial training we may have been better able to capitalize on students' enthusiasm and the gains they made related to Motivational Interviewing and SBIRT, resulting in increased partici-pation in the booster training and even greater gains in self-efficacy, skills, and use of SBIRT.

Limited resources prevented us from being able to assess students' com-petency in delivering SBIRT with standardized patients or role plays with experienced clinicians or in practice with actual clients. Research suggests that self-reported skillfulness in an evidence-based practice is unrelated to actual proficiency levels in observed practice (Miller et al., 2004); therefore, we can conclude that clinicians reported using SBIRT more frequently and felt more confident doing so after our trainings but not that SBIRT was delivered with fidelity. Others have noted that effective implementation of SBIRT requires routine monitoring of SBIRT delivery with feedback by supervisors or others skilled in the approach, to prevent drift (Babor et al., 2017). There are tools to assist with observing and rating SBIRT proficiency, such as the SBIRT Checklist for Observation in Real Time (Vendetti, McRee, & Del Boca, 2017). We recom-mend including assessment of proficiency immediately after training in SBIRT and, ideally, periodically thereafter to help students regain skills that become deficient over time.

Facilitators of and Barriers to Implementing and Sustaining SBIRT Training

Key stakeholders associated with the implementation and sustainability of SBIRT training in graduate programs include core faculty members from each of the programs involved, as well as program administrators (e.g., training directors) and faculty and field placement supervisors. Overall, we found it challenging to engage all of the relevant stakeholders from each of the graduate programs involved. Some supervisors were more interested in and supportive of our efforts to train their students than others. We received some pushback from core faculty members of some programs in response to our request for them to encourage graduate students in their programs to attend the SBIRT trainings and implement the approach with their clients. Some faculty endorsed the myth that clients would become upset if students screened them for substance use or discussed substance use in session when the client presented to treatment for a different problem. Others felt that we were asking a lot of students to spend time outside of class learning SBIRT when their schedules are already full. On the other hand, some faculty acknowledged substance use screening and intervention as a training gap and enthusiastically encouraged, and some even required, students to participate in the SBIRT trainings. In discussions about sustaining the training after funding expired, many faculty embraced the idea of continuing to train students in SBIRT, but some were either unwilling or felt unable to incorporate substance use screening or brief intervention into their curriculum. Only one group, mental health counseling master's students, continues to receive training in SBIRT because the training is now provided as part of a required course devoted to substance use and addictive behaviors taught by the first author of this chapter.

On the basis of our experiences working with faculty stakeholders, we learned that it is imperative to garner buy-in early in the process of developing the SBIRT training from as many core faculty as possible, especially from program administrators, such as doctoral training directors. Myths and commonly held stereotypes about substance use and substance use treatment should be anticipated and refuted in early discussions about SBIRT training. Data presented early in this chapter about numbers of clients who present with substance use concerns and co-occurring substance use and mental health problems and the unmet treatment need, as well as the lack of training of mental health professionals to meet these needs, could be presented to stakeholders to bolster their buy-in. Sustainability may be better achieved if one or two faculty with expertise in assessment and evidence-based practices can be identified, trained in SBIRT, and coached on how to incorporate SBIRT into their courses; in essence, such stakeholders would serve as "champions" in support of integration of SBIRT training into the graduate and professional curriculum.

Field supervisors were among the most commonly cited facilitators of and barriers to implementing SBIRT in field placement sites among our psychology and mental health counseling trainees. When supervisors were open to the use of SBIRT, knowledgeable about SBIRT themselves, and discussed the students' experiences with SBIRT in supervision (e.g., providing feedback, brainstorming solutions to problems encountered), students found it easier to implement SBIRT with their clients. Supervisors lacking knowledge of SBIRT and not supporting its use with clients were among the most commonly reported barriers to students' implementation of SBIRT. We offered all faculty and field supervisors associated with the graduate training programs an abridged version of the face-to-face SBIRT training provided to students free of charge to enable supervision of students using SBIRT and promote its adoption in field placement sites. Of the 81 supervisors invited, 31 (39.5%) participated in the training. Approximately 1 year later, we surveyed all field supervisors (the response rate was about 25%) to ascertain their perceptions of their knowledge of motivational interviewing and SBIRT and their experiences providing supervision in SBIRT to graduate student trainees so we could determine their SBIRT training needs and desires. Approximately 33% of supervisors said they knew "a good deal," and 20% said they were "very knowledgeable/expert," about motivational interviewing, whereas 20% said they knew "a good deal" and 12% were "very knowledgeable/expert" about SBIRT. Only about 33% of those who responded indicated that they had provided supervision in SBIRT, and only about 32% felt confident supervising students use of SBIRT, so it is not surprising that 42% reported discussing SBIRT in supervision rarely or never. The low participation rate in the supervisor training and the low response rate to our survey may reflect, in part, supervisors' enthusiasm for learning and adopting a new evidence-based practice. In addition, clinicians and supervisors are busy and may not have had the time to devote to such activities. It could be as well that supervisors who did not participate in either activity were already knowledgeable in SBIRT and felt they did not need additional training.

On the basis of our work with field supervisors, we identified several strategies to promote students' implementation of SBIRT and to better implement and sustain the SBIRT training. First, more supervisors need to be trained so that they can serve as SBIRT champions who encourage students' implementation of this intervention and so they can provide supervision of and feedback to students. Ongoing discussion of SBIRT skills, coaching, and supervision are necessary for mastery of SBIRT and for sustaining use of SBIRT with clients (Bray et al., 2014; Miller, Sorensen, Selzer, & Brigham, 2006; Ogden et al., 2016). From the data we gathered from field supervisors on their training preferences, it appears that most supervisors thought future SBIRT trainings would be helpful: About 25% preferred that future trainings be held outside of their organization, and a similar percentage preferred that the training be offered within their organization. Some supervisors indicated that receiving continuing education credit for attendance would entice them to participate, whereas others said that no remuneration was necessary for their participation. From these data we concluded that one-size-fits-all is not the best approach to training field supervisors and that greater effort should be made to assess individual supervisors' training needs and preferences. Some supervisors and students, especially those working with children and adolescents, indicated that SBIRT was not relevant to their setting or client population. More of a focus on the use of SBIRT with adolescents may have corrected the misperception that the intervention is not relevant for them. It seems that some individuals did not understand the concept of "universal screening" (i.e., screen all clients and patients, regardless of their presenting problems); greater emphasis on this concept may increase the perceived relevance of SBIRT for a larger number of supervisors, thus making it more likely they will participate in SBIRT training sessions for supervisors and implement this strategy within their setting.

Overall, we learned that successfully implementing and sustaining SBIRT training within a graduate program curriculum requires that SBIRT be integrated into the culture of the graduate program and fieldwork agencies. Accomplishing this is a challenging task that requires recruitment of SBIRT champions who are willing to learn something new, likely alongside the student learners, and devote time in their courses to teaching SBIRT to students. A train-the-trainer approach in which faculty and field supervisors are trained and then provided ongoing training, consultation, feedback, and support in their own use of SBIRT, and their teaching and supervising of the approach, is likely to be most effective. Ogden et al. (2016) described a train-the-trainer model used with social work faculty, field supervisors, and students that may serve as a template from which others can build their own training model appropriate for their students and training programs.

FUTURE DIRECTIONS FOR SBIRT TRAINING AND OUTCOME EVALUATION

On the basis of our experiences designing and implementing an SBIRT training program for mental health and psychology trainees, and our review of the extant literature evaluating SBIRT training approaches, we have several recommendations for future training efforts. First, there is a need for training curricula tailored specifically to mental health professionals. For example, inclusion of information on relationships between mood disorder symptoms and substance use, and unique motivations for and factors that contribute to maintenance of substance use among mental health populations, would be highly relevant. Most training programs, even if designed by psychologists, are created for and tailored to medical professionals (e.g., do not include information, examples, or images of mental health settings or populations). Our student trainees expressed a desire for materials that were more relevant to their training background and practice settings; however, we were not able to find any training resources tailored for mental health professionals from SAMHSA; the Institute for Research, Education & Training in Addictions; or entities that sell access to online SBIRT training modules (e.g., Kognito). Access to training programs and standardized patients specifically geared toward mental health providers who are trained to provide therapy (e.g., psychologists, mental health counselors) may increase the adoption of SBIRT into mental health provider graduate program curricula.

Second, standardized measures for the evaluation of SBIRT knowledge, self-efficacy, and use of skills in practice represent an area for future research that would enhance the generalizability of the results of SBIRT training outcome studies. Such measures would also allow for studies that directly compare outcomes to determine whether face-to-face or online trainings are more effective as well as the optimal length of a particular type of training to produce desired outcomes without being burdensome to the trainees or faculty involved.

Third, future research should test the effects of SBIRT training on client satisfaction with treatment and treatment outcomes. Fourth and last, there is a need for more researchers to objectively assess the frequency of SBIRT implementation after SBIRT training instead of relying solely on clinicians' self-reported implementation. For example, SBIRT could be monitored by means of documentation in client records or through observation (e.g., Seale et al., 2015).

CONCLUSION

The majority of people with substance use concerns or SUDs do not receive the treatment they need. Most mental health service providers do not receive training in substance use or substance use treatment, resulting in feelings of inadequacy in this area. With training in SBIRT, mental health service providers would receive the knowledge and skills they need to identify clients at risk for SUDs and provide them with brief interventions and referrals to the treatment they need to reduce their risk and improve their health. Research suggests that SBIRT training delivered in a variety of formats and modalities provides mental health service providers with knowledge of SBIRT and motivational interviewing they find useful to their careers and that bolsters their self-efficacy to deliver SBIRT. Indeed, service providers trained in SBIRT screen more clients for substance use and, in turn, provide brief motivational interventions and referrals to specialty treatment with greater frequency. We hope to see more graduate programs in mental health counseling and professional psychology adopt SBIRT training as part of their curriculum so that mental health services providers are prepared to meet the workforce demand for professionals who can address the needs of persons at risk for SUDs.

REFERENCES

Agley, J., McNelis, A. M., Carlson, J. M., Schwindt, R., Clark, C. A., Kent, K. A., . . . Crabb, D. W. (2016). If you teach it, they will screen: Advanced practice nursing students' use of screening and brief intervention in the clinical setting. *Journal of Nursing Education, 55,* 231–235. http://dx.doi.org/10.3928/01484834-20160316-10

Babor, T. F., Del Boca, F., & Bray, J. W. (2017). Screening, Brief Intervention and Referral to Treatment: Implications of SAMHSA's SBIRT initiative for substance abuse policy and practice. *Addiction, 112*(Suppl. 2), 110–117. http://dx.doi.org/10.1111/add.13675

Babor, T. F., McRee, B. G., Kassebaum, P. A., Grimaldi, P. L., Ahmed, K., & Bray, J. (2007). Screening, Brief Intervention, and Referral to Treatment (SBIRT): Toward a public health approach to the management of substance abuse. *Substance Abuse, 28,* 7–30. http://dx.doi.org/10.1300/J465v28n03_03

Beidas, R. S., & Kendall, P. C. (2010). Training therapists in evidence-based practice: A critical review of studies from a systems-contextual perspective. *Clinical Psychology: Science and Practice, 17,* 1–30. http://dx.doi.org/10.1111/j.1468-2850.2009.01187.x

Bernstein, E., Bernstein, J., Feldman, J., Fernandez, W., Hagan, M., Mitchell, P., . . . Owens, P. (2007). An evidence based alcohol Screening, Brief Intervention and Referral to Treatment (SBIRT) curriculum for Emergency Department (ED) providers improves skills and utilization. *Substance Abuse, 28,* 79–92. http://dx.doi.org/10.1300/J465v28n04_01

Borsari, B., Magill, M., Mastroleo, N. R., Hustad, J. T. P., Tevyaw, T. O., Barnett, N. P., . . . Monti, P. M. (2016). Mandated college students' response to sequentially administered alcohol interventions in a randomized clinical trial using stepped care. *Journal of Consulting and Clinical Psychology, 84,* 103–112. http://dx.doi.org/10.1037/a0039800

Bray, J. H., Kowalchuk, A., Waters, V., Allen, E., Laufman, L., & Shilling, E. H. (2014). Baylor pediatric SBIRT medical residency training program: Model description and evaluation. *Substance Abuse, 35,* 442–449. http://dx.doi.org/10.1080/08897077.2014.954026

Brener, L., von Hippel, W., & Kippax, S. (2007). Prejudice among health care workers toward injecting drug users with hepatitis C: Does greater contact lead to less prejudice? *International Journal of Drug Policy, 18,* 381–387. http://dx.doi.org/10.1016/j.drugpo.2007.01.006

Brener, L., von Hippel, W., Kippax, S., & Preacher, K. J. (2010). The role of physician and nurse attitudes in the health care of injecting drug users. *Substance Use & Misuse, 45*, 1007–1018. http://dx.doi.org/10.3109/10826081003659543

Broderick, K. B., Kaplan, B., Martini, D., & Caruso, E. (2015). Emergency physician utilization of alcohol/substance screening, brief advice and discharge: A 10-year comparison. *The Journal of Emergency Medicine, 49*, 400–407. http://dx.doi.org/10.1016/j.jemermed.2015.05.014

Burrow-Sánchez, J., Call, M. E., Adolphson, S. L., & Hawken, L. S. (2009). School psychologists' perceived competence and training needs for student substance abuse. *Journal of School Health, 79*, 269–276. http://dx.doi.org/10.1111/j.1746-1561.2009.00409.x

Cardoso, E., Pruett, S. R., Chan, F., & Tansey, T. N. (2006). Substance abuse assessment and treatment: The current training and practice of APA Division 22 members. *Rehabilitation Psychology, 51*, 175–178. http://dx.doi.org/10.1037/0090-5550.51.2.175

Clemence, A. J., Balkoski, V. I., Schaefer, B. M., Lee, M., Bromley, N., Maisonneuve, I. M., . . . Glick, S. D. (2016). Multispecialty Screening, Brief Intervention, and Referral to Treatment (SBIRT) training in an academic medical center: Resident training experience across specialties. *Substance Abuse, 37*, 356–363. http://dx.doi.org/10.1080/08897077.2015.1082953

Denering, L. L., & Spear, S. E. (2012). Routine use of screening and brief intervention for college students in a university counseling center. *Journal of Psychoactive Drugs, 44*, 318–324. http://dx.doi.org/10.1080/02791072.2012.718647

Dimoff, J. D., Sayette, M. A., & Norcross, J. C. (2017). Addiction training in clinical psychology: Are we keeping up with the rising epidemic? *American Psychologist, 72*, 689–695. http://dx.doi.org/10.1037/amp0000140

Edlund, M. J., Booth, B. M., & Han, X. (2012). Who seeks care where? Utilization of mental health and substance use disorder treatment in two national samples of individuals with alcohol use disorders. *Journal of Studies on Alcohol and Drugs, 73*, 635–646. http://dx.doi.org/10.15288/jsad.2012.73.635

Forsetlund, L., Bjørndal, A., Rashidian, A., Jamtvedt, G., O'Brien, M. A., Wolf, F., . . . Oxman, A. D. (2009). Continuing education meetings and workshops: Effects on professional practice and health care outcomes. *Cochrane Database of Systematic Reviews, 2*, CD003030. http://dx.doi.org/10.1002/14651858.CD003030.pub2

Hall, K., Staiger, P. K., Simpson, A., Best, D., & Lubman, D. I. (2016). After 30 years of dissemination, have we achieved sustained practice change in Motivational Interviewing? *Addiction, 111*, 1144–1150. http://dx.doi.org/10.1111/add.13014

Harris, B. R., Shaw, B. A., Sherman, B. R., & Lawson, H. A. (2016). Screening, Brief Intervention, and Referral to Treatment for adolescents: Attitudes, perceptions, and practice of New York school-based health center providers. *Substance Abuse, 37*, 161–167. http://dx.doi.org/10.1080/08897077.2015.1015703

Harwood, H. J., Kowalski, J., & Ameen, A. (2004). The need for substance abuse training among mental health professionals. *Administration and Policy in Mental Health, 32*, 189–205. http://dx.doi.org/10.1023/B:APIH.0000042746.79349.64

Knopf-Amelung, S., Gotham, H., Kuofie, A., Young, P., Manney Stinson, R., Lynn, J., . . . Hildreth, J. (2018). Comparison of instructional methods for Screening, Brief Intervention, and Referral to Treatment for substance use in nursing education. *Nurse Educator, 43*, 123–127. http://dx.doi.org/10.1097/NNE.0000000000000439

Lang, B., & Rosenberg, H. (2017). Public perceptions of behavioral and substance addictions. *Psychology of Addictive Behaviors, 31*, 79–84. http://dx.doi.org/10.1037/adb0000228

Lopez, M. A., Osterberg, L. D., Jensen-Doss, A., & Rae, W. A. (2011). Effects of workshop training for providers under mandated use of an evidence-based practice. *Administration and Policy in Mental Health and Mental Health Services Research, 38*, 301–312. http://dx.doi.org/10.1007/s10488-010-0326-8

Madson, M. B., Bethea, A. R., Daniel, S., & Necaise, H. (2008). The state of substance abuse treatment training in counseling and counseling psychology programs: What is and is not happening. *Journal of Teaching in the Addictions, 7,* 164–178. http://dx.doi.org/10.1080/15332700802269177

Martin, J. L., Cimini, M. D., Longo, L. M., Sawyer, J. S., & Ertl, M. M. (in press). Equipping mental health professionals to meet the needs of substance-using clients: Evaluation of an SBIRT training program. *Training and Education in Professional Psychology.*

McNeely, J., Kumar, P. C., Rieckmann, T., Sedlander, E., Farkas, S., Chollak, C., . . . Rotrosen, J. (2018). Barriers and facilitators affecting the implementation of substance use screening in primary care clinics: A qualitative study of patients, providers, and staff. *Addiction Science & Clinical Practice, 13,* Article 8. http://dx.doi.org/10.1186/s13722-018-0110-8

Miller, W. R., Benefield, R. G., & Tonigan, J. S. (1993). Enhancing motivation for change in problem drinking: A controlled comparison of two therapist styles. *Journal of Consulting and Clinical Psychology, 61,* 455–461. http://dx.doi.org/10.1037/0022-006X.61.3.455

Miller, W. R., Sorensen, J. L., Selzer, J. A., & Brigham, G. S. (2006). Disseminating evidence-based practices in substance abuse treatment: A review with suggestions. *Journal of Substance Abuse Treatment, 31,* 25–39. http://dx.doi.org/10.1016/j.jsat.2006.03.005

Miller, W. R., Yahne, C. E., Moyers, T. B., Martinez, J., & Pirritano, M. (2004). A randomized trial of methods to help clinicians learn Motivational Interviewing. *Journal of Consulting and Clinical Psychology, 72,* 1050–1062. http://dx.doi.org/10.1037/0022-006X.72.6.1050

Ogden, L. P., Vinjamuri, M., & Kahn, J. M. (2016). A model for implementing an evidence-based practice in student fieldwork placements: Barriers and facilitators to the use of "SBIRT." *Journal of Social Service Research, 42,* 425–441. http://dx.doi.org/10.1080/01488376.2016.1182097

Oxman, A. D., Thomson, M. A., Davis, D. A., & Haynes, R. B. (1995). No magic bullets: A systematic review of 102 trials of interventions to improve professional practice. *Canadian Medical Association Journal, 153,* 1423–1431.

Pantalon, M. V., Abujarad, F., Martel, S., Cheung, K., Tetrault, J., Butner, J., & D'Onofrio, G. (2015). "Coach Vicky": A web-based, self-directed brief intervention training program. In *The 39th Annual National Conference of the Association for Medical Education and Research in Substance Abuse Book of Abstracts.* Washington, DC: Association for Medical Education and Research in Substance Abuse. Retrieved from http://docplayer.net/49842196-Association-for-medical-education-and-research-in-substance-abuse-39th-annual-national-conference-1976-2015-november-5-7-2015.html

Patient Protection and Affordable Care Act, Pub. L. 111-148, 42 U.S.C. §§ 18001–18121 (2010).

Putney, J. M., O'Brien, K. H., Collin, C. R., & Levine, A. (2017). Evaluation of alcohol Screening, Brief Intervention, and Referral to Treatment (SBIRT) training for social workers. *Journal of Social Work Practice in the Addictions, 17,* 169–187. http://dx.doi.org/10.1080/1533256X.2017.1302884

Sacco, P., Ting, L., Crouch, T. B., Emery, L., Moreland, M., Bright, C., . . . DiClemente, C. (2017). SBIRT Training in social work education: Evaluating change using standardized patient simulation. *Journal of Social Work Practice in the Addictions, 17,* 150–168. http://dx.doi.org/10.1080/1533256X.2017.1302886

Satre, D. D., Leibowitz, A. S., Mertens, J. R., & Weisner, C. (2014). Advising depression patients to reduce alcohol and drug use: Factors associated with provider intervention in outpatient psychiatry. *The American Journal on Addictions, 23,* 570–575. http://dx.doi.org/10.1111/j.1521-0391.2014.12140.x

Satterfield, J. M., O'Sullivan, P., Satre, D. D., Tsoh, J. Y., Batki, S. Julian, K., . . . Wamsley, M. (2012). Using standardized patients to evaluate SBIRT knowledge and skill acquisition for internal medicine residents. *Substance Abuse, 33*, 303–307. http://dx.doi.org/10.1080/08897077.2011.640103

Scott, D. M., McLaurin-Jones, T., Brown, F. D., Newton, R., Marshall, V. J., Kalu, N., . . . Taylor, R. E. (2012). Institutional incorporation of Screening, Brief Intervention, and Referral to Treatment (SBIRT) in residency training: Achieving a sustainable curriculum. *Substance Abuse, 33*, 308–311. http://dx.doi.org/10.1080/08897077.2011. 640135

Seale, J. P., Johnson, J. A., Clark, D. C., Shellenberger, S., Pusser, A. T., Dhabliwala, J., . . . Clemow, D. (2015). A multisite initiative to increase the use of alcohol screening and brief intervention through resident training and clinic systems changes. *Academic Medicine, 90*, 1707–1712. http://dx.doi.org/10.1097/ACM.0000000000000846

Senreich, E., Ogden, L. P., & Greenberg, J. P. (2017). Enhancing social work students' knowledge and attitudes regarding substance-using clients through SBIRT training. *Journal of Social Work Education, 53*, 260–275. http://dx.doi.org/10.1080/10437797. 2016.1266979

Stoner, S. A., Mikko, A. T., & Carpenter, K. M. (2014). Web-based training for primary care providers on Screening, Brief Intervention, and Referral to Treatment (SBIRT) for alcohol, tobacco, and other drugs. *Journal of Substance Abuse Treatment, 47*, 362–370. http://dx.doi.org/10.1016/j.jsat.2014.06.009

Substance Abuse and Mental Health Services Administration. (2005). *Results from the 2004 National Survey on Drug Use and Health: National findings* (HHS Publication No. SMA 05-4062). Rockville, MD: Author.

Substance Abuse and Mental Health Services Administration. (2011). *White paper on the evidence supporting Screening, Brief Intervention and Referral to Treatment (SBIRT) in behavioral healthcare.* Retrieved from https://www.samhsa.gov/sites/default/files/ sbirtwhitepaper_0.pdf

Substance Abuse and Mental Health Services Administration. (2019). *Key substance use and mental health indicators in the United States: Results from the 2018 National Survey on Drug Use and Health* (DHHS Publication No. PEP19-5068). Rockville, MD: Author. Retrieved from https://www.samhsa.gov/data/sites/default/files/cbhsq-reports/ NSDUHNationalFindingsReport2018/NSDUHNationalFindingsReport2018.pdf

Substance Abuse and Mental Health Services Administration, Center for Behavioral Health Statistics and Quality. (2019). *2017 Mental health client-level data (MH-CLD) annual report.* Rockville, MD: Author. Retrieved from http://www.samhsa.gov/data/ report/2017-mental-health-client-level-data-mh-cld-annual-report

Tanner, T. B., Wilhelm, S. E., Rossie, K. M., & Metcalf, M. P. (2012). Web-based SBIRT skills training for health professional students and primary care providers. *Substance Abuse, 33*, 316–320. http://dx.doi.org/10.1080/08897077.2011.640151

Tetrault, J. M., Green, M. L., Martino, S., Thung, S. F., Degutis, L. C., Ryan, S. A., . . . D'Onofrio, G. (2012). Developing and implementing a multispecialty graduate medical education curriculum on Screening, Brief Intervention, and Referral to Treatment (SBIRT). *Substance Abuse, 33*, 168–181. http://dx.doi.org/10.1080/08897077. 2011.640220

van Boekel, L. C., Brouwers, E. P. M., van Weeghel, J., & Garretsen, H. F. L. (2013). Stigma among health professionals towards patients with substance use disorders and its consequences for healthcare delivery: Systematic review. *Drug and Alcohol Dependence, 131*, 23–35. http://dx.doi.org/10.1016/j.drugalcdep.2013.02.018

Vendetti, J. A., McRee, B. G., & Del Boca, F. K. (2017). Development of the SBIRT Checklist for Observation in Real-time (SCORe). *Addiction, 112*(Suppl. 2), 34–42. http://dx.doi.org/10.1111/add.13657

Wakeman, S. E., Pham-Kanter, G., & Donelan, K. (2016). Attitudes, practices, and preparedness to care for patients with substance use disorder: Results from a survey of general internists. *Substance Abuse, 37,* 635–641. http://dx.doi.org/10.1080/ 08897077.2016.1187240

Wamsley, M., Satterfield, J. M., Curtis, A., Lundgren, L., & Satre, D. D. (2018). Alcohol and drug Screening, Brief Intervention and Referral to Treatment (SBIRT) training and implementation: Perspectives from 4 health professions. *Journal of Addiction Medicine, 12,* 262–272. http://dx.doi.org/10.1097/ADM.0000000000000410

Whittle, A. E., Buckelew, S. M., Satterfield, J. M., Lum, P. J., & O'Sullivan, P. (2015). Addressing adolescent substance use: Teaching Screening, Brief Intervention, and Referral to Treatment (SBIRT) and Motivational Interviewing (MI) to residents. *Substance Abuse, 36,* 325–331. http://dx.doi.org/10.1080/08897077.2014.965292

Wilkey, C., Lundgren, L., & Amodeo, M. (2013). Addiction training in social work schools: A nationwide analysis. *Journal of Social Work Practice in the Addictions, 13,* 192–210. http://dx.doi.org/10.1080/1533256X.2013.785872

14

The Role of Public Policy in Advancing SBIRT Implementation and Dissemination

Brett Harris

Health care professionals often use the transtheoretical model (Prochaska, DiClemente, & Norcross, 1992) to encourage their patients or clients to reduce their alcohol or drug use during screening, brief intervention, and referral to treatment (SBIRT); however, there are multiple influences outside of an individual's control that affect alcohol and drug use behaviors. An ecological approach considers not only individual factors but also interpersonal, organizational, community, and policy-level factors as they relate to SBIRT. For example, on an organizational level, SBIRT is a protocol that can be integrated within organizations to influence alcohol and drug use among entire client populations. This chapter focuses on public policies that facilitate or impede the adoption, implementation, and impact of SBIRT. Such policies include behavioral incentives, the allocation of programmatic resources, the establishment of health promotion offices and agencies within government, access to resources by means of eligibility criteria, and restrictions on how programmatic resources may be used. Advocates play a key role in advancing policies through education, organizing groups to support health policy–related issues, monitoring implementation, and encouraging participation in the political process (McLeroy, Bibeau, Steckler, & Glanz, 1988).

http://dx.doi.org/10.1037/0000199-015
Screening, Brief Intervention, and Referral to Treatment for Substance Use: A Practitioner's Guide,
M. D. Cimini and J. L. Martin (Editors)

SETTING THE STAGE: THE HEALTH CARE ENVIRONMENT AND SUBSTANCE USE TREATMENT

In 2008, major laws were enacted that greatly influenced the way substance use services were embedded and delivered within health care systems. Before that time, substance use disorders (SUDs) were primarily treated outside of a health care environment in a specialty service sector that received little reimbursement and was staffed by professionals with limited training. Only about 40% of adults reported that their insurance paid for their services, leaving many to pay out of pocket or forgo services (Buck, 2011).

The Paul Wellstone and Pete Dominici Mental Health Parity and Addiction Equity Act of 2008 mandated that services for mental health and substance use be covered by insurance at a level similar to that of medical and surgical services. This meant that the financial requirements and treatment limitations insurance programs placed on mental health and substance use benefits could be no more restrictive than those placed on medical and surgical benefits. These parity provisions were extended to all children's state health insurance programs in 2009 (Buck, 2011).

The Patient Protection and Affordable Care Act (ACA) of 2010 included several provisions that affected access to and delivery of SUD treatment services. First, the ACA greatly expanded the Medicaid-eligible population. Approximately 17.5% of newly eligible individuals had a mental health disorder or SUD. Second, it created subsidized insurance for purchase through state exchanges, making care affordable for individuals at elevated risk (Croft & Parish, 2013). Third, the law mandated that programs providing insurance on the exchange include mental health and substance use services as part of their essential benefits and that these benefits be provided at full parity to medical and surgical benefits (Buck, 2011; Croft & Parish, 2013). Last, the ACA facilitated primary and behavioral health integration so that mental health and substance use services would be available and more easily accessible in mainstream health care settings (Buck, 2011).

Alcohol misuse screening and counseling is a preventive service that all ACA marketplace health plans and others must cover for adults without charging a copayment or coinsurance (Centers for Medicare & Medicaid Services, n.d.). Although screening and counseling for drug use is not included, the U.S. Preventive Services Task Force's (2019) recent recommendation to screen adults for drug use may be influential in getting this service covered in the future SBIRT, an evidence-based integration model that encompasses alcohol and other drug screening and counseling, expands the reach of substance use services by placing them in mainstream medical settings frequented by a vastly larger patient population than traditional SUD treatment. Many medical and behavioral health professionals—including physicians, nurse practitioners, physician assistants, psychologists, and social workers—are able to conduct SBIRT, making SBIRT services more widely available (Buck, 2011). Hence, because of the ACA, SBIRT is implemented with a great number of patients presenting in a variety of settings, making it more likely that those at risk for SUDs will receive prevention and early intervention services before problems become more severe.

Although ACA provisions have supported uptake and access to SBIRT, a 2012 U.S. Supreme Court ruling declaring Medicaid expansion unconstitutional severely hindered its impact (Rosenbaum & Westmoreland, 2012). The ruling left the decision up to states and, as of late 2019, 14 states opted against expansion. This left more than 2 million low-income adults in a "coverage gap," nine out of 10 of whom reside in the South, increasing geographical and racial disparities in health care coverage, access, and outcomes. Because these individuals are low income, work part-time jobs, or are in and out of the workforce, they will continue to fall through the cracks of the employer-based system. Given that marketplace plans cost almost 80% of the income of non-insured individuals in these states, this option is unaffordable (Garfield, Orgera, & Damico, 2019), limiting access to mental health and substance use prevention, intervention, and treatment services, including SBIRT. This uncovers major limitations of the ACA that resulted from the way it has been interpreted in the years since its passage.

SBIRT AND PUBLIC POLICY

This section describes additional policies that greatly influence the adoption and delivery of SBIRT. These policies include service delivery requirements, allocation of funding, restrictions on use of funding, performance measurement, and reimbursement.

SBIRT Reimbursement

The Centers for Medicare & Medicaid Services and the American Medical Association approved billing codes for screening and brief intervention in 2007 and 2008, respectively. Current Procedural Terminology® codes (American Medical Association, 2017) are reimbursable by public and private insurance, whereas Healthcare Common Procedure Coding System and G codes are reimbursable only through Medicaid and Medicare, respectively (Fussell, Rieckmann, & Quick, 2011). Combinations of these codes, detailed in Table 14.1, may be selected and approved for use by state Medicaid plans. More than half of states have active SBIRT billing codes (Hinde, Bray, Kaiser, & Mallonee, 2017). To find out if your state has active billing codes, view the SBIRT Reimbursement Map developed by the Institute for Research, Education & Training in Addictions (2017).

The purpose of the billing codes is to incentivize the delivery of screening and brief intervention and to generate revenue, making the services sustainable in the absence of external funding. A study of seven federally funded SBIRT programs found that SBIRT in outpatient and emergency department

TABLE 14.1. Billing Codes for Screening and Intervention

Payer	Code	Description	Fee schedule (USD)
Commercial insurance, Medicaid	99408	Alcohol and/or substance abuse structured screening and brief intervention services, 15–30 min	33.41
Commercial insurance, Medicaid	99409	Alcohol and/or substance abuse structured screening and brief intervention services, 30 min	65.51
Medicare	G0396	Alcohol and/or substance abuse structured screening and brief intervention services, 15–30 min	29.42
Medicare	G0397	Alcohol and/or substance abuse structured screening and brief intervention services, 30 min	57.69
Medicare	G0442	Prevention: screening for alcohol misuse in adults, including pregnant women, once/year. No coinsurance, no deductible for patient.	17.33
Medicare	G0443	Prevention: up to four, 15-min, brief face-to-face behavioral counseling interventions per year for individuals, including pregnant women, who screen positive for alcohol misuse. No coinsurance, no deductible for patient.	25.14
Medicaid	H0049	Alcohol and/or drug screening	24.00
Medicaid	H0050	Alcohol and/or drug service, brief intervention, per 15 min	48.00

settings, even with below-average patient flows (9,000 and 42,000 screens per year in emergency departments and outpatient settings, respectively), can be sustained through insurance. However, sustainability in inpatient settings requires above-average patient flow. With increased Medicaid coverage under the ACA, the number of required screens for sustainability of SBIRT could drop (Cowell, Dowd, Mills, Hinde, & Bray, 2017).

In real-world settings, public health professionals in states with active codes have highlighted the availability of billing codes as a mechanism for funding SBIRT. Unfortunately, billing codes have not adequately incentivized delivery of SBIRT, and states have not seen upticks in billing claims and payments after the activation of their codes. Major reasons cited for not using existing billing codes include not knowing how to use them, low reimbursement rates, and time constraints and competing demands (Fussell et al., 2011). Use of billing codes can be very complicated, often requiring the guidance of an organization's billing department. In addition, clinicians often note that they are unable to bill for screening and brief intervention in addition to the other counseling services they are delivering within a single patient visit and that reimbursement rates are higher for the other counseling codes. The billing codes for brief interventions require that the intervention last 15 minutes. Brief interventions can be effectively administered in less than half of that time, creating a disincentive for busy practices. Even with the aforementioned barriers, many clinicians continue to prioritize and deliver SBIRT (Harris, 2016a); they simply will not receive reimbursement for doing so. Conversations between state health and behavioral health agencies and public and private insurers are critical to iron out policy that ensures providers get adequate reimbursement.

Underuse of SBIRT billing codes can also be explained by contracts set forth by managed care organizations (MCOs) that bundle services. In this case, health systems get paid for a predetermined set of services and cannot bill individually for screening and brief intervention, erasing any incentive that available billing codes would provide. For these systems, it is critical for advocates to work with Medicaid officials to include substance use prevention within MCO contracts and to encourage MCOs to incentivize prevention (Community Catalyst, 2018). This tactic was taken by the state of Oregon, a topic that is described in greater detail in the next section.

To complicate matters further, states create their own stipulations for billing, including the type of providers who are allowed to bill for services, screening tools that are approved for use, and specific requirements for training. In many states, including Oregon, Indiana, New Jersey, and Connecticut, the list of providers who are eligible to bill for SBIRT services is restrictive, not allowing for the billing of services by nonlicensed social workers or health educators. In fact, it took a concerted advocacy effort in Indiana to expand the state's list of eligible SBIRT providers. Wisconsin and New York have a more expansive list. In New York State, for example, all providers with licenses from the New York State Education Department (e.g., psychologists, social workers, nurse practitioners, physician assistants, registered nurses) are eligible to bill for their services as long as they complete the state's 4-hour training program. Services delivered by unlicensed providers such as health educators can be billed under the supervising physician as long as the provider has completed the state's 12-hour program (New York State Department of Health, 2016). This creates an incentive for hiring unlicensed providers, whose services cannot typically be billed, in order to take the burden off busy licensed providers. Contact your state Medicaid department to learn about eligible SBIRT providers in your state.

Although reimbursement is commonly believed to be an important factor in the adoption of SBIRT, medical providers are often altruistic and put the needs of their patients first. In a study of school-based health center directors and clinicians, student need was the foremost reason that directors selected specific practices to adopt in their clinics. Billing and reimbursement ranked second, far below need, along with recommendations by state health departments and the American Academy of Pediatrics (Harris, 2016a). When asked specifically about what factors would motivate clinic directors to adopt and clinicians to implement SBIRT, billing and reimbursement ranked at the bottom of the list; instead, the benefits and cost-effectiveness of SBIRT compared with other preventive services, its effectiveness at preventing or decreasing alcohol use, its fit with their patient population, and recommendations by professional associations, ranked higher (Harris, 2016a).

Performance Measurement

The U.S. Preventive Services Task Force (2018) recommended that all patients 18 years and older receive screening for risky or hazardous alcohol use and, if positive, brief counseling to reduce their use. In 2019, the task force updated its recommendations to include screening for drug use when diagnosis, treatment, and appropriate care can be provided or referred. As such, the implementation of SBIRT to identify individuals at risk, provide brief intervention, and connect those with possible SUDs to treatment has been seen as increasingly critical to policymakers and health care providers. The National Committee on Quality Assurance (NCQA; 2017) researched the uptake of alcohol screening and brief intervention and found a shortage of screening. In addition, they found that when screening was conducted, many clinicians failed to appropriately identify or follow-up with patients. In 2018, the Unhealthy Alcohol Use Screening and Follow-Up (AST) measure was one of seven newly added measures to the Healthcare Effectiveness Data and Information Set, health care's most widely used performance improvement tool. The AST assesses the percentage of health plan members 18 years of age and older who were screened for unhealthy alcohol use and, if positive, received appropriate follow-up care within 2 months (NCQA, 2018). This measure was also one of the first to be reported using electronic medical record data collected during patient visits. In fact, with funding from the Substance Abuse and Mental Health Services Administration (SAMHSA) and the Centers for Disease Control and Prevention through FEI Systems, an AST learning collaborative was convened to assist health plans in adding this measure to their quality performance matrix (NCQA, 2018). By using the AST, health care providers will be more likely to consistently conduct alcohol screening and follow-up, and it will become standard care within a greater number of health care organizations.

Although not required, using performance metrics is a helpful way to track and increase uptake and delivery of services. Oregon turned on its SBIRT codes in 2009 but did not see an uptick in screening or brief intervention. When it received a $1.9 million waiver to transform its Medicaid system in 2012, it created Coordinated Care Organizations to prioritize prevention and reduce the cost of care. SBIRT became one of 17 performance measures for the Coordinated Care Organizations. The SBIRT measure stipulated that 12% of Medicaid visits by patients age 12 years and older would be billed with SBIRT codes. After their implementation in 2013, immediate and yearly upticks in SBIRT billing were observed (see Figure 14.1). The 12% threshold for visits billed with SBIRT codes was surpassed by 2015 (Winkle, 2016).

FIGURE 14.1. Monthly Counts of SBIRT Codes Submitted to Oregon (OR) Medicaid

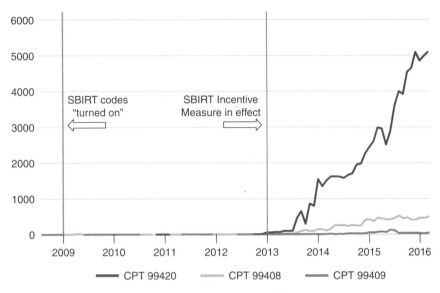

Note. SBIRT = Screening, Brief Intervention, and Referral to Treatment; CPT = Current Procedural Terminology.

Allocation of Funding

On the basis of the potential of SBIRT to reduce alcohol use and prevent negative or severe health outcomes, the federal government allocated considerable funds to facilitate and study its use. Part of the Department of Health and Human Services, SAMHSA's Center for Substance Abuse Treatment began its SBIRT discretionary grant program in 2003. Through subsequent cycles, SAMHSA has funded 29 states, two tribal councils, and one U.S. territory by means of its state cooperative agreements. It has also funded 12 college and university campus-based programs to prevent underage drinking and demonstrate the integration of SBIRT in the context of school health care and 17 medical residency cooperative agreements to encourage the use of SBIRT among physicians during their training. SAMHSA also funded 74 medical professional training programs, including nurse practitioners, physician assistants, psychologists, social workers, and pharmacists, to provide education and training in SBIRT to students entering key professions (SAMHSA, n.d.).

Goals of the state cooperative agreement program included expansion of substance use services into medical and other community settings; provision of support for clinically appropriate treatment services for individuals with mild, moderate, or severe SUDs; improvement of linkages between SBIRT providers and SUD treatment programs; and identification of systems and policy changes needed to increase access to SUD treatment in both generalist and specialty settings. The program also funded three cross-site evaluations to assess impact, implementation, and sustainability across medical systems and settings (Bray, Del Boca, McRee, Hayashi, & Babor, 2017). The results of the evaluations revealed decreases in alcohol and drug use at a 6-month follow-up (Aldridge, Linford, & Bray, 2017); assessed economic and financial sustainability, discovering how many patients are required to come through specific service lines such as inpatient, outpatient, or emergency departments to sustain SBIRT services with insurance payments (Cowell et al., 2017); identified a dose–response relationship for the brief intervention, indicating that more intensive brief treatment facilitated better outcomes than brief intervention among patients at higher risk (Aldridge, Dowd, & Bray, 2017); and uncovered facilitators of and challenges to implementation (Singh, Gmyrek, Hernandez, Damon, & Hayashi, 2017). Singh et al. (2017) found that having site champions promoting the use of SBIRT and having consistent staffing available to deliver the intervention facilitated sustainability. On the other hand, lack of funding; inconsistent staffing; and systemic changes, such as a lack of coordination between a health care and referral agency and a lack of integration among various behavioral health screenings, hindered efforts at sustaining SBIRT services across sites (Singh et al., 2017). This information is critical in advocating for additional federal funding to support SBIRT implementation as well as for promoting, adopting, implementing, and sustaining SBIRT within states and health systems in the absence of grant funding.

Many sites receiving grant funds—primary care outpatient clinics and hospitals—were able to sustain provision of SBIRT services when their grants ended. The cross-site evaluation found that, among 103 original sites in six SBIRT state grantee programs, 69 continued providing services, and new sites were added, bringing the final total to 88 sites providing SBIRT services in hospitals (including emergency departments, trauma, inpatient, obstetrics/gynecology, and surgery), primary care clinics, family medicine clinics, pediatrician offices, and school-based clinics across the six states (Singh et al., 2017). One program that was sustained after termination of grant funds was Project Renew, an SBIRT project implemented in all eight of New York City's sexual health clinics as part of a larger New York State SBIRT cooperative agreement funded between 2011 and 2016. In all, 130,597 substance use screenings were conducted, with 51% of patients screening positive for substance misuse. At a 6-month follow-up, patients reported reduced substance use, fewer days of depression and anxiety, and improved overall health compared with measures at baseline (Harris, Yu, Wolff, Rogers, & Blank, 2018). On the basis of the identified need and positive outcomes, the city incorporated SBIRT in sexual health clinics into its city-wide ThriveNYC initiative (City of New York, 2017), effectively sustaining the services in all eight clinics for the foreseeable future.

An important factor to consider when examining the impact of funding allocation is restrictions placed on funding. Through the 2013 funding cycle, SAMHSA SBIRT cooperative agreement funds could not be spent on individuals under age 18. With increased advocacy from professional associations and possibly by other demonstration programs funded under private foundations, such as the Conrad N. Hilton Foundation, in 2016 SAMHSA loosened restrictions and permitted funds to be spent on services for adolescent populations between ages 12 and 17 years. Adolescence is a period during which early intervention can prevent a lifetime of negative consequences (Levy, Williams, & Committee on Substance Use and Prevention, 2016); hence, funding services for this population can have a far-reaching impact while also increasing the availability of demonstration and evaluation results that may encourage a widespread uptake of SBIRT in other locations and for other populations.

In addition to federal funding specifically allocated for SBIRT there are funding sources that states and localities can explore to support SBIRT implementation. These sources include the Substance Abuse Prevention and Treatment Block Grant (see https://www.samhsa.gov/grants/block-grants/sabg), the Maternal and Child Health Services Block Grant (Title V; see https://mchb.hrsa.gov/maternal-child-health-initiatives/title-v-maternal-and-child-health-services-block-grant-program), Department of Education formula grants (see https://www2.ed.gov/fund/grant/about/formgrant.html), and opioid overdose prevention-related grant funding. All of these funding sources have been used to successfully support SBIRT, including to fund screening, training of nurses and other school personnel, and as an upstream prevention initiative to complement other opioid overdose prevention efforts.

Local advocacy is critical in accessing these funding sources given that the relevance of SBIRT for advancing different causes is not always obvious to people unfamiliar with SBIRT. It requires extensive knowledge of SBIRT, strategic planning, identification of key stakeholders, and persistence to obtain non–SBIRT-specific sources of funding for SBIRT.

State and Local Laws

Recognizing the impact of substance use on their communities, in particular in the context of the opioid epidemic, two states—Massachusetts and New Jersey—have either enacted or begun to enact laws regarding SBIRT. Both of these laws require that SBIRT be conducted in schools. The Massachusetts Society for the Prevention of Cruelty to Children received funding through a grant from Community Catalyst's Conrad N. Hilton Foundation to advocate for SBIRT legislation on the state level. The bill—An Act Relative to Substance Use, Treatment, Education and Prevention—was signed into law on March 14, 2016 (HR 3817, Commonwealth of Massachusetts). The act requires that each school district develop and file a policy regarding substance use prevention and education with the Department of Elementary and Secondary Education. The law also requires that each school district use a verbal screening tool, CRAFFT 2.0 (Center for Adolescent Substance Abuse Research, 2016), to screen students for SUDs at two different grade levels (grades 7 and 9 are recommended) starting in the 2017–2018 school year. Schools are then required to report aggregate data to the Department of Public Health within 90 days of the screening. The state's Department of Public Health has a variety of training programs available to prepare schools to deliver SBIRT according to the law. As of December 2017, 99% of school districts submitted policies with the Department of Elementary and Secondary Education (Wulfson, 2018). In New Jersey, a similar bill, requiring that SBIRT with verbal screening be conducted annually in grades 9 through 12, was sent to the Senate in 2018 (State of New Jersey, 2018). Considerable advocacy is required to advance state school-based SBIRT policies, and whether other states will follow the lead of Massachusetts and New Jersey remains unclear.

Enacting federal and state laws are difficult, time consuming, and subject to change when the political environment changes. Working with state or federal agencies to create regulations may be easier. For example, in 2012 the Massachusetts Department of Public Health School-Based Health Center Program stipulated in its contract with health centers that each medical provider was required to incorporate SBIRT into routine adolescent visits and meet specific performance measures. Targets included that 75% of school-based health center patients ages 12 to 18 years seen by the medical provider be assessed for substance use using the CRAFFT screening tool at least once during the school year and that 100% of students screened receive a brief intervention (including positive reinforcement for those who are not using). By 2013, 64.3% of patients were screened, and 78% received a brief intervention (Massachusetts Department of Public Health, 2014). This example illustrates the importance of advocates working not only with federal and state legislators but also with federal, state, and local agencies.

State laws regarding the legalization of cannabis—both for medical and recreational use—have major implications for the implementation of SBIRT. As of late 2019, 33 and 11 states had legalized medical and recreational use of cannabis among adults, respectively (National Conference of State Legislatures, 2019a, 2019b). Colorado and Washington were the first two states to legalize its recreational use, in 2012 (Hudak & Wallach, 2014). With a robust state-wide SBIRT initiative, Colorado has taken action to modify its SBIRT model to address increasing use (Peer Assistance Services, 2018). Colorado provides guidance on use of a screening tool, the Cannabis Use Disorder Identification Test—Revised (Adamson et al., 2010); key points for brief intervention; the general effects of marijuana; safety concerns; addressing common misperceptions; concerns among special populations; and how to involve parents (Peer Assistance Services, 2018). Other states may consider following Colorado's lead, if they have not already, because perception of risk and harm continues to decrease and use continues to increase nationwide (Miech, Johnston, & O'Malley, 2017). States must be prepared to give guidance to health systems and community providers on screening and brief intervention for cannabis misuse to prevent more severe consequences, such as impaired driving and motor vehicle accidents, impaired cognitive function, depression, anxiety, suicidal ideation and behavior, and chronic bronchitis (Peer Assistance Services, 2018).

A further concern with the legalization of recreational cannabis use is increased use among pregnant women (Young-Wolff et al., 2017). Young-Wolff et al. (2017) found a near-doubling of pregnant women in California who tested positive for cannabis use between 2009 and 2016, with one in five pregnant women under age 25 testing positive. This study was conducted before cannabis was legalized in the state, suggesting that cannabis use may have increased even further among this population. As such, it is important for medical professionals to warn their pregnant patients, or patients who may become pregnant, of the risks.

As previously mentioned, the U.S. Preventive Services Task Force (2019) updated its recommendations to include screening adults for drug use. This provision includes the screening of pregnant women. Although promising for identifying use and providing guidance, intervention, treatment, and referral, some existing state laws criminalize prenatal drug use, inhibiting pregnant women who are using drugs from honestly responding to screening questions and getting the care they need. As of 2019, 23 states and the District of Columbia consider substance use during pregnancy to be child abuse, and 25 states and the District of Columbia require health care professionals to report suspected prenatal use (Guttmacher Institute, 2019). This is an example of policies working against each other, underscoring the importance of lawmakers working together to identify and remedy conflicting directives for the benefit of their constituents.

Role of Advisory Committees and Advocacy

To successfully effect change it is important to involve experts and key stakeholders in advisory roles. For example, policy steering committees and advisory committees have been set up as part of SAMHSA state cooperative agreements and often include representation from various state agencies, insurers, SUD treatment providers, schools, school-based health centers, community-based organizations, and professional associations. Members of the committees help provide expertise as states develop plans and policies that relate to SBIRT. Having such a wide variety of key stakeholders involved in the planning process ensures that the policies that are developed are feasible, practical, and sustainable and meet the needs of the patients they are intended to serve.

Advocates can effect change by promoting policy and regulatory action. These individuals may engage in activities that increase public awareness about substance use, its impact on specific populations, and policies relating to substance use. For example, advocates may emphasize the connection between early initiation of alcohol use and future SUDs as they push for laws mandating routine screening in schools. Advocates may also encourage lobbying; organize coalitions that support substance use prevention–related issues; and provide policymakers, the general public, and target populations with policy options (McLeroy et al., 1988). Community Catalyst funded consumer advocates to advance SBIRT policies in their states, resulting in a law that requires SBIRT to be conducted in Massachusetts schools (Wulfson, 2018).

It is important for advocates to be equipped with background information, research on the health impact and cost-effectiveness of SBIRT, guidelines for implementation, success stories, and audience-specific messages. Harris (2016a) found that, although a variety of substance use- and SBIRT-related information is important, some messages are more important to certain audiences than to others. For example, the information a clinic director uses to make program adoption decisions is different from the information a clinician uses to assess whether a service is worth the effort to implement with fidelity. Furthermore, regardless of whether the information is conveyed in person or in writing, the time that advocates have with their audience is usually limited, meaning that only a few bullet points can be shared or will be remembered. These findings underscore the importance of tailoring messages to an audience and a venue.

Consumer advocates must engage community members and providers to generate demand for SBIRT. These activities may include launching a public education campaign to increase public awareness of SBIRT, or engaging with professional associations, and describing the implementation of SBIRT as part of a multipronged effort to combat the opioid crisis ravaging a community (Harris, 2016a). Advocating for funding may include meeting with state Medicaid officials and working with local entities to earmark existing funding streams for SBIRT (Community Catalyst, 2018).

Advocacy was critical in the uptake of SBIRT for adolescents in the United States, in particular because the U.S. Preventive Services Task Force does not have sufficient evidence to recommend it, giving SBIRT an "Insufficient Evidence," or "I," rating (U.S. Preventive Services Task Force, 2018). There are clear reasons for the lack of evidence, including a burdensome student assent and parental consent requirement that deters researchers and a natural increase in substance use as individuals moves through adolescence to adulthood, canceling out potential reductions that may result from SBIRT (Sterling, Kline-Simon, Wibbelsman, Wong, & Weisner, 2012). Even so, the "I" rating has the potential to severely limit the use SBIRT.

Considering the significant amount of time required to translate research into practice, advocacy is critical for the timely advancement of SBIRT with adolescent populations. In 2011, the American Academy of Pediatrics (AAP) issued a policy statement recommending that pediatricians provide substance use education and screening to adolescents during routine clinical care using the SBIRT model; specifically, the statement recommended that pediatricians become knowledgeable about adolescent alcohol, drug, and cigarette use and screen all adolescents using developmentally appropriate screening tools and intervention strategies. The statement also encouraged pediatricians to advocate that health care and payment organizations provide mental health and substance use services to all ages and developmental stages at the same level and quality as with other medical services

(Committee on Substance Abuse, 2011). In 2016, the AAP revised the policy statement to emphasize the significant public health impact of adolescent substance use and urged continued research into the most effective intervention strategies (Levy et al., 2016). In every iteration of the policy statement, the AAP provided background information about SBIRT and guidelines for conducting SBIRT with adolescent patients. The AAP has also developed clinical reports, an implementation guide, and information about developmentally appropriate screening and assessment instruments.

Thanks to the support and advocacy of the AAP, the U.S. Preventive Services Task Force "I" rating has not prevented individuals, policymakers, and organizations from recognizing the importance of implementing SBIRT for adolescents. In fact, the task force publicizes the AAP recommendation that pediatricians provide substance use education and screening to adolescents during routine clinical care using the SBIRT model along with their rating so as to place the rating in context. Because the AAP is such a well-respected association, its recommendation carries a significant amount of weight in advancing SBIRT with adolescents.

The AAP recommendation, as well as the recommendations of other professional organizations, has had a significant impact on decisions to adopt SBIRT and to implement it with fidelity (Harris, 2016b). For example, in 2013 the Conrad N. Hilton Foundation initiated a new 5-year Youth Substance Use Prevention and Early Intervention Strategic Initiative to ensure youth substance use is identified and addressed using SBIRT. Since then, the foundation has provided more than $61 million to fund 75 research, training, implementation, communications, and policy-related programs. Awards went to primary care organizations, foundations, universities, professional associations, and nonprofit agencies (Abt Associates, 2018). Through these grant awards, 911,230 providers received information and materials related to SBIRT, 34,541 providers received SBIRT training, and more than 73,000 youth across 802 sites were screened for substance use. Of the adolescents screened, 14% received a brief intervention and 2% received a referral to treatment. Research grantees produced a total of 364 publications, brief reports, and conference presentations contributing to the evidence base for youth SBIRT (Abt Associates, 2018).

One project funded by the Conrad N. Hilton Foundation was an advocacy model developed by Community Catalyst (2014). This project selected consumer advocates in Georgia, Massachusetts, New Jersey, Ohio, and Wisconsin to improve insurance coverage for early screening and intervention, increase the number of locations in which these services are provided, and increase the number and type of professionals who can provide these services. Consumer advocates, including youth organizations, parent groups, faith groups, organizations working to address addiction, and health care providers, created public education campaigns about the scope of the youth substance use problem and the best policy solutions (Community Catalyst, 2014). This work was critical in helping pass the bill in Massachusetts requiring schools to provide substance use screening and education and in developing a similar bill affecting schools in New Jersey, described earlier in this chapter (State of New Jersey, 2018; Wulfson, 2018).

The impact of AAP advocacy sets an example for other professional organizations, including nurse practitioners, physician assistants, social workers, mental health counselors, psychologists, and pharmacists, all of whom can play a key role in the implementation of SBIRT. Integrating SBIRT into university training programs for health care professionals, as SAMHSA has begun to do through its professional training grants, will increase the extent to which professionals will be informed about and able to conduct SBIRT when they enter the workforce. These same professionals ideally will help advocate for SBIRT within their professional organizations to further encourage its implementation and dissemination.

CONCLUSION

Policy serves as part of a multipronged effort for preventing and reducing substance use and associated consequences. Policies that influence SBIRT range from the ACA, Medicaid expansion, and mental health and substance use parity to SBIRT billing codes, funding allocation, restrictions on the use of funds, and requiring service delivery. Advocacy is key to enacting policy change, and continued advocacy is essential to ensure that laws remain in place. With 70,236 drug overdose deaths in 2017 (Scholl, Seth, Kariisa, Wilson, & Baldwin, 2018), there is not a more critical time for policies to promote the use of SBIRT. SBIRT can play a key role in preventing initiation of opioid or other drug and alcohol use and helping, in the form of intervention or referral to treatment, those at high risk for health consequences associated with substance use and individuals with SUDs.

REFERENCES

Abt Associates. (2018). *Substance use prevention: Evaluation report*. Westlake Village, CA: Conrad N. Hilton Foundation. Retrieved from https://gallery.mailchimp.com/39ee06752b10a8f76880922e6/files/6f9e7d57-e90c-4447-834e-136cb4b018c1/MEL_SUP_10.17.18_SCREEN.pdf

Adamson, S. J., Kay-Lambkin, F. J., Baker, A. L., Lewin, T. J., Thornton, L., Kelly, B. J., & Sellman, J. D. (2010). An improved brief measure of cannabis misuse: The Cannabis Use Disorders Identification Test—Revised (CUDIT–R). *Drug and Alcohol Dependence, 110*, 137–143. http://dx.doi.org/10.1016/j.drugalcdep.2010.02.017

Aldridge, A., Dowd, W., & Bray, J. (2017). The relative impact of brief treatment versus brief intervention in primary health-care screening programs for substance use disorders. *Addiction, 112*(Suppl. 2), 54–64. http://dx.doi.org/10.1111/add.13653

Aldridge, A., Linford, R., & Bray, J. (2017). Substance use outcomes of patients served by a large US implementation of Screening, Brief Intervention and Referral to Treatment (SBIRT). *Addiction, 112*(Suppl. 2), 43–53. http://dx.doi.org/10.1111/add.13651

American Medical Association. (2017). *Current procedural terminology (CPT®) 2017 standard*. Chicago, IL: American Medical Association Press.

Bray, J. W., Del Boca, F. K., McRee, B. G., Hayashi, S. W., & Babor, T. F. (2017). Screening, Brief Intervention and Referral to Treatment (SBIRT): Rationale, program overview and cross-site evaluation. *Addiction, 112*(Suppl. 2), 3–11. http://dx.doi.org/10.1111/add.13676

Buck, J. A. (2011). The looming expansion and transformation of public substance abuse treatment under the Affordable Care Act. *Health Affairs, 30,* 1402–1410. http://dx.doi.org/10.1377/hlthaff.2011.0480

Center for Adolescent Substance Abuse Research. (2016). *CRAFFT 2.0.* Retrieved from https://sbirt.webs.com/CRAFFT%202.0%20Combined.pdf

Centers for Medicare & Medicaid Services. (n.d.). *Preventive care benefits for adults.* Retrieved from https://www.healthcare.gov/preventive-care-adults/

City of New York. (2017). *ThriveNYC: Year Two update.* Retrieved from https://thrivenyc.cityofnewyork.us/wp-content/uploads/2019/08/Thrive-Year-Two-Update-Report.pdf

Committee on Substance Abuse. (2011). Substance use Screening, Brief Intervention, and Referral to Treatment for pediatricians. *Pediatrics, 128,* e1330–e1340. http://dx.doi.org/10.1542/peds.2011-1754

Commonwealth of Massachusetts. An Act Relative to Substance Use Treatment, Education, and Prevention, HR 3817, 189th Leg (Mass 2015–2016).

Community Catalyst. (2014). *Consumer advocates take new approach to keep youth on healthy path.* Retrieved from https://www.communitycatalyst.org/news/press-releases/consumer-advocates-take-new-approach-to-keep-youth-on-healthy-path

Community Catalyst. (2018). *Advocate toolkit: Funding Screening, Brief Intervention and Referral to Treatment (SBIRT) with young people.* Retrieved from https://www.communitycatalyst.org/resources/publications/document/2018/Funding-Youth-SBIRT-Toolkit.pdf

Cowell, A. J., Dowd, W. N., Mills, M. J., Hinde, J. M., & Bray, J. W. (2017). Sustaining SBIRT in the wild: Simulating revenues and costs for Screening, Brief Intervention and Referral to Treatment programs. *Addiction, 112*(Suppl. 2), 101–109. http://dx.doi.org/10.1111/add.13650

Croft, B., & Parish, S. L. (2013). Care integration in the Patient Protection and Affordable Care Act: Implications for behavioral health. *Administration and Policy in Mental Health and Mental Health Services Research, 40,* 258–263. http://dx.doi.org/10.1007/s10488-012-0405-0

Fussell, H. E., Rieckmann, T. R., & Quick, M. B. (2011). Medicaid reimbursement for screening and brief intervention for substance misuse. *Psychiatric Services, 62,* 306–309. http://dx.doi.org/10.1176/ps.62.3.pss6203_0306

Garfield, R., Orgera, K., & Damico, A. (2019). *The coverage gap: Uninsured poor adults in states that do not expand Medicaid.* San Francisco, CA: Kaiser Family Foundation. Retrieved from https://www.kff.org/medicaid/issue-brief/the-coverage-gap-uninsured-poor-adults-in-states-that-do-not-expand-medicaid/

Guttmacher Institute. (2019). *Substance use during pregnancy.* Retrieved from https://www.guttmacher.org/state-policy/explore/substance-use-during-pregnancy

Harris, B. R. (2016a). Communicating about screening, brief intervention, and referral to treatment: Messaging strategies to raise awareness and promote voluntary adoption and implementation among New York school-based health center providers. *Substance Abuse, 37,* 511–515. http://dx.doi.org/10.1080/08897077.2016.1175400

Harris, B. R. (2016b). Talking about Screening, Brief Intervention, and Referral to Treatment for adolescents: An upstream intervention to address the heroin and prescription opioid epidemic. *Preventive Medicine, 91,* 397–399. http://dx.doi.org/10.1016/j.ypmed.2016.08.022

Harris, B. R., Yu, J., Wolff, M., Rogers, M., & Blank, S. (2018). Optimizing the impact of alcohol and drug screening and early intervention in a high-risk population receiving services in New York City sexual health clinics: A process and outcome evaluation of Project Renew. *Preventive Medicine, 112,* 160–167. http://dx.doi.org/10.1016/j.ypmed.2018.04.018

Hinde, J., Bray, J., Kaiser, D., & Mallonee, E. (2017). The influence of state-level policy environments on the activation of the Medicaid SBIRT reimbursement codes. *Addiction, 112*(Suppl. 2), 82–91. http://dx.doi.org/10.1111/add.13655

Hudak, J., & Wallach, P. A. (2014). *Legal marijuana: Comparing Washington and Colorado.* Washington, DC: Brookings Institution. Retrieved from https://www.brookings.edu/blog/fixgov/2014/07/08/legal-marijuana-comparing-washington-and-colorado/

Institute for Research, Education & Training in Addictions. (2017). *SBIRT reimbursement map.* Retrieved February 2019 from https://my.ireta.org/sbirt-reimbursement-map

Levy, S. J. L., Williams, J. F., & Committee on Substance Use and Prevention. (2016). Substance use screening, brief intervention, and referral to treatment. *Pediatrics, 138,* e20161211. http://dx.doi.org/10.1542/peds.2016-1211

Massachusetts Department of Public Health. (2014, Spring). *Massachusetts SBIRT news* (No. 2). Retrieved from https://www.masbirt.org/sites/www.masbirt.org/files/documents/SBIRT%20News/Spring%202014%20SBIRT%20Newsletter.pdf

McLeroy, K. R., Bibeau, D., Steckler, A., & Glanz, K. (1988). An ecological perspective on health promotion programs. *Health Education Quarterly, 15,* 351–377. http://dx.doi.org/10.1177/109019818801500401

Miech, R., Johnston, L., & O'Malley, P. M. (2017). Prevalence and attitudes regarding marijuana use among adolescents over the past decade. *Pediatrics, 140,* e20170982. http://dx.doi.org/10.1542/peds.2017-0982

National Committee on Quality Assurance. (2017, July 11). *NCQA updates quality measures for HEDIS 2018.* Retrieved from https://www.ncqa.org/news/ncqa-updates-quality-measures-for-hedis-2018/

National Committee on Quality Assurance. (2018, May 8). *New HEDIS measure strengthens alcohol screening and follow up.* Retrieved from https://www.ncqa.org/news/new-hedis-measure-strengthens-alcohol-screening-and-follow-up/

National Conference of State Legislatures. (2019a, October). *Marijuana overview: Legalization.* Retrieved from https://www.ncsl.org/research/civil-and-criminal-justice/marijuana-overview.aspx

National Conference of State Legislatures. (2019b, October). *State medical marijuana laws.* Retrieved from http://www.ncsl.org/research/health/state-medical-marijuana-laws.aspx

New York State Department of Health. (2016). *Medicaid expands coverage for Screening, Brief Intervention, and Referral to Treatment (SBIRT).* Retrieved from https://www.health.ny.gov/health_care/medicaid/program/update/2016/2016-04.htm#sbirt

Patient Protection and Affordable Care Act, Pub. L. 111-148, 42 U.S.C. §§ 18001–18121. (2010).

Paul Wellstone and Pete Dominici Mental Health Parity and Addiction Equity Act of 2008, Pub. L. 110-343, 26 U.S.C. § 9812, 29 U.S.C. § 1185a, and 42 U.S.C. § 300gg-5.

Peer Assistance Services. (2018). *Marijuana clinical guidance: Information to guide work with adolescents and adults.* Retrieved from https://static1.squarespace.com/static/577554cb37c5816f7a87d32e/t/5bdc8204cd8366c2a7bfb516/1541177861340/18-32546_Marijuana+Clinical+Guidance+8.5+by+11+updated+9.18.pdf

Prochaska, J. O., DiClemente, C. C., & Norcross, J. C. (1992). In search of how people change: Applications to addictive behaviors. *American Psychologist, 47,* 1102–1114. http://dx.doi.org/10.1037/0003-066X.47.9.1102

Rosenbaum, S., & Westmoreland, T. M. (2012). The Supreme Court's surprising decision on the Medicaid expansion: How will the federal government and states proceed? *Health Affairs, 31,* 1663–1672. http://dx.doi.org/10.1377/hlthaff.2012.0766

Scholl, L., Seth, P., Kariisa, M., Wilson, N., & Baldwin, G. (2018). Drug and opioid-involved overdose deaths—United States, 2013–2017. *Morbidity and Mortality Weekly*

Report, 67, 1419–1427. Retrieved from https://www.cdc.gov/mmwr/volumes/67/wr/mm675152e1.htm?s_cid=mm675152e1_w

Singh, M., Gmyrek, A., Hernandez, A., Damon, D., & Hayashi, S. (2017). Sustaining Screening, Brief Intervention and Referral to Treatment (SBIRT) services in health-care settings. *Addiction, 112*(Suppl. 2), 92–100. http://dx.doi.org/10.1111/add.13654

State of New Jersey. (2018). State of New Jersey, 218th legislature (Senate, No. 491). Retrieved from https://www.njleg.state.nj.us/2018/Bills/S0500/491_I1.HTM

Sterling, S., Kline-Simon, A. H., Wibbelsman, C., Wong, A., & Weisner, C. (2012). Screening for adolescent alcohol and drug use in pediatric health-care settings: Predictors and implications for practice and policy. *Addiction Science & Clinical Practice, 7*, 13. Advance online publication. http://dx.doi.org/10.1186/1940-0640-7-13

Substance Abuse and Mental Health Services Administration. (n.d.). *Screening, Brief Intervention and Referral to Treatment (SBIRT) grantees*. Retrieved from https://www.samhsa.gov/sbirt/grantees

U.S. Preventive Services Task Force. (2018, November). *Unhealthy alcohol use in adolescents and adults: Screening and behavioral counseling interventions*. Retrieved from https://www.uspreventiveservicestaskforce.org/Page/Document/UpdateSummaryFinal/unhealthy-alcohol-use-in-adolescents-and-adults-screening-and-behavioral-counseling-interventions

U.S. Preventive Services Task Force. (2019, September). *Draft recommendation statement: Illicit drug use, including nonmedical use of prescription drugs: Screening*. Retrieved from https://www.uspreventiveservicestaskforce.org/Page/Document/draft-recommendation-statement/drug-use-in-adolescents-and-adults-including-pregnant-women-screening

Winkle, J. (2016). *The story behind Oregon's SBIRT incentive measure and its impact on implementation*. Retrieved from https://my.ireta.org/sites/ireta.org/files/Winkle%20webinar%20handouts.pdf

Wulfson, J. (2018). *State requirement for districts to implement a substance use related verbal screening tool*. Malden: Massachusetts Department of Elementary and Secondary Education. Retrieved from http://www.doe.mass.edu/sfs/safety/verbalscreening.html

Young-Wolff, K. C., Tucker, L. Y., Alexeeff, S., Armstrong, M. A., Conway, A., Weisner, C., & Goler, N. (2017). Trends in self-reported and biochemically tested marijuana use among pregnant females in California from 2009–2016 [Letter]. *JAMA, 318*, 2490–2491. http://dx.doi.org/10.1001/jama.2017.17225

INDEX

ABOUT THE EDITORS

M. Dolores Cimini, PhD, is a New York State licensed psychologist and director of the Center for Behavioral Health Promotion and Applied Research at the University at Albany, State University of New York. She is also a senior research scientist in the University at Albany's School of Education. Dr. Cimini has led comprehensive efforts in research-to-practice translation at the University at Albany for 3 decades with over $9 million in grant support from the National Institute on Alcohol Abuse and Alcoholism, National Institute on Drug Abuse, Substance Abuse and Mental Health Services Administration (SAMHSA), U.S. Department of Education, and U.S. Department of Justice. The screening and brief intervention program developed by Dr. Cimini, the STEPS Comprehensive Alcohol Screening and Brief Intervention Program, has earned 10 national awards for best practices and innovation in behavioral health care and was listed in SAMHSA's National Registry of Evidence-Based Programs and Practices in January 2014 after undergoing rigorous peer review. Dr. Cimini is the past chair of the American Psychological Association's Board for the Advancement of Psychology in the Public Interest. She serves as a consulting editor for the *Journal of American College Health* and has published book chapters and professional articles in both national and international refereed journals. Dr. Cimini was recognized by the White House as a Champion of Change in 2012, as well as for her contributions to science, technology, engineering, and mathematics in 2018.

Jessica L. Martin, PhD, is a New York State licensed psychologist and an associate professor of counseling psychology within the Department of Educational and Counseling Psychology at the University at Albany, State University of New York. Dr. Martin's research expertise is in the area of substance use among college students and, more specifically, the identification of individual, psychosocial, cultural, and contextual risk and protective factors for alcohol use and co-occurring psychological disorders and health-risk behaviors. In addition, she conducts research on substance use training for psychologists and dissemination and implementation of substance use preventive interventions. Dr. Martin served as coprincipal investigator and project evaluator on a SAMHSA-funded screening, brief intervention, and referral to treatment training grant for which she and Dr. M. Dolores Cimini established a comprehensive training collaborative among five graduate programs in professional psychology. Dr. Martin has received over $1.1 million in federal funding to support projects aimed at reducing alcohol use and health disparities. She has published book chapters and numerous peer-reviewed articles on these topics in national and international scientific journals. She chairs the Education and Training Committee for the Society of Addiction Psychology (Division 50, American Psychological Association), is a member of the Society of Counseling Psychology (Division 17, American Psychological Association), and serves on the editorial boards for *Addiction Research & Theory* and *Journal of Studies on Alcohol and Drugs*.